Japanese Taiwan

SOAS Studies in Modern and Contemporary Japan

Series Editor: Christopher Gerteis, SOAS, University of London (UK)

Series Editorial Board:
Steve Dodd, SOAS, University of London (UK)
Andrew Gerstle, SOAS, University of London (UK)
Janet Hunter, London School of Economics and Political Science (UK)
Helen Macnaughtan, SOAS, University of London (UK)
Timon Screech, SOAS, University of London (UK)
Naoko Shimazu, Birkbeck, University of London (UK)

Published in association with the Japan Research Centre at the School of
Oriental and African Studies, University of London, UK.

SOAS Studies in Modern and Contemporary Japan features scholarly books on
modern and contemporary Japan, showcasing new research monographs as well as
translations of scholarship not previously available in English. Its goal is to ensure
that current, high-quality research on Japan, its history, politics, and culture, is
made available to an English-speaking audience. The series is made possible in part
by generous grants from the Nippon Foundation and the Great Britain Sasakawa
Foundation.

Published:
Women and Democracy in Cold War Japan, Jan Bardsley
Christianity and Imperialism in Modern Japan, Emily Anderson
The China Problem in Postwar Japan, Robert Hoppens
Media, Propaganda and Politics in 20th Century Japan,
The Asahi Shimbun Company (translated by Barak Kushner)
Contemporary Sino-Japanese Relations on Screen, Griseldis Kirsch
Debating Otaku in Contemporary Japan, edited by Patrick W. Galbraith,
Thiam Huat Kam, and Björn-Ole Kamm
Politics and Power in 20th-Century Japan, Mikuriya Takashi and
Nakamura Takafusa (translated by Timothy S. George)

Forthcoming:
Japan's Postwar Military and Civil Society, Tomoyuki Sasaki

Japanese Taiwan

Colonial Rule and its Contested Legacy

Edited by Andrew D. Morris

Bloomsbury Academic
An imprint of Bloomsbury Publishing Plc

B L O O M S B U R Y
LONDON · OXFORD · NEW YORK · NEW DELHI · SYDNEY

Bloomsbury Academic

An imprint of Bloomsbury Publishing Plc

50 Bedford Square
London
WC1B 3DP
UK

1385 Broadway
New York
NY 10018
USA

www.bloomsbury.com

BLOOMSBURY and the Diana logo are trademarks of Bloomsbury Publishing Plc

First published 2015
Paperback edition first published 2016

British Library Cataloguing-in-Publication Data
A catalogue record for this book is available from the British Library.

ISBN: HB: 978-1-4725-7672-9
PB: 978-1-350-02257-7
ePDF: 978-1-4725-7673-6
ePub: 978-1-4725-7674-3

Library of Congress Cataloging-in-Publication Data
A catalog record for this book is available from the Library of Congress.

Series: SOAS Studies in Modern and Contemporary Japan

Typeset by Integra Software Services Pvt. Ltd.

Contents

List of Illustrations

List of Tables

Notes on Contributors

Joseph R. Allen is Professor of Chinese Literature and Cultural Studies and Chair of the Department of Asian Languages and Literatures, University of Minnesota. He has held a National Endowment for the Humanities Fellowship, two Fulbright Research Fellowships, and a Faculty Fellowship in the Humanities at Harvard University. Trained in classical Chinese poetry, his early work included *In the Voice of Others: Chinese Music Bureau Poetry* (University of Michigan Center for Chinese Studies, 1992). He has focused on Taiwan and cultural studies in his recent works, including "Picturing Gentlemen: Japanese Portrait Photography in Colonial Taiwan" (*Journal of Asian Studies*, 2014) and *Taipei: City of Displacements* (University of Washington Press, 2012), and he is winner of the 2014 Joseph Levenson Book Prize in Chinese Studies, Post-1900.

Paul D. Barclay is Associate Professor and Chair of the Asian Studies Program at Lafayette College, and General Editor of the East Asia Image Collections Digital Archive. He has published articles in *Journal of Asian Studies*, *Japanese Studies*, *Taiwan Genjūmin Kenkyū (Studies on Indigenous Peoples of Taiwan)*, *Humanities Research*, and *Social Science Japan Journal*. He is a recipient of awards from the National Endowment for the Humanities, Social Science Research Council, Taiwan Ministry of Foreign Affairs, and the Japan Society for the Promotion of Science.

Evan N. Dawley is Assistant Professor of History at Goucher College. After completing a Ph.D. in Chinese History at Harvard, he worked for several years as a historian with the U.S. Department of State. He has also taught at Reed College, the George Washington University, and Georgetown University. He co-edited, with Tosh Minohara and Tze-ki Hon, *The Decade of the Great War: Japan and the Wider World in the 1910s* (Brill, 2014). He is currently working on a book manuscript about the construction of Taiwanese ethnic consciousness in the port city of Jilong from the 1880s to the 1950s.

Chih Huei Huang is an anthropologist at the Institute of Ethnology, Academia Sinica, in Taiwan, and has conducted extensive fieldwork in Japan. Since 1995, she has translated a series of early-twentieth-century reports on the customs of Formosan Indigenous Peoples completed by the Japanese Governor-General's Office and has published several papers in Japanese and Chinese on the postcolonial situation and ethnic relationship between Okinawa and Taiwan. Her interests also include the re-establishment of Taiwan–Japan relations and translating academic knowledge into legal action to support Indigenous rights and culture. Her chapter in this volume, presented in an earlier version, won the Best Paper Award at the first Asia Future Conference (Bangkok, 2013).

Andrew D. Morris is Professor of History at California Polytechnic State University, San Luis Obispo. He is the author of *Colonial Project, National Game: A History of Baseball in Taiwan* (University of California Press, 2010), *Marrow of the Nation: A History of Sport and Physical Culture in Republican China* (University of California Press, 2004), and co-editor (with David K. Jordan and Marc L. Moskowitz) of *The Minor Arts of Daily Life: Popular Culture in Taiwan* (University of Hawai'i Press, 2004).

Marc L. Moskowitz is Professor in the Department of Anthropology at the University of South Carolina. Focusing on the intersection between gender and popular culture in Chinese-speaking Asia, he is a recipient of the ACLS-NEH, Chiang Ching-Kuo, Fulbright, and Fulbright-Hays Awards. He is the author of *Go Nation: Chinese Masculinities and the Game of Weiqi in China* (University of California Press, 2013), *Cries of Joy, Songs of Sorrow: Chinese Pop Music and its Cultural Connotations* (University of Hawai'i Press, 2009), *The Haunting Fetus: Abortion, Sexuality and the Spirit World in Taiwan* (University of Hawai'i Press, 2001). He edited *Popular Culture in Taiwan: Charismatic Modernity* (Routledge, 2010) and co-edited (with David K. Jordan and Andrew D. Morris) *The Minor Arts of Daily Life: Popular Culture in Taiwan* (University of Hawai'i Press, 2004). He also has directed and produced the ethnographic films *Dancing for the Dead: Funeral Strippers in Taiwan* (2011) and *Weiqi Wonders: Conversations About the Game of Go in China* (2012).

Corrado Neri holds a doctorate in Chinese Film Studies from the University of Ca' Foscari, Venice, and the University of Lyon 3. He is now Assistant Professor at the Jean Moulin University, Lyon 3. He has conducted extensive research on Chinese cinema in Beijing and Taipei and published many book chapters and journal articles in English, French, and Italian. He is author of *Tsai Ming-liang* (Cafoscarina, 2004) on the famed film director and *Âges inquiets: Cinémas chinois, Une représentation de la jeunesse* (Tigre de Papier, 2009). He co-edited (with Kirstie Gormley) the French/English bilingual book *Le Cinéma taïwanais/Taiwan Cinema* (Asiexpo, 2009) and (with Florent Villard) *Global Fences: Literatures, Limits, Borders* (IETT, 2011).

Jens Sejrup is a postdoctoral research fellow at the Centre for East and South-East Asian Studies, Lund University, Sweden. A Japan specialist, he holds a Ph.D. in East Asian Studies as well as an MA in Japanese Studies from the University of Copenhagen. Jens has published several research articles and book chapters, including "Instrumentalized History and the Motif of Repetition in News Coverage of Japan-Taiwan Relations" (*Pacific Affairs*, winner of the 2014 EastAsiaNet Award for Best Academic Article) and "Awakening the Sufferers: Reflections on Public Relations, Activism, and Subalternity in Postcolonial Controversies between Taiwan and Japan" (*Public Relations Inquiry*, winner of the 2012 Young Scholar Award from the European Association of Taiwan Studies). Jens serves as a steering committee member of the Nordic Association for the Study of Contemporary Japanese Society.

John R. Shepherd, Associate Professor of Anthropology at the University of Virginia, is the author of *Statecraft and Political Economy on the Taiwan Frontier, 1600–1800* (Stanford, 1993) and *Marriage and Mandatory Abortion among the 17th-century Siraya* (American Ethnological Society, 1995), and the co-editor of *Death at the Opposite Ends of the Eurasian Continent: Mortality Trends in Taiwan and the Netherlands, 1850–1945* (Aksant, 2011). Shepherd is currently engaged in research on the mortality transition in late-nineteenth- and early-twentieth-century Taiwan, the 1918 influenza epidemic in East Asia, and the practice of footbinding in Taiwan.

Scott Simon is Professor in the School of Sociological and Anthropological Studies and Research Chair in Taiwan Studies at the University of Ottawa. He specializes in the political anthropology of indigeneity and development in the Austronesian communities of Taiwan and is the author of the books *Sadyaq balae! L'autochtonie formosane dans tous ses états* (Presses de l'Université Laval, 2012), *Tanners of Taiwan: Life Strategies and National Culture* (Westview Press, 2005), and *Sweet and Sour: Life Worlds of Taipei Women Entrepreneurs* (Rowman & Littlefield, 2003).

Acknowledgments

This volume originated in a conference on "East Asian Dialogues: The Cultural Flow between Taiwan and Japan," organized by Marc Moskowitz at the University of South Carolina in February 2010. We are grateful to Gordon Smith, Director of the USC Walker Institute of International and Area Studies, and Dean Kinzley, Associate Director of the Walker Institute and Director of the USC Center of Asian Studies, for having made funding for this conference possible.

We would also like to thank Mark Selden, Leo Ching, Jennifer Liu, and several anonymous reviewers for their constructive input into this volume, and Eriko Takamine for her help with copyediting. We are also grateful to series editor Christopher Gerteis and Bloomsbury editorial assistant Emma Goode for their good cheer and their willingness to include the history of Japanese Taiwan in this exciting new SOAS Studies in Modern and Contemporary Japan series.

Finally, I would like to thank my wife Ricky, my daughter Shaina, and my son Aaron for their love and support as I edited this volume and always.

Andrew D. Morris

Part One

Making Japanese Taiwan

Introduction: Living as Left Behind in Postcolonial Taiwan

Andrew D. Morris

In 2011, the new National Museum of Taiwan History committed to a bold interpretation of history and the role of the museum in twenty-first-century society. They published, with much fanfare, a comic book by young historian/artist Li Guanru titled *The End of Summer, 1945*. Drawn in the prototypical iconographic style of Japanese *manga*, *The End of Summer* traced the recently uncovered history of Lü Yanping, a Taiwanese woman who was able, as Miyashita Heiko, to study in Japan and then to study medicine at Taihoku Imperial University.

Lü/Miyashita's work on a rescue team put her in great danger during the massive American bombing of Taihoku (Taipei) on May 31, 1945, and she died as one of the many thousands of tragic victims of this attack on the modern seat of Japan's prize colony. Her fate is significant; Li's rendering of her death situates this comic book as a direct descendant of dramatized true war horror stories like *Barefoot Gen* and *Grave of the Fireflies*. Indeed, like these celebrated works of *manga* and *anime*, *The End of Summer* focuses on innocent Japanese victims of the violence of World War II. And one clear implication of this historical intervention is just that simple and intentional: that many Taiwanese men and women died in this war as Japanese. This is a compelling association in today's Taiwan, where real and imagined traces of "Japaneseness" are treasured for their marking Taiwan as separate from "China" proper. The last chapter of Li's comic contains one dramatic and powerful line that all the bloggers love: "We're not Japanese, or Chinese, or even Taiwanese. What we have here is just family" (Li 2011: 218–19). If this is true, then the Japanese Taiwan that Li works to redraw into being is thus scarred and blessed just enough by a half century of colonialism to be exempt from the unificationist expectations that would be placed upon a more Chinese "renegade province."

Living representatives of the tragedy of Japanese colonialism also haunt our recent past. One of these was Wu Lianyi, an ethnic Taiwanese resident of the Red River Delta region of northern Vietnam, who died in December 2006 at the age of 83. Wu's tenure far away from home was no act of historical wishful projection, however. He had been there for sixty-two years, after being assigned to Japanese-occupied Vietnam for the purpose of carrying out agricultural reform during World War II. And there he stayed, during many subsequent decades of turmoil and trauma in East and Southeast Asia.

Wu graduated in 1943 from southern Taiwan's Tainan District Kagi Agriculture and Forestry Institute (*Tainan shūritsu Kagi nōrin gakkō*), the Kagi (Jiayi) school best known for its history of baseball excellence under Japanese colonialism (Morris 2010: 31–44). The next year, Wu, then known as Arai Yoshio, arrived in northern Vietnam under the auspices of the Taiwan Development Company Ltd. (*Taiwan takushoku kabushiki kaisha*) to supervise cotton and jute cultivation (Jiang 2009: 1–2).[1] When the war and dreams of a Greater East Asia Co-Prosperity Sphere ended, the formidable process of repatriating some 6 million Japanese military and colonial personnel from China, Southeast Asia, and their former colonies began. However, Wu and the 700-some other ethnic Taiwanese working in Vietnam no longer enjoyed their former privileges as Japanese subjects and were not included in the repatriation plans of the overmatched Japanese agencies. More than one hundred desperate Taiwanese tried to buy or steal boats and navigate by themselves the 900 miles back to Taiwan in the South China Sea but none of them seem to have survived (Jiang 2009: 7). In May 1946, roughly one hundred more Taiwanese former colonial agents were able to make it back to Taiwan via a Japanese military ship (Zhang 1997: 20). Wu was not among them, having fled Hanoi because of the presence of Republic of China (ROC) forces, who he feared would take revenge on Taiwanese who had served the Japanese. His work for Ho Chi Minh's Viet Minh, the independence movement that hundreds of former Japanese soldiers also assisted (Spector 2007: 129–30), guaranteed that Wu would not be welcomed back home by the anti-communist ROC. Indeed, as Tessa Morris-Suzuki (2012) has written, "the carving up of the space of Japanese empire left hundreds of thousands of people stranded on the wrong side of re-drawn frontiers, a plight that was aggravated as new political tensions turned these frontiers into the frontlines of global confrontation."

Even by the 1990s, when Cold War obstacles had faded away, complications related to the lack of formal diplomatic relations between Taiwan and Vietnam prevented Wu from being permitted to return to Taiwan. In 1991, a television interview on the Tokyo Broadcasting System won him sympathy in Japan, and in 1992 he pleaded with the Japanese Embassy in Vietnam to "take responsibility" for his fate and to send him back to Taiwan (Xu 2007; Jiang 2009: 10–11). The lengthy efforts of many advocates in Taiwan, including the alumni association of his alma mater (now known as National Jiayi University), allowed Wu finally to visit Taiwan for three months in 1994. After being met at Chiang Kai-Shek International Airport by an older sister and a younger brother whom he had not seen in half a century, Wu visited his parents' graves and took part in a graduation ceremony at his alma mater in Jiayi. He, of course, could not speak Taiwan's national language of Mandarin, spread in his absence by the ROC regime since 1945, and in fact had even forgotten his Taiwanese; perhaps fittingly, Wu could only communicate with his long-lost fellow ex-colonial subjects in Japanese. He returned to his family in northern Vietnam and spent the remaining twelve years of his life there (Jiang 2009: 11).

Wu was a "left behind" counterpart of sorts of Nakamura Teruo (Attun Palalin), the Amis Aborigine soldier of the Japanese Imperial Army who was discovered in Morotai, Indonesia, in 1974 as the famed last holdout of World War II. The fact that Nakamura, this most loyal of the Shōwa emperor's many millions of soldiers, was not even "really" Japanese was jarring to many Japanese citizens who just hoped to put all of these three-decades-old memories behind them. It was jarring to Nakamura himself as well. When told that Taiwan was now part of China, he could only answer, "I've been Japanese for a long time." He had a new official Chinese name as a new citizen of the ROC—Li Guanghui—although the new Mr. Li did not speak any Chinese language. He lived for five more years, pitied and soon forgotten in both Japan and his new/old home of Nationalist Taiwan, before dying of lung cancer in 1979 (Trefalt 2003: 164–76).

These three subjects of the Shōwa emperor—Lü/Miyashita, Wu/Arai, and Nakamura/Li—and the absurd quality of their Japanese lives and Taiwanese deaths stand as potent symbols of how many Taiwanese people have lived and seen themselves as "left behind" by their Japanese rulers, teachers, neighbors, and friends after the end of colonial rule seven decades ago. The compelling nature of this historical consciousness—the omnipresence of the Japanese legacy in what its KMT (*Guomindang*, or Chinese Nationalist Party) rulers for decades referred to as "the real China"—is crucial to understanding Taiwan's postwar and postcolonial moments.

Making Japanese Taiwan: Wilderness to colony

Taiwan was Japanese for fifty years, four months, and twenty-seven days. Since "Retrocession" (*Guangfu*) to direct Chinese rule—that October 1945 "brilliant return," that victorious moment of great pregnancy, significance, anticipation, disappointment, and ultimate redemption—Taiwan has also been imagined to be Japanese in many different ways by many different observers. This volume is an attempt to understand the many dimensions, memories, ideals, and transformations of this Japanese history of Taiwan.

The chapters in this volume are divided into two parts: "Making Japanese Taiwan" and "Remembering Japanese Taiwan." These parts address the five decades of Japanese rule and the seven decades of Taiwan's status as a "left behind" former colony, respectively; however, this neat division is complicated by the fact that many of these pieces move back and forth in time and over this 1945 boundary. Some of the pieces look at specific moments of the creation of Japanese Taiwan, while others engage with the complicated ties between history and memory, or the long-lasting influence that Japanese colonial rule had on the essence of Taiwanese life: How did the colonial regime understand the different peoples of their new colony? How did the colonial officials, civil servants, and other Japanese subjects living in Taiwan try to reshape Taiwanese lives for their own benefit and for the benefit of the empire? How did they attempt to explain this conquest and enterprise to the subjects of imperial Japan? What happened to these Japanese people and ideas when Taiwan became part of the ROC in 1945? How did they think they had actually changed Taiwanese history? How did the different peoples of Taiwan understand the surrender of Japan, the moment of "Retrocession," and their new lives under ROC rule? How did they try to make sense of the Nationalist regime with respect to the departed Japanese? What elements of Japanese culture did people in Taiwan miss or imagine still remained? My collaborators and I want to understand how the Japanese imagined, ruled, misunderstood, changed, left, and remembered Taiwan, and how the people of Taiwan experienced and remembered these processes as well (Figure 1.1).

Figure 1.1 Wedding picture: Huang Cong (left) and Huang Shu (Nakahara Masao, right), Taichū (Taizhong), 1937. Photo courtesy of Ilon Huang.

Two important elements of this history stand out. The first has to do with the ways that the question of Taiwan's "Chinese" heritage was imagined during and after the end of Japanese colonial rule. In Taiwan today, explicit recognition of the importance of the colonial era provides an important political context for Taiwanese people's (i.e. *benshengren*, the ethnic Han whose families immigrated to Taiwan during the seventeenth to nineteenth centuries) notions of exactly how "Chinese" they are, and how this formulation determines their relationship with the People's Republic of China (PRC) regime on the mainland. What has been studied less thoroughly, however, is the way that this "Chinese question" was phrased and understood by Japanese and Taiwanese subjects in the colonial era; this is an approach that many of us pursue in this volume. The second unique aspect of this volume is the way that many of its chapters frame the "Japaneseness" of colonial and postcolonial Taiwan by explicitly centering the history of Taiwan's Austronesian Aborigine, or Indigenous, population. The Aborigines (*Yuanzhumin*), though constituting only 2 percent of the island's population during the modern era, were an early focus, if not an obsession, of the Japanese colonial government. Because the camphor, timber (specifically Formosan cypress), marble, and tea resources that the Japanese hoped to exploit were largely concentrated in the Aboriginal highlands of central Taiwan, the institution of extractive colonial rule had an especially significant impact on these Indigenous Peoples' political, social, and cultural status. (See Figure 4.1 in Chapter 4 for a map of the distribution of Taiwan's Indigenous populations.) Japan's "civilizing mission" toward these native peoples of "darkest Taiwan"—as opposed to the behavior of Taiwan's Han Chinese population that could only antagonize and steal from them (Barclay 2007: 77)— would be one of the most important justifications for their rule of Taiwan. Having their "very own 'savages'" whom they could raise and modernize was a virtual raison d'être of Japan's colonial enterprise (Tierney 2010: 63, 82). Indeed, the 1935 state documentary *Southward Expansion into Taiwan* made the case that Taiwan "had been regarded by the Qing Government as a wasteland with uncivilized inhabitants. But through the assimilation process the Japanese Government has succeeded in turning them into loyal subjects of the Empire" (*Nanshin Taiwan* 1935). Thus, just as the history of Native North Americans is central to any serious understanding of American and Canadian history, Taiwan, and this colonial era in particular, is also best comprehended with serious investigation of the positions and experiences of the Indigenous Peoples who lived under this system.

The four chapters in the first part, "Making Japanese Taiwan," all treat the first decades of the colonial era, three of them addressing the active process of imaging, mapping, defining, and categorizing the new colony. Joseph Allen, in his "Colonial Itineraries: Japanese Photography in Taiwan," shows us the implications of the Japanese introduction of modern photography and photographic album collections to Taiwan. Allen reads these collections, many of which chronicled the very conquest of the island, the Japanese narrative of its transformation from malarial wild open space to a controlled and civilized colony, as providing to the Japanese viewer of the 1890s "infinitely repeatable" voyages of "wonder and discovery." These were not just flat pictures of a far-off island but an extremely advanced technology that Japanese artists and publishers deployed and that allowed viewers to transport themselves to a new sort of colonial time. Photos in these albums were organized chronologically, allowing the viewer to move from a precolonial primitive wilderness to a modern colony. As chief civil administrator Gotō Shinpei wrote in 1901, "[r]uling Taiwan is much more complicated than we originally thought, since today on the island of Taiwan thousands of years of living history exist simultaneously" (Tierney 2010: 43). His difficulty as an administrator (having to master several different eras simultaneously!) was a boon, however, to the developing Japanese ideologies of progress and historical development; these photographic albums provide a rich source for the study of the logic and conceit of colonial rule. Many of these chronological accounts also created a sense of colonialism in time and space. The albums were designed to take the viewer from the northern city of Taihoku, where visiting photographers would have started their journeys, into a "pristine and primitive" past as they moved southward into Aboriginal territories or perhaps the even more exotic offshore holdings like Red-Headed Islet (Kōtōsho, today's Lanyu). This colonial time thus also allowed the viewer to move from present to past but to a "past that anticipate[d] the future" of the Japanese empire. Japan's initial experiment in colonialism in Taiwan constituted much more than simple southward expansion of the borders of the empire; it also, as the twentieth century dawned, opened up entirely new understandings of the interaction of time and space.

Paul D. Barclay also pursues the Japanese quest to understand Taiwan in his "Tangled up in Red: Textiles, Trading Posts, and the Emergence of Indigenous Modernity in Japanese Taiwan." Where Allen addresses the Japanese imagination of Taiwan as presented through photography, Barclay studies the Japanese project of transforming the Indigenous barter/gift economy to one of regulated modern commerce. The accomplishment of lifting the Indigenous population of Taiwan from the violent and subjective nature of their "primitive" systems of exchange, while at the same time protecting them from the ravages of laissez-faire capitalism, was meant to broadcast two ideologies about the balance of power and morality in turn-of-the-century East Asia: the transcendent benevolence of Japanese imperialism and the moral bankruptcy and obsolete inefficiency of the Chinese/Qing approach to ruling Taiwan. Trade under Japanese rule would no longer be about crass calculations of gifts (although Japanese officials and anthropologists seemed to track these minutely, down to the last flower hairpin, cigar, or monkey bone), arranged marriages, or vengeful violent attacks. Instead, Indigenous participation in the modern economy of Taiwan would serve as a site for colonial officials to influence tribal life and customs through pedagogy, grace, and punishment as well as trade. The Japanese did not imagine themselves to be innocents in this process; high-ranking colonial official Mochiji Rokusaburō, frustrated at the problem of the Aborigines "blocking" Japanese access to their new colonial landholdings, in 1902 publicly stated his conclusion that they would have to hold on to their own "barbarian nature" to beat the natives (Tierney 2010: 44).[2] But the prerogative to move between civilization and violence and to define these poles belonged to the Japanese. On their island, as Barclay shows, these almost-former "savages" and "headhunters" would have to learn how to farm and not rely simply on the atavistic violence that lay at the heart of their hunting culture. Taiwan's Indigenous Peoples would have to conform to new practices of wage labor, commodity production, set prices, public works projects, and occasional official embargoes—the practices that constituted modern economic life in the Japanese empire. The native "handicrafts" produced under this regime in time became part of the broad, commodified, and simply fun understanding of colonial power, as visitors to Taiwan could purchase at tourist-friendly "trading posts"—and drape themselves in—authentic "Aborigine cloth" made by these erstwhile primitives.

Scott Simon continues with this focus on Japanese efforts to define the culture, society, and borders of Taiwan's Aboriginal tribes in his "Making Natives: Japan and the Creation of Indigenous Formosa." Simon begins by describing the current movement for an official "autonomy" for the Indigenous Peoples of Taiwan, rooted in understandings not only of Dr. Sun Yat-sen's century-old thoughts on the place of minorities in the ROC but also of similar contemporary movements for autonomy for the first peoples of Canada and New Zealand. However, Simon also shows how many of the definitions, narratives, assumptions, and boundaries claimed and explained by Aborigine advocates today are actually direct products of Japan's project to bring their tribal ancestors under colonial rule a century ago. Simon's familiarity with the vast anthropological scholarship on Taiwan's Aborigines allows him to explain how the political and economic customs of these native peoples functioned before Japanese colonial rule and how the Japanese appetite for camphor and timber led them to vast exercises of classification and categorization of people, commodities, and land. What appear to be perfectly natural tribal boundaries today are actually the product of colonial administrative redistricting and imposed agricultural changes, new irrigation systems built by the Japanese, and forced relocation and resettling programs of violent and rebellious Indigenous communities. Like Allen, Simon demonstrates the effects of a colonial definition of time itself, where utterly contemporary affairs can only be understood and comprehended from within the plans and dreams of a governmental system that has been gone for seven decades (Figure 1.2).

The final chapter in this part, John Shepherd's "Ethnicity, Mortality, and the Shinchiku (Xinzhu) Advantage in Colonial Taiwan," presents another artifact of the complicated ethnic spectrum in colonial Taiwan. Some 15 percent of Taiwan's population during the colonial era belonged to the ethnic/linguistic minority known as the Hakka (*Kejiaren*), mainly from China's Guangdong Province. As described above, Japanese colonial officials maintained a regime of finely detailed household linguistic, ancestral, biological, and medical data about the residents of their treasured colony, all the while reminding themselves and their Taiwanese subjects about the difference between their modern rule and life in "filthy...unhealthy China" (M. Liu 2009: 86–8). Shepherd's work reminds us of the very real medical dangers of Qing and early Japanese Taiwan, such as malaria, and respiratory and diarrheal diseases. But instead of merely presenting the truism of Japanese

Figure 1.2 Taiwanese policeman Huang Shu (Nakahara Masao, right) and fellow officer, participating in flood rescue operation, Taikō (Dajia), around 1940. Huang/Nakahara was the commanding officer at the Citongjiao police station on the outskirts of Shōka (Zhanghua). Photo courtesy of Ilon Huang.

advances in fighting or eradicating these diseases, Shepherd makes exhaustive use of census data to show glaring differences in mortality rates between Hakka and Hoklo Taiwanese (the Minnanyu speakers who constitute the majority of the Han population on Taiwan) and among the different prefectures of the colony. These marked mortality discrepancies (which heavily favor the Hakka) help explain one oft-forgotten fact about Japanese Taiwan: the endurance of great variations in hygienic and community customs among ethnic groups that had very little to do with the colonial rationality and efficiency that is so often reified in Taiwanese memories of their Japanese heritage.

Remembering Japanese Taiwan:
Colorful bloom or poisonous weed?

Taiwan loves cherry blossoms. In fact, it loves almost everything Japanese. For a nation that ruled the island for 50 years, often with an iron fist, Japan has left a very favourable impression. In the latest triumph of Japanese soft power in its former colony, tens of thousands of Taiwanese have taken up planting cherry trees to revel in their colourful bloom for a few precious moments each spring—just like in Japan. "When you see the flowers, you almost feel as if you're in Japan," 50-year-old businesswoman Susan Wu said.

—Agence France-Presse, March 25, 2012 (Yeh 2012: 2)

This volume will also be useful for its attempt to provide links between the Japanese colonial era and Taiwanese contemporary culture; the six chapters in the second part of this volume, titled "Remembering Japanese Taiwan," share this goal. Stuart Hall, in his 1996 article "When Was 'The Post-Colonial'?," described the importance of seeing the "forms of transculturation, of cultural translation, destined to trouble the here/there cultural binaries for ever" (Hall 1996: 247). The book (especially the chapters in Part Two) follows this prescription as it recognizes and centers the impossibility of true decolonization—especially in Taiwan, where Japanese colonization was followed immediately by another form of colonial rule under the Chinese Nationalist Party. Only with the historicization of early KMT rule in Taiwan can we truly understand the current moment, as noted above, of Taiwanese reveling in the "colourful bloom" of colonial nostalgia and indeed going far out of their way to accentuate just what still is truly "Japanese" about Taiwan today (Figure 1.3).

By 1945, the wartime exploitation of Taiwan, its people (taken to serve as soldiers and as "comfort women"), its treasure, and its food had become truly unbearable. Most Taiwanese people were initially elated that the Japanese colonial authorities—the true endgame of their decades of "assimilation" policies now painfully clear—would be leaving their island and that Taiwan would achieve "Retrocession" to direct Chinese rule. Many elites turned their attention to the imminent arrival of Chinese forces on Taiwan, forming Preparatory Committees to Welcome the National Government, distributing ROC flags, promoting the study of Mandarin Chinese, and fervently organizing basic propaganda projects on behalf of their new Chinese rulers (Phillips 2003: 43–4). A famous photo represents the mixture of enthusiasm and lack of concrete knowledge about the ROC that characterized that moment: a banner stretching across the modern Taihei District Block 1 of Taihoku (soon to become Yanping North Road, Taipei), reading "WELCOME, Residents United," and displaying the ROC flag backwards, Sun Yat-sen's beckoning but unfamiliar twelve-ray white sun hovering in the upper-right corner instead of the upper left (Guan 1981: 116).

Figure 1.3 Huang Ba (Nakahara Torao), son of Officer Huang/Nakahara in
Figures 1.1 and 1.2. Nicknamed Tora ("Tiger"), Huang/Nakahara was the only
Taiwanese student in his otherwise all-Japanese first-grade class, at Shōka (Zhanghua)
Elementary School (Shōka jinjō kokumin shōgakkō), 1944. Photo courtesy of Ilon Huang.

However, the Nationalists' errors and brutal missteps in late 1940s Taiwan
soon led many Taiwanese people—especially those elites who had prospered as
assimilated Japanese subjects—to start imagining their island's Chinese history as
one of irretrievable loss, decline, and fall. This stance, as Bissell explains, is the basis
for the construction of colonial nostalgia—"sentimental ... indulgent ... reaction"
(2005: 215, 221–4), perhaps, but compelling as an explanation of all that many
in Taiwan felt that they had lost since 1945.[3] This historical recognition of the
importance of the colonial era provides an important context to Taiwanese people's
notions of their "Chineseness," or, often, their relative lack of such a quality.

Selbin's clear explanation that remembering "places the past in the service of the present," and that "there is a societal memory which is up for grabs, a battlefield where various groups struggle to protect and extend their interpretations of society's past" (Selbin 1997: 125), is useful shorthand for the clear historicity of Taiwanese people's nostalgia for the Japanese era. As described above, Japanese colonialism in Taiwan functioned largely as a signifier of the difference between modern Japanese and obsolete Chinese rule, and, therefore, of Japan's role as the former ruler and champion of East Asia. The widespread popular dissatisfaction that the Nationalists faced in late 1940s Taiwan quickly led to serious and sustained efforts to reform KMT rule, to stress their "new" orientation and goals, and to attract Taiwanese party members and followers from all walks of life (Myers 2009: 187–92). However, the dark 1950s joke related by Melissa Brown in her book *Is Taiwan Chinese?* suggests that the damage to the reputation of the KMT had already been done: "The Japanese were lucky because the Americans only dropped atomic bombs on them; Americans dropped Chiang Kai-shek on us" (Brown 2004: 241). At the same time, it is tantalizing to wonder if Chiang's postwar "policy of magnanimity,"[4] as explained in Chih Huei Huang's chapter in this volume, actually served to enable pro-Japan nostalgia in postwar Taiwan. Chiang believed—even to the point of supporting the maintenance of Japan's emperor system—that Japan and his ROC on Taiwan should be allies based on their shared Asian culture and their common anti-communist position (Z. Huang 2009: 165–7). Could his publicly benevolent position toward his defeated enemy have emboldened further Taiwanese people's warm feelings toward their former colonial rulers?

On one level there has existed for more than six decades a fundamental wariness on the part of many Taiwanese people toward the Nationalist party/state. In the 1980s, one Taiwanese person told anthropologist Hill Gates, "Under the Japanese, we learned to trust the word of the authorities. The Nationalists betrayed that trust; they will never have it again" (1987: 45). On another level, the populist resentment of mainlander privilege in Taiwan gave rise to the intellectual movement toward "Taiwan history" (*Taiwanshi*). Jeremy Taylor has described this representation of the past as significant for two distinct but related reasons: (1) its clear opposition to official Nationalist histories (literally *Guoshi*) and (2) its focus (usually favorably) on the Japanese colonial era as a moment that "represent[s] an experience that differentiates Taiwan from China" (2005: 166).

It was one thing for newly constituted Taiwanese citizens of the ROC to express their resentment at a regime that scorned and punished them, their families, and/ or their communities for having lived under Japanese colonial rule and then to indulge in (for some, perhaps, cheap, and for others, well-earned) after-the-fact preference or nostalgia for the departed Japanese. However, it should appear as something very different today for Taiwanese people, perhaps born several decades after the events of the KMT's program of "White Terror," to actively remember and recreate these memories of victimhood. While I feel strongly that categories of Holocaust suffering should not be cited lightly, the scholar Marianne Hirsch's notion of "postmemory" is useful here. In discussing how photographs fit within the memories of family members murdered in the Holocaust, Hirsch has identified this "powerful and very particular ... often obsessive and relentless" form of memory, which is "distinguished from memory by generational distance and from history by deep personal connection ... [and] mediated not through recollection but through an imaginative investment and creation" (1997: 22). "Postmemory" becomes an apt mode of understanding the dynamic tension between contemporary Taiwanese nationalism, resentment of KMT governance, and nostalgia for Japanese colonialism that is so foundational today. Indeed, the "postmemory" of Japanese Taiwan—a fifty-year period imagined and remembered over a period of seventy years—has truly become, in Hirsch's words, a specter of "incomprehensibility and presence, a past that will neither fade away nor be integrated into the present" (1997: 40).

Andreas Huyssen sees this articulation of past as memory as a fissure that "should be understood as a powerful stimulant for cultural and artistic creativity" (1995: 3). Also there are many Taiwanese and Japanese artifacts of this impulse to remember, many decades on, a progressive and mutually beneficial colonial moment in Taiwan. On a visit to Taiwan in July 2011, the first television program my children and I watched upon arriving was a daytime public television broadcast of the 2009 animated film *Hatta Is Coming!! The Story of Water in the Southern Island.* This film is a hagiographic treatment of Hatta Yoichi, the Japanese hydraulic engineer beloved in Taiwan for his work to design both the Jiayi-Tainan Canal and the Wushantou Dam in Tainan; both of the massive and transformational projects were completed in 1930. While glorifying his engineering triumphs, the film also instructs contemporary viewers about the intimate history of Japanese–Taiwanese cooperation, friendship, and understanding during this golden age of colonial rule. Taiwanese subjects marvel at the incredible technology bestowed on them by Hatta and the colonial regime, while the film emphasizes that Hatta "never distinguished between Japanese and Taiwanese" and thus exemplified the *isshi dōjin* ideology of impartial assimilationist colonial rule (Ishiguro 2009).

This film, produced in Japan, is a prime example of "imperialist nostalgia," which "uses a pose of 'innocent yearning' both to capture people's imaginations and to conceal its complicity with often brutal domination" (Rosaldo 1989: 108).[5] What is important to grasp, however, is that such colonial-nostalgic hyperbole actually seems to reflect a widely held view of Hatta's legacy in contemporary Taiwan. The 2005 *Record of Taiwan Great Men* praised his "rational and humane management style" and marveled at his canal project as "a green magical miracle" (Tang 2005: 107, 109). More recently, the official ROC government publication *Taiwan Review* cited former grand justice Su Junxiong's praise for Hatta: "In the face of colonial rule, he ignored the distinctions of class, title, ethnicity or race, showing a broad-mindedness rare among members of the ruling class" (Gao 2011). Also, in May 2012, former ROC president Lee Teng-hui called Hatta "the best example of the 'Japanese spirit'" in a highly publicized visit to the Wushantou Dam. Lee "choked [up] several times and almost burst into tears as he recalled Hatta's contributions and humanity." (He also, revealingly, took this opportunity to explain that he had "declined an invitation to attend President Ma Ying-jeou's inauguration ceremony on Sunday as 'a form of silent protest' about Ma's [reunification] policies"[6] [Wang 2012b: 1].) The moment of Japanese nostalgia and identity in Taiwan—via the maneuvers of figures like Lee—has become synonymous with opposition to "China" in any possible form. Indeed, Leo Ching has recently written on others of Lee's generation whose memoirs of their colonized lives harken back to the peace, stability, and discipline of Japanese Taiwan and mourn the postwar loss of the "Japanese spirit" (Ching 2012: 215–20).

Cultural artifacts such as this film about the hydraulic/social engineer Hatta are a handy reminder of the virtual omnipresence of expressions of nostalgia for the colonial society that predated Taiwan's era of Chinese rule beginning in 1945. In other words, these feelings go far beyond the common academic view that Japanese colonial rule provided important material benefits that help us to understand Taiwan's subsequent development.[7] Taiwanese people's attachment to their status as former subjects of the Shōwa, Taishō, and/or Meiji emperors thus is crucial to understanding their notions of their relationship to Chinese culture and the Chinese governments that rule both their own island and the mainland just ninety miles away. Taiwan–PRC relations have long been, and surely will long be, complicated by memories of Taiwan's half century as part of the Japanese empire; our volume will bring out this seldom-explored element of this important trans-Chinese rivalry and misunderstanding.

The first chapter in this part is Evan N. Dawley's "Closing a Colony: The Meanings of Japanese Deportation from Taiwan after World War II," a study of the newly arrived ROC government's role in the massive task of repatriating Taiwan's Japanese residents to their home islands. Dawley refers to the two-year duration of this process, from 1945 to 1947, as a moment when Taiwan functioned as a "multi-national society" made up of Japanese, Chinese, and Taiwanese (this latter group, of course, comprised of former Japanese subjects and newly anointed Chinese citizens of the ROC) people all competing for valuable and scarce resources (as well as political power) in the aftermath of World War II. The triumphalism of the arriving Chinese victors of the war, the obviously close ties between so many Taiwanese and their Japanese spouses, children, friends, teachers, and neighbors, and the real and imagined involvement of Japanese subjects in the anti-ROC uprising following the February 28th Incident (*Ererba shijian*) in 1947 combined to make this a very tense time. However, Dawley reveals the histories of those Japanese who made the most of their lame-duck status in Taiwan, working earnestly and enthusiastically to help the Chinese regime rebuild the island to which their own government had dedicated so many financial and ideological resources. Helping to reconstruct China's Taiwan was a way, for some of the more introspective Japanese technicians and soldiers kept behind, to pay penance for the wrong that their imperial military had done on the mainland, while for others it could serve as a way of continuing the imperial fight against communism in East Asia.[8] This work thus helped many Japanese to deal with their newfound and jarring status as "fourth-rate" losers, and this dedication meant much to Taiwanese residents who were starting to wonder how they would fare under Chinese rule. Their gathering and waving Japanese flags to bid some of the last Japanese deportees goodbye was a meaningful gesture—not only showing politeness and regard but also appropriating a belonging to Japan, a "left behind" status that would come in handy in critiquing Chinese governance of Taiwan for many decades.

Chih Huei Huang, in her "Ethnic Diversity, Two-Layered Colonization, and Modern Taiwanese Attitudes toward Japan," adds one more variable to this already complicated postwar and postcolonial discourse—that of ethnicity within the "Taiwanese" population and how Taiwanese (Hoklo), Hakka, and Aborigine intellectuals have configured their views of the Japanese era since the end of World War II. As with Shepherd's piece above, her investigation of views unique to the Hakka people of Taiwan complicate even more the ethnic and ideological profile of postwar Taiwan. Anne McClintock asked in 1992, "Can most of the world's countries be said, in any meaningful or theoretically rigorous sense, to share a single … 'post-colonial condition,' or 'post-coloniality?'" (1992: 87) Huang's fine distinctions here show that this concern for a diversity and multiplicity of postcolonial ways of seeing can be extended to the island of Taiwan itself.

Many native Taiwanese writers and intellectuals, dismayed by the sudden destruction of their high hopes for a democratic Chinese Taiwan after 1947, swore loyalty to Japanese culture and spirit and vowed never to speak Mandarin. Hakka residents of Taiwan who identified with the tight-knit Hakka community on the mainland, however, sympathized much more with the idea of "China" than those Taiwanese who saw themselves only as residents of this small island. Having been largely left out of Hoklo majority imaginations of Taiwanese culture for centuries, Hakka people identified more with the *waishengren* "provincial-outsiders" (the "mainlanders" who relocated to Taiwan between 1945 and 1949) arriving from China after World War II and the powerful mainland-centric notion of Taiwan as merely one province of a greater Chinese republic. And in turn, these *waishengren*, the newest group of immigrants in Taiwan's layered history, immediately came face to face with the original peoples of Taiwan, the Aborigines. Conflicts between these two groups over land, the vision of constructing a truly Chinese society, and memories of World War II (one group fought fiercely *against* the Japanese while the other fought loyally *for* them) added one more fault line to this tumultuous landscape. As Huang explains, "Taiwanese society is still entangled in three 'postwars'"; a discriminating eye with regard to Taiwan's complex ethnocultural diversity is crucial to an understanding of how Japanese Taiwan has been remembered. Taiwanese people of any background who lived and negotiated these tensions never could have understood outsiders' Cold War-inflected assumptions of a Chiang Kai-shek-worshiping, communist-hating uniformity achieved under ROC rule.

A chapter of my own follows, in which the possibility, trauma, resentment, and nostalgia that defined early ROC Taiwan emerged on, of all places, the baseball diamond. This game had been brought to Taiwan by the Japanese and had very shallow roots in mainland China. After 1945, it emerged as an important site for the negotiation of many ideas about how Chinese or Japanese the future of Taiwan would be. The game thrived at the semipro level (and with some American support—again Cold War-inflected) during the 1950s without much notice by the ROC regime, which had imported soccer and basketball as their "national" games. The official position of the game in Taiwan changed in the mid-1960s, however, with the emergence of Oh Sadaharu, the Chinese-Japanese star player of Tokyo's Yomiuri Giants.

In "Oh Sadaharu/Wang Zhenzhi and the Possibility of Chineseness in 1960s Taiwan," I look at the clashing Taiwanese and mainlander understandings of Oh (Wang, in Chinese) and his accomplishments. Taiwan's mainlander population, though greatly diverse in terms of socioeconomic status and prospects (Fan 2011: 82–109), was at this time largely unified by notions of diaspora and exile (Lupke 2009: 247). Safran's classic categories of a diasporic identity—characterized by an experience of dispersal from the homeland, collective memories of that homeland, a belief that the émigrés are not accepted in their new land, a desire for return, support of their homeland, and a collective identity constructed around their place of origin (1991: 83–4)—characterize well the dual position of privilege and trauma that defined the public mainlander identity when Oh became an important part of popular culture in Taiwan.

The ROC regime invited Oh to Taiwan and played up his identity as Wang, the (half-) ethnic Chinese Superman triumphing over Japanese discrimination with unbeatable Chinese morality, patriotism, and drive. Wang became all Oh, though, till the moment he opened his mouth; having grown up in Japan, he spoke almost no Chinese and seemed in his demeanor and professional identity to be Japanese through and through. This fact electrified Taiwanese fans, who harkened back to the colonial support of the game and thrilled to the home run feats of Oh, the man (like so many of them) who was born under Japanese rule.

Oh's background made him a handsome and conquering mirror image of the Taiwanese former subjects of the Japanese empire. Where many Taiwanese saw themselves as having been blessed by the gaze of Japanese emperors and cursed by the coming of the backward Chinese Nationalists, Oh had risen from the kitchen of his father's modest noodle shop by the grace of the "Japanese" game of baseball. In Joyce Liu's words, "the denouncement of the primary uncultivated … Chineseness, and the identification with … the sacred Japanese spirit is … the key to the understanding of identity in colonial Taiwan" (2009: 267). In the 1960s, Taiwanese nostalgia for the colonial moment was still based largely on the accompanying scorn for a retrograde "China." Oh/Wang thus provided a specific site where this complicated nexus of Taiwanese, Chinese, and Japanese could be imagined, explained, and cheered on.

Corrado Neri's "Haunted Island: Reflections on the Japanese Colonial Era in Taiwanese Cinema" takes us directly into the swirling representations of the Japanese–Taiwanese relationship that Taiwanese films have refracted during the colonial period and since the late 1980s. Although questions of Chinese culture and identity, history, and memory dominated Taiwanese film for more than four decades after 1945, Taiwan's democratization resulted in a return to the seemingly organic search for the meanings of Japanese Taiwan. Some of these films explore love between Japanese and Taiwanese people, while others experiment with grisly fantasies of sexualized revenge. Some straightforwardly celebrate a civilizing, modernizing Japanese influence, while others posit the reverse and interrogate the ways in which Taiwanese culture changed the culture of the colonial metropole.

The most famed example of how film can demonstrate the compelling nature of this complicated historical consciousness is the wildly popular 2008 Taiwanese feature film *Cape No. 7* (*Haijiao qi hao*). This film is about nothing so much as those "left behind" in different ways in the history of interchange between Taiwan and Japan (Wei 2008). *Cape No. 7* is the second-highest grossing film in Taiwanese history (behind only *Titanic*), beloved for the ways in which rowdy fun, romance, community bonds, and moments of great melodrama in the southern rock-and-roll scene are all defined totally by the legacies and losses of colonialism. However, it horrified film critics and scholars, who saw the work as an example of the culture of "obsequious flattery of Japan" (*mei Ri*), of Taiwanese people's "desire to be colonized," as a "poisonous weed," and as proof that "Taiwan cannot escape the devil's clutches of Japanese culture" (Lin 2010: 139–40, 150, 158). The fact that some of these critiques, once posted online, became popular reading in the PRC (Lin 2010: 158) served only as the clearest reminder of how these Taiwanese expressions of intimacy with Japan often are meant distinctly to (and do successfully) infuriate PRC nationalists who believe that the "loss" of Taiwan keeps today's China from its true destiny. (And fans of this genre that we might call postcolonial pornography have also enjoyed *Cape* director Wei Te-Sheng's latest film *KANO*, an epic about the colonial-era baseball team cited above and their physical demonstration of the successes of Japanese colonial rule. A 2012 press release from the city government of Jiayi, home of this school, refers us to that 1930s Japanese moment when "a group of people shared common goals, mutual respect and tolerance…. a simple town full of human touch" [Chiayi City Government 2012].)

Neri investigates several other works of Taiwanese cinema as well. Where slasher films, soft porn, and teen coming-out dramas may not seem the logical place to look for the specter of a colonial power long departed, he makes a compelling case for the important intersection here of history, gender, and memory. Much of the last three decades of Taiwanese film has been defined by the filmic value that a cherry blossom, a Japanese boyfriend, or a commemorative railroad token can deliver to an on-screen representation of this eternally postcolonial island. And Neri's conclusion on *Blue Brave*, director Hung Chih-yu's otherwise unremarkable 2008 portrayal of Hakka resistance of the Japanese invasion, has striking implications: What does it tell us about Taiwan when the only character in such a film "who has the privilege and the right to speak" is a paternalist conservative Japanese medic? Seven decades after the end of Japanese colonialism in Taiwan, is the benevolent Japanese verdict on this era all that the market will bear?

Jens Sejrup's "Reliving the Past: The Narrative Themes of Repetition and Continuity in Japan–Taiwan News Coverage" immediately follows and manages to show how this default Japanese aesthetics and sensibility dominates not only art but the real world of presidential and party politics. Former ROC president Lee Teng-hui's fondness for the Japanese trump was mentioned above; Sejrup discusses Lee's early 2000s gambits of staging "private," "medical," or "family" visits to Japan when all observers knew that these were meant to be provocative performances of a Taiwanese debt to Japanese achievement, progress, sacrifice, and beauty. Hill Gates described a Mrs. Lim Fumiko, a teacher educated under the Japanese, as an example of those many Taiwanese with "deep respect and admiration for Japan's culture and achievements, and with a sense of having lost membership in a progressive and respected nation only by historical accident" (1987: 212). Lee has worked since his presidency to validate, normalize, and reify this very sensibility, a move that he seems to believe can only be achieved while simultaneously trying to ridicule and humiliate PRC nationalists who believe in their own Chinese claim on the island. Lee's project is one of positioning Taiwan as still part of a Japanese East Asia, a Taiwan of "Japanese mornings" where a life of left-behind Japanese culture could hopefully transcend the temporal and geographical divides between Japan and Taiwan, or even between colonial/wartime Taiwan and the twenty-first-century Taiwan home of the ROC regime.

Sejrup seeks to find, in effect, how and why on earth Lee's position as eternal colonial subject has become such an authoritative one. Drawing on the trappings and gestures of Lee's visits to Japan, as well as those by 2008 presidential election opponents Frank Hsieh and Ma Ying-jeou, Sejrup describes the contemporary political value in Taiwan, supported vigorously by much of the Japanese media, of a sensibility conspicuously informed by Japanese education, culture, and history. Hsieh in his campaign even labeled his plan to renegotiate Taiwanese values and culture and to resolve domestic political conflict a "Taiwan Restoration" (*Taiwan weixin*, directly copying the name of 1868's Meiji Restoration) (Sejrup 2012: 753). One does wonder about the implications for democracy in Taiwan when the leaders of its "Left" (as the Democratic Progressive Party and Taiwan Solidarity Union position themselves) remember so fondly Taiwan's rule by an empire responsible for as much violence toward the body and soul as was Japan's. As in Allen's, Simon's, and Neri's pieces described above, Sejrup's work again illustrates how the categories of history, memory, alienation, present-day politics, and anxiety about the future swirl back and forth and truly mutually constitute each other in often the strangest of ways.

One final way in which Japanese culture is remembered and relived in Taiwan today can be seen in Marc L. Moskowitz's chapter "Drinking Modernity". While the uninformed observer might imagine that Taiwan's contemporary coffee culture was a simple case of Starbuckolonization or one more instance of seeming Asian mimicry of the innovative ways of Western late capital, Moskowitz provides an alternate history of the career of coffee in Taiwan. The coffee houses that are so popular in Taiwan today are descendants of traditional Chinese teahouses, Japanese hostess clubs, postwar Chinese coffee shops catering to mainlanders and American soldiers alike, postwar Japanese coffee chains, and the martial law-era popularity of Nescafé in Taiwan. Even the Starbucks branches that seem ubiquitous are as much a testament to the marketing genius of Uni-President Enterprises Corporation, the Japanese-influenced Taiwanese conglomerate that has also filled the island with 7-Eleven, Carrefour, and Mister Donut franchises, as they are to simple one-directional cultural imperialism. Starbucks's regime of sanitized uniformity has been partly confounded in Taiwan by the gendered history of coffee there and the history of coffee establishments as a clearly sexualized sphere. The sensual experiences of coffee and their close links to the sexualized economy of male-dominated hostess culture remind us how often and how thoroughly moments in contemporary Taiwan can still be intruded upon by the "left behind" traces of Japanese rule.

Conclusion: Competing nostalgias—
China and Japan in modern Taiwan

Living as "left behind" in some way seems to be what makes Taiwan Taiwan. Where else can one imagine a former president posing for photos in full comic book "cosplay" attire, as 81-year-old Lee Teng-hui did in 2004? (See his 2004 turn as World War II veteran–turned–feared school principal Edajima Heihachi of the comic book *Charge!! Men's Private School* [*Sakigake!! Otokojuku*] in Huang 2004: 3.) While much of Lee's presentation and advertisement of his famed Japanophilia seems calculated to antagonize PRC nationalists, it is undeniable how meaningful his "left behind" status is to him and how much it has benefited him and others like him politically.

Another typical example of this nostalgia can be seen in the Zhanghua City Butokuden (*Zhanghua shi wudedian*) in Figure 1.4. The original structure was built in 1930 by the Shōka municipal police department for the purposes of judo and kendo training. After the arrival of the Nationalists in 1945, like so many other essentially Japanese structures (Shintō shrines, for example), it was converted into a Martyr's Hall. It was restored after the September 21, 1999, earthquake at a cost of NT$22.5 million, and in 2001 its Japanese-era name was restored to it (*Taiwan dabaike quanshu* 2014) and a statue of a "Japanese" martial artist was gratuitously erected at its entrance. The generally shabby condition of the unambiguously "Chinese" Confucius statue less than a mile east on Gongyuan Road provides a useful contrast: the compelling political charge that the Japanese connection provides to this small city in central Taiwan made the Butokuden a much better investment of public funds.[9]

Academics—especially those educated by the Japanese—also figure prominently in this discourse. Historian Huang Wen-hsiung is a generation younger than Lee, but after pursuing study in Japan in the 1960s, he became a powerful voice for the benevolence of the colonial empire that he was only able to enjoy living under until the age of seven. In many, many dozens of books that one can only conclude are written very intentionally to antagonize, Huang has tried for almost four decades to build a case for the great contributions of the Japanese Empire to the fate of modern Taiwan, China, and Korea. One recent example is his 2002 book *Modern China Was Created by Japan*, in which Huang goes far beyond his typical nostalgic enthusiasm for Japan's contributions to Taiwanese history to make the case that both modern regimes of China's twentieth century were "created" by the Japanese and their political, religious, moral, cultural, artistic, military, agricultural, and technological work on behalf of the Chinese people. A longtime supporter of Taiwanese independence, Huang provides a vivid example of the surprising ideological power of this Japan–Taiwan nexus even today. Although not as inflammatory, the "mainlander" analog to this essentialist and ahistorical position can be seen in Professor Su Jiahong's recent book, *We Are All Mainlanders: 400 Years of Immigration from the Mainland across the Sea to Taiwan*, and his study of "50 Years of Imperializationist Education under Japanese Occupation and the Unchanging Chinese Mind" (Su 2008: 76–103). It is a triumphalist and clichéd reading, to be sure, but one that is representative of the Nationalist position today: that Taiwan's past and, of course, future are Chinese through and through.

Figure 1.4 Zhanghua City Butokuden (*Zhanghua shi wudedian*). Photo by Andrew D. Morris.

The student of Japanese Taiwan quickly becomes accustomed to the weight of the legacy of "China" in colonial and postcolonial Taiwanese discourse. A recent example of the capacity for "China" to stand for that which is harmful, oppressive, and destructive can be seen in the Sunflower Student Movement that thrived during the spring of 2014. University students in Taiwan demonstrating against the KMT's secret approval of a Cross-Strait Service Trade Agreement (*Haixia liang'an fuwu maoyi xieyi*) with the PRC posted, above the front entrance of the parliament (*Lifa yuan*) building, large yellow signs sarcastically renaming the institution the "Parliament of the Chinese Party for Selling out Taiwan" (*Zhongguodang mai Tai yuan*) ("Heixiang" 2014; Mair 2014). A "Chinese" counter came the week that this manuscript was submitted for publication, from Lien Chan, former ROC premier and vice president and KMT chairman. Attempting to help his son Sean in his campaign for Taipei mayor in November 2014, Lien told a pro-unificationist crowd that opponent Dr. Ko Wen-je was a "bastard" who was morally compromised by coming from a family who had been "imperialized" (*huangminhua*) under Japanese rule: "I absolutely cannot stand the thought of having someone whose grandfather changed his surname to a Japanese one during the Japanese colonial era as mayor of Taipei" (members of the audience helped fill out this characterization with catcalls that Ko came from a family of "traitors" [*Hanjian*]) (Lin 2014; Loa 2014).

The chapters in the book on the early colonial period provide important investigations of the meanings of "China" or of the Qing Dynasty legacy in Japanese

Taiwan. In Allen's study, the modern regime of photography provides a way to show the emptiness, the undefined vacancy that characterized the island to many Japanese in the late nineteenth century. How flawed and unserious a colonial power, in other words, would the Qing have had to be in order to leave this bountiful island so formally, administratively, and economically blank and unmarked? Barclay's emphasis on the Japanese project to teach and civilize the Aborigines through trade and commerce helps us to understand another dimension of their disregard for the unsophisticated and undisciplined model of Qing rule of Taiwan. Simon's study fits here as well, as he shows us the power within colonial discourse of the trope of mistreatment of the Indigenous Peoples by the Qing/Chinese (these categories were often carelessly conflated). Combined with Shepherd's piece on the incredibly thorough compilation of the medical biodata of Taiwan's population, this all helps us to understand Angelina Yee's characterization of colonial-era understandings of the Chinese mainland as "primordial ... asleep ... dormant," a virtual opposite of what is remembered as the palpably modern and alive society in Japanese Taiwan (2001: 91).

Contributors to the second half of this volume then demonstrate how this refraction of the "Chinese" crosses the 1945 boundary and seeps into the postcolonial as well. The popular affection for the departing Japanese that Dawley explains was often simply the flip side of the gloating stereotypes that Taiwanese residents reserved for the incoming KMT "blanket soldiers" and "old taro" (*láu-ōo-á*) "provincial outsiders" from all over the poor war-torn mainland. My chapter traces this Taiwanese/mainlander rivalry to the person of Oh Sadaharu and his successes in the "Japanese" game of baseball, while Huang complicates this picture even further by reminding us of the unique positions, loyalties, and resentments of Taiwan's often-overlooked Aborigine and Hakka populations. Finally, Neri and Sejrup show how strong the common Hoklo nostalgia for the good old colonial days still is today; clearly the democratic era has allowed, and has been largely constituted by, newer and more intense imaginations of what the Japanese left behind in Taiwan. For those who are proud of what they remember and imagine as their Japanese heritage, every instance of KMT misrule can be understood as direct proof of this Chinese party's unfitness to rule Taiwan, and by extension, the timeless appropriateness of the long-gone "Japanese spirit."

The existence of this powerful nostalgia in Taiwanese society is evocative, especially when one considers the competing nostalgias that existed in the minds of the millions of "mainlanders" who found themselves stuck in Taiwan for the next several decades (see Corcuff 2011: 40–1). These more recent Chinese immigrants to Taiwan left their families and communities behind in the mainland that many of them would never see again; it is easy to imagine the modern conveniences and conformist politics of the KMT's 1950s–1960s "Free China" seeming a poor substitute for all that they had abandoned to go to Taiwan with the Nationalists. Grasping the power of these opposed but vibrant nostalgias,[10] by two groups who very rightfully imagined themselves to have been "left behind" by the traumas of East Asia's mid-century wars and turmoil, allows us to have an even richer understanding of what life was like for so many people in postwar, post-"Retrocession" Taiwan.

Notes

1   Gotō Ken'ichi studies the notion, especially after 1935, that Taiwan should play more of an active role in Japan's advance into Southeast Asia. Besides schools like Wu's alma mater, the Imperial Subject Service Society established three schools especially for the purpose of training Taiwanese youth to build a modern and Japanese Southeast Asia (Gotō 2004: 31–41).

2   This could also include the direct sponsorship of headhunting raids by allied tribes against those judged to be in the way of colonial progress, as in the officially sanctioned 1903 Bunun-on-Atayal grotesquerie described elsewhere by Barclay (2007: 79).

3   Bissell's epigram citing Don DeLillo from *Underworld* —"Longing on a large scale is what makes history"—is thus very appropriate here.

4   Later ROC authors were clear to specify that the wisdom of Chiang's "*yi de bao yuan*" policy came from Chapter 63 of the *Daodejing* (Chang 1968: 206), thereby rooting his treatment of the vanquished Japanese in an essentially Chinese benevolence.

5   However, Rosaldo misses out entirely on the significance of Japanese colonialism by simply calling this nostalgia part of the "white man's burden."

6   One month earlier Lee had called Ma "pathetic" and accused him of "cheat[ing] his people" for putting forward an official position that Taiwan and China are two administrative areas of the same country (Wang 2012a: 3).

7   For a recent investigation of these claims, see Booth 2007.

8   In 1949, this phenomenon took a more controversial turn when Chiang Kai-shek invited General Okamura Yasuji, former commander-in-chief of the China Expeditionary Army, to lead a group of former Japanese officers to train Nationalist forces. See Barak Kushner's (2013) nuanced description of this arrangement, which lasted until 1969.

9   Min-Chin Chiang also cites this Butokuden as an example of the ambiguous treatment of "colonial heritage" sites in contemporary Taiwan (2012: 35–7).

10   Chen Kuan-Hsing has summed up this tension by saying simply that " 'colonialism' does not seem to exist in the structure of historical memory for *waishengren*, just as 'Cold War' does not occupy a central place in that of *benshengren*" (2005: 52–3).

2

Colonial Itineraries: Japanese Photography in Taiwan

Joseph R. Allen

The timely convergence of Japan's colonization of Taiwan and the development of third-generation photographic materials and processes, especially the introduction of celluloid film and the perfection of the halftone printing process, resulted in the medium holding a position of importance in the Japanese colonial effort that exceeded even the one it held in the early British, French, and German colonial regimes. Although the earliest Japanese photographs of the island, by Matsuzaki Shinji, documenting the 1874 Meiji military expedition to the east coast of the island, were made with the cumbersome wet-plate techniques (which required an on-site darkroom), photography from the colonial period proper was produced with high-speed dry plate/film media and reproduced in halftone printed volumes.[1] Regarding the improved technology of the 1890s, Beaumont Newhall wrote as follows:

> This important invention [i.e., halftone printing] was perfected at precisely the time that the technical revolution in photography was taking place. Dry plates, flexible film, anastigmat lenses and hand cameras made it possible to produce negatives more quickly, more easily, and of a greater variety of subjects than ever before. The halftone enabled these photographs to be produced in limitless quantities in books, magazines, and newspapers. (Newhall 1964: 175)

It is this turn-of-the-century photographic technology and outlook that Japan brought to its early colonial project in Taiwan.[2]

Since the entire Japanese colonial period (1895–1945) fell under the gaze of an increasingly widespread and sophisticated photographic technology (with ever faster film, smaller cameras, and higher-definition mass printing), the medium was a constantly evolving instrument in the construction of Taiwan's colonial modernity. It provided a continuous and detailed visual construction of the colonial enterprise that was interwoven with, and conditioned by, its other discursive systems:

This project was supported by a Faculty Research Grant from the Ministry of Education of Taiwan, ROC, administered through the Taipei Economic and Cultural Office in Chicago. Research was conducted at Taiwan Studies Research Materials Center, National Taiwan Library, which holds the contents of the Japanese Colonial Library; I especially want to thank Chen Limei and the staff of that center for their help.

cartographic, demographic, and natural history. More importantly, it provided early heuristic models by which the island came to be known: the "landscape" for the equally constructive colonial maps.[3] First, photographs of Taiwan promoted the new territorial possession as part of the Japanese national imaginary—up to that point, Taiwan had been a relatively obscure island far from the Japanese cultural reach. As Yuko Kikuchi has observed, "From a vague characterization as a peripheral part of China, Taiwan came to be defined [in the Japanese consciousness] as an independent cultural entity with distinctive characteristics" (Kikuchi 2007: 4). This is an important shift in the conditionality of the island. Before that time, the island had been seen either as a belated addition to the Qing dynasty or, more locally, as a collection of enclaves exiled from the southeast coast of China—both early forms of conditionality. In 1895, the island suddenly became a part of, or an attachment to, Japan.

Early colonial photography in Taiwan

The Japanese colonial camera focused on the tropical novelties of Taiwan that found resonance with cultural constructions already present in Japan, on subjects that were wondrous but not alien. As James R. Ryan has demonstrated, European colonial photographies also often offered views and subjects that matched the expectations and prejudices of audiences at home; in many cases, the objects being photographed were integrated with the production of Orientalism and its knowledge regime. In Japan's case, its colonial photography seems more closely linked to its own domestic experience with modernization, wherein it, too, was the subject of the colonial gaze, what Thomas Lamarre calls the Japanese "doubly colonial situation" and C. J. Hsia identifies in Taiwan as the "double transplantation of cultural dependency" (Hsia 2002: 17; LaMarre 2009: 261). This condition of being colonially "doubled" characterizes many aspects of Meiji Japan, including its photography. This is another difference between European and Japanese colonial photography: the Japanese professed colonial ideology of "shared culture" (*dōka*), which claimed a cultural and racial affinity with other East Asian peoples, seems to have reduced the potential exotic nature of the colonial subject.[4] For example, photographs with explicit sexual content, which are common in European colonial photography, seem to have *not* attracted the Japanese camera; there are no equivalents to French postcards of Algerian harem girls, nudes of the "Venus of the Hottentots," or the bare-breasted geishas of Beato.[5] And although there is plenty of evidence of racism in Japanese colonial policy, particularly as directed toward the Aboriginal peoples, the situation was also complicated by the ambiguous position of the Japanese vis-à-vis elite Chinese culture. Given the esteemed position that some aspects of Chinese culture held in Japan, especially as related to literature and the arts, the efforts of the Japanese to place that culture within a colonial relationship created a complication of subjectivities that was nearly impossible in other, more clearly racialized colonial worlds.[6]

The album constructions

Early Japanese colonialist photography not only produced individual images of the island but also placed those images in composite visual narratives that presented detailed and integrated knowledge of the island for viewers. The earliest of those narratives are in the albums of halftone printed images (*shashinchō*), dating from 1896. Within the Japanese holdings of the National Taiwan Library (*Guoli Taiwan tushuguan*), which were transferred from the Japanese Colonial Library of Taiwan (*Taiwan sōtokufu toshokan*) in 1946, are approximately 145 such albums.[7] Although the Colonial Library was not established until 1914, its collection dates from the first years of the colony. These earlier works were probably first collected by Gotō Shinpei, the island's celebrated civil administrator from 1898 to 1906. Gotō was known for his rigorous academic approach to colonization, and he maintained a large library in his official residence (Peattie 1984: 82–9; Takekoshi 1907: 21–2).

The albums in the National Taiwan Library date from 1896 to 1941 and represent both governmental and commercial publications; they range in length from a diminutive thirteen pages to two-volume tomes with thousands of images. The photography contained in the albums is of many genres, such as formal portraits, studio compositions, candid shots, architectural photos, landscapes, aerial photography, and aesthetic studies. The thematic range is also wide, covering almost every possible subject and event on the island: from naked hunters to the visiting crown prince; from native flora and fauna to colonial monuments; and from local opera to Shinto rituals. The collection offers an early manifestation of what Susan Sontag calls the "voraciousness" of the twentieth-century photographic medium (1973: 146). Although some of these volumes have been mined for photographs in support of historical and cultural studies in Taiwan, the photography and the albums have seldom been considered in and of themselves, especially as part of the machinery of colonization.

At the time of publication, these albums were at the leading edge of the development of halftone printing in the world.[8] Their "first viewers" were elite Japanese. In fact, the primary audience for the 1896 album, *Album Commemorating the Military Triumph in Taiwan*, may have been the imperial household itself. For the audience in Japan, the albums functioned as a graphic representation of the young nation's modern possessions, while for those Japanese on the island, the albums were guidebooks for their sojourn. The albums were also part of the apparatus by which Japan projected its new presence in the international community of colonial powers, which it was eager to join as an equal—the English-language captions in several of the early albums are an index of that interest. And whether intended or not, I assume the Taiwanese colonial subjects, especially the cultural and economic elite, also "learned" of their island from these visual narratives. This is in part because precolonial identity formation of the Chinese population on the island was largely contingent on other geographic and cultural references—either subethnic identities within the island community or ancestral alliances to southeast China. In fact, we might argue that there was no real Taiwanese identity before the disparate groups within the Chinese population were drawn together by the Japanese colonial government's *hontōjin* (islander) appellation, which established an identity in a binary construction with the Japanese *naichijin* (homelander) population.[9] In this sense, the Chinese population learned to become "islanders" because of its conditional relationship with a colonial power, and that knowledge was constructed by the various colonial media and technologies.

Albums of the early colonial period

Eight photographic albums held in the National Taiwan Library collection were published during the first decade of the colonial period, a decade that centers on the decisive rule of Governor-General Kodama Gentarō and his civil administrator Gotō Shinpei. These albums not only plot the general lines of colonial rule during this early critical decade but also encompass most of the important photographic genres found in the entire album collection: military and civil itineraries, commemorative occasions, portraiture, scenery, architecture, and local customs and people.[10] The first two albums, considered in detail below, exhibit early examples of this diversity, even as they establish two models for cultural engagement with the island: the narratives of the expedition and the tour. They also represent two principal rationales and implied audiences for the albums in the collection: governmental instruments for the colonial office and commercial products for the Japanese tourist.

In the following discussions, I will consider photographs not so much as individual representations of specific subjects but rather as contributions to the album as a structural form.[11] To use the language of film studies, I am more interested in the montage, rather than the mise-en-scène, of the work. By employing some of the language of film studies (such as "shot," "scene," and "sequence") in analyzing these albums, I suggest that the albums be considered a genre in which the individual photographs (the "shots") are composed into readable, integrated sequences. The photographic structure anticipates the visual narrative of film and the modern photo essay (Greenough 2009: 176–89).

The conquest narrative

Album Commemorating the Military Triumph in Taiwan, published in Japan in May of 1896, presents multiple narratives, both verbal and visual, describing the 1895 Japanese military expedition to occupy the island. The latter half of the album is composed of a detailed, seventy-eight-page written account of the expedition, which concludes with a review of the accomplishments and final days of Imperial Prince Kitashirakawa, the most celebrated of its military leaders. The album's central heuristic design—the southward movement along the west coast of the island, ending in the heroic sacrifice embodied by the death of the prince (although he actually died of malaria)—determines how we read the composite work.

The visual narrative in *Military Triumph* begins graphically with a large tipped-in map that traces the progress of the expedition from the north to the south, plotting the footprint of conquest with red-tinted portions (as if the blood of sacrifice has stained the map). In its materiality, the map is also a manifestation of colonial ambitions: it employs the Western-style cartography that the Meiji government made part of its modernity project, into whose fold the colony was quickly incorporated. This is seen in many of its conventions, such as longitude and latitude designations; legends of landforms, civil works, and local products; hachure-marked topographic shapes; and details of scale. Thus, in two ways, the map declares the island to be a colonial possession: we own it, and we own it as a modern object.

Following the map, the sequence of photographs begins with a series of portraits. First, there are the paired, unlabeled portraits of the Meiji emperor and his heir apparent, both in modern military garb (Figure 2.1).[12] These are followed by individual photographs of the leaders of the expedition and administrative officials, headed by that of the late Prince Kitashirakawa (Figure 2.2). The entire photographic sequence concludes with scenes commemorating the military sacrifices made in the Sino-Japanese War, including depictions of the Yasukuni Shrine for the war dead in Tokyo. Thus, the opening gallery of portraits establishes the colonial authority and order behind the driving force of the narrative, while the concluding images provide its commemorative finale.

The photographic narrative contained within that frame of portrait and commemorative arch is, however, much more fragmentary and episodic than the written or cartographic one. Instead of a steady march to the south, the photographs

Figure 2.1 Meiji emperor (right) and his heir apparent (the future Taishō emperor), unlabeled opening photograph. *Taiwan gun gaisen kinen shashinchō* (1896). Courtesy of National Taiwan Library.

下 殿 王 親 川 白 北 故
Late Marshal H. I. H. Prince Kitashirakawa.

Figure 2.2 Prince Kitashirakawa, military commander of the 1895 expedition, part of the portrait gallery. *Taiwan gun gaisen kinen shashinchō* (1896). Courtesy of National Taiwan Library.

present a series of interrupted and largely unintegrated moments along the way; in this sense, the photographs *are* resistant, a la Mitchell, to the narrative drive of the accompanying essay. Of the approximately eighty-five photographs in the album, less than a dozen are actually of the expedition itself, and even these are often somewhat peripheral to the story of conquest. For example, the two depicting the critical approach toward Taipei (soon to be Taihoku) are typical in that they present the troops not in combat but rather on the journey toward that combat or at rest away from it: the first depicts the troops relaxing amid the rice paddies and bamboo groves of the countryside, and the next shows them gathered at a railroad bridge along the Jilong River, which the train and the troops follow toward the city. In part, this reflects an issue of technology: working with the still relatively clumsy equipment (at least, large cameras and tripods), it was much easier to photograph the troops in camp instead of on the battlefield. Even if this presentation is driven by practicalities, the ideological effect is to represent the military as a "civil" force, an instrument of control but not violence, what I call the ideology of "encampment." This is a representation that also resists the narrative of conquest.

Although there are similar depictions of military forces in states of encampment in other colonial photography (and probably for similar reasons), the ubiquity of scenes of encampment seems special to expeditionary photography in Taiwan and may represent a self-conscious effort to present a position of "civility" on the island. The most iconic example of this type of photography is an image of the military commander Prince Kitashirakawa at the very beginning of the expedition. In this photograph, which has been repeatedly printed in colonial and postcolonial publications, Kitashirakawa and his support staff are in camp with their tents and the wild rushes of the Taiwan plain in the background (Figure 2.3). While the others stand or sit on the ground, the prince poses casually, legs crossed, cigarette in hand, in an overstuffed chair. The chair is a sign not only of his stature in the group but also of the coming of Meiji modernization to the island and is in direct contrast to the untamed landscape and his temporary military quarters. The other men in the photo gaze directly at the camera, but Kitashirakawa looks away, as if pondering the upcoming battles, offering a dignified three-quarter profile, the common pose of the photographic portrait (Tagg 1993: 34–40; Allen 2014). This photograph has become an emblem of the man and the times because it is loaded with visual signifiers of that early colonial moment—civilization has arrived amid the wild Taiwan landscape, and its leader, who will sacrifice his life to the expedition, is aristocratic and contemplative.[13]

Figure 2.3 Prince Kitashirakawa encamped on arrival to Taiwan, May 29, 1895. *Taiwan meisho fūzoku shashinchō* (1903). Courtesy of National Taiwan Library.

This pose of the military at rest permeates the photographic record of Taiwan expeditionary narratives throughout the subsequent decades—in the later years, these were primarily expeditions against Taiwan's Indigenous Peoples. For example, the expeditions of 1911, 1913, and 1914 were thoroughly documented in photographic albums, some with hundreds of images. Despite the overt violence these expeditions entailed, the photography most often conveys a sense of discipline and rescue. We see the troops poised, orderly, and calm, ready for battle but not in battle; sometimes they are even shown in playful moods and activities, such as in a 1914 album that depicts them in wrestling matches and swimming in Taroko Gorge.[14] Regardless of the intervening narrative and its violence, at the conclusion of these albums, the troops inevitably return in triumph, not in a raucous display of bravado but rather in orderly ranks returning to recognized sites of civilization. Even the 1931 album documenting the expedition against the Aboriginal peoples after the infamous and brutal Musha Incident (*Musha jiken*; see Chapter 4 of this volume) contains many more photographs of the military at rest and en route rather than of actual fighting or battles.[15] For example, rather than photographs documenting the bombing of the villages or its aftermath, we have an elegant portrait of the planes and pilots, the misty mountains providing a backdrop for the young men and their sleek machines that will deliver "modernity" to those very hills (Figure 2.4).

Figure 2.4 Airplane and pilots for the Musha (Wushe) expedition of 1930. *Musha tōbatsu shashinchō* (1931). Courtesy of National Taiwan Library.

The visual record is not always completely one of deferred violence, however. Even the 1896 *Military Triumph* album demonstrates some attempt to record the effects of battle. Midway through the album, there is a small embedded narrative of violent conquest in three images. The first, a two-page panorama shows Japanese troops crossing a river; below it, a second panorama shows them firing artillery at some distant enemy; then, on the next page are two gruesome photographs of the Taiwanese dead. "Ready, aim, fire," the sequence seems to say. Yet a comparison of the dates and place-names in the captions reveals that the sequence is really a montage of shots of different parts of the expedition edited for narrative effect. Occasionally, later albums contain depictions of such violence, most often the burning of Indigenous villages, but sometimes the actions documented are much more graphic and horrific, showing the actual level of violence used against these peoples. For example, an album recording the 1913 campaign against the Aborigines in the Giran (Yilan) area has a montage of captured prisoners: three group photographs and then a final shot of a beheading, taken freeze-frame (the effect of the new photographic technology) just as the head falls away from the body (Figure 2.5).[16] The force of colonial rule does not get much more explicit than that. Nonetheless, the depiction of violence in these albums never seems to reach the level of sensationalism that Ryan describes in the commercial photography of the British campaigns in India and elsewhere, despite the fact that photographic technology during the Japanese campaigns had shed most of the limitations that had restricted the medium in British military campaigns fifty years earlier (Ryan 1997: 75–6). The ideology of the encampment and the masking of violence seem to be central forms in the Japanese colonial depiction of conquest, even when it is no longer technologically determined.[17]

When the *Military Triumph* album is considered as a constructed whole, the photographs actually tell a story more about the surroundings of the march rather than the march itself. Most project a lyrical image of the object of the expedition (the exotic tropical island) that diverts, if not resists, the central narrative of conquest. For example, a sequence of photographic montages that depict the city, its people, and environs follows the two photographs of military forces en route to Taipei. These montages offer a view of the island on the eve of colonial possession—Chinese, locally oriented and undeveloped in the modern sense. This condition is well illustrated by a page of Taipei street scenes, in which fruit stands, washerwomen, and sedan chairs appear; only the railroad suggests the recent changes to the island (see Figure 2.6). All things await the coming of colonization.

Throughout these early albums, shots are gathered together in a coordinated display. The coordination of the images range from vaguely thematic to highly structured narratives, but they all exhibit the editorial hand. Some of the montages even have the trompe l'oeil effect of earlier, hand-built photo albums, typically with the photos "trimmed" and "overlapped" on the page, sometimes even with "curled" edges (see Figures 2.8 and 2.9). The self-consciousness of the montages is clear, and the "handling" of the images is made palpable through this manipulation of advanced printing techniques.

The urban monument is a type of image that commonly occurs in these coordinated montages. When used to represent the precolonial urban condition, the monument most often portrayed is the city gate, which bears high symbolic

Figure 2.5 Leftmost two photos of montage of Japanese violence against Giran (Yilan) Aboriginal people, prisoners and beheading. *Tōbatsu guntai kinen shashinchō* (1913). Courtesy of National Taiwan Library.

value: the gate was both the emblem of the Chinese city and its central defense structure. In representations of the impact of colonization, on the other hand, the images are of the architecture of the modern state and its technology: European-style buildings, city boulevards, railroad stations, waterworks, and the like

Figure 2.6 Taihoku (Taipei) street scenes ca. 1895. *Taiwan gun gaisen kinen shashinchō* (1896). Courtesy of National Taiwan Library.

(see Figure 2.9). In some albums, the two types of urban monuments are joined to form a montage narrating architectural change on the island, particularly in Taihoku, which was obsessively photographed. This is most clearly seen in an album documenting the 1915 renovation of the downtown commercial district, in which benchmarking is made explicit with comparative before-and-after photographs of the specific sites (see Figure 2.7).[18] Such comparisons constitute the ideological equivalent of the conquest narrative, this time celebrating the renovation rather than the occupation of the object.

Japanese colonial albums that are grounded in a conquest narrative are essentially diachronic in construction and in the past tense: we need to move through time in order for that conquest to unfold and it must have been completed in order to have been recorded. In this narrative the subject/object of the conquest needs to remain, but its condition must change from disequilibrium to equilibrium. Thus, the precolonial becomes colonial, the savage becomes civil, and the traditional becomes modern. Even the cartographic representation of the conquest is marked by change: the terrain conquered by the expedition has turned red.

The tour narrative

Although the 1899 *Album of Famous Sites in Taiwan* contains remnants of a conquest narrative, its overall content and rationale diverge substantially from those of the

日丁一街武文――ヨリ方西

(葛) 上   圓

Figure 2.7 Before (bottom) and after (top) photographs of downtown Taihoku commercial district street renovations. *Taihoku shiku kaihen jinen shashinchō* (1915). Courtesy of National Taiwan Library.

1896 *Military Triumph* album. The difference is evident in its size alone. Approaching the dimensions of a small handbook (19 by 12 cm) and designed as an early travel guide for the Japanese visitor, its format can be seen as an emblem of the innovative, forward-looking approach toward development of the island that Kodama and Gotō brought with them in 1898. Under their leadership, the island was not only transformed economically and socially but also moved fully into the Japanese national imaginary, now as a destination not for the soldier but for the tourist.[19]

As a temporally contingent technology, photography is the perfect tool for bringing the past into the present while making the present instantly into the past. This is the condition of "temporal duality" that Rosalind Morris traces to the writings of Oliver Wendell Holmes and that informs Roland Barthes's *Camera Lucida* (Morris 2009: 11–13; Barthes 1981: 15). In the conquest narrative discussed above, that double condition is achieved by positing both the precolonial and the colonial in the same spatiotemporal plane. This flattening out of the past and present is also central to the imagery of the *Famous Sites* album, yet there, a new dimension also allows the reader to anticipate the future. The 1899 album relies on the familiar geographic itinerary—the movement from the northern seaport and capital southward down the west coast—but reconfigures that old itinerary by implying a new agent of travel. Here, the reader does not follow the postfactual record of a military force that moved down the island in pursuit of conquest; rather he (and it would almost certainly be "he") is invited to be a tourist, either actual or imaginary, and to make his way into wonder and discovery. It is an itinerary of the future as much as of the past and present. Unlike the conquest, this journey is infinitely repeatable. That reorientation away from the completed/successful government expedition and toward the invitation to embark on a commercial tour is one of the most distinctive moves this album makes; it is also a reorientation that permeates later albums in the collection. From this point onward, Taiwan is a site not just of military occupation but also of individual exploration; it is not just a possession but also a commodity.[20]

The visual narrative of the *Famous Sites* album is embedded in an elaborate set of written contexts: captions, notes, essays, and guides. In addition to the short Japanese-only captions, a set of background notes collected at the end of the album contextualizes the individual images and montages. These notes range from a single line that merely identifies the location of the photographed object to a dozen or more lines that offer significant details about the image. Not coincidentally, the opening and closing montages are given some of the most detailed notes, suggesting their important role in framing the album. For example, the notes for the two images of the opening montage (after the formal portraits) total twenty-four lines. The note for the second image, captioned "The Memorial Monument for Prince Kitashirakawa's Expedition" (*Kitashirakawakyū seitō kinenhi*), includes the entire text of the inscription on that monument. The longest single note, however, accompanies the montage of four city gates (see Figure 2.8); although the captions merely name the gates, the note itself is titled "A History of Taihoku City Wall" (*Taihokujō no enkaku*) and recounts the background to the building of the city going back to Shen Baozhen's memorials of 1875 (*Taiwan meisho shashinchō* 1899: 5–6, 9–10).[21] Thus, these photographic notes provide substantial contextualization for the image/object itself as well as more wide-ranging information that might appeal to the curious tourist.

Significantly, the album also contains two essays: "The Island of Taiwan" (*Taiwantō*) and "A Taiwan Travel Guide" (*Taiwan ryokō annai*). The essays are not linked directly to the photographs but do provide information about the images. "The Island of Taiwan" is composed of short paragraphs on a set of general topics, such as geography, weather, flora and fauna, and so on. The last of these topics is "cities and towns" (*toyū*), which the essay explores by listing urban sites along the expected itinerary from the north

Figure 2.8 Montage of Taihoku city gates. *Taiwan meisho shashinchō* (1899). Courtesy of National Taiwan Library.

to the south (Taihoku to Kōshun [Hengchun]) and providing short introductions to the east coast and the Hōko (Penghu) Islands. In contrast, "A Taiwan Travel Guide" is much longer (twenty-seven pages) and more complex. For example, its treatment of individual cities, presented in almost exactly the same order as in "A Taiwan Travel Guide," is fully developed and includes various levels of practical information, such as ferry and train schedules, pricing for rickshaws, and an explanation of alternative transportation around the flood-damaged railroad bridge for those wanting to take the train going south from Taihoku (*Taiwan meisho shashinchō* 1899: 4, 40). The information on the capital is the most detailed and provides a full overview of the official colonial presence in the city along with extensive notes on shopping and entertainment. Most noteworthy, the section concludes with a list of all streets in the city by district, accompanied by approximations of the Taiwanese pronunciations transcribed into Japanese katakana. The note to this listing suggests the new position the island was then taking in Japanese social consciousness:

> There are occasions when travelers from abroad have difficulty in negotiating the city despite the fact that they know [how to read] the names of the streets and districts in question. This is because they are not familiar with the native language, and thus their pronunciation of the place-names is not intelligible. We have therefore provided pronunciations for the following streets and districts for the convenience of the recently arrived. (*Taiwan meisho shashinchō* 1899: 35)

This passage is explicit about the volume's intended audience: the new resident or curious colonial tourist who wants to interact with the local culture. This new reader can also be deduced from the language of the essays themselves, which is much less formal than that of the 1896 album, with extensive use of *furigana* notation, not just for Chinese place-names and rare kanji but for almost every kanji, even common terms. Only newspapers of this era matched this blanket usage of *furigana* as the new imperial media carried out its popular explication of Japan's expanded polity.[22]

The commercial orientation of the *Famous Sites* album is also elaborately confirmed by its back matter: of the album's 200 pages, fully half are dedicated to commercial advertising. The commodities and services advertised are diverse and their media presentation varied, yet the tourist is clearly implied in many of their designs. Ads for hotels and restaurants, sake and tobacco, clothing and shoes, various publications, and dry goods stores are common. Many of these print ads contain different types of illustrations, including occasional photographic images. These usually occur in the most upscale advertisements, such as for the Hiryoku Restaurant in downtown Taihoku and the Fukukōkan Hotel in the port city of Kīrun (Jilong). And just in case a tourist needs his or her portrait taken while in town, advertisements for five different photographic studios, including one called the "Southward Advance Studio" (*Nanshinkan*), are included. The popular orientation of the album is also testified by its availability at various bookstores and other commercial establishments in both Taiwan and Japan.[23]

The primary visual structure of the album is geographic and brings the reader, like "A Taiwan Travel Guide," from Kīrun (the northern point of disembarkation for ships from Japan) steadily southward through city, town, and countryside to the southern tip of the island, followed by brief stops on the east coast plain of Giran and the Hōko Islands to the west. Although there is nothing remarkable about the way this tourist itinerary mirrors the military one (much of it due to the practicalities of travel), it, nonetheless, provides a structure of discovery of the island that restates the conquest narrative in a future tense. This itinerary is repeatedly employed throughout the colonial and postcolonial periods in a variety of media. In terms of geographic measure, the northern capital and environs are vastly overrepresented in the album. Although these photographs include images of the premodern city (again, the city gates being emblematic [see Figure 2.8]), they are outnumbered by images of the new, modern city with its colonial architecture, namely post office, police station, hospital, office buildings, pharmaceutical plant, weather station, and so on (see Figure 2.9).

Yet, when the photography moves away from the city, it withdraws from this colonial presence, encountering more and more of the precolonial conditions, especially vistas of the countryside—this part of "A Taiwan Travel Guide" is called "South from Taihoku" (*Taiwan meisho shashinchō* 1899: 40). Leaving the city, the reader moves metaphorically not only into the past but also into the future, toward the natural world that is both pristine and primitive, both inviting and forbidding. Placing the 1899 album in its historical context, we can argue that this itinerary plots the future both at a personal level (the travel plans of the tourist) and at the institutional level

Figure 2.9 Montage of new colonial buildings (clockwise from top left: weather observatory, hospital, pharmaceutical factory, post office). *Taiwan meisho shashinchō* (1899). Courtesy of National Taiwan Library.

(as virgin terrain for the colonial machine and emerging tourist industry). Thus, the episodic sights/sites over which the viewer's gaze would have moved can be read as a narrative of curiosity and anxiety: sites would have enticed with their tropical wonders and local curiosities even as they put one on edge with their forbidding jungles and savage practices.

Almost all post-1899 albums in the National Taiwan Library's collection reproduce this southward itinerary that moves away from the colony, the modern, and the present into the primitive, the past, and, at the same time, the future. In later albums, the island's central regions are more fully represented, with their deep forests and soaring mountains; this is a result of the enduring colonial presence on the island that forced precolonial conditions deeper into the isolated interior *and* brought the technology of photography into those very regions, which became more and more part of the potential itinerary of the visitor. (In fact, Barclay notes that "Japanese tourism in Indigenous Taiwan was not even feasible until the rash of Taishō period Indigenous revolts were put down in 1923" [2010: 104].) Over time, the lofty mountains of central Taiwan were increasingly celebrated and coveted: celebrated as the vestiges of the exotic and coveted as resources for the colonial industry, including the tourist industry. An album from 1927 embodies this dual status of the interior. A documentary on the aggressive logging industry accompanies elegant mountain scenery and ethnographic portraits of the Indigenous Peoples.[24]

The photographic itinerary in the *Famous Sites* album ends at a point at the greatest geographical and cultural distance from the capital: the island of Kōtōsho

("Red-Headed Island," today's Orchid Island) off the southeast coast; Torii Ryūzō established this in his ethnography as the most "untouched" of the Aboriginal areas. Once there, the itinerary is reintroduced in ethnographic terms with scenes of local customs and type portraits, providing another version of the past and the undiscovered, of both "traditional" China and the "primitive" island. The final montage in the album propels us as far into the native as we want to go: opium, the Aboriginal family, and head-hunting. These are the colonial objects that remain "unconquered." This last montage stands in counterpoint to the album's opening images, which celebrate the Japanese leadership of the island, including the commemorative monument to Prince Kitashirakawa. The narrative between the first and final frames of the album (from imperial presence to Aboriginal head-hunting) is not entirely linear, but it does follow a general movement from the colonial to the precolonial, from the modern to the traditional, and from the present to the past. Yet this is a past that anticipates the future, which will someday look like the colonial present but for now invites its discovery.

Later albums often contain detailed elaborations of this regressive itinerary, concluding with shots and sequences that emphasize the natural and still to be colonized—typically flora, fauna, and the Indigenous Peoples themselves. For example, the large 1918 *Picture Album on the Colonization of Taiwan* is based on an expansion of the southward narrative that makes a complete circuit of the island, north to south along the west coast, then south to north along the east.[25] As the circuit passes through specific sites, each is explored in depth, both visually and verbally, including subnarratives on the exploration of the primitive. Thus, when the viewer arrives at Taichū (Taizhong), he or she finds a detailed investigation of the mountain interior that lies to the east before the journey continues southward. After completing the entire circuit, the album concludes with a series of photographic essays that elaborately plot other regressive "narratives." First, there is a lineage of agricultural products from the most to the least colonized: sugar, camphor, salt, tobacco, rice, and tea. This is followed by a short sequence of type and custom photographs focusing on the Taiwanese, both commoners and elites. From there, the album moves on to less cultivated flora: bamboo, palms, and various fruits and trees. After that, the viewer is introduced to the Indigenous Peoples, the most distant of the colonial "products"—the human equivalent of wild fruit.

Still, the narrative move toward the primitive is not yet over. This last section on the Indigenous Peoples is prefaced by a short essay and a map that presents the modern anthropological understanding of the Indigenous groups (à la Torii), followed by a montage of photographs depicting the guard line separating the tribal land (or reservation) from the rest of the colony. After the montage, a sequence of photographs of the Indigenous Peoples again moves toward the primitive: the first page shows a village in the capital area with Aboriginal children in a relatively modern school; in the pages that follow, the conditions photographed as well as the photography itself move away from this ideal of colonial modernity, ending with old photographs of the Yami people of Kōtōsho taken from Torii's earlier photographic work. Thus, the *Colonization* narrative that began with the crisp official portrait of the Taisho emperor and empress, with their sixteen-petal chrysanthemum crest (Figure 2.10), concludes with a grainy image, captioned "Savage Chieftain Couple of Kōtōsho," of a Yami couple in their exotic conical headgear and he in his loincloth; indeed, the low quality of the photograph does not allow us to reproduce it here.

The 1899 *Famous Sites* album, I would argue, contains not one narrative but two, which come together to produce the necessary conditions for a commercially successful travel guide: the promise of convenience *and* the excitement of adventure. This very much prefigures travel materials from the 1930s, which Paul D. Barclay says "conjure the danger and exoticism of the old head-hunting days [i.e., contemporaneous with the 1899 album], while reminding consumers that all had been made safe for sight-seeing amongst the colorful Indigenous Peoples of Taiwan" (Barclay 2010: 104). Likewise, the *Famous Sites* offers a successful conquest narrative in the opening pages, wherein the capital is depicted as modern and progressive, featuring a life of creature comforts—this is intensely reinforced by advertising that offers a variety of goods and services. The conquest narrative is complemented by the regressive narrative of the southern itinerary, which builds on an anxious fascination with the exotic and suggests the future. The albums that follow in the collection modify and reinterpret these two narratives; nonetheless, their heuristic strength remains vital. For example, when the Japan Tourist Bureau published volume 3 of the photographic magazine *Lure of Taiwan* in 1937, some features were new, such as the opening photograph of a young Taiwanese "geisha" dressed in a traditional *qipao* smoking a cigarette—an alluring blend of the

Figure 2.10 Taishō emperor and empress, opening page. *Taiwan takushoku gachō* (1918). Courtesy of National Taiwan Library.

traditional and the modern.[26] Despite such innovations, the structure of the visual narrative remains largely that of the 1899 *Famous Sites* album. The magazine still leads us from the modern and metropolitan capital toward the exotic; the section on the capital opens with the depiction of another woman in a *qipao* standing in front of a DC-2 named "Fuji" (Figure 2.11), and the last main section is labeled (in English) "Jolly time with aborigines: Santeimon near Heito" (Pingdong) and features scenes of folk dances.

Epilogue: Beyond the colony

The narrative structures of the Taiwan colonial itinerary construe the island as a location of conditionality. It is presented as a geographic and cultural entity known only through the rationale of the colony: a place in which to be stationed or to tour but not a place of full unmediated residence. These narratives and their projected

Figure 2.11 "Fuji." Lead photograph in "Snapshots of the Capital" section. *Kamera de mita Taiwan (Lure of Taiwan)*, Vol. 3 (1937). Courtesy of National Taiwan Library.

conditionality remained viable even after the Chinese government "recovered" the island from the Japanese in 1945 and the Republic of China and its Nationalist (KMT, *Guomindang*) government were exiled there in 1949. Once again, the island was attached to a distant national narrative, belonging conditionally to another northern place.

During the postwar period, the southward itinerary, beginning in Taipei and proceeding south along the west coast, became so standard in travel literature as to be unremarkable.

Even the conquest narrative finds its postwar equivalent. During the martial law period (1949–1987), that conquest took two forms: one is in the Sinification (*Zhongguohua*) of the island's cultural forms (and the masking of the Japanese legacy); the other is the Americanization of the island with its Cold War allegiances (often cast in terms of "internationalization"). In these narratives, the overt conquest itinerary is lost, but its ideology remains: the island is represented as a site of comfort (for the recent Chinese immigrant) and convenience (for the American traveler). In the 1970 *Pictorial History of Taipei*, for example, the historical images are overwhelmingly from the pre-Japanese period, foregrounding the island's Chinese heritage. *Pictorial History* largely ignores the rich resources from the Japanese period: of 160 photographs, only about twenty are identified from the Japanese period. At the same time, glitzy presentist publications such as *Taipei Pictorial* (*Taibei huabao*) and *New Image of Taipei* typically feature either the architectural monuments in the Chinese neoclassical (Northern Palace) style promoted by the Nationalist government in its attempt to make the city "more Chinese" or the architecture of international modernism. For example, a layout in the 1981 *New Image* features the flamboyantly neoclassical Grand Hotel along with the glass-and-brick Lai Lai Sheraton (*Taibei xin xingxiang* 1981: 118–19).

Following the lifting of martial law in 1987, the ideological direction of these earlier narratives began to be reversed. In the new political climate, these narratives are cast primarily in the ideology of the *bentuhua* (nativistic) movement, wherein nationalist and internationalist rhetoric is replaced with celebration of local Taiwanese cultural forms. In this celebration of the local, the Japanese experience is re-presented as central to the meaning of Taiwan; in doing so, archival materials (such as photographs from the albums under discussion here) have flooded the public forum, where they have met with a largely nostalgic reception: the "good old colonial days" standing in counterpoint to the more recent and much resented forty years of political oppression under Nationalist martial law. There are numerous examples of these new *bentuhua* narratives, but none is as telling as the catalog for a 2004 exhibition sponsored by the Taipei City Cultural Affairs Bureau in celebration of the 120th anniversary of the building of the Taipei city wall (Wei and Gao 2004). The catalog is elaborately illustrated with maps, historical photographs, and images of objects and materials from the exhibition. Although the exhibition and its catalog ostensibly trace the entire historical period of the island through a series of six general topics, in all cases, the balance of materials is severely canted toward images from the Japanese colonial period.

As the term *bentuhua* implies, this is a narrative of the island not as an itinerary but rather as a residency; it is an attempt to remove Taiwan's long-standing conditionality, to take control of the future of the island through the selective recovery of the past or, as the title of the last chapter of the *Viewing Taipei* catalog puts it, "The Past: Seeing the Present, Knowing the Future." Needless to say, this is very much an attempt to foreclose the conditionality of another potential conquest narrative that is on everyone's mind, on both sides of the Taiwan Strait.

Notes

1   Kinoshita Naoyuki mentions Matsuzaki Shinji's work but says that "his photographs of Taiwan have never been found" (2003: 33). There is, however, a small set of reproductions from his expedition in a photo album dating to 1915, *Taiwan shashinchō*, held by the National Taiwan Library, call no. 0748–12; and in Davidson (1903: opposite 127). There is no direct evidence regarding the equipment Matsuzaki used on the Taiwan expedition, but on another expedition a year later, he produced collodion prints (see Kinoshita 2003: 33, fig. 8), so we assume that he was also using wet-plate technology in Taiwan.

2   I include a detailed account of that technology and its transfer to Taiwan in Allen (2014).

3   See Ryan (1997: 21–2) for the interrelationship of cartography and photography in the construction of the British colonial imaginative geography. For a review of Japanese maps of the island, see J. Allen (2005).

4   On *dōka* policy, see Peattie (1984: 96–108). Ching (2001) explicates the false promises of that policy and the complications of ethnicity in the Japanese colonial condition. We should note that the Aboriginal population was definitely not considered part of this *dōka* policy. See Kleeman (2003: 19–22) on the complete "otherness" of the Aboriginal peoples in Japanese policy and representations.

5   On the Algerian postcard, see DeRoo (2002) and compare with Alloula (1986); on the Hottentot Venus, see Ryan (1997: 144–5); on Felice Beato, see Hight (2002). This is not to say there is not some sexualized photography from colonial Taiwan (especially of Aboriginal women), but it is certainly less frequent, at least in the albums in the NTL collection.

6   On the "problematic subjectivity" of the Japanese colonizer in relation to Chinese elite culture, see Allen (2007: 180–4).

7   The Japanese library was destroyed in 1945 during Allied bombing raids, but fortunately the library holdings had been moved for safekeeping. The collection is now held in the Taiwan Studies Research Materials Center (*Taiwanxue yanjiu ziliao zhongxin*) of the newly built (2004) National Taiwan Library in Zhonghe.

8   For example, these are contemporaneous with and similar to the 1897 halftone printed photographic survey *The Queen: Her Empire and the English-Speaking World* (Ryan 1997: 183–6). Halftone printing is first seen in Japanese newspapers in 1904

(Junkerman 2003: 187); the *Taiwan nichinichi shinpō* newspaper produced its first halftone image on the front page on May 3, 1905.

9   Note that the Austronesian Aboriginal peoples (who are Malayo-Polynesian) were not included in the *hontōjin* grouping.

10   In chronological order, these albums are *Taiwan gun gaisen kinen shashinchō* (1896), NTL call no. 0748–93; *Taiwan meisho shashinchō* (1899), NTL call no. 0748–29; *Shashin kurabu: Ichimei Taiwan jimbutsu shashinchō* (1901), NTL call no. 0743–3; *Taiwan miyage shashinchō* (1902), NTL call no. 0748–2; *Taiwan meisho fūzoku shashinchō* (1903), NTL call no. 0748–83; *Taiwan fūzoku to fūkei shashinchō* (1903), NTL call no. 0748–81; *Kodama sōtoku gaisen kangei kinenchō* (1906), NTL call no. 0748–4; *Gotō danshaku sōbetsu kinenchō* (1906), NTL call no. 0748–97. The first purely ethnographic album in the collection was not published until 1910 (Torii 1910, NTL call no. 0762–3), but its investigations and photography date from these early years, and several of these eight albums contain examples of Torii's work.

11   This is similar to what Roland Barthes has called the "concatenation" of connotation in the syntax of the photo essay (1977: 24–5).

12   The photographs are unlabeled and undated, but the one of the Meiji emperor is similar to a famous portrait by Uchida Kuichi dating from 1872 or 1873 (see Worswick 1979: 41; Junkerman 2003: 55, plate 30). The pose and attire are almost identical, but judging from the mustache and goatee, the photograph here is later than the one by Uchida; in this sense, it is closer to the undated and unattributed portrait found in Japan Photographers Association 1980: 96. The accompanying photograph of the heir apparent (i.e., the future Taishō emperor) also seems unique in the photographic record of the Japanese imperial family.

13   Oddly enough, this photograph does *not* appear in the *Military Triumph* album. I found the photograph first in the 1903 *Taiwan fūzoku to fūkei shashinchō*.

14   *Tōban guntai kinen shashinchō* (1914), NTL call no. 957-23043-3, no pagination.

15   *Musha tōbatsu shashinchō* (1931), NTL call no. 0748–77. For an analysis of the violence and narratives surrounding this expedition, see Ching (2001: 133–73).

16   *Tōbatsu guntai kinen shashinchō* (1913), NTL call no. 0748–70, no pagination.

17   There are, however, Japanese examples of more graphic depictions of the battle narrative, such as that of the Russo-Japanese War of 1904–1905 (see Japan Photographers Association 1980: 124–41). Parr and Badger note the early linkage of war photography and the photobook, with war providing an obvious narrative line for any photo essay in 2004: 36.

18   *Taihoku shiku kaihen jinen shashincho* (Taihoku: n.p., 1915), NTL call no. 0748–20.

19   This album is also a testimony to the rapidly expanding photographic industry on the island; according to *Taiwan shishō meikan* (1901), NTL call no. 0743–1, there were at least nine photographers with studios in the Taihoku area in 1900.

20   In some ways, this southward exploration is an early and abbreviated version of the Japanese *nanshin* (southward advance) ideology that defines later imperial expansion into Southeast Asia and the South Seas. During the early colonial period, this southward advance was reenacted in miniature on the island itself. Later manifestations of this policy have been well studied and recently reviewed in Taylor (2004).

21   Note that the pagination is by individual sections and is not continuous in the album.

22   The 1902 *Taiwan miyage shashinchō* has such coverage, but none of the other albums from this early period do. The contemporary colonial newspaper *Taiwan nichinichi shinpō* widely used *furigana*, although not quite as extensively as did these essays.

23 Retail establishments selling the volume are listed just before the publication page: six locations in Taihoku, three in Kīrun, and four in Tokyo.
24 *Arisan Niitakayama keishoku shashinchō* (1927), NTL call no. 0748–49.
25 *Taiwan takushoku gachō* (1918), NTL call no. 0748–23.
26 *Kamera de mita Taiwan*, Vol. 3 (1937), NTL call no. 0748–131.

3

Tangled up in Red: Textiles, Trading Posts, and the Emergence of Indigenous Modernity in Japanese Taiwan

Paul D. Barclay

Introduction: Entangled objects on a savage border

For a major exhibit titled "Rainbow and Dragonfly," held from September 2014 through March 2015 at the National Taiwan Museum in Taipei, a large billboard greets visitors and passersby with four distinct examples of Taiwanese indigenous textile manufacture, of varied pattern and ages, all dominated by the color red. Inside, displays of Atayal cloth occupy fully one-half of the palatial museum's first floor. It is a complex installation: 100-year-old disembodied fabrics are juxtaposed with updated designs on sleek black mannequins; colonial-era ethnological surveys share space with large color photos of contemporary weavers consulting them; and, numerous imperial-era postcards illustrate the diversity, antiquity, and daily uses of the displayed fabrics. The National Taiwan Museum was established by the Taiwan Government-General in 1908, while its current structure was completed in 1915. The "Rainbow and Dragonfly" exhibit, housed in a neoclassical neocolonial edifice, is in good measure a dusting-off, repackaging, and repurposing of the artifacts collected among Indigenous Peoples during the Japanese occupation.

As Chih Huei Huang argues in Chapter 7 of this volume, the intellectual climate of post–martial law Taiwan has overdetermined positive endorsements of the Japanese occupation, or at least a willingness to entertain the possibility that it was not an era of unmitigated exploitation. The "Rainbow and Dragonfly" exhibit bears out Huang's contention. It reveals how colonial ethnography, museum practices, and photography were (and remain) active partners in the sustenance and revival of Atayal culture:

Thank you to Janice Matsumura, Scott Simon, Robert Blunt and an anonymous reader for reading drafts of this chapter and providing helpful comments and advice. Thanks to Hu Chia-yu for sharing her vast knowledge of Indigenous textiles, Taiwan museums, and cultural revival. This research was made possible by grants from the ROC Ministry of Foreign Affairs, the National Endowment for the Humanities, and the Japan-U.S. Friendship Commission, and with the support of the Institute of Taiwan History at Academia Sinica.

which is also packaged in this exhibit as an element of Taiwan's national heritage. The national maps that frame the exhibit mark out Atayal and Paiwan homelands as visually consistent, recognizable, and commensurate units of Taiwan's composite national "geobody"—the symbol of bounded and inviolable territory that both mobilizes and defines the nation (Winichakul 1994). This exhibit disrupts our ability to imagine modern Taiwan without its indigenous complement—or indigenous Taiwan without its modern complement. Despite its awareness of the interpenetration of past and present, however, it says little about the journey of its artifacts from sites of local use to the display cases of the museum. A recounting of this forgotten story will reveal that global chains of commerce, technological adaptations, colonial collecting, and traditional Atayal textile production have been entangled in Taiwan for 150 years. This chapter will demonstrate how this entanglement produced a historical formation that I call "indigenous modernity." The argument is built on an investigation of the historical interplay between Japanese colonists and Taiwan Indigenous Peoples centered on prestations, exchanges, appraisals, and reappropriations of red-dyed thread, yarn, and cloth. In the course of this entanglement, "modernity" and "indigeneity" have emerged as two sides of the same coin, in all their complexity and ambiguity. To pick up this thread, so to speak, we must begin with the opening of treaty ports during the late Qing dynasty.

In the aftermath of the 1858 Arrow War and Lord Elgin's 1860 sacking of Beijing's Summer Palace, the Qing court opened two Taiwanese ports to foreign trade as part of a series of concessions to stop the British from destroying their capital. The next decade saw a steep increase in foreign calls to Taiwanese ports, setting off a lucrative tea, camphor, and sugar export boom. Taiwanese merchants and laborers organized and directed most of the trade, while a few scattered Western missionaries, exporters, and a lone British consul constituted the meager foreign presence in 1860s Taiwan (Gardella 1999: 167; Hevia 2003: 31–48). To reach the interior beyond the areas of Han settlement, where much of Taiwan's camphor was produced, nineteenth-century sojourners relied upon seasoned Qing subjects called *tongshi* (interpreters) for a number of services (Barclay 2005b: 323–60). Among them, the selection of gifts was conspicuous. A famous 1869 encounter between US Consul to Amoy Charles Le Gendre and the Paiwan chief Tauketok in southern Taiwan illustrates the importance of such gifts in borderland diplomacy during the treaty-port period (Shufelt 2010: 40–1). In a consular report, Le Gendre wrote,

> I gave the chief one hundred and eighty yards of red camlet, a small pistol, a single-barrel shot gun (unserviceable), and a spear ... an ivory spy-glass and case ... some beads, and a quantity of rings, bracelets, and a case of gin ... Tauketok had not expected this attention, and he was evidently much touched by it. "If you have brought all this to buy me," said he, "you have taken a useless care, for you had my word; but if you hand me these presents as a token of friendship, I receive them with pleasure." (1871: 33)

Le Gendre's gift was a pivotal event in the history of Indigenous–outsider relations. At stake in this encounter, for outsiders, was the security of maritime commerce at the height of the second industrial revolution. Qing relations with industrializing empire-states like Japan and the United States were beginning to hinge on Beijing's ability to make its entire realm, including southern Taiwan, safe for commerce. Tauketok, the reputed leader of a confederation known as "The Eighteen Tribes of Langqiao," was also deeply invested. Le Gendre himself first sought Tauketok out to find a way to protect shipwrecked merchants off the coast of southern Taiwan. Before Le Gendre's visit, numerous European and American sailors had been either robbed or murdered by Langqiao residents. Le Gendre's diplomatic efforts ended with Tauketok agreeing to induce erstwhile southern coastal wreckers to honor flag signals from distressed Western sailors, and with a pledge from Qing officials to erect a lighthouse to aid merchants in these treacherous waters (Yen 1965). Red was the color of choice for these flags, a sample of which was presented to Tauketok during these negotiations (Fix 2009: 247). According to Le Gendre's travel notes, a more rigorous and attentive program of gift distribution to the southern coastal tribes was needed to keep his agreement with Tauketok in force (2012: 316).

Le Gendre's dramatization of Tauketok's eager acceptance of "tokens of friendship," and insistence that he would not "be bought," is problematic for a number of reasons. Other travelers to Taiwan recorded Tauketok's businesslike collection of cash fees for the upkeep of stranded sailors (Hughes 1871–2: 32). Le Gendre himself remarked in unpublished writings that Tauketok's leadership of the Eighteen Tribes was financially draining, and that the leader was known to drive hard bargains for ransoms of foreigners (2012: 267–9). Douglas Fix has argued that when Le Gendre arrived in Langqiao in 1867, Tauketok's influence was at an apogee. By 1869, his hold on power had become precarious in part for lack of funds (Fix 2009: 246–7). In light of these considerations, Le Gendre's testament to Tauketok's incorruptibility commands attention less as a transcript of a verbal exchange than as a thinly disguised barb at Han Taiwanese and resident "mandarins."

Like so many other travelers to Taiwan during the treaty-port period, Le Gendre had an ax to grind with the local Qing officials who seemed to thwart his every initiative, and Hakka intermediaries who sought to profit from their monopoly on access to interior settlements. The everyday forms of resistance Le Gendre faced are unsurprising, since his ability to propose measures to the Qing and indeed travel to the interior of Taiwan were a direct result of the success of British arms in mainland China. Thus, Le Gendre and other foreign writers generally considered Indigenous Peoples trustworthy, and able to deal in good faith; they represented the antithesis of profit-oriented, greedy Chinese subjects they encountered on a daily basis.

Charles Le Gendre left his post with the US government in 1872 to enter the hire of the Japanese empire as a highly placed advisor on Formosan affairs. This new position gave additional institutional weight to his pronouncements and a platform to convey them across empires and regime changes through bureaucratic channels and published reports. Subsequently, Le Gendre's treaty-port discourse on Han avarice and Indigenous sincerity was institutionalized in Japanese government and commercial circles in the writings of high-ranking China hands such as Mizuno Jun and Ueno

Sen'ichi, over the final two decades of Qing rule in Taiwan. In Japanese colonial times Indigenous sincerity was reconfigured as "gullibility" or even "innocence," a foil to Chinese perfidy.

While much has rightfully been said about the formation of group identities, ethnic boundaries, and oppressive machinery along the axes of race, gender, and class, it is also true that estimates of cultural capacity, moral probity, and technical competence can weigh heavily in the construction of identities, both emically and etically speaking (Adas 1989; Stoler 1997: 203–5; Hsieh 1998: 97–103). In colonized Taiwan, the trope of the "innocent" Indigene validated Japanese policies to exclude Han Taiwanese from the lively "border trade" and redirect the flow of income into state coffers. It also rationalized the policy of confiscating Indigenous landholdings and making them either state property or selling them off to logging companies. (This resembles the US disposal of forest lands in White Earth, Minnesota, during the same time period, also premised on the trope of indigenous economic incompetence [Meyer 1991: 384].) Lastly, officials, writers, and scholars deployed this discourse to position the Japanese as honest brokers and teachers who would defend Indigenous People from greedy Han interpreters, squatters, and merchants, while teaching them how to be rational economic beings. In other words, a triad of interlocked stereotypes—impartial Japanese, avaricious Chinese, and innocent Indigenous People—allowed colonists to portray their civilizing mission in terms of benevolent disinterest, despite their own participation in an avowedly rapacious enterprise.

The patent hypocrisy and lack of self-awareness so evident in Japanese colonial discourse on Chinese greed and Indigenous gullibility was arguably symptomatic of a larger crisis, one that we still face. As was the case with their German and American contemporaries, Japanese public intellectuals found it difficult to reconcile the seemingly amoral values of capitalism—the much-vaunted engine of modern progress—with the principles of nationalism. How could capitalism, a system that enshrined individualism, ruthless competition, and the pursuit of profit, be understood in terms of national mission, when the nation was being imagined as a fundamentally communitarian enterprise (Marshall 1967; Noble 2002)? Like Max Weber's "indolent Catholics" (1958: 39–42) and Frederick Jackson Turner's "primitive Indians" (1994: 38), Japan's "greedy Chinese" and "gullible Indigenes" provided the defining negative examples for imagining capitalism as a virtuous and coherent system whose triumph was inevitable and desirable in the long run—despite short-term crises such as violent strikes, frontier wars, industrial accidents, or urban blight.

As Weber suggested, both in his formulations and his unwitting revelations, "The Spirit of Capitalism" is indeed part and parcel of modernity. This ethos includes an unwavering belief in the rationality, universality, and utility of an economic system that originates in Europe and is based on the continuous accumulation of surplus as determined by quantitative evaluations of profit and loss on a regularly scheduled basis. In Weber, the existence of "modern" and "traditional" societies is postulated through the use of the comparative method and is presented in a sober style. Nonetheless, he did not adopt the methodological relativism familiar to academic sociologists today. Instead, Weber began with the axiom that "the West" was uniquely rational. Moreover, his sweeping pronouncements about non-Western civilizations were made, by his own admission, for the sole purpose of putting his own milieu into conceptual relief. As foils to progress, the guilds, churches, unions, local chieftains, service providers, state officials, and petty merchants who stand in the way of a system that promises to deliver the "greatest good for the greatest number," as determined by the black ink on corporate balance sheets, annual GDP totals, or healthy national budgets, are relegated to the dustbin of history.

In other words, Le Gendre's stereotypical descriptions of "the Chinese" actually foreshadowed Weber's comparative method. Whereas Weber elevated his peevishness with "greedy" Neapolitan cabdrivers to the status of sociological data, Le Gendre's annoyance at the many obstacles he faced in Taiwan found expression in a discourse that rendered machine-powered industry, free-trade, and other capitalist institutions normative. Analogously, it is not hard to figure out why Qing officials would prevaricate, intimidate, mask, and otherwise frustrate foreign interlopers whose sole mission was to render them obsolete by entering into direct relationships with the producers, consumers, and congregations who populated the Qing realm. Once recorded in scientific journals, trade reports, newspaper articles, and other media, Le Gendre's statements effectively reified behaviors that were largely structured by treaty-port encounters with the consul himself into a preternatural Chinese racial essence.

This line of argument is not advanced to suggest that Le Gendre, Weber, and their contemporaries were being dishonest, or even racist, in their attempts to define capitalism or economic rationality. The point here is to understand the persistence and consistency of Anglophone and Japanese discourse vis-à-vis Chinese and Taiwan Indigenous Peoples in the face of the copious empirical counterexamples provided in the same reports. The attributes imputed to Indigenous Peoples and Chinese in the period under discussion were immune to empirical correction because they had in fact become axiomatic.

Like any other colonial project, however, the Japanese enterprise contained its own internal contradictions and factional struggles. There was much more to the discourse generated by cross-border exchanges during the period of Japanese colonial rule than the formation of a progressive, national, modernist self against the foil of backwards "savages" and avaricious sons of Han. In this volume, Scott Simon (in Chapter 4) notes that the ethnonym "Atayal" is a Japanese-era creation. And as he demonstrates, this imposed category has become an object of heated political contestation in the postcolonial period. "Atayal" is externally imposed, it is in some sense careless of local aspirations and realities, and it surely took on a life of its own in Japanese official and scholarly documentation. On the other hand, the ethnonym "Atayal" was generated in the heat of particular encounters, ones where Atayal peoples were active and agentive. Moreover, this category was also contested among Japanese colonists and did not represent a monolithic "Japanese view" of Indigenous ethnicity. Rather, the colonialist use of the term was harnessed to a dissenting view that rested uneasily with the triumphalist discourse outlined above.

Yamaji Katsuhiko has studied the centrality of Atayal textiles and Paiwan woodcarving to Japanese–Indigenous relations over the past century. Early Japanese descriptions of Atayal cloth merely stated their distinctiveness as exemplars of a unique cultural ensemble. By the 1920s, however, antiseptic descriptions gave way to aesthetic engagement (Yamaji 2011). To be sure, this external affirmation of local genius also deployed an allochronic discourse that participated in the making of the modern progressive self. Nonetheless, there is a difference that must be emphasized: in the Japanese discourse on "Atayalness," the unmarked subject was a disenchanted, soul-less denizen of the Weberian "iron cage." This subject's existence was rendered impoverished without the rejuvenating presence of the indigenous other. In a word, indigenous modernity partakes in the progressive discourse described so ably by a generation of critics who linked affirmations of industrial progress to race-making in the era of high imperialism (1870s to the 1910s). But indigenous modernity is not simply a triumphalist discourse. Its resting point, or state of equilibrium, is not the "end of ideology" or the creation of an odorless, colorless utilitarian market space. Rather, indigenous modernity is a subject position that seems to grow ever more needy of timeless, authentic, and enchanted others to replenish its world weariness in the face of a capitalist time-space premised on the end of limits. The cultural and political history of Taiwan in the post–martial law era has seen the strengthening of multiculturalism as a mainstream element of national identity in tandem with its high-speed economic growth. In this milieu, much of the multicultural element is supplied by Taiwan Indigenous Peoples as avatars of authenticity and diversity. This development is fully consistent with an indigenous modern ethos, though there are many other factors at work here as well.

In his 1991 book *Entangled Objects*, Nicholas Thomas devised a framework for elucidating the long-term imbrication of indigenous renaissance with colonialism and its legacies. Thomas proposes the "entanglement" metaphor as an alternative to "incorporation" (a triumphalist or extinction narrative of global capitalism's rise to dominance) or "comparison" (the critique or lionization of capitalism through comparison with putatively alternative economic logics). The "entangled objects" model, which I employ in this analysis, steers a course between ascertaining the rate and extent of the periphery's transformation by the core ("incorporation") and the meticulous reconstruction of internally coherent, ideal-typical systems of meaning ("comparison") (Thomas 1991).

From an "incorporation" perspective (to illustrate), Le Gendre's presentation of the red cloth to Tauketok is salient because it facilitated an agreement between a US emissary and a powerful chieftain. The arrangement was but one in a series of ad hoc accords whose breakdown fomented the Japanese invasion of Taiwan in May 1874. As a result of this invasion, the Qing initiated more aggressive policies against Indigenous Peoples from 1875 through 1895, further eroding their autonomy. Shortly thereafter, mechanized Japanese military might brought Indigenous populations to heel beginning in 1903. By 1915 or so, Japan delivered the coup de grâce to Indigenous sovereignty, ushering in an era of subordinate existence in the global division of labor and the colonial racial pecking order. In this rendering, "one hundred and eighty yards of red camlet" are fungible—any gift might have served the same function. This conclusion is at odds with the inordinate attention paid to the specific contours of materiality by contemporary observers. Moreover, as an extinction narrative, the "incorporation model" does little to help us understand current developments in Indigenous Peoples' rights-recovery and renaissance, or the continued attractions of primitivist consumerism (Comaroff and Comaroff 2009).

Using the "comparative" method would lead us in a different direction, and also raises problems. Based on the voluminous travel reports and diplomatic correspondence available for southern Taiwan and anthropological fieldwork studies of Paiwanese kinship, political structure, and ideology, one could ascertain the role of red camlet in the redistributive political economy of the "Eighteen Tribes of Langqiao." Using models constructed by political anthropologists of Polynesia, one could then hypothesize to what extent Tauketok was a "chief" or a "big man," or try to figure out how his brushes with the global economy transformed his leadership style from one type to the other.[1] Having established the internal logic of Langqiao's political economy, and the meaning of gifts within it, one could then contrast it with the logic of monopoly capitalism and national sovereignty to identify what is distinctive, autochthonous, and original about Paiwanese social organization. Like "incorporation" analyses, "comparativist" studies yield important insights. But as Thomas notes, the methodological insistence upon "difference" in comparative work has a tendency to consign actors in these systems to parallel or siloed temporalities, an analytical fiction that is belied by the phenomenon of meaningful cross-cultural exchange.

An "entangled objects" analysis instead lingers a bit longer on the materiality of Le Gendre's gift to take notice of the fact that Indigenous People refashioned imported red cloth to create "traditional clothing" (Figure 3.1). These garments in turn took on a variety of local meanings, values, and usages that had little relevance to the story of international relations, but were, nonetheless, crucial for social reproduction in Taiwan Indigenous societies (Harrison 2003: 337). Following Le Gendre's red camlet through another iteration, we observe that traditional Indigenous cloth was in turn reappropriated by Japanese of various stripes for a multitude of purposes during the colonial period (and beyond). As museum pieces, objects of study, and popular items at souvenir stands, Atayal textiles came to symbolize either a particular ethnic group or Taiwan's non-Han population in general. Fast-forwarding to contemporary times, Taiwan Indigenous Peoples have refashioned elements of Japan's colonial-period repository of material culture. The revival of Atayal weaving practices, partly based on consultation of textiles collected during colonial times and preserved in Japan, now illustrate claims of Atayal distinctiveness and autochthony (Yoshimura 2007: 166–7; Yamaji 2011: 402–5; Tamoto 2012).

All of this is not to argue that exchanges between agents of nation-state-sponsored capitalism and representatives of local systems were symmetrical. Richard White's classic *The Middle Ground*, a study of the Great Lakes area of North America, explicitly links the microhistory of gift presentation on capitalism's frontiers with a macroanalysis of shifting imperial power relations. As nation-states like the United States reterritorialized the old frontier zones of the French and British dynastic empires, Native American "wiggle room" to play competing empires off against each other disappeared. When Indigenous bargaining power was thus reduced, the "gifts" that once lubricated frontier diplomacy also dried up (White 1991). Returning to Taiwan, Westerners like Le Gendre, Hakka leaders,

Figure 3.1 An Atayal couple with garments that display the use of imported dyed threads, buttons, and shells. The abundance of large shells on the man's cape and cap signify high social standing. In addition, he is wearing two government-issued badges that identify him as a "headman." Item wa0103, "Richly attired Atayal man and woman," East Asia Image Collection, Lafayette College.

and Qing magistrates sought Tauketok's favor because his mediation was critical for solving political problems in the vacuum left by a Qing dynasty (Le Gendre 2012: 267–80) that was more focused on border issues in Central Asia than on the empire's southern flank (Larsen 2008: 60–1). After the Qing began to collapse under its own enormous weight and Japan annexed the island, the Taiwan Government-General expelled Western rivals for "the Indigenous trade," and sought either to pension off or kill local big men like Tauketok.

In the new dispensation, "tokens of friendship" were reconfigured as "rewards for good behavior." Japanese administrators designed Indigenous Trading Posts to effect this reconfiguration; these enterprises buttressed claims to Japanese normativity, supplied museums and tourist shops with evidence of Atayal dexterity and artistry, and provided the grounds for investigations into Chinese and Indigenous "character." In addition, trading posts were weapons of territorial conquest. After "Indigenous Affairs" were turned over to the Police Bureau in 1903, the tribes who had resisted the Qing were forced to surrender their firearms or face crippling embargoes on daily necessities. Because of these dramatic effects, many narrative histories of Taiwan, if they mention Indigenous Peoples at all, consider the post-1903 military offensives as the start of meaningful Japanese "Indigenous policy."

However, if we wish to understand indigenous modernity as manifest in current cultural politics and in colonial-era practice, revisiting the inaugural years of Japanese occupation is of utmost importance. During this "lost decade" Japanese officials probed the opaque side of the "savage border" in search of allies and obedient imperial subjects. Indigenous emissaries to feasts and parleys posed for photographs and paintings; Indigenous artifacts were collected by rural officials in exchange for tobacco and red thread; and "Indigenous textiles" purchased in cross-border trade were boxed up and shipped to Japanese museums and industrial expositions. By producing and circulating curios, photographs, reports, and illustrations that portrayed Taiwan Indigenous Peoples as racially and culturally distinct from each other and from Han Taiwanese, Japanese impresarios filled in the blank spaces on census maps with ethnic groups in possession of their own languages, artistic sensibilities, and forms of subjectivity (Figure 3.2).

As others have argued, this colonial repository of visible signs of reified traditional culture is important because the contemporary world is politically and economically dominated by settler-states and their majority populations. Indigenous peoples, for both commercial and political reasons, find themselves forced to perform identities that meet the expectations of outsiders. It is these expectations, rather than any emic sense of affiliation, that coalesced for Taiwan Indigenous Peoples in the early twentieth century (Tamoto 2012: 91–113; Geismar 2013).

Figure 3.2 A diorama from the 1913 Osaka Colonial Exhibition with Atayal red-striped capes prominently displayed as "The household of the Taiwanese Natives and its customs and manners." Item ip1472, "Grandcolonial Exhibition at Tennoji Park," East Asia Image Collection, Lafayette College.

The era of red-cloth diplomacy:
Tokens of friendship and the innocent Indigene

Just two years after US Consul Le Gendre's 1869 parley with Tauketok, the disappearance of fifty-four shipwrecked Ryukyu islanders on Taiwan's southern peninsula brought Meiji Japan's first official visitors to Taiwan. In particular, the observations of Mizuno Jun merit scrutiny because he would return to Taiwan as the top civilian official in the Government-General at its inception in 1895. In 1873, Ambassador Soejima Taneomi dispatched a 22-year-old Mizuno, who was studying Chinese on the continent, from Hong Kong to Danshui to investigate conditions surrounding the deaths of the Ryukyuans (Mizuno 1930: 188; McWilliams 1975: 237–75). Upon arriving at Dakekan (modern Daxi in Taoyuan), Mizuno's party trekked eastward on a steep "woodcutter's path" toward the so-called "savage border." Mizuno was told that areas of Chinese habitation were marked by the russet color of denuded forests, while the Indigenous areas were still lushly green. Mizuno's informants told him that this divide ran the length of Taiwan, patrolled by armed Han and Indigenous guards on either side.

In a clearing used to initiate cross-border parleys, on May 23, 1873, Mizuno hailed a group of passing Atayal people. The men fled to the hills at the sight of Mizuno's armed Chinese guides. Two Atayal women, however, stayed behind. They explained that their village had been the victim of a ruse. Chinese traders had promised the delivery of Western goods to lure unsuspecting Atayal people into the clearing. The Chinese subsequently kidnapped the Atayal men and ransomed them later in exchange for titles to land. To overcome their reticence, Mizuno offered to distribute large quantities of red cloth, a la Le Gendre, if the two women could bring an Atayal headman down from the mountains. Mizuno noted that Taiwan Indigenous Peoples coveted red cloth most of all. The next morning Mizuno presented the two women with gifts of red cloth, matches, obsidian (or glass), small daggers, and pearls. That afternoon, the chief sent a different women's contingent down the mountain. Mizuno supplied each with a "foot or two" of red cloth. Finally, Mizuno presented the chief with a live pig and two large jars of *shōchū* liquor. With this presentation of "tokens of friendship," Mizuno had accomplished the "principal goal of his mission, to look into savage strengths and weaknesses, degrees of intelligence and ignorance, and manners and customs" (Mizuno 1930: 188–93). Although Mizuno did not establish population figures, estimates of military strength, or routes to interior villages, the intelligence he collected on his mission to Dakekan was put to use a quarter-century later. As first governor-general Kabayama Sukenori's civil administrator, Mizuno issued proclamations and oversaw policies based on his estimation that the *seiban* (raw savages, i.e. unassimilated) were collective victims of the Han Taiwanese. At the same time, Mizuno's narrative provided a guide for subsequent administrators and travelers regarding the linguistic and logistical means to engage in commerce and diplomacy with Indigenous People.

A year after Mizuno's journey to Dakekan, the Japanese government dispatched a punitive expedition of some 3,600 men to Taiwan's southern Hengchun peninsula, ostensibly to avenge the December 1871 murders of the shipwrecked Ryukyuans. The Japanese expedition lasted from May through December of 1874. The Japanese occupation terminated with a complex agreement that acknowledged Qing sovereignty over Taiwan, declared the "justice" of Japan's mission, and solidified Japan's claims to Okinawa (Gordon 1965: 171–85; Yen 1965; Eskildsen 2002: 388–418). In response to this near loss of imperial territory (Hengchun), and real loss of a stalwart tributary vassal (the Ryukyus), the Qing court took steps to extend administration into the Indigenous territory. From 1875 through 1895, Taiwan's circuit attendants and governors feverishly built roads, forts, a lighthouse, and even an Indigenous school system to bolster Qing sovereignty throughout Taiwan. This policy was known as "opening up the mountains and pacifying the savages" (*kaishan fufan*) (Chang 2008: 1–30).

During *kaishan fufan*'s peak period of intensity, Japan's foreign minister Aoki Shūzō dispatched up-and-coming career officer Ueno Sen'ichi to Taiwan on a commercial intelligence gathering mission (Hayashi 1979). In January 1891, Ueno left for Dakekan (Mizuno's 1873 destination) "to meet the chief (*doshū*)" of an "important Indigenous area." In his report, which was filed with the army and published in a geography journal, Ueno stated that purchasing presents for the Indigenous People was "most necessary" for entering the "savage border." Accordingly, Ueno brought along "liquor, tobacco, glass beads, Western red-dyed thread, brass buttons, white ceramic buttons, etc." (Ueno 1892: 21–48; Sanbō 1895). Ueno ordered the guide to arrange a parley with the paramount chief. The Atayal deputation consisted of a chief named Watan Yū, his wife and daughter, and three retainers. Ueno distributed the aforementioned cloth, beads, and buttons. Like so many Japanese officials who followed him, Ueno insisted that presents to Indigenous Peoples were to be distributed equally, from the youngest child to the paramount chief. If one Indigene were treated too kindly, and another too carelessly, hard feelings would result. In return for these "tokens of friendship," chief Watan produced sweet potatoes and a bundle of rice stalks from a "head-carrying bag" and presented them to Ueno. After this exchange of gifts, the chief, along with the other five, stood up at once and took turns striking Ueno in the chest with their right arms. Ueno asked the Chinese-language interpreter (*tsūben*) what this meant, and the Indigenous-language interpreter (*tsūji*) replied that it was a sign of affection and happiness. Interestingly, Ueno's Chinese retainer was denied the same courtesy. The snub was attributed to long-standing hatreds between the Chinese and Indigenous People in the area. According to Ueno, the Indigenous People were simple and trusting, but they were also quick to anger and never forgot a slight (Ueno 1892: 42–5; Sanbō 1895).

Less than five years after Ueno's mission, the Taiwan Government-General set up shop in its new capital of Taihoku (Taipei). On August 29, 1895, forty-six men under the Dakekan garrison commander Watanabe trekked southeast from the walled city to initiate official relations with the Indigenous People. The previous day, Watanabe sent an Indigenous interpreter (*seiban tsūji*) to arrange the meeting. After a half-hour wait, seven Indigenous emissaries, two of them women, arrived at the clearing. Following Ueno Sen'ichi's instructions, which were in turn informed by Le Gendre's and other foreign reports, the soldiers distributed gifts of liquor, tobacco, silver coins, and tinned mackerel. Like Ueno, Watanabe was careful to distribute all gifts equally among the emissaries. According to Watanabe's report, these Dakekan residents valued manufactured goods highly, as they swaddled the empty liquor vessels, great and small, into bundles to carry back to their villages. Yet, the chief showed no interest in the silver coins he was given (*Tokyo Asahi shimbun*, September 28, 1895; *Fūzoku gahō*, November 28, 1895). On September 2, the government organized a follow-up mission of similar size, headed by future Taihoku prefectural governor (*chiji*) Hashiguchi Bunzō. This meeting commenced with the distribution of red cloth, tinned meat, handkerchiefs, ornamental hairpins, short daggers, tobacco, and alcohol (Hashiguchi 1895b: 313–8, 1896). Hashiguchi wrote that the Dakekan men were adorned with trademark Atayal red-striped capes and emphasized the importance of red serge (a rough woolen), which he distributed in equal shares. To produce the distinctive red garments, Hashiguchi reported, the women took the serge apart and wove the dyed thread together with locally produced ramie fiber (Hashiguchi 1895b: 313–4).

Like Le Gendre and Mizuno before him, Hashiguchi also extrapolated specific brief encounters into general assessments of his hosts' general character. Hashiguchi alluded to the powerful attraction of imported textiles by noting that the Indigenous People insisted upon keeping the blankets Hashiguchi's men "lent them" during the cold journey from the rendezvous point to the Dakekan garrison. Based on this incident, he surmised the "*seiban*" (savages) lacked the intellectual equipment to discriminate between gifts and loans—he also believed they operated with an impoverished vocabulary of about 300 words. With the promise of additional wool blankets, Hashiguchi lured five of the Dakekan Indigenous People to Taihoku for meetings with Governor-General Kabayama (Hashiguchi 1895b). During these meetings, where the delegation was duly feasted, a number of photographs and sketches were made of the red-caped Atayal visitors. The event entered the annals of Japanese lore as the "first meeting between the Japanese government and the Indigenous People" and fixed the image of red-caped Atayal peoples as representative of all non-Han people in Japanese mass media (Hashiguchi 1895b: 317; Jiryū 1895).

Based on his experience at the Dakekan mission, Hashiguchi, as director of the Office of Industrial Promotion (*Shokusan-bu*), proposed that each Japanese garrison near the Indigenous territory stock gifts for distribution to neighboring tribes. The Civil Affairs bureau accordingly sent memoranda to the subprefects of Tainan, Miaoli, Yunlin, Yilan, Hengchun, and Puli explaining their importance. Hashiguchi's list of recommended gifts, dated September 11, specified the quantities and types of gifts to be stocked—scarlet cotton fabric, red beads, flower hairpins, cigars, daggers, red blankets, red serge, and hand towels—and their exact values in monetary terms. Every item on the proposed inventory matched one that was distributed by Hashiguchi to the Dakekan emissaries three days earlier, on September 8, 1895 (Hashiguchi 1895a). In January 1896, Miyanohara Tōhachi, the Dakekan district head, applied to the Government-General for 143 yen to conduct "Indigenous Feasts." Miyanohara acknowledged that a recent rash of murders and beheadings by Indigenous People could be attributed to Japanese disarmament policies that left Chinese dwelling near the "savage border" defenseless against Indigenous raids. Nonetheless, Miyanohara's recommendations reflected a common Japanese official reflex to consider the Indigenous People as victims of the Chinese. Miyanohara suggested that signposts be erected along the "natural border" between Chinese and Indigenous People. Han Taiwanese would then be strictly forbidden to cross the line. The Indigenous People would also be admonished—at banquets held under government auspices (Inō 1918: 5–7). Miyanohara's request for 143 yen was turned down, but his strategy was institutionalized soon after in a new organ of Japanese colonial administration: the *Bukonsho* (Pacification-Reclamation Office).

To promote the exploitation of the camphor forests, Governor-General Kabayama requested 236,871 yen as start-up money to establish the Bukonsho. In March 1896, Kabayama's proposal was approved, but his request to deploy twenty policemen in each of the twelve proposed stations, at a total cost of 111,181 yen for the first year of operation, was turned down. Instead, each station would be staffed by one interpreter, two assistants to the chief, and two "operatives"; only eight out of the twelve stations would have a chief, for a total of sixty-three officials (Inō 1918: 10–11).

A review of the Bukonsho experiment is of special interest, because it tested the limits of the methods inspired by Le Gendre, Mizuno, Ueno, and Hashiguchi. Hashiguchi's successor at the Shokusan-bu, Oshikawa Norikichi, ordered the inaugural class of Bukonsho chiefs to meet with headmen on appointed days, distribute presents, and announce that attacks on Han settlers and neighboring Indigenous tribes must cease. Oshikawa also circulated a list of questions that charged Bukonsho officials with surveying the political, demographic, mineral, vegetative, and military situation beyond the savage border. This tall order was informed by the belief that Indigenous People treasured their gifts and would do just about anything to receive them. Oshikawa stated that compliant villages would be rewarded with further gifts, while disobedient ones would be punished by withholding presents (Inō 1918: 14–15).

In addition to noting their power as diplomatic instruments, the Japanese administrative record contained much evidence of the power of red-dyed textiles to cement profitable trading relationships. On September 30, 1895, an anonymous Civil Affairs translator (*tsūyakukan*) told a Japanese metropolitan readership that such gifts might even open Taiwan's interior to Japanese camphor merchants. He optimistically reported the cost of gifts to Indigenous chiefs as 1 yen per camphor tree in Miaoli. The gifts included red, black, brown, or purple cloth scraps for women, and guns, swords, sake, and tobacco for men. To obtain the camphor trees, he wrote, local Chinese also traded Nanjing coins or rings and bracelets made of pearl and lead. The return on these gifts was indeed hefty: the selling price of a camphor tree was 60 or 70 yen. This particular correspondent surmised that the Indigenous People did not understand the value of currency, nor the difference between silver or gold. He wrote that they accepted one or the other based on color preferences for yellow or white and that one could even use shards of glass or chunks of metal for currency in some areas ("Taiwan tsūshin" 1895).

In October 1895, Ueno Sen'ichi's 1891 report resurfaced in a commercial guide published by the Japanese Ministry of Agriculture and Commerce in Tokyo. The guide reiterated Ueno's advocacy of red cloth as a rain-making gift and as the price of entry to the "savage territory." Moreover, Ueno's capsule history of "Chinese-savage" (*Shinajin-seiban*) interaction, which attributed the loss of land to Chinese settlers to Indigenous simplicity, illiteracy, and inability to plan ahead, was duly reported. The Chinese, according to Ueno's now recycled report, were greedy, cunning, and unscrupulous, and robbed Indigenous People of their lands. As a result, the Indigenous People became sworn enemies of the Chinese (*Taiwan sangyō ryakushi* 1895: 40–1, 52–3).

Thus, the notion of Taiwan Indigenous Peoples as simplistic, irrational peoples who were prone to violence when wronged gained traction in Japanese rhetoric and policy through the force of repetition. But as Japanese merchants and officials gained experience in Taiwan's interior, other reports undermined this view. A November 1896 report issued by the Industrial Promotion Section began its discussion of camphor with a predictable admonition to stock "liquor-meat-cloth," especially Western imported dyed red cloth, as a prerequisite to trade. It then mentioned, in contrast to the above rhetoric, that the residents of Beipu were dishonest Indigenes who would not honor commitments. This behavior necessitated the stationing of *aiyong/aiyū* guards to protect camphor workers in Xinzhu. This report also mentioned that some headmen in Qing times required frequent cash payments, in addition to feasts and gifts, to keep the peace—suggesting that at least some Indigenous Peoples valued money (*Taiwan sōtokufu minseikyoku* 1896: 15).

A contemporary series of internal memoranda from the Luodong section chief for Indigenous Affairs retained the language of Chinese bad faith while it tempered the rhetoric of Indigenous ignorance or disinterest in commerce. Until honest, fair-dealing Japanese immigrants could insert themselves into the "Indigenous Trade," he warned, the profitable trade would remain in the hands of unscrupulous Chinese, who had the bad habit of cheating Indigenous People and setting off violent cycles of revenge feuds (Taihoku-shū 1924: 141). To move the trade away from the "crooked Chinese," the Luodong office began to broker marriages between the commercially minded *jukuban* (cooked savages, i.e. acculturated) men of Alishi village and daughters of the Atayal Nan'ao villages further inland to strengthen ties with the mountain peoples behind the Yilan plain. The district office held a large wedding banquet in May 1899 to celebrate one such marriage. Over 100 Nan'ao guests were feted. The Japanese rural officers also encouraged the adoption of Indigenous males into *jukuban* households to facilitate plains–mountain commerce. The Government-General then recruited these bicultural couples as go-betweens and spies to keep tabs on conditions in the mountains. According to the official who promoted this policy, it was the lure of trade goods and wealth that inspired the Nan'ao villagers to place their daughters and sons among the trading villages at the foot of the mountains (Taihoku-shū 1924: 172).

Despite contrary evidence anchored in the experiences of local Japanese officials who dealt with Han and non-Han Taiwanese on a daily basis, the notion that Indigenous People were irrational when it came to trade and money persisted throughout the period of Japanese rule. This belief was often invoked to argue for government supervision of trade between Han and Indigenous Peoples. One Wang Jiasheng, writing for the mass circulation daily *Yomiuri shimbun*, claimed that the large feasts and giveaways attending initial overtures to interior tribes (in this case Paalan, Teuda, Wandai, and Truku near Musha [Wushe]) were making Indigenous People into craven and shiftless dependents. These men, who were so simple that they measured a precious necessity like salt by the "hat-full," were being spoiled by the distribution of free salt and liquor. The same author also reported on Han–Indigenous trading practices, corroborating the many other reports that described the cunning nature of Han merchants. Like the Luodong district officer discussed above, Wang recommended that the government supervise this cross-border trade (1896).

As we have noted, many a Japanese observed that Indigenous Peoples were acutely sensitive to the "equal distribution of gifts." Did this behavior mean that Indigenous Peoples were egalitarian, unselfish, and innocent of the notion of profit? Numerous Japanese writings intimate a child-like glee among Indigenous Peoples at receiving gifts, one likely to expire as soon as the gift was consumed. One writer opined that the type of gift did not matter, but the number of gifts was crucial, and that these should be the same for all. Such an interpretation would explain why Japanese officials sometimes gifted indiscriminately, giving every settlement or headman the same treatment. On the other hand, detailed lists of gift items in the manuscript records of traveling district officials reveal that more expensive gifts were earmarked for headmen, suggesting that gifts reinforced local hierarchies (Barclay 2005: 93–6).

At distribution events, a Japanese official could proclaim that his emperor would not play favorites. But distributing gifts evenly among villages was an affront to those who accepted them in order to bolster their prestige or power vis-à-vis local rivals. According to Irie Takeshi, an infantryman whose story appeared in the December 10, 1896, issue of *Fūzoku gahō* (Customs pictorial), Puli prefect Hiyama Tetsusaburō doled out the expected blankets and jars of liquor at his wedding to the daughter of the Paalan chief near Musha. Complications arose, however, when Hiyama, unable to distinguish Teuda and Truku men from the Paalan men, distributed gifts to everyone. Angered by the fact that their rivals also got the gifts, the Musha men ambushed the other guests after the banquet and took their gifts at gunpoint. Irie reported that the Musha men asserted their right to receive the gifts first and then to redistribute them to other locals as they saw fit. After all, they were the area's dominant village. Moreover, their chief had conducted a marriage alliance with Hiyama (Irie and Hashimoto 1896: 29–30). Hiyama's successor Nagano Yoshitora in Puli triggered the same response by distributing presents to Teuda emissaries after a feast in 1898. On their way back home, the Teuda men were ambushed by Musha men. In the ensuing battle, Teuda and Musha suffered fifteen and two casualties, respectively ("Hokuban" 1898: 5).

Trading posts, behavior modification, and punitive embargoes

Saitō Otosaku, chief of the Bukonsho in Linyipu, institutionalized the growing chorus of criticisms directed at Hashiguchi's gifting policy in an 1898 white paper. In his preface, Saitō criticized the shortcomings of the overly generous approach:

> One must take care in distributing gifts to the Indigenous Peoples; if it is done carelessly it can lead to feelings of injustice and foment anger, or it can cause lethargy and shiftlessness... We must not distribute gifts without a reason; we must certainly not distribute luxury goods; we must not give in to demands for goods; when gifts are requested, we should give no more than is absolutely necessary. (Inō 1918: 102)

In language that reflects a newfound confidence in the Japanese government's ability to command, rather than placate, Saitō composed a well-calibrated scale of gift categories. He reserved the Hashiguchi-style "tokens of friendship" for first-time visitors to government offices. Return "guests" would have to earn their "gifts." For example, to receive goods classified in Saitō's top-shelf categories, Indigenous People would have to perform "labor on roadwork, afforestation projects, or stock-raising/ farming enterprises... or service as savage auxiliaries (_banhei_)." Such efforts would be rewarded with "thick cotton shirts; black cloth, light cloth, table salt, matches, etc."; "buttons, all colors of wool thread, combs, tobacco, Nanjing Pearls, etc."; and, for especially meritorious service, guns and ammunition.

Saitō recommended that farm tools, seeds, and stock be freely distributed because they would wean the Indigenous Peoples from their hunting economy. He argued that firearms and ammunition, though necessary for the time being, should be phased out, because hunting in and of itself was a vestige of savagery. Saitō also envisioned the government-managed trade as a source of profit. Lesser categories in Saitō's typology, which ranged from hoes and hatchets to hairpins and fans painted with _nishiki-e_ scenes, were to be stocked as trade items. A plan that may have been influenced by Saitō's report was implemented in Yilan in mid-1901. It restricted trade to government-licensed agents who would operate with set exchange rates. For example, one deer pelt was listed as equivalent to two feet of red woolen or nine catties of table salt; one bear bladder equaled two iron pots or one suckling pig; three catties of wood ears equaled five catties of salt or a skein of thread; and so on. The government would profit from this trade and use the proceeds for "Indigenous betterment," which meant building schools and transporting and lodging chiefs' families who came down the mountain to enroll in the pilot education programs (Taihoku-shū 1924: 304–10). The conversion of gift-distribution centers into trading posts was at the heart of Saitō's template for reform and was central to the trade-for-education program attempted in Yilan in 1901. Both schemes sought to alter the political economy, and economic ethos, of Indigenous settlements by using trade goods as incentives and trading posts as schools of commerce. While there may have been some altruism involved here, and a genuine attempt to give Indigenous Peoples a "fair shake" vis-à-vis their wealthier Han neighbors, these trading posts quickly turned into instruments of punishment and conquest, or income generation for the Japanese state.

In 1899, Gotō Shinpei launched the Government-General's camphor monopoly, along with other measures, to increase revenue to support his vision of an efficiently run, surplus-extracting colony. As Antonio Tavares has shown, the official Japanese plan for camphor—to export large quantities of uniform quality with profits accruing to Japanese capitalists—posed a direct threat to the Atayal, Saisiyat, and other northern Indigenous Peoples whose leaders were accustomed to leasing forest land, collecting tolls, or organizing production themselves. Accordingly, cases of Indigenous violence against Japanese officials piled up (Tavares 2005: 361–85). In response, the Bukonsho was abolished in June 1898 and rural installations for government–Indigenous relations began to emphasize the importance of "embargoes," "smuggling," "illicit trade," and "contraband." As Atayal, Sediq, and other northern tribes put up stout armed resistance to logging-company encroachments, government officials began to worry less about the injury done to Indigenous Peoples by crafty Chinese than to express outrage that Han traders would subvert Japanese bans on weapons, ammunition, or even salt to blacklisted tribes.

Taihoku prefectural governor Murakami Yoshio urged that the tribes responsible for a June 1900 armed uprising, which cost over 1,000 Chinese and Japanese lives and destroyed much property, be completely cut off from trade and from receiving gifts. Friendly villages would have only a partial ban on trade, in Murakami's plan. Murakami sent out strict regulations in December 1900, requiring merchants to be registered, and calling for a complete ban on guns and salt to troubled areas like Dakekan. Murakami believed that villages could be crushed and brought to heel after a few months of deprivation of life's necessities (Inō 1918: 163). In September of the same year, the Balisha district chief in Yilan sent out a similar memorandum, calling for selective trade embargoes against villages who defied the government's authority or disrupted the peace. He stipulated that feasting and trade would be permitted for tribes who had made amends for their crimes or who were above suspicion. Such a policy might have seemed wildly optimistic in the era when Ueno and Hashiguchi were being led by their guides into terra incognita to purchase interviews with "demanding" headmen and chiefs. Yet, by 1900, by following the Bukonsho charter's directive to regularly supply gifts to headmen as an incentive to "heed invitations to arrive and be transformed" (*shōrai kika*), the Yilan district offices had perhaps rerouted enough traffic, or created enough new demand, to be in a position to open and close the spigot (Taihoku-shū 1924: 248).

In 1902, two major developments conspired to minimize the centrality of the diplomatic and pedagogical functions of "entangled objects" and accentuate the punitive power of their regulation. First, the Ri Aguai rebellion, which pitted an Indigenous–Hakka–Han coalition of camphor producers against the Government-General, taught the Japanese that force would be required to make northern Taiwan's interior safe for capitalism. Under Ri Aguai's domination, camphor production was too decentralized, too beholden to "toll state" politics that ran on "bribes," and too unproductive to meet the camphor monopoly's requirements for black ink on the annual colonial management balance sheet (Tavares 2005). Second, Gotō Shinpei, through a combination of adroit manipulation and cold-blooded assassination, brought the Japanese campaign against armed Han resistance to completion that same year. In late 1902, an "Indigenous Affairs Section" was placed under the Police Bureau (Kondō 1992: 38). One of the architects of this policy, Mochiji Rokusaburō, went so far as to claim that ungovernable Indigenous Peoples, while technically human beings in a sociological sense, could be considered "animals" insofar as they fell outside of the jurisdiction of any internationally recognized authority (Inō 1918: 182). Henceforth, the Japanese police would fortify, lengthen, and gradually march inward a "guardline" of electric wires, scorched earth, and heavily armed garrisons to interdict arms, salt, and migration between the plains and the mountains, until Indigenous Peoples in the north were completely disarmed. The implementation of this ambitious plan was interrupted by the Russo-Japanese War, but resumed in earnest afterwards. The era of "red-cloth diplomacy" was over.

In July 1905, Government Order #56 strictly regulated all merchants in the "Indigenous trade." Although private traders were still allowed to operate, they required government permits to enter Indigenous territory. All trade items were to be registered and declared, along with the names of all employees and coworkers (Inō 1918: 408–10). The long list of "surrender ceremonies" that punctuate the annals of Indigenous Administration after 1906 shows that resumption of borderland trade was important to Indigenous leaders. In January 1906, the four villages of Fanshuliao (Akō Prefecture) promised not to seek contraband trade goods from camphor workers on the "savage border" as a condition of resuming trade. In May 1906, the Musha tribes agreed to leave their weapons at home to conduct business at trading posts and to stay at specially designated lodgings during sojourns for commerce, in order to participate in the trade (Inō 1918: 465, 457). In the summer of 1909, the Government-General put strict embargoes and rations at the center of its much publicized and documented "Five-Year Plan to Subdue the Indigenous Peoples."

On October 9, 1909, after applying for terms of surrender, certain Dakekan tribes were permitted "one rice-bowl of salt per month per person," as "gifts," though not as a "trade item." After agreeing to cease head-taking, surrender their guns, and submit to biannual inspections for weapons, Teuda's terms of surrender on October 17, 1909, stipulated that Indigenous People could not negotiate the price of goods at the re-opened trading posts. Moreover, matches, salt, and daggers would be excluded from the list of trade items and supplied as "gifts" to the Teuda in amounts determined by the Government-General. The following day, the Malepa tribes submitted to similar terms, accepting a ban on trade in salt, matches, and daggers in exchange for subsistence-level handouts. On November 11, 1909, the Xakut tribes also surrendered, again foreswearing the right to trade in salt, matches, and daggers (Inō 1918: 723–5).

On April 1, 1910, the Government-General began to operate its own trading posts, instead of merely supervising trade at government offices. The management of this trade was entrusted to the Taiwan Branch of the *Aikoku fujinkai* (Japanese Women's Patriotic Association) (Inoguchi 1921: 63; Uesugi 1992: 59), while the former system of privately run licensed trading posts remained as a parallel system operated by Han Taiwanese. Echoing Saitō Otosaku's memorandum of 1897, this system announced its intention to reform Indigenous character by suppressing the instinct to hunt (Taiwan sōtokufu 1912: 55–6). Special commissioner Marui Keijirō inspected these trading posts in 1913 and urged that the *Fujinkai* be stripped of the contracts (and that private trading posts be abolished as well). In a painstakingly detailed accounting of exchange rates for adzuki beans and salt rations, among other commodities, Marui pointed out that the *Fujinkai* was indeed fleecing the Indigenous Peoples by taking too much profit.[2] He believed, consistent with earlier reports about Han avarice, that such unfair dealing would provoke Indigenous anger in the long run. Marui argued against the participation of Chinese merchants on the grounds that their bad moral character was corrupting, by its very nature. He even linked the presence of venereal disease among Indigenous Peoples to Chinese traders. As a substitute, he recommended the Saitō plan as the only way forward: use Indigenous consumer appetites and trade dependency as a lever to reform their character through the promotion of weaving, planting, and stock-breeding, and by taking away incentives to hunt.

A heavy hand was required, Marui argued, because Indigenous Peoples were still mentally deficient in terms of their capacity to function as economic moderns. For example, Marui suggested that Indigenous People only be paid in tools or other durable goods instead of cash for labor on roads and other public works. Why? They might foolishly spend their wages. Marui expressed frustration that Indigenous People would hike through kilometers of dense mountain trails to save six-thousandths of a yen on a catty of salt. He attributed this stubbornness to the well-known desire of Indigenous People to be treated fairly—if salt cost 5 *sen* per catty in Musha, he wrote, then Teuda men would not pay 5.6 *sen* for it at the nearest trading post, but would instead walk all the way to Musha to get the "fair price." Marui explained the Indigenous lack of understanding that the foregone productivity squandered on these long journeys offset the small savings in purchase price (Marui 1914: 29–36).

Soon after Marui's report was released in October 1914, Government Order #85 called for the establishment of official trading posts to replace the *Aikoku fujinkai* institutions. These posts would be operated by police captains (*keibu*) and assistant captains (*keibu-ho*), who would report to district heads. All posts would work with fixed barter schedules, to be set at the prefectural level. Following Marui's plan nearly to the letter, the circular that accompanied the new trading-post regulations stated as follows:

> The goal of trade in the Indigenous territory is completely for education. To have success, we will pay high prices for cereals, legumes, ramie, rattan, and wicker goods; we will sell farming implements, and pig and cattle stock, at low prices. We want to instill an agricultural ethos among them. We will pay low prices for deer antlers, deer penis, animal pelts, and bones, to discourage hunting.
>
> Moreover, villages which are not submissive will have their rations of salt severely limited. If we interrupt the flow of salt, that will give them some time to reflect upon their situation. This is a way to exercise coercion without resorting

to brute force. It is a "soft policy." We are willing to sacrifice profit for the government to attain our goal of making the Indigenous Peoples into farmers. (Inoguchi 1921: 531)

In the short term, the new policy did little to deter Indigenous People from hunting. In the February 1917 issue of the government organ *Taiwan Times*, Mori Ushinosuke explained that 70 percent of the value of Indigenous "exports" exchanged at trading posts was comprised of animal products obtained in the hunt. Mori wrote that Indigenous People could not afford metal pots, salt, or fabrics without hunting. Besides, hunting was the only way to put fresh meat on the table. Mori highlighted the economic irrationality of agriculture when prices for crops were so low: at the time of his writing, deer penis still brought 5 yen, bear bladders 10 yen, and a good set of deer antlers 30–40 yen (Mori 1917: 9–19). In short, a couple of well-aimed shots or smartly set traps could earn an Indigenous hunter more than he would otherwise earn through months of toil in the fields or on road crews.

As we have seen in the foregoing, Indigenous Peoples were demonstrably motivated by the prospect of cash earnings, material benefit, and personal advantage according the records of the Government-General itself. But these anecdotal examples, no matter how legion, did little to disrupt the view that Indigenous Peoples were ipso facto irrational, childlike creatures who lived on the "fruits of the chase" and required tutelage. An article titled "The Economic Sensibilities of Savages and [Savage] Customs," which appeared in a policeman's journal thirty years after the Government-General squashed the possibility of free-market conditions obtaining along the Han–Indigenous border (Masuya 1935: 8–9), is but one of many examples of this resilient trope.

The 1935 article maintained that Indigenous Peoples did not customarily buy or sell goods based on considerations of market price, but relied upon the "traditional value" of a good as an index of its worth. Indigenous People were also likely to spend all of the money at their disposal and be flat broke. With so much home-brewed liquor to be had for free, there was little incentive for drink-loving Indigenes to worry about having cash on hand. This article is illustrated with a large photograph of several Tsuo men downing bamboo cups of wine with apparent gusto. The author concluded, after proposing his generalizations up front, that some Indigenous People did maximize profit and adopt a market mentality. He congratulated the police on their good work by noting that the Indigenous Peoples were losing their backwards habits and becoming more like Japanese (Masuya 1935: 8–9).

It is clear, then, that Japanese policies in economic tutelage were intended to produce a docile, disarmed, "reformed" colonial Indigenous subject who was amenable to labor dragoons and militia service, and who maintained a fixed address. With set prices at the posts, and an onerous licensing system that restricted entry into the market, the posts could not have been intended to produce the profit-seeking, utility-maximizing *homo economicus*. Although the trading posts and related stratagems did not create Indigenous subjects who were recognizably "modern" in the liberal political economic sense, I would argue that they produced modern Japanese subjects. If indeed capitalism is a coherent and consistent system for wealth production, one based on principles such as "comparative advantage," "free markets," "competition," and "transparency," its history seems to be one of the "state of exception" (Dudziak 2012). The progressive narrative that naturalizes capitalism draws upon on a well-established body of authoritative writings produced by eminent men. This rhetoric, which can be found in Adam Smith's groundless assertion that the British wage system had made the rudest of Englishmen wealthier than the most powerful of African kings (2002: xxxii, 13), was elaborated by Marx (1978: 437), was given academic polish by Weber, and finds recent expression in the work of Niall Ferguson (2008: 18). The invidious comparisons employed by all of these writers—which rest on very thin or nonexistent empirical bases—warn us that, for all of its problems, the world was much worse off without capitalism. In the early twentieth century, Japanese colonialists in Taiwan, and the many who read their pronouncements in Japan and abroad, could rest assured that the land grabs, frontier wars, monopoly licenses, fixed prices, and coercive migration policies that attended development were stopgap measures, collateral damage in a just war to provide the "greatest good for the greatest number."

Takekoshi Yosaburō, perhaps Japan's most famous whig public intellectual, articulated such a view in a famous book that was published concurrently with Weber's *The Spirit of Capitalism and the Protestant Ethic* in 1905. To justify the launch of offensive, set-piece mechanized warfare against the Atayal peoples of the north, Takekoshi wrote:

> Almost everybody who has come in contact with the savages declares that they are all quite capable of being raised from their present state of barbarism, and I am very strongly of the same opinion. But it is a question how much longer the Japanese authorities will be willing to pursue their present policy of moderation and goodwill, and leave nearly half the island in their hands. If there were a prospect of their becoming more manageable in ten or even in twenty years, the present policy might possibly be continued for that length of time, but if the process should require a century or so, it is quite out of the question, as we have not that length of time to spare. This does not mean that we have no sympathy at all for the savages. It simply means that we have to think more about our 45,000,000 sons and daughters than about the 104,000 savages. (Takekoshi 1907: 230)

Conclusion: The making of Indigenous modernity in Japanese Taiwan

By Takekoshi Yosaburō's reckoning, the policies articulated by Hashiguchi Bunzō and implemented at the "Indigenous Affairs" field offices had put the bright future of his 45 million fellow Japanese at risk. Gathering intelligence among and building relationships with the ethnically variegated and politically decentralized Indigenous population was turning out to be a time-consuming and delicate project. For

Governor-General Kodama Gentarō, Takekoshi, and a host of other Taihoku-based and Tokyo-oriented "big-picture" thinkers, this experiment had failed to enrich the nation, and was therefore slated for termination. Following suit, subsequent writers have considered these early years to have been ones of passivity regarding "Indigenous policy." Outposts were lightly staffed and underfunded, to be sure. Moreover, most of the government's resources were poured into the war against the so-called "bandits" (*dohi*) from 1896 through 1903—who were mostly non-Indigenous, as far as the Japanese could tell. Therefore, there is some truth to the view that the era of "red-cloth diplomacy" was a historical cul-de-sac. But for the ethnologists whose taxonomic work, photography, collecting, and display efforts are still bearing fruit in exhibitions such as "Rainbow and Dragonfly," the years 1895–1903 were remembered as a golden age.

To bring our story full circle, then, we return to the National Taiwan Museum, where ethnologist Mori Ushinosuke (1877–1926) curated Indigenous artifacts. Mori was an interpreter for Tokyo University anthropologist Torii Ryūzō, who made four anthropological surveys of Taiwan between 1896 and 1900. Mori was also a junior contemporary, and sometimes rival, of the famous historian, folklorist, and ethnologist Inō Kanori (1867–1925).[3] To this day, Mori's photographs are prominently displayed in the National Taiwan Museum's permanent exhibit and in other museums to illustrate the material life of Indigenous Peoples.

Mori, Torii, and Inō, between 1895 and 1915, constructed the modern taxonomic system, racial cartography and baseline ethnography of Taiwan Indigenous Peoples. During the first decade of colonial rule, at the Bukonsho outposts, government halls, and army garrisons, anthropologists photographed, measured, interviewed, and collected artifacts from the Indigenous representatives who showed up to receive gifts or have a social drink. Inō Kanori's field notes, Torii Ryūzō's published travelogues, and Mori's serialized memoirs all describe the period as a time when demobilized Japanese soldiers, Han–Indigenous interpreters, ethnologists, government officials, and Indigenous headmen assembled to conduct business, exchange information, and size each other up. In Taihoku, on March 1, 1896, for example, Inō met twenty-seven Atayal men and women from the Wulai area, accompanied by Xindian garrison soldiers, who came to receive gifts. Inō, who worked for the government as an editor and education-policy advisor that year, exploited the occasion to conduct an impromptu investigation of the Wulai peoples.

In the era before participant observation, anthropologists like Inō worked quickly and gathered evidence opportunistically. Unsurprisingly, red textiles acted as the prompt to initiate the interviews that constituted his brand of "fieldwork." The precious materials also functioned as the currency of access. In the "course of distributing various items colored red, which they generally like, such as scraps of red cloth, red yarn, red Japanese flags and ornate hairpins," Inō tried to characterize the mental life (*shisō*) of the Atayal guests. There are echoes of Ueno Sen'ichi's 1891 report in Inō's 1896 update, but there are important differences. Like Ueno, Inō observed a reverence for the gifts, polite manners in receiving them, and a lack of selfishness among the recipients: they insisted that everyone receive the same gifts.

But Inō's report did not compare the Atayal people (as he would later call them) favorably to the Han Taiwanese, nor did he dwell on their simplicity or innocence (Inō 1896: 274–6). Instead, Inō learned the local names for the numerous types of clothing and adornment that were fashioned from these gifts and illustrated his account with several carefully labeled sketches. Having established that the female visitors from the Wulai area were similar in appearance to the women brought from Dakekan by Hashiguchi in 1895 (see above), Inō classified them as coethnics. To the question "by what name do you refer to yourselves?" Inō heard the reply, "'Taiyal" from members of each contingent. Inō recorded this term in Roman script, announcing a new scientific outsider's perspective on non-Han peoples in Taiwan. As he noted, the Qing terms *shengfan* and *shoufan* (literally "raw" and "cooked savages") were externally imposed political categories. "Atayal," in contrast, was a self-designated ethnonym, according to Inō (1896: 301–13).

A little over a year later, in May 1897, Inō visited the Wulai-area villages. He was greeted with some enthusiasm, and put up for the evening, by a headman named Watan Yūra. Watan and others recognized Inō from their March 1896 Taihoku meeting. Inō was accompanied by the ex-army interpreter Jiku Shō Min (Inō 1992: 7). Like Le Gendre and Mizuno before him, Inō found himself in the company of Taiwanese who lived on the margins of, and in many senses beyond, the Chinese society that had evolved in Taiwan under Qing administration. In 1897, the Government-General was at war with Han rebels throughout Taiwan. As the official records of Indigenous Administration indicate, an alliance between the Japanese and Indigenous Peoples held advantages for both sides in the early days of colonial rule. Thus, Inō's relatively positive assessments of Indigenous character, like Le Gendre's, were in large measure formed in political conditions that favored good relations between outsiders and Indigenous Peoples.

The following year, in 1898, Inō launched a bulletin to publish research on Taiwan Indigenous Peoples. For the inaugural issue, he published a photo montage with representatives of eight tribes. The Atayal man in the montage was from the Wulai area, probably a member of the troupe that visited Taihoku in 1896. Due to technological constraints, and the infrequent access Inō had to sitters, Inō's montage was cobbled together out of black-and-white studio portraits and field photographs of uneven quality. This illustration could not capture the brilliant reds that were distributed to Atayal woman at Japanese outposts as the raw materials for the textiles that would in turn mesmerize Japanese souvenir-hunters, ethnographers, and art fanciers. To remedy this problem, Inō commissioned a color painting as a substitute for display at the 1900 Paris Universal Exposition. While the photo montage displayed the Atayal man and woman in a simple vest and Chinese blouse, respectively, the painting took considerable artistic license to adorn them in ornate, bright red traditional Atayal clothing (Hu 2007).

Mori Ushinosuke returned to Inō's site in late 1902 and early 1903 to photograph Watan Yūra and his family. Mori took multiple portraits of individuals and groups from Wulai and Rimogan (just upriver), as well as shots of architecture and material culture. The photographs that resulted from these encounters became iconic. Five were exhibited in nearly life-size reproductions for the 5 million visitors who attended the 1903 Osaka Industrial Exhibition. The Osaka posters were transported to the 1904 St. Louis Exposition and then picked up by American news services for further reproduction. It would not be an exaggeration to say that Inō's and Mori's Wulai photographs became the face of Indigenous Taiwan to Japan and the world between 1900 and 1920 (Barclay 2015).

At the height of their popularity, Mori's Wulai photographs were reproduced in Japanese geography textbooks, while Inō's ethnic map also found its way into the Japanese school curriculum (Monbushō 1910: 21; Tanaka 1911: 102). By 1912, then, any primary or high school teacher in Japan could demonstrate that Taiwan was inhabited by a number of ethnic groups each in possession of its own customs, languages, and territories, with the blessings of the Ministry of Education. This was a true accomplishment for the ethnologists. At this time, the overwhelming image of Taiwan's Indigenous Peoples, even in textbooks, but especially in newspapers, photo albums, and postcards, was of armed savage enemies of the state who would either soon go extinct or assimilate to Japanese culture.

As the frontier wars over camphor wound down in the 1910s, Atayal villages near Jiaobanshan and Wulai became hotspots for Japanese tourists and visiting dignitaries. The Atayal textiles that incorporated the red threads that were introduced in the treaty-port period could now be obtained at tourist-friendly "trading posts" as authentic "Indigenous cloth." During Japanese colonial rule, these garments made the transition from items of local consumption and everyday use into exported, high-quality handicrafts and art objects. In 1920, the protagonist of Satō Haruo's novella *Musha* reported that the trading posts were stocking inferior knockoffs of the "genuine Indigenous textiles" he sought (1998: 29), while visiting Crown Prince Hirohito himself viewed an Atayal weaving demonstration in a Taiwan exhibition hall in 1923. The prince reportedly expressed admiration for their purity, color, and boldness of expression ("Chinki na bussan" 1923: 2). The Indigenous trading posts and weaving demonstrations were also on the itineraries of Prince Chichibu in 1925 and Prince Asaka in 1927. A photo of the sword-bearing Asaka and his police escorts towering over three female Atayal weavers was splashed on the cover of the December issue of the *Taiwan Times* ("Chichibunomiya denka" 1925: 12; "Kappanzan bansha" 1927: front piece).

In 1933, the eminent scholar and critic Ozaki Hotsuma urged colonial officials to enforce Japan's "Important Arts Preservation Law" in Taiwan so that traditional Atayal textiles, along with Paiwan woodcarvings, could be preserved as "national treasures." Ozaki rued the extent to which Indigenous culture had been degraded in Taiwan since its golden age. Ozaki believed that Atayal artistic abilities had peaked in the distant past, when the world's most archaic form of linear patterned cloth had emerged in the mountains of Taiwan. As a repository for scholarly and artistic appreciation, he argued that these artifacts, if preserved, would reflect well on the empire itself. For Ozaki, the "normally administered areas" of Han residence possessed nothing of interest, except for derivative pieces imported from the continent (Ozaki 1933: 2).

Like the Japanese aesthetes who praised the genius of Goryeo-era pottery while Japanese merchants undercut its production by flooding Korea with cheaper manufactured wares (Atkins 2010: 124), Ozaki did not connect the current "degraded state" of Atayal weaving to Japanese imports or other policies that eroded traditional forms of production. As early as 1900, the Government-General began to facilitate the construction of textile factories in Xindian. The local "Indigenous Affairs" field office recorded with satisfaction that Atayal women were being trained in Xindian and in Wulai to run the machines ("Banjin banchi" 1900: 47). By 1938, journalist Harrison Forman, who shot numerous photographs at the same Indigenous village visited by Princes Hirohito, Chichibu, and Asaka in the 1920s, observed that Atayal textiles had become luxury goods for local people. Traditional clothing required two weeks of labor to produce a single garment, wrote Forman, while second-hand Japanese clothing sold for about the price of two day's labor on a road gang (Forman 1938: 16–17). In a letter to the editor of *Natural History*, Forman lamented that "the women too are dressed by the Japanese in cotton kimonos (Figure 3.3), which are symbolic of a movement that will rob another one of the few remaining native groups of the world of their own traditions and culture" (Forman 1941: 182).

Today in Taiwan, the fruits of colonial anthropological preservation work have been put to use in museum displays, textile manufacturing, book publishing, and

Figure 3.3 This photograph was taken by American journalist Harrison Forman in 1938, probably in Musha (Wushe). He titled it "Taiwan-woman weaving." While the ostensible subject of the photograph is native Atayal textile-manufacture, the photograph itself suggests that most Atayal people actually wore imported factory-produced clothing by this time. From the American Geographical Society Library, University of Wisconsin-Milwaukee Libraries. Harrison Forman Collection—Taiwan, *American Geographical Society Digital Archive, Asia and Middle East* (Milwaukee, WI: University of Wisconsin-Milwaukee), Digital ID: fr200018.

Indigenous activism. The imperial Japanese footprint is recognizable not only at the "Rainbow and Dragonfly" exhibit but also at the permanent and special exhibitions at the Taiwan University Anthropology Museum in Taipei and the National Historical Archives and Museum in Nantou. These displays put the Taiwan Government-General and the activities of its agents in a favorable light and provide confirmation of Chih Huei Huang's contention in Chapter 7 that many contemporary Taiwanese view the period of Japanese rule less harshly than the progressive Japanese intellectuals or embittered mainlanders who have done so much to shape the historiography of Japanese colonialism in Taiwan. In other locales, such as Xincheng/Taroko, the story is different. Here, the township government of Xiulin has organized forums and commemoration events to mark the 100th anniversary of the Taroko Battle (*Tarokoban tōbatsu*) of 1914. In this series of battles, which the local keepers of memory date back to 1896 (see Simon, Chapter 4), thousands of Japanese troops attacked east-coast Taiwan from the mountains and the ocean to decimate villages, take prisoners, and collect weapons (Xiulin xiang gongsuo 2014). It was a bitter war that ended with mass surrender ceremonies for the Taroko and with a great triumphal arch in Taipei for the Japanese, in 1914 (Otani 1914: 22). The concomitant unfolding of both Japanese legacies, one preservationist and culture affirming, and the other death dealing and sovereignty destroying, are the historical antecedents of indigenous modernity in today's Taiwan.

Notes

1   Matsuoka (2012: 42–7) summarizes this body of scholarship.
2   For a detailed analysis and description of the official trading posts, see Barclay (2005c: 1–36).
3   See Chen (2014) and Yang (2005) for intellectual biographies of Inō and Mori, respectively.

4

Making Natives: Japan and the Creation of Indigenous Formosa

Scott Simon

Among the Austronesian-speaking groups now known as the Indigenous Peoples of Taiwan, memories of the Japanese period continue to influence the ways in which people define communities in terms of culture, place, and nascent nationhood. The Japanese, in order to extract natural resources from Taiwan's mountain regions, forced the formerly nomadic groups who had hunted and practiced swidden agriculture on the territory for millennia to settle into fixed communities and adopt new livelihoods. In order to better control and regulate these people, the Japanese created new ethnic and community identities, which, rather than constituting pure cultures awaiting anthropological study, are political categories still contested by local people over seven decades later. An examination of the Japanese colonial period, and especially memories thereof, is thus important to an understanding of contemporary political dynamics, even those usually framed in terms of twenty-first-century political innovations like the 2007 United Nations Declaration on the Rights of Indigenous Peoples and Taiwan's 2005 Basic Law on Indigenous Peoples. The current demands for Indigenous autonomy, a leitmotif of global indigenism (Niezen 2003), comprise the most recent arena for the mobilization of colonial memory as the boundaries between communities are debated by local political actors. The point is that these contested boundaries were initially drawn by the Japanese state, which took control of Taiwan's mountainous regions by seizing the power to name groups and relocate people. This means that today's political debates about Indigenous rights are rooted in an unfolding political dynamic that predates both the global Indigenous rights movement and even the arrival of the ROC on Taiwan. What we know today as Indigenous Formosa is a co-creation of the resulting relationship between the Japanese state and diverse political constellations among many Austronesian peoples across the island.

Field research between 2004 and 2007 was made possible by a grant from the Social Science and Humanities Research Council of Canada. The author would like to thank Paul Barclay for his generous comments on this chapter, and all of the Sediq, Truku, and other people in Taiwan who have shared so much of their time and knowledge with me over the years.

Introduction

Ever since the Japanese left Taiwan, the notion of "autonomy" (*zizhi*) has been employed both as a mode of governance and as a utopian vision for Taiwan's Indigenous social movements. In the 1945 "Outline for the Takeover of Taiwan" (*Taiwan jieguan jihua gangyao*), the incoming Republic of China government promised the island's "savage tribes" (*fanzu*) the same self-determination and autonomy (*zijue zizhi*) initially pledged to China's national minorities by Dr. Sun Yat-sen (Fujii 2001: 156). Yet, as Chih Huei Huang shows in this volume, when leaders of Tsou and Atayal groups demanded self-rule on their own terms in 1947, they were jailed or executed. Nearly four decades later, Taiwanese anthropologists argued that the lack of legal guarantees for Indigenous autonomy constituted a human rights issue for the very same peoples (Li 1983: 50).

Autonomy subsequently became a rallying cry of the social movements of the 1980s and 1990s (Allio 1998; Rudolph 2008: 77), emerging as the object of constitutional debate (Lin 2000). In 1994, the term "Indigenous People" (*Yuanzhumin*) was added to the ROC Constitution, but revised again to "Indigenous Peoples" (*Yuanzhuminzu*) in 1997. Article 10 of the additional articles promises them political rights in subsequent laws "according to the will of the *peoples*."[1] In 1999, Amis legislator Cai Zhong-han of the ruling Nationalist Party (KMT) drafted the first of many proposed laws on Indigenous autonomy. In 2005, autonomy was included in the Basic Law on Indigenous Peoples, and in 2010, the Executive Yuan proposed a draft law on Indigenous autonomy.

The basic idea is that Indigenous governance should happen on the basis of territorially based peoples, and on a total of 1,664,085 hectares amounting to 44.9 percent of Taiwan (Pan 2005: 115). Proponents of Indigenous autonomy, regardless of their broader political affiliations, argue that autonomy will empower Indigenous Peoples and permit the flowering of their unique cultures (Simon and Awi 2013). They envision autonomy in terms of large mutually exclusive ethnic territories, a political realization of maps such as in Figure 4.1.

The ethnic groups and boundaries of the Atayal/Sediq/Taroko/Truku peoples were fiercely contested during the entire time that I have worked and conducted research with those groups since 2001. In 2004, after the Executive Yuan recognized the existence of the Truku tribe as independent from the Atayal, Truku advocates associated with the Presbyterian Church of Taiwan began to lobby for the creation of a Truku (or Taroko) Indigenous Autonomous Region.[2] They drafted a Truku Constitution and drew up a map of the Truku territory that included three contiguous townships in Hualian and one in Nantou (Simon 2007). These would be known in Chinese as the Qilai, Batuolan, Wanrong, and Deluwan (from the Chinese rendering of Truwan) regions (Siyat 2004: 172). While doing research with the Truku in Fushi and Hsilin villages of Hualian from 2004 to 2006, I found that the Presbyterians promoted Truku autonomy as a moral good, yet were also opposed by other people in the same communities, including the leaders of prominent community development associations. In 2005, I visited Nantou, which Truku nationalists perceive to be their

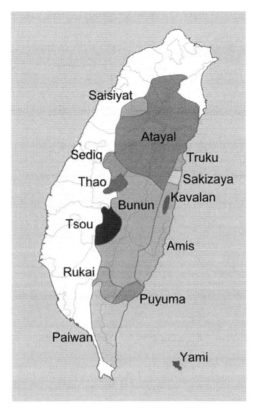

Figure 4.1 General distribution map of Taiwan's Indigenous population. Courtesy of Wikimedia Commons.

ancestral home, and found absolutely no support for the existence of a Truku tribe or the establishment of a Truku Autonomous Zone. In fact, the cadres of the Ren'ai Township Office seemed surprised when I showed them a published map identifying them as part of the Deluwan region (Siyat 2004: 172). They said that they had not been consulted at all.

Opponents to the Truku in Hualian allied themselves with those in Nantou to form the Sediq tribe, which was recognized in 2008. I had conducted six months of field research in Ren'ai Township's Seediq community of Gluban in 2007, during which time I lived in the home of a Seediq advocate. (I use "Seediq" in this chapter only in reference to Gluban, in deference to local usage. Otherwise, I use "Sediq" to refer to the entire tribe.³) During the study, I was struck by the fact that Fushi and Hsilin community leaders debated the boundaries of their identities and communities, to the point where they became sworn enemies and refused to cooperate on community projects, whereas those in Gluban seemed to avoid such conflicts. At the same time, and not unlike Michael Rudolph, who also did research in Hualian (Rudolph 2004), I found widespread apathy among ordinary people for the political ambitions of their presumed leaders. Instead of seeing new ethnic identities and autonomous zones as a form of empowerment, people in all three villages viewed proposed changes cynically as political manipulations of a small minority. Some opposed to the formation of a Truku nation argued that the name represents only those who descended from the ancestral village Truku Truwan (Truku meaning "terraced steps in the mountains", and Truwan referring to "place of origin") and that it should not be applied to the other groups in the population. They argued that there are three formerly hostile enemy groups (Truku, Teuda, Tkedaya, see below), and that only the word *sediq* (for "human being") can unite members of all three related ethnic groups. Others said that the name Taroko was chosen because of the name recognition of Taroko National Park, which they perceive as a colonial imposition. Those opposed to Sediq as an ethnonym emphasized the overly broad definition of the word as "human being." As one elder man in Gluban said to me, "You can't restrict that word to one small ethnic group. You [the foreign anthropologist] are also Sediq. You are also human." On both sides, people opposed to the new terms merely kept their official household registration as Atayal or changed their legal identity and claimed that they had been coerced to do so.

Many proponents of Indigenous autonomy, including those on both sides of the Truku versus Sediq debate, see themselves as part of an international social movement allied with the First Nations of Canada and the Maori of New Zealand, two countries with which the ROC has signed agreements of cooperation on Indigenous issues. They advocate a form of Indigenous autonomy, or self-rule, based on their understandings of those countries as models. KMT actors have portrayed autonomy as part of Sun Yat-sen's vision for Chinese minorities. But neither of these narratives can explain why "Indigenous" seems to fit these communities so well, nor why the boundaries of "nation" and "community" are so hotly contested. They can also not explain why the Truku of Fushi Village in Hualian are divided into so many competing factions, whereas the Sediq of Gluban in Nantou seem united in comparison. Picking up cues from the elites in both villages, who seemed to relish discussions of the Japanese period with me, I suggest in this chapter that all expressions of indigeneity in Taiwan have roots in the histories of actual kin groupings in the Japanese period. Their political ambitions may thus sometimes articulate with, but cannot be reduced to, the demands of urban-based social movements or the global Indigenous rights movement. They are also deeply rooted in the experience of Japanese colonial administration and "savage management."

Anthropological approaches to political economy make it possible to disentangle such notions as "nation," "community," and even "culture," especially near the borders between anthropology and history. These concepts are often reified to the point where scholars and others may perceive such social creations as a "Sediq nation," a "Truku community," or "Chinese culture" as things with lives and histories of their own rather than as relations between people. As Eric Wolf argued, "Only by understanding these names as bundles of relationships, and by placing them back into the field from which they were abstracted, can we hope to avoid misleading inferences and increase our share of understanding" (1982: 3). In this chapter, I look at the formation of Truku and Sediq communities to explore how nations and communities were created through the negotiation of relationships as capitalist modes of production expanded around the world.

In the case of Taiwan's Indigenous Peoples, this happened under Japanese tutelage, largely after the conquest of the Taroko Gorge in 1914. After that year, Taiwan's Indigenous Peoples endured the same measures taken in colonial situations worldwide: population transfers and the creation of reserves, the transformation of traditional laws, struggles over natural resources, and policies requiring new forms of capitalist productivity (Balandier 1966: 37). The central issue is that colonial administration imposed on these peoples a new mode of production, defined as "a specific, historically occurring set of social relations through which labor is deployed to wrest energy from nature by means of tools, skills, organization, and knowledge" (Wolf 1982: 75). Colonialism transformed them from a kin-based mode of producing through hunting and swidden agriculture for subsistence needs to a market-based mode of producing industrial goods for capital accumulation. It was the Japanese who contributed the most to the incorporation of Taiwan into the world economy. Below I will examine the following questions: How did Japanese rule contribute to the creation of Indigenous communities and nations? To what extent were these relations influenced by pre-existing relationships? What does this mean for the creation of a "Truku Nation" or a "Sediq Nation" in a time of Indigenous nationalism and demands for substantial land-based autonomy?

Political anthropology of Indigenous Taiwan

In western Taiwan, Indigenous Peoples were first incorporated into new modes of production after the Dutch established a small colony near Tainan from 1624 to 1661 (Andrade 2008). Under subsequent waves of Chinese colonists, the plains Aborigines were assimilated, annihilated, or forced to withdraw from the lowlands during the reigns of Koxinga (1661–1683) and the Manchu Qing Dynasty (1683–1895). Qing administrators called these peoples *shoufan* (literally, cooked savages), in contrast with the unassimilated *shengfan* (raw savages) of central and eastern Taiwan who were not subject to Qing political institutions. The history of the *shoufan*, based largely on Qing colonial sources, has been well documented by anthropologists and historians (Linck-Kesting 1978, 1979; Shepherd 1993; Zheng 1995; Brown 2004). The *shengfan* largely escaped Qing political control until 1874. Military expeditions by the Qing against *shengfan* began in earnest after that year, when Japan used Qing inaction in those territories to argue that no state exercises sovereignty over *shengfan* territory (Chang 2003). Less than twenty years later, and before most Truku or Sediq had capitulated to state control, Japan took control of Taiwan in the 1895 Treaty of Shimonoseki. As Barclay describes in this volume, it was Japan that finally incorporated these peoples into the modern nation-state and into capitalist modes of production.

For political anthropologists, the important issue is that Truku and Sediq communities were *stateless*, making them effectively what Clastres called "society against the state" (Clastres 1977). In addition to great linguistic diversity, there was diversity in political structure between the different Austronesian groups on Taiwan on the eve of Japanese rule. The idea that various bands, with fluid memberships, constituted larger "tribes" or "ethnic groups" with fixed territorial boundaries was not a part of their lives before the arrival of the state.

The Atayalic groups, who lived at altitudes in the mountains between 500 and 1,200 meters above sea level, were very small. Before the Japanese period, Atayal groupings had an average population of only fifty people, compared to 400–600 for the Paiwan, 700 for the Amis, and 800 for the Puyuma (Rudolph 2003: 361). The small size of the population precluded the need for complex political organization. Without institutionalized positions of power or clearly defined territories, Atayal groupings were what many anthropologists call acephelous ("headless") societies and were described by Japanese-era anthropologists as "incomplete societies" (Wang 2006: 30).

Each small group lived in the mountain rainforests, primarily subsisting from slash-and-burn agriculture of sweet potatoes and millet, supplemented with hunting and trapping. They moved from a site when it became less fertile, allowing the site to be reclaimed by rainforest. These practices of frequent moving and claiming of new territories contributed to frequent war and headhunting expeditions. Each group sought land that was fertile, easy to defend, far from the tombs of other groups, and acceptable after consultation with divinatory oracles (Kojima [1915] 1996: 65). In the Sediq/Truku language, the word for such a small group is *alang*. Unlike the Chinese lineage, it is not organized around a written genealogy and surname and is much more open to adoption of new members. Instead of surnames, Sediq and Truku people use their personal name followed by their father's name. The *utux* (spirits) potentially included patrilineal and matrilineal ancestors, as well as individuals from enemy tribes who were incorporated into the *alang* after their heads were taken and transformed into *utux* through post-headhunting rituals (Simon 2012).

These groups caused problems for state administrators. They were highly mobile groups who moved through the mountain forests without clearly defined territories, fixed forms of political leadership, or permanent populations. They reinforced their own population boundaries through blood, sacrificing pigs to incorporate new members, but also fighting over hunting territories and hunting the heads of enemy groups in elaborate headhunting rituals. The general tendency was to form confederations of people residing along the same river, but in which villages were extremely autonomous (Mabuchi 1974: 186). Politician-intellectual Takekoshi Yosaburō described the Atayal groups thusly: "They live mostly in mountain recesses, are extremely ferocious and attach great importance to head-hunting … They are divided into many small tribes, the members of which are like one family, under the patriarchal rule of the chieftain" (Takekoshi 1907: 219). When people reminisced about the past to me, they brought up this history, pointed out the frequent migration, and said, "We love freedom." This vision of the world is very different from that of nation-states, autonomous zones, or even agricultural villages—all of which have clear territorial boundaries, fixed populations, and names that contain some and exclude others. The Japanese, however, wanted to incorporate these Atayal forests into the modern economy of camphor.

Indigenous communities and the camphor economy

During the Qing Dynasty, Taiwan was already involved in the harvesting and export of camphor, primarily for use in medicine and in Hindu rituals in India. After 1890, it was also used in the production of celluloid, smokeless gunpowder, and plastic. Taiwan and Japan, both of which had naturally occurring camphor laurel trees (*Cinnamomum camphora*), emerged as the world's most important producers of this substance. Between 1860 and 1895, Taiwan's camphor industry spread into Indigenous areas of northern Taiwan. Camphor harvesting involved camphor workers (*naoding*), who had the dangerous task of cutting down camphor trees. They were managed by camphor foremen (*naozhang*), usually Hakka or plains Aborigines, who rented land from local Indigenous People or paid them off with barters of salt, cloth, pigs, cows, alcohol, or gunpowder (Lin 1997: 126–30). Often regarding camphor workers as their enemies, Indigenous People launched headhunting expeditions against them and destroyed the camphor stoves used in processing (Davidson 1903: 425; Lin 1997: 135). Indigenous violence against the camphor industry caused wide fluctuation in world camphor prices and brought Taiwan's camphor exports down to nearly zero in 1861 and 1885. Conflicts grew as the Qing pushed back the frontier lines, but the Han Chinese were disadvantaged in warfare against the Indigenous groups on treacherous mountain terrain and furthermore lost troops to malaria (Lin 1997: 48, 169). Through endemic violence on Taiwan's "frontier zone," settlers from China, Indigenous groups, and state agents all negotiated their rights in the new industry, an arrangement that largely allowed the Indigenous Peoples to maintain autonomy and their traditional collective land ownership of forests. As Tavares noted, the Qing was not unexceptional in their decision not to impose new institutions on local communities; most Old World agrarian-based empires retained traditional priorities and generally left these stateless peoples to rule their own communities according to their own customs (Tavares 2005: 361–85).

It was Japan that first imposed capitalism and new forms of property rights on Taiwan's Indigenous People. The Japanese annexation of Taiwan gave Japan an effective monopoly over world camphor supplies. They established a state monopoly in 1899, making it obligatory for the wood and oil be sold to the Taiwan Camphor Bureau. The *Bukonsho* (Pacification-Reclamation Office) was established to control Indigenous communities and reclaim land for the camphor industry. Bukonsho officials were supposed to learn Indigenous languages and customs, protect Indigenous communities from outside exploitation, and gradually "civilize" Indigenous People through peaceful means. In reality, however, the post was so poorly paid that it did not attract good officials, and by 1898 had to be replaced with police control. Davidson's suggestions that Japan make the island's Indigenous Peoples into wards of the state on the model of the American reserve system went unheeded at the time. The Japanese government, which established clear legal frameworks for the property rights of Han Taiwanese over farmland, simply declared that "all forests and prairie lands for which no title deed or other positive evidence of ownership exists is hereby declared government property." The Japanese claimed the sole right to grant land concessions in the forests, but did in some cases recognize the rights of Indigenous People to receive compensation for camphor lands (Davidson 1903: 440, 429–31). Nonetheless, the lack of clarity and consistent practices on Indigenous property rights led to conflict in the camphor areas and to violent resistance.

By 1903, the Japanese had lost over 1,900 lives to the Indigenous People in over 1,132 different incidents (Takekoshi 1907: 229). Across the island, these conflicts contributed to processes of ethnogenesis, in terms of both external identification and internal ethnic subjectivity, as we will see below. The 1902 Nanshō (Nanzhuang) Incident—or Ri Aguai rebellion—in the camphor-producing district of Byōritsu (Miaoli), for example, led to the formation of the Saisiyat (Saisiett) tribe. In 1904, this group of formerly "cooked savages" was reclassified as "raw savages" due to the violence of this historical incident (Tavares 2005: 376). The Atayalic and Saisiyat groups, which were mostly concentrated in camphor-rich areas, were contrasted as dangerous "northern savages" (*hokuban*) against the more cooperative Bunun or "southern savages" (*nanban*). This division was concretized in an October 1903 incident in which the Japanese convinced their Bunun allies to entrap and murder more than 100 Atayal men near Hori (Puli), after which they redeemed the heads with Japanese officials (Barclay 2007: 79).[4]

The Atayalic groups, who occupied prime camphor land in the northern forests of Taiwan, proved especially difficult to classify and control. Survey anthropologist Inō Kanori (1867–1925) considered them Taiwan's most primitive tribe due to their residence deep in the mountain forests and low degree of contact with the Chinese (Barclay 2007: 72). Anthropologists generally agreed that the eastern groups, all of whom referred to themselves in various dialectical variants of the word *sediq* (human being), were linguistically and culturally distinct from the other two Atayal groupings (Squliq and Ci'uli) who called themselves *tayal* (also "human being" in their language). According to the Taiwan Government-General Provisional Committee on the Investigation of Taiwanese Old Customs, the Sediq included groups also known as Musha, troku, tawca', tawsai, Taroko, and Mokkōban, all of whom referred to themselves in their own language as simply "human beings," or *sajiq* (Kojima [1915] 1996: 5). It was only in the 1930s, as we see below, that Mabuchi Tōichi had disentangled the relations between these subgroups and classified the Sediq as comprised of the three groups of Truku, Teuda, and Tkedaya.

By 1935, anthropologists used genealogical, linguistic, and cultural criteria to classify all Indigenous communities into nine tribes. Their results were published by the Institute of Ethnology at Taihoku Imperial University as the authoritative *Formosan Native Tribes: a Genealogical and Classificatory Study* (Taihoku teikoku daigaku 1935). The first volume of this treatise uses geography, oral history, and mythology to justify the resulting classifications. The second volume, labeled "data," gives detailed genealogical charts of all the Indigenous communities. For the purpose of this chapter, what is important is that this study finalized nine as the number of Indigenous groups and established the names by which they would be known. The Atayal included all of the Sediq groups discussed in this chapter.

These colonial categories were accepted by the states on Taiwan until after 2000, when a Democratic Progressive Party (DPP) government opened up the possibility of new Indigenous identities. The new identities, however, also had roots in the

Japanese period. Most of all, memories of colonial violence—in processes observed elsewhere in Taiwan and beyond—led to the crystallization of new identities (Simon 2003; Conway 2009). Older members of Sediq communities argue that Japanese administrators grouped them all with the Atayal *because* of these violent incidents, the administrative logic being that the other Atayal groups would control the rebellious eastern groups on behalf of the Japanese. These colonial attempts to reorganize bundles of local relationships remain at the heart of controversies over tribal names and Indigenous autonomy.

Creating Taroko identity

Hualian and Nantou have different histories of conquest, resistance, and colonial administration, making it necessary to study the local histories of both regions in order to understand how colonialism shaped social identities in the two places. Each location has its own local scholars, and all of them are linked to political struggles. In Hualian, the most detailed scholarship on colonial relocation and community history was done by the anthropologist Masaw Mowna (Chinese name: Liao Shou-chen), who self-identified as Sediq.[5] Masaw (1939–1999) became Xiulin Township's first university student when he entered the National Taiwan University Department of History in 1961. After his graduation, he audited courses with the anthropologist Li Yih-yüan, beginning a lifetime of research and writing on Indigenous Taiwan. In 1976, he was elected Xiulin Township magistrate. In 1984, he was sent to prison, where he wrote his work on the Amis tribe. In 1998, he became an anthropology instructor at Tzu Chi University in Hualian. As an outspoken opponent of the independence of the Truku tribe from the Atayal tribe, he wrote several opinion pieces in the newspapers and established the Xiulin Kele Cultural Heritage Association in 1998 to oppose Truku nationalism. His detailed research on Sediq migration to Hualian, based on interviews with seventy-five local elders as well as studies of Japanese archival records, was published by the Academia Sinica Institute of Ethnology in two installments in 1977 and 1978. Because of his political actions and strong opposition to Truku independence, Masaw is revered as an intellectual only by local people who support recognition as Sediq. The competing Truku nationalists remember him more for his drinking habits and for corrupt politics.

All studies demonstrate the continuing importance of the *alang* as the fundamental form of social organization, even after groups were moved into administrative villages, as can be seen in the case of Fushi Village. The main part of that village has six main kin communities, now largely organized around church membership, but each of which was formed during the colonial period when Japanese administrators forced people of different *alang* to live together in the same village. The people of Fushi, with the exception of those who entered the community through marriage and a minority of people who moved in of their own volition, speak the Truku dialect.

Masaw traced the historical origin of all three Sediq subethnic groups (Truku, Teuda, and Tkedaya) in Hualian to Nantou, documenting their history of intergroup conflict and nomadic migration in search of game. He divided Sediq eastward migration into three periods. First, prior to 1914, groups migrated eastward by themselves along different river systems. The second and third periods, in which the Japanese encouraged or forced resettlement on the eastern plains, followed the 1914 Taroko Battle and the 1930 Musha Incident.

Masaw traced the origin of each *alang* to its earliest known ancestor. During the precolonial period, there was considerable movement, often in search of wildlife, arable land, or even access to salt from the ocean. With the accord of the elders, some allied groups could decide to settle together in the same location. Yet new *alang* were formed if, under population pressure, one or two younger members migrated through the mountains in search of new territory. Kin-based groups such as Bsngan, Kele, Xoxos, and Skadang already had identities as *alang*. The descendants of Lapaq Wattan, for example, recall moving down to the east so that they could benefit from arable land and access to the ocean for salt. They called their new settlement Busengan (Bsngan), meaning "trading place." Kele was founded by a fusion of two kin groups who migrated down the Liwu River, settled together in the mountain area of Sidakang, and ended up in a formerly Amis area at what is now the Asia Cement Plant. Both of these were near Xincheng, which was established by the Qing to prevent Japanese encroachment on the northeast coast. The new arrivals established barter relations with the Han who lived there. Xoxos and Skadang have similar stories of their ancestors settling in the mountains above Bsngan (Masaw 1977: 126–7, 90, 113–15). A close reading of this history leaves an impression of these groups as marked by both fusion, as groups moved together, and fission, as segments moved out in search of better territory. There were attempts to create confederacies of related *alang*, usually in the same rivershed, but also warfare and competition over hunting grounds.

As discussed above, the Qing had not brought these "raw savages" under state rule, and the Japanese, after taking Taiwan in 1895, had to launch military campaigns to subordinate the mountain tribes and access mountain resources. In Hualian, people of Kele and Bsngan commonly refer to the Xincheng Incident (1896) and the Weili Incident (1906) as their first anticolonial acts, as they were unsatisfied with the way that the Japanese violated *gaya* in their search for camphor (Chin 2002: 218). Some members of the community remember the role of Lee Ah-long, a Han or plains Aborigine merchant and former officer in the Qing military who instigated Indigenous violence against Japan (Yamaguchi 1999; Walis and Yu 2002). The longest and most violent battle, however, was the Taroko Battle of 1914. In 1910, Governor-General Sakuma Samata declared the second "Five-Year Plan to Pacify the Savages." In May 1914, Japanese troops began a military offensive, with troops arriving both from Musha (Wushe) in the West and from Karenkō (Hualian) in the East. The Japanese sent in 6,000 soldiers, twenty-nine artillery units, and nineteen tanks and had battleships for reinforcement (Walis and Yu 2002: 154). Including military and police, they mobilized a total of 20,748 men. In Hualian, Japanese troops first attacked and occupied the communities near Xincheng, including Bsngan and Kele, where they gained formal surrender by village leaders (Masaw 1978: 81–2). In the mountains, some 2,000–3,000 young Indigenous warriors continued to resist the troops armed only with bows and arrows and hunting rifles. Familiar with the treacherous terrain, the high mountain groups were able to resist invasion with guerilla fighting tactics for nearly three months. People of Xoxos and Skadang recall luring Japanese troops into the narrow gorge of the Skadang River and killing them by causing a landslide. Official records document the deaths of sixty-one Japanese soldiers and fifteen police officers, as well as the wounding of 125 soldiers and twenty-five police officers, but no records seem to have been kept of Indigenous losses (Fujii 1997: 266, Walis and Yu 2002: 155).

Although they eventually surrendered and recognized Japanese sovereignty over their territory, this event crystallized their identity as Truku. Taroko, the Japanese pronunciation of this group's name, became a place name and would in the 1930s become the name of a national park. In so far as the memory of violent resistance contributes to identity, this moment of anticolonial resistance and violent oppression is similar to the February 28th Incident as lived by the Taiwanese as a whole (Chang 2000; Simon 2003). Truku pride about their fierce resistance in the battlefield is reflected in their narratives about Sakuma's death. Japanese records showed that he returned to Japan and died a year later, when he became a deity (*kami*) enshrined in state Shinto. Truku elders, however, claim that he was killed in battle and that his return to Japan was a fraud. One older Truku hunter even claimed to know the true site of Sakuma's remains in the mountains. Whether such stories are true or not, they illustrate well how colonial memory contributes to ethnic identity. Truku identity may have been strengthened around the Taroko Battle, and this was especially true for the people of Skadang and Xoxos, but the Japanese did everything possible to prevent further colonial uprisings. The battle for Taroko, moreover, had little to do with the Truku in the ancestral homeland or with competing Teuda and Tkedaya groups. It also meant different things to the Truku of the plains villages, who capitulated earlier, and to those of the mountains, who resisted more fiercely.

The politics of relocation further reshuffled the bundles of relations that make up these tribal groups. After the 1914 defeat, most Truku communities were encouraged by the Japanese to leave their mountain villages and resettle in the plains. In an attempt to avoid further violence, the Japanese broke up existing communities during relocation. According to the accounts of elderly villagers, members of the same *alang* were intentionally placed in different locations throughout Hualian. People of various *alang*, including those of previously hostile groups, were also included in the same village. These different groups were encouraged to keep the other groups under surveillance, reporting any suspicious behavior to the Japanese police. This led to a reduction in the number and size of mountain groups. The Japanese constructed new irrigation systems for the new plains villages and taught the villagers modern forms of agriculture and management of rice paddies. Twenty-eight *alang*, however, refused to move, including Skadang and Xoxos in the Taroko Gorge area, where the battles had been the fiercest. This resettlement process, which broke up existing kin groups only to place families in different administrative villages surrounded by families from formerly hostile groups, destroyed many precolonial social institutions, including ritual groups (Masaw 1978: 109, 4–5).

Following the 1930 Musha Incident, which did not involve the participation of Hualian groups, almost all groups were forced to resettle in the plains, as Japan did not wish to risk another violent incident that could hamper camphor production. The only exceptions were the three bands of Skadang, Xoxos, and Senlingan, who were encouraged instead to practice agriculture on their mountain lands (Masaw 1977: 75–9). The Japanese used the opportunity of these forced relocations to split up the former communities while creating citizens of modern villages. To give just one example, the families of Tobogo, whose high mountain settlement was bombed by the Japanese, were scattered throughout at least eight villages in Hualian.

Memories of the colonial period still influence day-to-day social relations—even between individuals in the same communities. In Hualian, for example, people still recall how one individual had participated in the Takasagozoku Youth Corps (*Takasagozoku seinendan*) and subsequently became a police officer. He participated in surveillance of the emerging local Presbyterian church and imprisoned the founder of the True Jesus Church. After the Japanese left, however, he himself became a Presbyterian pastor, which his peers describe as an opportunistic move to take a job that would give him access to the post-war food aid from Christian organizations. When I suggested that he may have had a conversion experience like Paul on the road to Damascus, they questioned the sincerity of his faith. People on both sides of local political debates pointed out that he has a long-standing pattern of taking from both sides. He contributed to the creation of a Truku dictionary (a paid position), yet simultaneously joined forces with the opponents of Truku identity to lobby for the creation of a Sediq tribe on the same territory. The important thing here is that people recall memories of his collaboration with the Japanese to highlight his untrustworthiness today.

Xoxos scholar Tera Yudaw, who studied history and served as a primary school principal, wrote a nationalist treatise on the Truku people (Tera 2003) and was one of the main proponents of Truku name rectification leading up to their recognition in 2004. He subsequently emerged as the main proponent of the establishment of a Truku Autonomous Region. He and the Truku networks, mostly affiliated with the Taroko Synod of the Presbyterian Church, thus attracted the ire of people in both Hualian and Nantou who identified alternatively as Sediq. Likewise, the Truku nationalists have tense relations with Sediq advocates in both places.

Creating Sediq community

Especially due to the contested meaning of the Musha Incident in the national imagination of Chinese, Taiwanese, and Indigenous nationalists—as Huang shows elsewhere in this book—local scholars in Nantou play an important role in the interpretation of Sediq history. Two prolific Seediq historians are Takun Walis and Dakis Pawan, both of whom have been active in Sediq nationalist advocacy. Takun is an economist trained at National Taiwan University, and Dakis is a retired schoolteacher who now specializes in Seediq language revival. Local Han Taiwanese scholars have also made important contributions and have been largely successful at learning from and representing Sediq perspectives of events. Deng Shian-yang, born in 1951 in Nantou, was trained as a medical technician, made many Indigenous friends while working at the Puli Christian Hospital, and began doing research on Indigenous history. At the fiftieth anniversary of the Musha Incident, he began doing archival and interview research on the subject after his father gave him a collection of Japanese archives and photos (Chou 2000: 30).

As in Hualian, the communities in Nantou were originally egalitarian groups marked by processes of fission and fusion. The Sediq of Nantou, however, had earlier contact with the state system and established chiefdoms under indirect rule of the Qing Dynasty in the nineteenth century (Deng 1998: 28). The Tkedaya communities had their historical origins in the village of Taya-Truwan, but various groups split off from this original group in search of new food sources. During the Qing Dynasty, they had formed the Musha confederation of ten Tkedaya *alang* plus the Teuda *alang* of Boalum that had performed pig sacrifices to break away from the Teuda and join the Tkedaya Confederacy. This confederacy dissolved after 1895, when the Japanese played the different groups against one another to gain control of the territory (Deng 1998: 52–3).

Still living in the ancestral homeland, the Nantou Sediq relish the story of how their ancestors emerged from a rock in the Central Mountain Range. Some of them even make a treacherous pilgrimage through the forest to that sacred site. They identify themselves as belonging to the three dialect groups of the Truku, Teuda, and Tkedaya, and maintain relations with the same groups in Hualian. They discuss known individuals in Hualian as relatives, friends, allies, co-ethnics, or despised traitors with an emotional vigor unlike discussion of any other neighboring groups such as the Atayal or Bunun. Some Sediq nationalists argue that the Nantou Sediq and Hualian Truku form different Indigenous nations and can list examples of long-standing differences in weaving patterns, facial tattoos, songs, dance steps, or spoken dialects to prove their point. At the same time, they refer to the Nantou Sediq as those of the "ancestral land" and those in Hualian as those of the "land of emigration," regretting what they perceive as a political manipulation to form the Truku tribe and thus divide existing groups (Simon 2009). The same individuals thus make the apparently inconsistent arguments that they are of the same tribes, yet of a different nation, than those in Hualian.[6]

Hara explains the contemporary split in terms of competing political factions formed around Presbyterian synods in Hualian and Nantou, as well as the different demographic weight of the subgroups in Hualian and Nantou (Hara 2003, 2004). Whereas the Truku have an absolute majority in Hualian, each subgroup represents only about one-third of the total population in Nantou. This makes it easier for the Truku to impose their name on tribal formation in Hualian than in Nantou. This sociological interpretation is correct and points toward a deeper meaning of events. It is important to also keep in mind, however, that the three groups were also enemy groups and considered each other to be legitimate victims of headhunting rituals as early as the Japanese period, if not before. In 1897, for example, Tkedaya men from Musha presented one Truku and one Teuda head to the Japanese as a sign of their loyalty to Japan (Barclay 2008: Chap. 3).

The contemporary factionalism is thus built upon social divisions exacerbated by violent events during the colonial period.

The Sediq, also known during the Japanese period as the "Mushaban" (Musha savages) for the area of their residence, presented a paradox to the Japanese. Following the 1914 pacification of the Taroko Gorge, the Japanese invested heavily in Indigenous areas, setting up schools, police stations, medical clinics, and Shinto shrines in villages across Taiwan. Musha, an important camphor production town, was perceived to be a model Indigenous village. Mona Ludaw, a local chief, was educated by the Japanese and he even participated in a trip of Indigenous leaders to visit Japan. Two local Sediq policemen, brothers Dakis Nomin and Dakis Nawi still remembered by their Japanese names as Hanaoka Ichirō and Hanaoka Jirō, were decorated for their loyalty to the Japanese emperor. Yet Musha was the lieu of the most violent and most surprising resurrection against Japanese administration. The warriors were all Tkedaya men from the six villages of Mahebo, Boalum, Suku, Hogo, Taya-Truwan, and Rodof.

Early in the morning of October 27, 1930, while most Japanese officers were distracted by the preparations for ceremonies to celebrate the thirty-fifth anniversary of Japanese rule on Taiwan, over 300 Sediq warriors led by Mona Ludaw attacked twelve police stations. They killed the Japanese officers present, cut off communication lines to the outside, and seized all the guns and ammunition they could find. That afternoon, as Japanese officials, teachers, and their families gathered in Musha for a sports event, they descended upon the crowd in a frenzy of murder. A total of 134 Japanese were killed on site (Ching 2000: 797–8). The historical reasons for the violence are varied, ranging from resentment toward colonial control and imposition of new modes of production to Mona Ludaw's personal grudge against a Japanese policeman who had refused to accept a wedding toast of alcohol from his son two weeks earlier (Deng 1998: 55–66). Mona Ludaw himself sent a message to the Japanese, saying that this was revenge because the Japanese police had not honored agreements to loan firearms and provide ammunition to Sediq hunters and because of a record of onerous corvée labor without adequate compensation (Barclay 2008: Chap. 1).

The Japanese military responded immediately, in two months of attacks using 1,305 police officers and 1,303 military troops, as well as headhunters from enemy tribes, to punish the six communities involved in the uprising (Deng 1998: 72–86). They even resorted to aerial bombings and used chemical gasses that had been banned in international agreements (Chou 2000: 18). During this initial chaos, Mona fled to the mountains and committed suicide. From an initial population of 1,234 in those six communities, at least 644 were killed in the first reprisals. Deng notes that 290 (45 percent) of them chose to commit suicide rather than be killed. Some 561 survivors were placed in detention centers in Shibao and Rodof, as well as in Teuda and Truku communities. A year later, the Japanese mobilized Teuda warriors to attack the detention centers of Shibao and Rodof in what is remembered locally as the "Second Musha Incident." This led to a further 195 deaths and nineteen suicides (Deng 1998: 85, 87, 92). The remaining 298 survivors, mostly women, children, and elderly people, were relocated from their highland villages to a lowland village surrounded by the waters of two rivers, which was called Kawanakajima (island between the rivers). Placed under direct military surveillance, and required to have military escorts if they crossed the suspension bridge to leave the village, the villagers remember this situation as being like a concentration camp. They also recall that there were further suicides and deaths from tropical diseases that they had never encountered in the highlands. In October 1931, the Japanese arrested and executed an additional twenty-three men from Kawanakajima (Chou 2000: 18). Mona Ludaw's body, found in 1933 by a hunter—likely Truku, since the Japanese had resettled that group into former Tkedaya highlands areas—was subsequently exhibited in the Taiwan Imperial University Institute of Ethnology.

The survivors from the six rebellious villages had to adapt to a new environment and soon created a new local identity based on their common historical suffering. Under ROC rule, the former Kawanakajima became incorporated into the village of Qingliu (literally "clear flow"). Qingliu is also important politically as a voting district, which includes not only Kawanakajima but also the upstream communities on the Beigang River of Nakahara (a Tkedaya group that was relocated from the highlands by the Japanese to make way for a hydroelectric dam in 1939) and Mebara (an Atayal group that had previously settled the area). Local people still refer to these hamlets by their Japanese names more often than by their Chinese names. Kawanakajima is also referred to as Alang Gluban, which local elders say means "the place where skulls are washed." They say that their ancestors used to hunt heads and would stop to wash the skulls at the confluence of rivers. All three names thus refer to the flowing waters around the village. This environment was propitious during the Japanese period for the construction of a modern irrigation system and the introduction of paddy agriculture. The farmers of Gluban now produce what they call Kawanakajima rice, and the rice harvest is one of the major events of the year.

The aftermath of the Musha Incident led to a radical reshuffling of all Sediq communities. As mentioned above, almost all Sediq communities in the mountain ranges were forcefully relocated into the plains after 1930 and dispersed across villages to break up kin networks that could potentially contribute to anticolonial resistance. In order to prevent the survivors at Gluban from returning to their home villages, the Japanese moved enemy Teuda and Truku groups into those six locations. The Japanese put all of these communities under strict police control, but they also built up other institutions of schools, shrines, and irrigation associations. The forests were freed up for camphor production, and Sediq hunters were encouraged to become farmers on reserve land (*banjin shoyōchi*) (Yan and Yang 2004: 232–3). The main goal was to reduce Indigenous territory, while limiting their movement and submitting them to state authority. This process accelerated during the Imperialization campaigns (*kōminka*) of 1939–1945, which Leo Ching has defined as a change in governmentality from subjugation to acculturation (2000: 802). Supposedly under the direct order of the emperor, Japan began referring to the Indigenous Peoples as *Takasagozoku* (high sands tribes, referring to an archaic Japanese term for Formosa, elicits positive connotations of bravery in

Japanese) rather than as savages (*seiban*) in 1935 (Yamaguchi 1999: 32). The Japanese encouraged them to adopt Japanese names, pray in Shinto shrines, and serve in the military. In Kawanakajima, there were so many volunteers that they had to resort to a lottery to decide who would get the glory of joining the Japanese military (Walis and Yu 2002: 166). As Huang also shows in Chapter 7 of this volume, former members of the Japanese military are still praised in the village for their "Japanese spirit" of hard work and community solidarity. These elders say that they joined the Japanese because the Japanese convinced them it was to prevent an American occupation of their lands.

After the transfer of Taiwan to the ROC, the Musha Incident was incorporated into the Chinese nationalist imagination as the Wushe Rebellion, an act of anti-Japanese resistance on behalf of the Chinese nation (Chou 2000: 25). Local leaders, however, were also able to express their own version of events. Pihu Walis of Hogo, who was only 14 years old at the time of the event, lost his father to the bombings and his mother to suicide. He ended up as a police assistant in Kawanakajima and married the daughter of Hanaoka Jirō. After the arrival of the ROC, he studied medicine and was elected as the first magistrate of Ren'ai Township in 1951 (Chou 2000: 38–9). Under his influence, the first memorials to the Musha survivors were erected in Qingliu and Wushe in the 1950s. The township office, which also organized commemorations of the event and played a role in the 1973 repatriation of Mona Ludaw's body to Wushe, has been a training ground for local leaders and has played an important role in the promotion of Sediq national identity and tribal autonomy. In the 1980s and 1990s, there was a blossoming of local scholarship on the Musha Incident, with a focus on Taiwanese rather than on Chinese history, and with an affirmation of Sediq identity (Chou 2000: 29). Scholars affiliated with the Presbyterian Church of Taiwan argued that the Musha Incident happened because the Japanese violated *gaya* and that such resistance necessarily points the way toward formal Indigenous autonomy (Pusin 2002; Walis 2002).

The Musha Incident and its aftermath are commemorated in the Survivors Memorial Hall, a local hall and exhibit space that is sometimes shown to visitors. The memories of Mona Ludaw and the Musha Incident, although the object of a film (2011's *Warriors of the Rainbow: Seediq Bale*) by the Taiwanese director Wei Te-sheng, remain contested in the village. Some Seediq nationalists and young people, especially those who were recruited to work in the film as advisors, language teachers, and actors, have gained new pride in Mona Ludaw and their village's history of resistance. Some proudly observe that they are descendants of his clan. Others, however, also regretted that Mona's action led to the destruction of their families. Many older people refused to talk about it with their families, with the hope that their children would instead focus on the future. This changed only when Mona's remains were returned to the community and elders began new reflections on their history (Takun 2010). In Gluban, however, the prevailing sentiment is a consensus that he was a Sediq hero who defended the traditional law of *gaya* against colonial perpetrators. Sediq identity, conceived in the aftermath of the Musha Incident, was thus incubated in the political field of Ren'ai Township and largely separated from developments in

Hualian. Colonial violence forged a unitary Seediq identity in Gluban and made that village into the epicenter of Sediq national identity.

Conclusion

For anthropologists and historians looking at language and power, the power to name is the central issue. An examination of Japanese colonial governance shows that the Japanese fully used the power to name to implement their rule on Taiwan. The Japanese were the first to use the word "Sediq" to refer to an ethnic group rather than, as had been done by the people themselves, to distinguish human beings from animals. They were also the first to settle Taiwan's nomadic Indigenous groups into villages with place names fixed on maps. The Japanese also gave Japanese surnames to Sediq and Truku people who had not used surnames in the past. All of these foreign names were transformed into Chinese versions after the transition to ROC rule. Japanese and Chinese rule were thus both modern forms of governance that positioned peoples and territories in similar ways. As we can see from the local histories unraveled in this chapter, these names made bundles of relationships into social realities that could be named and discussed as if they were entities with histories of their own. The Japanese thus created not just physical communities such as Fushi and Kawanakajima but also the categories through which the people in those places imagine their futures. Without that history, the Sediq and Truku would have neither the concept of territorially based nations nor the identities that were crystallized in colonial violence.

These processes were part of global changes. Attention to political economy reminds us further that these governance modes were imposed upon Taiwan, as they were around the world, in order to facilitate the spread of new modes of production for the capitalist world market. In Taiwan's case, the lure of camphor brought both Japanese and Chinese into the mountain forests, where they met Indigenous Peoples who resisted the territorial intrusion and new modes of production. Indigenous groups eventually capitulated to the new political systems, even taking leading roles in local politics (Simon 2010). With democratization and the emergence of new social movements, some of them started demanding recognition as Indigenous nations with the right to legal and political autonomy, not unlike people in similar situations around the world (Miller 2003). When they did so, however, they imagined those new possibilities through the prism of their colonial experience.

On the very day that I finished the first draft of this chapter in December 2010, for example, representatives from Gluban, Fushi, and Indigenous villages across Taiwan met at the Council of Indigenous Peoples in Taipei to revise a proposed law on Indigenous autonomy. Although this law failed to pass before the end of the legislative session, Indigenous leaders continued to hope for some form of autonomy in the future. Even if a future government were to implement a policy of Indigenous self-government, however, there is no guarantee that it will be implemented in the ways envisioned by its most fervent advocates. Studies of the future of Indigenous autonomy in Taiwan often point out obstacles to autonomy such as Taiwan's lack of international space, uncertain relations with China, or the need to compromise with non-Indigenous citizens of Taiwan (S. Allen 2005). Legal studies of Taiwan's proposed autonomy laws also suggest that Taiwan's Indigenous self-government could be even weaker than similar systems in the United States and elsewhere (Ericsson 2004). These political and legal studies are useful. Historical studies are also necessary, as they illustrate how the colonial experience shaped both the possibilities of autonomy and the internal contradictions that make it a difficult goal to achieve. Colonial memories, evoked and reinvigorated as relationships are built and factions reinforced, shape the way in which Indigenous architects draw the blueprints of autonomy.

Notes

1   The use of the plural in the translation follows debates in international indigenous law about the distinction between "Indigenous People" and "Indigenous Peoples," a distinction rendered in Chinese as that between *Yuanzhumin* and *Yuanzhuminzu*.

2   Although some Taroko nationalists argued for the use of the word "Taroko" instead of "Truku," saying that it is more inclusive of two other subgroups, the Council of Indigenous Peoples (CIP) ultimately decided that they would be called the Truku in English publications.

3   Sediq nationalists often provide three separate spellings for this word in publications, in order to include the dialect differences between the three subgroups, in which the word is pronounced *sejiq, sediq,* or *seediq.* The CIP is inconsistent about their usage in English publications.

4   For an anthropological reflection on the Bunun strategy of Indigenous–state relations from a Bunun perspective, see Yang (2005).

5   In accordance to Sediq naming, his name is Masaw and his father's name is Mowna.

6   The use of the word "nation" is intentional; some ethnic nationalists use the word *guo* in Chinese (e.g. *Saideke guo*) to make their point. When speaking with me, they are enthusiastic about the Canadian use of the term "First Nation" and see it as applicable in their case.

Ethnicity, Mortality, and the Shinchiku (Xinzhu) Advantage in Colonial Taiwan

John R. Shepherd

Ethnic differences past and present

A prominent feature of Taiwan's political scene today is the salience in public discourse of "ethnicity" or "provenance." Political affiliation is often discussed in terms of ethnically based voting blocs, usually "mainlanders" (*waishengren*) versus "Taiwanese" (*benshengren*), the former usually tending toward pan-Chinese loyalty and the latter often toward pro-Japanese nostalgia. Within the group known as "Taiwanese," further distinction is made between the majority Hoklo (Minnan speakers) and the minority Hakka (Kejia speakers) (Chang 1994: 93–150; Martin 1996: 176–95). The salience of ethnicity in politics today matches the important role attributed to ethnic differences in the early history of Chinese/Manchu Taiwan, when strife between settler groups led to violent disturbances and even rebellion against the Qing (Lamley 1981: 282–318; Shepherd 1993). In both past conflicts and the modern competition for votes and resources, partisans make strong claims for the depth of the cultural differences that divide their groups. Accordingly, the study of ethnicity and identity politics has become a prominent feature of modern scholarship on Hakka and Taiwanese (Chen et al. 1994; Constable 1996; Leong 1997), and multiple conferences have been devoted to a new field of "Hakkaology."[1]

The origins of this ethnic competition lie in the early settlement history of Taiwan. During the eighteenth and nineteenth centuries, Taiwan was a frontier of Chinese agricultural settlement open to migrants from adjoining provinces on the southeast coast of China, namely Hoklo from Fujian and Hakka from Guangdong. The oftentimes turbulent process of frontier settlement resulted in the creation of mutually antagonistic and residentially segregated communities based on provenance and speech group. Conflicts between Hoklo and Hakka were frequent and reinforced their identities as separate ethnic communities (Lamley 1981; Shepherd 1993: 310–39).

The two immigrant groups, Hoklo and Hakka, shared many Han customs, including patrilineal ancestor worship, strong parental authority over married adult sons, equal property inheritance among brothers, and folk religious practices.

Hoklo and Hakka practiced similar forms of marriage and adoption, including "little daughter-in-law" marriage ("minor" marriage), and had similar levels of marital fertility. But there were also differences, most notably mutually unintelligible languages, different patron deities, and the Hakka refusal to bind the feet of daughters (Chuang 1994; Shepherd et al. 2006: 121–61). This latter distinction meant that female Hakka were able to perform field labor and contribute economically to their families in ways denied to adult Hoklo women, over 90 percent of whom were footbound (till 1915, when the Japanese banned the practice).[2]

Despite the many similar customs shared among the groups, the remaining differences, whether in language, footbinding, or historical experience, became the focus of separate ethnic identities that perdured into the twentieth century. Study of the Japanese colonial period in Taiwan, however, rarely attends to the differences between Hoklo and Hakka, focusing instead on the position of Taiwanese in general (*hontōjin* in the Japanese censuses) vis-à-vis the resident Japanese colonialists (*naichijin*). This neglect exists despite the resources available for exploring differences between the Hoklo and Hakka found in the unique censuses and vital statistics reports compiled by the Japanese colonial government.[3] No study has ever before noted the sharp distinction in death rates between Hoklo and Hakka, and the discovery of these sharp differences in the vital statistics of the colonial period poses a demographic puzzle. Did the cultural differences between the groups have important consequences for differential mortality? Or, did the regional concentration of nearly two thirds of the Hakka in one prefecture confer an *environmental* advantage that reduced the mortality rates not just of Hakka but of *all* the groups living in that prefecture? This chapter seeks to exploit Taiwan's rich demographic data sources to examine the role ethnicity may or may not play in accounting for the significant differences in death rates within the Taiwanese population.

First, we must consider the public health, policing, and local control systems that produced the information contained in Taiwan's censuses and annual vital statistics reports analyzed in this chapter. In the 1895 conquest of Taiwan, well-organized and well-equipped Japanese forces were hindered as much by unfavorable climate and disease as by military resistance in driving armed opposition from the field. From the very beginning of their rule, the Japanese armed forces and the civilian administrators posted to Taiwan suffered high death rates. There they confronted unfamiliar diseases like malaria and bubonic plague (which arrived in Taiwan in May 1896), in addition to well-known scourges such as smallpox, cholera, and pulmonary tuberculosis. Alarmed by the high incidence of diseases of all kinds and the lack of public health infrastructure, the Japanese invested significant resources in medical services, sanitation, smallpox vaccination, and epidemic control. Via the study of modern European methods, Meiji reformers had learned much about new advances in germ theory, medicine, and sanitation and implementation of public health measures in Japan proper, and they readily applied the new knowledge to their Taiwan colony. These efforts were directed first at preserving the health of the Japanese colonizers, but gradually extended to the Taiwanese population as a whole; plans for economic exploitation of the island could not succeed unless health conditions could be improved for all imperial subjects (Goto 1904: 585–98; Takekoshi 1907).

In the first years of colonial rule, the Japanese also confronted open resistance, and, when that was suppressed, occasional scattered instances of banditry and rebellion. To minimize these threats, the security-conscious Japanese created a policing system that exercised close control over the subject Taiwanese population. They did this by creating a dense network of police stations and charging police with surveillance of households, aided by a mutual security system that held household heads responsible for any illegal activities (Chinese *baojia*, Japanese *hokō*). Each household was required to record the names, birthdates, parentage, provenance, and other information of each of its members in a register maintained at the local police registry office. Heads were required to report any changes in household membership, whether birth, death, migration, adoption, or marriage. Movements between households were carefully tracked in both sending and receiving registry offices. Regular inspection visits by police ensured that the information in the registers was kept up to date.[4]

The Japanese regime assigned numerous duties to the policing system that were not strictly limited to guaranteeing local security. In addition to its security function, the registration system produced the population data required by economic development and administrative planning, and in public health programming. Responsibility for aspects of public health and sanitation was also assigned to the police and *hokō* hierarchy. A local medical officer or trained policeman was required to assign an official cause of death for each such event reported. Aggregating the changes in the population recorded through the household registration system produced the annual vital statistics reports and detailed census returns. The data on death rates and causes of death, which provide insights into the prevalence of disease in the population, were, subsequently, used by public health administrators. This system of continuous registration yielded the extremely high-quality demographic data we have at our disposal for the Japanese period.[5] Given the turbulent history of communal strife in Qing Taiwan and the continuing importance of cultural differences in the organization of local society, the registration system also took care to record the provenance of *hontōjin* residents: the Hoklo Minnan-speaking majority (82 percent of Taiwan's population in 1920) or the Hakka minority (15 percent). The household registers and censuses and vital statistics created by the Japanese assigned individuals to provenance groupings (Fujian and Guangdong) based on ancestral origin and descent (through the presumed biological father, or mother if father was unknown) rather than ethnicity or language. For the great majority provenance and ethnolinguistic affiliation coincided unproblematically. The 1915 census reports that more than 99 percent of those registered as Fujianese were also Minnan speakers and 85 percent of Guangdongese were Kejia speakers. However, approximately 15 percent of Guangdongese (from Chaozhou Prefecture) were speakers of a language closely related to Minnan rather than Kejia (*Dai-niji rinji* 1917: 1159; Shepherd et al. 2006: 128). This is an important but statistically minor exception to the practice of equating the provenance categories of Fujianese and Guangdongese to Hoklo and Hakka, respectively. Japanese anthropologists, scientists, and statisticians thus kept their statistics in this manner, noting simply "Fukken" for our category of Hoklo and "Kanton" for the Hakka subjects of Taiwan.

A surprising gap: Hoklo versus Hakka crude death rates

Comparing Hoklo and Hakka crude death rates in the colonial period reveals a striking contrast that gives apparent support to claims that these groups are divided by significant cultural differences. As shown in Table 5.1, the death rates of the Hakka minority were 20–30 percent lower than those suffered by the Hoklo. Table 5.1 is drawn from the reports of causes of death by ethnic group and sex for the period 1906–1931. The death rates are computed by dividing three-year averages by the population totals reported in the censuses of 1905 (adjusted to a midyear population 1907), 1915, 1920, 1925, and 1930. The left columns report the crude death rates for all causes. To facilitate comparison, the two rightmost columns index the death rates by sex in each period on the Hoklo rates, which represent more than 80 percent of Taiwanese. (Because the Hoklo and Hakka populations had similar age distributions, we can discount the possibility that the differences in crude death rates are affected by differences in age structure between the ethnic groups [Shepherd 2011a: 130].)

The crude death rates by sex for each cultural group presented in Table 5.1 reveal sharply lower death rates for both Hakka men and women compared to their Hoklo counterparts. The Hakka death rates remain significantly lower than Hoklo rates from 1906 to 1931. What factors could account for this striking divergence? One possibility is that the Hakka are relatively free of a particular disease or set of diseases that plague the Hoklo.

To assess the possibility that particular diseases raise death rates among the Hoklo compared to the Hakka, we explore the leading causes of death in the two groups. Cause of death data is reported in the vital statistics by provenance grouping and by sex through 1931. However, due to inconsistencies in the definition of cause groups and the quality of reporting of the cause of death in the early years, we provide rates for some causes only for the latter two periods, 1924–1926 and 1929–1931.[6]

Table 5.1 Crude death rates by ethnicity, all causes, 1906–1931.

Year	Crude Death Rates by Ethnicity, Deaths per 100,000				Indexed Rates, Hoklo = 100	
	Hoklo		Hakka		Hakka	
All Causes	Male	Female	Male	Female	Male	Female
1906–1908	3,617	3,548	2,454	2,365	68	67
1914–1916	3,305	3,075	2,289	2,165	69	70
1919–1921	3,038	2,823	2,586	2,384	85	84
1924–1926	2,681	2,406	2,151	1,968	80	82
1929–1931	2,356	2,123	1,856	1,719	79	81

Source: Vital statistics from the *Taiwan jinkō dōtai tōkei*, and populations at risk from the Taiwan censuses for the relevant years.

Note: This and several following tables use "Hoklo" and "Hakka" to denote the Taiwanese people distinguished by the Japanese as tracing their ancestry to Fukken and Kanton, respectively.

Table 5.2 reports the death rates by cause for the leading causes of death. Death rates by cause are computed as a ratio of the deaths assigned to a specific cause (three-year averages) to a midyear census population; these crude rates (because they are not broken down by age) can be referred to as cause-specific death rates (Barclay 1958: 151–5). To facilitate comparison, the rightmost columns index the Hakka death rates by sex in each period on the Hoklo rates. Each of the leading causes shows significant differences between the groups.

Table 5.2 Cause-specific crude death rates by leading causes and by ethnicity and sex, 1906–1931.

Cause of Death*	Cause Specific Crude Death Rates by Ethnicity, Deaths per 100,000				Indexed Rates, Hoklo = 100	
Year	Hoklo		Hakka		Hakka	
Malaria	Male	Female	Male	Female	Male	Female
1906–1908	365	392	290	308	*79.5*	*78.6*
1914–1916	340	351	221	221	*65.0*	*63.0*
1919–1921	214	212	198	179	*92.5*	*84.4*
1924–1926	177	172	145	146	*81.9*	*84.9*
1929–1931	71	68	75	73	*105.6*	*107.4*
Respiratory Tuberculosis						
1906–1908	191	104	84	51	*44.0*	*49.0*
1914–1916	189	109	75	38	*39.7*	*34.9*
1919–1921	237	150	96	44	*40.5*	*29.3*
1924–1926	227	137	108	53	*47.6*	*38.7*
1929–1931	195	124	95	48	*48.7*	*38.7*
Respiratory Diseases						
1924–1926	848	700	639	535	*75.4*	*76.4*
1929–1931	733	611	590	510	*80.5*	*83.5*
Diarrhea, Enteritis						
1924–1926	352	353	190	192	*54.0*	*54.4*
1929–1931	369	384	195	202	*52.8*	*52.6*
Certain Diseases of Infancy						
1924–1926	145	112	139	106	*95.9*	*94.6*
1929–1931	138	106	115	79	*83.3*	*74.5*
Certain Diseases of Infancy as Infant Death Rate						
1924–1926	32.9	25.5	32.3	24.7	*98.2*	*96.9*
1929–1931	28.7	22.4	25.9	18.0	*90.2*	*80.4*

* Certain Diseases of Infancy as Infant Death Rate is calculated as deaths per thousand live births. Vital statistics from the *Taiwan jinkō dōtai tōkei*, and populations at risk from the Taiwan censuses for the relevant years.

We begin our discussion of the leading causes with malaria. Malaria was a leading cause of death in nineteenth- and early twentieth-century Taiwan, and it alone accounted for 10 percent or more of all deaths, 1906–1916, in both ethnic categories. Malaria was an early target of Japanese colonial public health efforts, which included attacking mosquito-breeding sites to reduce transmission and distributing quinine to ease symptoms. As can be seen in the table, malaria death rates declined noticeably from 1919 to 1931 (Kip 2009). Still, malaria accounts for significant differences between the groups. The Hakka show substantially lower rates, compared to the Hoklo, for all years except 1929–1931. Within each group the sex differential in malarial death rates is small. Malarial death rates are highest in warmer climates, which are most favorable to the propagation of anopheline mosquitoes and the malaria plasmodium. The key factor determining divergences in malaria death rates is most likely to have been differential rates of exposure, as differences in disease resistance are unlikely to have been significant: the high rates among Hakka in 1929–1931 rule out any genetic protection (e.g. sickle cell, thalassemia) and only severe malnutrition compared to the Hakka would lower the resistance of the Hoklo and increase their chances of dying from malaria (Packard 2007: 29, 98). One possibility is that the Hakka had means to avoid exposure (e.g. screening, protective clothing, domestic animals that drew anophelines away from human targets) that were unavailable to Hoklo, but this is also unlikely given the high rates in 1929–1931. More likely is that the Hakka occupied areas less favorable to malaria-bearing mosquitoes except under unusual climatic conditions. Thus in 1929–1931, when unusual weather fostered mosquito breeding and transmission rose, the Hakka, lacking immunity built up from previous exposures, fell victim to malaria. The possibility that differences in the regional distribution of the groups affected their death rates will be explored in detail below.

Prevalence of respiratory tuberculosis was higher among the Hoklo than the Hakka, and in both groups there is a significant male disadvantage. Hypotheses accounting for differentials in the incidence of respiratory tuberculosis emphasize variables that lower resistance and immune response, such as malnutrition,[7] and concurrent diseases (comorbidity), and variables that amplify exposure to infection, such as active cases among family members, crowded living and work spaces, and poor ventilation. One or many of these factors may underlie the higher Hoklo rates. The Hoklo dominance in urban areas, where respiratory tuberculosis rates were highest, contributes to their high rates.

"Respiratory diseases" is a broad category including pneumonia, bronchitis, influenza, and other respiratory diseases. This broad class of diseases was the leading cause of death of Taiwanese in all periods, as was common for early twentieth-century populations in Japan, Europe, and the United States in the pre-antibiotic era (Preston 1976). Hakka and Hoklo suffered from high rates of these diseases and show a marked male disadvantage. In both groups, pneumonia death rates were the highest of the three named diseases; cases of pneumonia often bring on death after a person has been stricken by some other disease. The Hakka advantage in lower respiratory death rates, though substantial (20–25 percent), is less than in the case of respiratory tuberculosis (50–60 percent). Many factors could account for the higher Hoklo rates—rates of malnourishment (pneumonia is nutritionally sensitive) are unlikely to have systematically distinguished the Hoklo from the Hakka, but lowered resistance due to a heavier incidence of concurrent diseases and higher exposure rates remain likely possibilities.

Diarrhea and enteritis is our next disease category. The disdvantage of the Hoklo when compared to the Hakka in diarrhea and enteritis death rates is the second greatest (45 percent), after respiratory tuberculosis, of the leading causes. What can explain such a sharp difference? Differential exposure (perhaps resulting from climatic factors favoring bacterial growth?) and resistance are possibilities, but differences in food and drink sanitation practices could also play an important role. Evidence here supports the reputation of the Hakka for better sanitation. It is important to note that diarrheas, because they interfere with the absorption of nutrients when the immune system is most in need of them, can be important causes of the worsening of concurrent diseases. Diarrheas thus are linked to nutritional distress on the immune system and are debilitating infections that can leave the victim vulnerable to opportunistic infections, which are nutritionally sensitive, including respiratory diseases, pulmonary tuberculosis, and other bacterial infections such as whooping cough and pneumonia (Lunn 1991: 131–45). Higher rates of diarrhea and enteritis thus could play an important role in raising the rates of death from other diseases as in the "pneumonia-diarrhea-malnutrition" complex in children (Omran 1971: 509–38). Diarrheal diseases are an important cause of infant mortality and a large proportion of deaths due to diarrhea occur in infancy and early childhood.

Certain diseases of infancy is a cause category restricted to deaths occurring in infancy and includes causes occurring overwhelmingly in the first month of life, such as congenital malformation, debility, prematurity, and birth trauma. The Hakka advantage in this category over the Hoklo is small compared to the other leading causes. To get a more precise picture, we can refine these measures by limiting the denominator to the exposed population of infants. The "certain diseases of infancy" category reports only deaths in the first year of life, which enables us to report an "infant death rate" computed as deaths per thousand live births. The computation of certain diseases of infancy as an infant death rate confirms our impression of the small Hakka advantage in this disease category.

The most striking feature of these tables is that the Hakka advantage was consistent across all causes, rather than concentrated in one or two, and that the advantage was continuous across all periods despite fluctuations in rates. The interaction among the diseases compounded the Hoklo disadvantage: higher rates of diseases like diarrheas and malaria likely weakened resistance to the two categories of respiratory disease. Then, lower rates amplified the Hakka advantage by leaving that population better able to resist the other diseases. The consistent Hakka advantage suggests that some factor related to Hakkaness was beneficial to health and longevity. What were the possibilities?

The spatial distribution of the Hakka and Hoklo populations

As a consequence of the frontier settlement process, the Hakka were not dispersed as widely as the Hoklo, but were heavily concentrated in specific localities. The uneven distribution of the two groups was a result of two aspects of the frontier settlement process. Immigrants arriving on the turbulent frontier sought to settle among their fellow co-ethnics for reasons of security and mutual aid, and boundaries between the groups hardened when friction and communal strife drove them further apart. In addition, factors of timing in arrival, availability of unopened land, and migrant preference for areas most resembling hometown ecologies where their skills could be put to best advantage led to separate bands of settlement. These factors led to Hoklo domination along the coast and on the coastal plain, and Hakka concentration in the interior hills (Lamley 1981: 299–300; Shi 1987: 86–7, 180; Shepherd 1993: 315).

The question is, how much was the Hakka mortality advantage determined by the environments to which Hakka settlement was restricted? We look at the regional distribution of the ethnic groups in two ways: first we examine the ethnic composition of each prefecture's population in Table 5.3. In 1920, the Hoklo population from Fujian dominated demographically throughout the island and were the majority ethnic group in every prefecture except Shinchiku (Xinzhu), Taitō (Taidong), and Karenkō (Hualian) (in the latter two prefectures, mountain Aborigines dominated). Hakka were the majority population in Shinchiku and constituted significant minorities in Taichū (Taizhong) and Takao (Gaoxiong).[8]

Table 5.3 Composition of prefectural populations by provenance, by percent of Taiwanese, 1920.

Prefecture (*chō*)	Fujian/Hoklo	Guangdong/Hakka	Total % of Taiwanese*	Number of Taiwanese
Taihoku (Taibei)	98.7	0.8	99.5	658,184
Shinchiku (Xinzhu)	37.4	62.1	99.5	549,401
Taichū (Taizhong)	88.3	10.9	99.2	754,466
Tainan (Tainan)	98.5	0.7	99.2	922,337
Takao (Gaoxiong)	80.3	15.3	95.6	509,270
Taitō (Taidong)	11.8	3.9	15.7	35,260
Karenkō (Hualian)	23.7	14.1	37.8	37,589
TAIWAN	82.3	15.0	97.3	3,466,507

Source: Dai-ikkai Taiwan kōkusei chōsa, yōran hyō, Taishō kyū nen (Taihōku: Taiwan sōtoku kambō, rinji kokusei chōsabu, 1922 [hereafter *Census of 1920, yōran hyō*]), Tables 5.1, 5.2–5.7.

*Not included here are the additional Taiwanese subcategories "other Han," "cooked savages" (*jukuban*, i.e. assimilated plains Aborigines) and "raw savages" (*seiban*, i.e. unassimilated Aborigines).

Table 5.4 Distribution of the provenance groups among the prefectures, 1920.

Prefecture	Fujian/Hoklo (%)	Guangdong/Hakka (%)
Taihoku	22.8	1.1
Shinchiku	7.2	65.7
Taichū	23.4	15.8
Tainan	31.9	1.2
Takao	14.3	15.0
Taitō	0.1	0.3
Karenkō	0.3	1.3
TAIWAN	100	100
Total Number	2,851,353	519,770

Source: Census of 1920, *yōran hyō*, Table 5.1, 5.2–5.7.

A different perspective emerges when we examine the distribution of the two ethnic groupings across the prefectures (Table 5.4). In 1920 the bulk of the large Hoklo population was concentrated in Tainan in the south, the mid-island prefecture of Taichū, and in Taihoku in the north. In all, these three prefectures accounted for 78 percent of the total Hoklo population. In 1920 the Hakka population was even more heavily concentrated in the northern prefecture of Shinchiku, followed by Taichū in the center and Takao in the south. These three prefectures accounted for 96.5 percent of the total Hakka population, and nearly two thirds of the Hakka population was concentrated in the single prefecture of Shinchiku.

It is also important to point out that Taiwan's small urban population was overwhelmingly Hoklo. Five cities (Taihoku, Kīrun [Jilong], Taichū, Tainan, and Takao) were recognized in the 1925 census and they accounted for approximately 8 percent of the total Taiwanese population (Barclay 1954: 116). In 1926, 9.8 percent of the Hoklo population and only 0.9 percent of the Hakka population lived in these five cities. The Hakka population was thus overwhelmingly rural, while nearly a tenth of the Hoklo population lived in the small major cities. It is also likely that the larger and more urban Hoklo population was stratified internally to a greater degree than the Hakka and showed greater extremes of both wealth and poverty. Note also that Shinchiku City, the largest city in Shinchiku Prefecture, was too small to be included as one of the five largest cities.

Because of the marked regional concentrations, especially of the minority Hakka population, generalizations based on all-island data about the separate ethnic groups must raise an immediate question: Was the selected characteristic the result of cultural differences or the result of differences linked to regional ecology, such as climate, epidemiology, agrarian economy, wealth, access to ports, administrative influence, and so on? While discussing the differences and similarities between the ethnic groups in the following sections, we must not lose sight of the possibility that these regional concentrations were likely to have an important influence on the disease and mortality patterns we observe.

Crude death rates by ethnicity and prefecture

The vital statistics volumes report births and deaths by both prefecture and ethnicity; this enables us to test whether the Hakka advantage so visible in the all-island data actually was enjoyed by the local populations of Hakka, regardless of where they lived. The same data enable us to see whether some Hoklo also benefited from living in healthy districts apparently dominated by Hakka.

Table 5.5 presents the average crude death rates by both prefecture and ethnic group from 1920 to 1931. We will focus our discussion on the prefectures (shown in boldface) that have the more significant concentrations of Hakka population (only 4 percent of Hakka lived outside the three prefectures of Shinchiku, Taichū, and Takao). The Hakka death rates are indexed on the Hoklo rates in the rightmost pair of columns in Tables 5.1, 5.2, and 5.5–5.9.

Did Hakka uniformly have the lowest rates of death regardless of prefecture? Alternatively, if regionally specific factors are more important than ethnicity, did Hoklo living in prefectures where Hakka had low rates of death also enjoy lower rates than Hoklo elsewhere? We can begin this inquiry with Shinchiku Prefecture, where 66 percent of Taiwan's Hakka population was concentrated. The Hakka in Shinchiku

Table 5.5. Crude death rates by ethnicity and prefecture, 1920–1931.

1920–1931	Crude Death Rates by Ethnicity, Deaths per 1,000				Indexed Rates, Hoklo = 100	
	Hoklo		Hakka		Hakka	
Prefecture	Male	Female	Male	Female	Male	Female
Taihoku	23.7	22.1	13.2	15.1	55.9	68.2
Shinchiku	**21.6**	**19.6**	**19.3**	**18.0**	**89.4**	**91.8**
Taichū	**25.7**	**22.6**	**21.3**	**18.5**	**82.9**	**81.8**
Tainan	28.6	25.7	19.5	20.2	68.2	78.8
Takao*	**28.2**	**26.1**	**31.0**	**27.5**	**110.0**	**105.2**
Taitō	25.6	22.7	27.8	27.6	108.6	121.5
Karenkō	29.1	26.2	23.6	22.7	80.9	86.4
TAIWAN	**26.2**	**23.8**	**21.3**	**19.6**	**81.3**	**82.3**

Source: Vital statistics from the Taiwan *Jinkō dōtai tōkei*, and populations at risk from the Taiwan censuses for the relevant years.

* Takao crude death rates include Hōko (Penghu). Figures for prefectures containing large average populations of Hakka (greater than 60,000) are shown in bold; prefectures not shown in bold have Hakka populations of less than 10,000.

had a clear advantage over their Hoklo neighbors in the twelve-year period shown in the table, although the advantage in Shinchiku was not as great as the average Hakka advantage for all Taiwan (see indexed columns). This is because Hoklo had their lowest death rates in Shinchiku, and this narrowed the gap between Hoklo and Hakka in that prefecture. Thus, Hoklo also benefited from living in Shinchiku and the healthier environment it provided, even if they did not benefit from any possible health benefits of cultural Hakkaness. Despite having higher average death rates than their Shinchiku compatriots, the Hakka in Taichū had a greater advantage over their Hoklo neighbors because the Taichū Hoklo death rates, although lower than the all-Taiwan Hoklo average, were much higher than those of the Shinchiku Hoklo. The Taichū environment likely benefited both groups, but the Hakka enjoyed a clear advantage over the Hoklo within this central prefecture.

Any assumption that Hakkaness everywhere conferred health advantages is contradicted when we look beyond the northern concentrations of Hakka in Shinchiku and Taichū. The advantage of being Hakka disappeared in the southern prefecture of Takao (where 15 percent of Hakka resided). In Takao the average Hakka death rate was higher than that of the Hoklo. So it appears that if some aspect of Hakkaness confers a health benefit in the northern climate of Shinchiku and Taichū, this factor is not effective when confronted with the southern environment of Takao. Clearly the southern Hakka, concentrated in the eastern parts of Takao (today's Pingdong), lack the health advantage enjoyed by their northern cousins. In Takao, the Hakka along with their Hoklo neighbors suffer death rates above the all-Taiwan Hoklo average. Both Hoklo and Hakka suffered from the unhealthy environment of the south.

The hypothesis that some aspect of Hakkaness conferred a health advantage is considerably weakened by the high death rates of the southern Hakka. Nevertheless, it is still the case that the Shinchiku and Taichū Hakka did better than their Hoklo neighbors, suggesting that environment is not the sole determining factor (we explore this further below).

Hoklo death rates also varied significantly by prefecture. The highest average Hoklo death rates occurred in the southern prefectures of Tainan and Takao (putting aside the very high rates occurring in the east coast prefecture of Karenkō suffered by small populations of Hoklo [most likely malaria related]). And the lowest Hoklo rates occurred in the northern prefectures of Taihoku and Shinchiku.

Analysis of the ethnic and regional pattern for the period prior to 1920 (not shown here) confirms these same patterns: lower rates in the north and higher in the south for both Hakka and Hoklo, and a significant Hakka advantage in the north but not the south (Shepherd 2011a). The strong regional differentiation that persists throughout the period was even more marked in the early years and predated colonial epidemic control efforts, but it diminished somewhat as rates overall moderated in the later years. The gradual decline in crude death rates between 1906 and 1931 reflects the effect that slow strengthening of colonial public health measures and improving of economic conditions had (see Table 5.1).

Using district-level date to refine the test of ethnicity versus locality

The crude death rates by prefecture and ethnicity (Table 5.5) have enabled us to refine generalizations about the health advantages and disadvantages of ethnic group membership that we derived from death rates by cause and ethnicity aggregated for the whole island (Tables 5.1 and 5.2). We have identified prefectures where the presumed health benefits of Hakka ethnicity failed to live up to the all-island pattern, and found that strong regional differences affect both ethnic groups. But so far our tests of the role of ethnicity versus locality have been applied only at the level of the prefecture, leaving open the possibility that health disadvantages and advantages (such as those of the Hakka in Shinchiku) were the product not of ethnicity within a prefectural context but of environmental differences among smaller areas. Because residence segregates ethnic groups in areas within prefectures (not just between prefectures), it is conceivable that the environments occupied by particular ethnic groups had an important effect on their death rates that was hidden when data are aggregated at the prefectural level. Is the impression that ethnicity played a significant role within the large prefectural units an effect of over-aggregation of data?

We can further refine our assessment of the role of ethnicity versus locality by focusing on subprefectural districts (*gun*) that had substantial populations of *both* ethnic groups. In Shinchiku, five of eight districts contained large populations of both Hoklo and Hakka: Shinchiku (Xinzhu), Zhongli, Daxi, Zhunan, and Byōritsu (Miaoli). In Taichū Prefecture, two districts containing large populations of both Hoklo and Hakka are Fengyuan and Nenggao (today's Puli). In Takao Prefecture, three districts contain large populations of Hoklo and Hakka: Qishan, Pingdong, and Chaozhou. Table 5.6 presents the district-level crude death rates by ethnicity for 1920–1931. Do the districts simply replicate the prefectural-level patterns of ethnic differences in mortality or do they reveal local influences that complicate the prefectural ethnic patterns?

In four of the five districts in Shinchiku, Hakka consistently had death rates for both males and females lower than Hoklo in agreement with the prefectural pattern. But in the fifth district of Zhongli, where both the Hoklo minority and the Hakka had death rates below the Hakka prefectural average, Hakka death rates were, nevertheless, consistently higher than Hoklo. Thus within Shinchiku, the Hakka advantage did not hold in every case. Whether Hakka crude death rates are higher or lower than Hoklo, it is interesting that the Hakka males always did better (index is lower) compared to their Hoklo counterparts than the Hakka females.

In Taichū, Hakka death rates were consistently lower than Hoklo rates in Fengyuan, but in Nenggao, the average Hakka female death rate was higher than that for Hoklo females. In Takao's Qishan and Pingdong death rates for both Hoklo and Hakka were lower than or very close to the prefectural averages for each group; Hakka death rates nearly equal those of Hoklo except in the case of males in Qishan, where the average Hakka male death rate significantly exceeded that of the Hoklo males. In Chaozhou death rates for both Hoklo and Hakka were substantially higher than the prefectural averages for both groups, and the Hakka male death rate

Table 5.6 Crude death rates by ethnicity and district, 1920–1931.

| District | Crude Death Rates by Ethnicity, Deaths per 1,000 | | | | Indexed Rates, Hoklo = 100 | |
| | Hoklo | | Hakka | | Hakka | |
	Male	Female	Male	Female	Male	Female
Shinchiku Pref.	**21.6**	**19.6**	**19.3**	**18.0**	**89.4**	**91.8**
Shinchiku *gun*	22.5	20.1	19.4	18.5	86.4	91.8
Zhongli	17.2	16.2	18.1	17.5	105.5	108.5
Daxi	21.7	20.3	19.1	19.2	88.1	94.8
Zhunan	22.3	19.6	19.7	18.0	88.3	91.8
Byōritsu (Miaoli)	23.1	19.5	20.2	17.7	87.2	91.0
Taichū Pref.	**25.7**	**22.6**	**21.3**	**18.5**	**82.9**	**81.8**
Fengyuan	22.7	19.6	21.1	17.2	92.9	87.8
Nenggao	25.5	20.8	25.0	21.7	97.7	104.8
Takao Pref.	**28.2**	**26.1**	**31.0**	**27.5**	**110.0**	**105.2**
Qishan	26.4	25.8	30.2	25.4	114.3	98.4
Pingdong	28.3	26.6	28.0	25.8	98.7	97.3
Chaozhou	33.9	31.5	35.2	31.0	103.9	98.3

Source: Vital statistics from the Taiwan *Jinkō dōtai tōkei*, and populations at risk from the Taiwan censuses for the relevant years.

exceeded that of the Hoklo males. In the Takao districts Hakka females consistently did better compared to their Hoklo counterparts than males, the opposite of the Shinchiku pattern, where Hakka males did better, even in Zhongli. These multiple differences among districts within prefectures reveal internal variations, which suggest that local environmental conditions were as important as ethnicity in determining levels of mortality.

We take a more focused look at sex differences in mortality by ethnicity and district in Table 5.7. Sex ratios of mortality are computed by dividing the male death rate by the female death rate; ratios above 100 indicate male rates exceed female.

Although in all the districts and in each ethnic group (with the sole exception of Daxi) male crude death rates exceed female rates, the degree of male-excess mortality varies. The sex ratio of mortality among the selected districts in Shinchiku is consistently lower among the Hakka than among the Hoklo. But even this aspect of Hakka population cannot be generalized beyond Shinchiku; the sex ratio of mortality among Hakka in the Taichū districts was as often higher as it was lower than the Hoklo sex ratio, and in the Takao districts it is consistently higher. We will discuss the possible significance of these findings below.

Table 5.7 Sex ratios of mortality by ethnicity and district, 1920–1931.

District	Sex Ratio of Mortality, Male CDR/Female CDR		Indexed Rates, Hoklo = 100
	Hoklo	Hakka	Hakka
Shinchiku Pref.	110.1	107.3	97.4
Shinchiku *gun*	111.8	105.2	94.1
Zhongli	106.2	103.3	97.2
Daxi	106.8	99.3	92.9
Zhunan	113.6	109.2	96.2
Byōritsu	118.7	113.9	95.9
Taichū Pref.	113.6	115.1	101.3
Fengyuan	116.2	122.9	105.8
Nenggao	123.0	114.8	93.3
Takao Pref.	107.9	112.9	104.6
Qishan	102.5	119.1	116.2
Pingdong	106.7	108.3	101.5
Chaozhou	107.4	113.6	105.8

Using household registers to refine the test of ethnicity versus locality

We can refine our tests of ethnicity versus locality even further by using the household register databases for two localities in Shinchiku.[9] The sites are located north of Shinchiku City, in the township of Zhubei, whose population is divided between a Hoklo area (Jiugang) and a Hakka area (Liujia).[10] The sites, because they combine two ethnic groups within a small area, give us the opportunity to see if ethnic differences in mortality persist even when two groups occupy much the same environment.

To create samples as ethnically homogeneous as possible, I have excluded from the sample individuals who had a birth mother or adopted mother whose registered provenance/ethnicity differed from their own (which almost always followed the registered provenance of the father) because they came from the comparison group. Comparing samples of people raised by fathers and mothers having the same ethnicity provides the clearest test of the effect of ethnic group membership.

Tables 5.8 and 5.9 present measures of mortality and life expectancy comparing the Hakka and Hoklo of Shinchiku's Zhubei between 1906 and 1945. Despite living in villages in close proximity to one another, these data show that the Zhubei Hakka enjoyed lower levels of mortality and higher levels of life expectancy than their Hoklo neighbors. Table 5.8 presents childhood mortality rates. In infancy (ages 0–1) and early childhood (1–5), both the Hakka males and females fared

Table 5.8 Age-specific death rates, Hakka and Hoklo, Zhubei, 1906–1945.

	Age-Specific Death Rates, per 1,000				Indexed Probability of Death, Hoklo = 100		Sex Ratio of Mortality	
	Hoklo		Hakka		Hakka		Male/Female	
Age Interval	Male	Female	Male	Female	Male	Female	Hoklo	Hakka
0–1	197.4	156.4	167.1	134.8	84.7	86.2	126.2	124.0
1–5	30.8	46.0	18.8	25.4	61.0	55.2	67.0	74.0
5–10	6.3	5.0	5.4	5.9	85.7	118.0	126.0	91.5
NN%	41.0%	24.2%	57.4%	54.7%	140.0	227.9	170.8	104.9

Table 5.9 Life expectancy at different ages, Hakka and Hoklo, Zhubei, 1906–1945.

Zhubei, 1906–1945	Life Expectancy at Different Ages, in Years				Indexed Life Expectancy, Hoklo = 100		Sex Ratio of Life Expectancy	
	Hoklo		Hakka		Hakka		Male/Female	
	Male	Female	Male	Female	Male	Female	Hoklo	Hakka
0	38.0	41.8	44.7	46.3	117.6	110.8	90.9	96.5
1	44.9	47.6	51.5	51.8	114.7	108.8	94.3	99.4
5	46.6	52.8	51.4	53.1	110.3	100.6	88.3	96.8
10	43.0	49.0	47.8	49.6	111.2	101.2	87.8	96.4
30	27.8	33.5	31.8	33.1	114.4	98.8	83.0	96.1
50	15.9	17.9	18.0	18.5	113.2	103.4	88.8	97.3

better than the Hoklo. The neonatal percentage (NN%) indicates the proportion of deaths in the first year of life occurring in the first month of life; such deaths are due primarily to the "certain diseases of infancy" discussed earlier. A higher neonatal percentage, combined with lower morality rates over the first year of life among the Hakka, suggests that Hakka infants suffered less from post-neonatal causes of death, primarily exogenous factors related to environmental conditions and exposure to communicable diseases. This advantage grew even greater in the next four years of life. Differences in breastfeeding patterns (duration, age at weaning) might be invoked to explain such differences in European populations, but we have no evidence that Hakka and Hoklo differed in this regard in Taiwan. The sex ratio of mortality is quite low among both groups at ages 1–4 and especially among the Hoklo; this indicates high excess female mortality that could be the result of female adoptions in both groups. Wolf has shown that adoption at young ages had an adverse mortality consequence (perhaps connected to premature weaning) particularly on young girls (Wolf 1995: 303). Lower rates of adoption (affecting primarily females) compared to Hoklo might also be invoked to explain the Hakka female advantage in ages 1–4 in Zhubei, but both the Zhubei Hakka and Hoklo adopted females and practiced little daughter-in-law marriage at high rates.[11] It is also significant that the Hakka male death rate at ages 1–4 shows almost the same advantage over Hoklo as the female in these years, which suggests factors other than adoption create the Hakka advantage in early childhood for both sexes. There is a big divergence in the sex ratios of mortality at ages 5–10; the Hakka ratio shows a female excess when the Hoklo ratio shows a substantial male excess.

Table 5.9 shows that the Hakka advantage in life expectancy persists for males throughout the life cycle, but diminishes rapidly for Hakka females to levels much closer to those of Hoklo females and even falls slightly below the Hoklo female life expectancy at age 30; this is related to higher probabilities of death at ages 30–45 for Hakka females. Differences in fertility might be suspected to contribute to higher death rates for women at these ages among a higher fertility group, but previous work shows no significant differences in fertility levels and patterns between the Hakka and Hoklo of Zhubei (Shepherd et al. 2006: 143). Note that in Table 5.9 the sex ratios of life expectancies always show greater male disadvantages among the Hoklo than among the Hakka. The sex ratios of life expectancies are much closer to being equal for the Hakka than the Hoklo, indicating a much larger gap in the life expectancies of Hoklo males compared to Hoklo females, a factor to be discussed below.

Comparison with rates for other parts of the island (Tables 5.5 and 5.6) shows that both the Hoklo and the Hakka benefited from the healthier environment of Shinchiku, but as these household register data show even in the circumscribed area of Zhubei, an additional Hakka advantage persisted. Both the Hakka advantage and the advantage conferred by the Shinchiku environment demand explanation. Analysis of regional differences in causes of death shows that Shinchiku Prefecture enjoyed significantly lower death rates due to diarrheas, respiratory diseases, and malaria and thus both Hakka and Hoklo in this region, compared to those in other parts of Taiwan, were benefited (Shepherd 2011a). But despite the shared advantage of residence in the Shinchiku environment, a Hakka advantage over the Hoklo persisted. Within the township of Zhubei, small environmental differences may have made a difference. In Zhubei, as in the Shinchiku area generally, Hoklo (Jiugang) lived nearer the coast, and Hakka (Liujia) in hillier country farther inland. Perhaps Hakka living upstream enjoyed cleaner sources of drinking water than Hoklo living downstream and this would have contributed to the difference in rates of diarrhea and enteritis.

Discussion

What aspects of Hakkaness contributed to higher survival in the Shinchiku (Xinzhu) environment remain a mystery. Was it greater resistance to disease or lower rates of exposure that explains the Hakka advantage? There are many popular notions about Hakka–Hoklo differences that could provide clues. Could the reputation for the greater orderliness and cleanliness of Hakka villages reflect a generally higher level of sanitation that had a positive impact on their health (Kleinman 1980: 338n; Y. Chuang, personal communication)? Could the reputation of Hakka for strong group solidarity imply a community that provided support for the sick and disadvantaged in ways that reduced death rates (Pasternak 1972: 128; Kleinman 1980: 338n)? Are there dietary and food preparation practices among Hakka that led to lower levels of diarrhea and enteritis? Or did lower levels of malaria in Shinchiku somehow differentially benefit the Hakka and lead to lower disease levels overall due to reduced negative impacts of comorbidity? Did the Hakka reputation for bodily cleanliness associated with regular afternoon bathing have positive health consequences or reflect sanitary practices that carried over into food and drink preparation (M. Cohen, personal communication; Oehler 1922: 352)? Why were respiratory tuberculosis rates so low among the Hakka? What does this reflect about the situation of Hakka in Shinchiku—is it an advantage of having so little of its population living in urban centers (note such an argument could not explain the differences within Zhubei)? Were there more scholars and medical professionals per capita among the Hakka than among the Hoklo (Kleinman 1980: 338n)? Was the Hakka population (or the Shinchiku population generally compared to all Taiwan) better educated (higher rates of school attendance?) and thus more familiar with germ theory and sanitary principles based on it? The hypotheses are many but the hard evidence for historians to test them is scarce.

Did Hakka women benefit compared to their bound-footed Hoklo counterparts from having natural feet and freedom of movement or suffer from heavy labor as Hoklo critics alleged? A health benefit from natural feet fails to explain why Hakka men shared the same health advantages as Hakka women over Hoklo counterparts. But perhaps the health of both male and female Hakka benefited from women's natural feet? Note that adult men are much more vulnerable than adult women to respiratory diseases (Table 5.2); perhaps the increased share of farm field labor borne by Hakka women reduced the exposure of vulnerable Hakka men to the elements and to the risk of death due to respiratory diseases, without jeopardizing the similar advantage of Hakka women over Hoklo in respiratory diseases? If Hakka men and women more freely switched off in otherwise gendered tasks when an opposite sex family member was sick, the sick person could be left to recover and over the long run both sexes would enjoy a health advantage. By comparison, the Hoklo gender division of labor denied Hoklo men any relief from male tasks. (Note that even after the demise of the footbinding practice from 1915, the sharper Hoklo gender division of labor likely continued to contrast with that of the Hakka.) This implies a lower sex ratio of mortality at adult ages for Hakka compared to Hoklo, which is supported by our data for Zhubei and Shinchiku (but not for the south). This gives a different meaning to the Hoklo critique of lazy Hakka men benefiting from the heavy labor of Hakka women.[12] The higher sex ratio of mortality among Shinchiku Hoklo suggests that Hoklo men as much as Hoklo women paid in poorer health the price of footbinding.

Overall, it is striking how many potentially viable hypotheses there are that could explain a Hakka health advantage. Yet we must remember that the actual advantage of Hakka over Hoklo within Shinchiku is moderate and that the mortality advantage disappears in the context of Takao. If a Hakkaness hypothesis survives further testing, it will be in a conditional form that acknowledges the overriding importance of environmental factors. Unfortunately, we have no reports of causes of death by both ethnic group and prefecture with which to pursue these questions. The reports of causes of death by prefecture analyzed elsewhere show a pattern of low rates for all leading causes for the population of Shinchiku that matches those shown for all Taiwan Hakka in Table 5.2 (Shepherd 2011a). This is consistent with the finding in Table 5.5 that the Shinchiku mortality advantage over the other prefectures was shared by both the Hakka and the Hoklo.

Conclusion

We have not completely dispensed with the possibility that ethnic cultural differences contribute to the mortality advantage. The Japanese regime's great attention to surveillance of public health and vital statistics allows us to find in Shinchiku the persistence of small mortality differentials that favor the Hakka compared to the Hoklo even within small districts where both groups lived in much the same environment. The many differences in lifestyle and customary practices between the two groups provide many possible factors that may have conferred health advantages within the overall environment of Shinchiku. For now, the historical data needed to test these possibilities are beyond the scope of this chapter.

Two things are certain: death rates in the Hakka minority in the colonial period were substantially lower than the Hoklo majority, and rates of mortality of both Hakka and Hoklo living in Shinchiku were low. This was not an advantage enjoyed by a wealthy minority (i.e. Japanese colonists) enjoying a higher standard of living and privileged access to modern health care in cities but rather one enjoyed by relatively poor populations concentrated in rural districts. The vital statistics data demonstrate that the Shinchiku mortality advantage predated significant colonial improvements in Taiwan's public health infrastructure and thus must owe much to a unique disease ecology in the region. Thus, the Hakka advantage cannot be primarily attributed to cultural differences between the Hoklo and the Hakka. Instead, it was the Hakka people's good fortune that a history of settlement combined with ethnic competition and strife left the bulk of Taiwan's Hakka population concentrated in areas of northwest Taiwan (modern Taoyuan, Xinzhu, and Miaoli). This region turns out to have been an environment that was, relative to the rest of the island, healthy and comparatively disease-free. Hoklo residing in that environment also benefited from its healthy qualities. That the southern Hakka did not enjoy a consistent advantage over Hoklo also undermines the case for a significant ethnic advantage and underlines the importance of environmental factors affecting disease. Thus what appeared on first viewing to be a difference attributable to cultural differences between the ethnic groups turns out to be primarily a product of the concentration of the Hakka in the salubrious environment of the Shinchiku region.

Notes

1   For example, see Hsu 2000 and Lagerwey 2005.
2   The colonial government had long opposed binding, which it considered culturally
     backward and an impediment to the full mobilization of female labor and Taiwan's
     economic development. But it prudently hesitated to risk intervening in so intimate
     a practice until it was sure that influential Taiwanese would not oppose a prohibition.
     Only in 1915, after twenty years of rule, and years of support for the efforts of
     Taiwanese anti-footbinding groups, did the colonial government take the steps of
     forbidding the binding of young girls' feet and ordering adult women to loosen their
     bindings. (Allowances were made for women whose feet were so misshapened that
     unbinding would make it impossible for them to walk.) See Wu 1986: 69–108.
3   For an excellent introduction, see Barclay 1954.
4   Ts'ai (2009) and Chen (1975: 391–416) document the local control systems; Wolf and
     Huang (1980: 16–33) describe the household registers.
5   See the discussion of data quality in Barclay 1954: viii, 10, 141–5.
6   For details on the quality of cause of death reporting, see Shepherd 2011b: 77–9.
7   Tuberculosis is a nutritionally sensitive disease; see The Conferees 1985: 305–8.
8   Here the relatively well-known Japanese names for prefectures are used in order to
     stay true to the censuses from which the data come; however, Chinese names are
     used for smaller towns whose Japanese names would not be widely known.
9   I want to express my thanks to the Program for Historical Demography at the
     Academia Sinica and its director, Yang Wenshan, and to Chuang Ying-chang, for
     providing access to the household register databases for these sites.
10 The registers come from the villages of Maoerding in Jiugang and the village of Liujia
     in Liujia; Chuang Ying-chang provides a comparative ethnography of the two villages
     in 1994.
11 Arthur P. Wolf found a mean age at adoption of four among the Hakka and a slightly
     lower age among the Hoklo (1995: 50–1, 54, 177).
12 Nicole Constable suggests that Hakka women shared this critique (2000: 365–96).

Part Two

Remembering Japanese Taiwan

6

Closing a Colony: The Meanings of Japanese Deportation from Taiwan after World War II

Evan N. Dawley

On August 15, 1945, one thing was clear: the Japanese empire, with its projects of military and civilian expansion, had been defeated. Less certain was what would become of those Japanese who had spread out through continental and maritime Asia since the late nineteenth century. The Japanese community in Taiwan, which had roots that extended five decades into the past, faced a complex dilemma. Would they remain in Taiwan, which was, for many, the only home they had ever known or would they move to metropolitan Japan, a homeland that they did not know well if at all? With the end of Japan's colonial project now imminent, and with it the loss of status as colonizers bringing civilization to a backwards people, it was no longer clear what it meant to be Japanese.

After the Nationalist Chinese government announced that the Japanese were not going to be allowed to remain, the removal of Japanese citizens from Chinese territory defined the context for multiple relationships in Retrocession-era Taiwan. Chinese and American authorities sorted the entire population into distinct categories, a victor's prerogative that also characterized other Japanese-occupied territories in Asia and assigned a specific territorial destination to each group (Watt 2009: 3–7). The almost 350,000 Japanese civilians then resident in Taiwan, previously called homelanders (*naichijin*), were designated as Overseas Japanese (Ch. *Riqiao*, J. *Nikkyō*) or as Overseas Ryukyuans (*Liuqiao/Ryūkyō*), depending upon the part of Japan from which they originated; Taiwanese, formerly known as islanders (*bendaoren/hontōjin*), became both provincials (*benshengren*) and compatriots (*tongbao*); mainland Chinese now became "outside-provincials" (*waishengren*). As a result of this sorting, from the summer of 1945 to the spring of 1947, Taiwan contained a multinational society in which the different groups pursued their own interests while they competed for the scarce necessities of daily life. In so doing, Japanese, Chinese, and Taiwanese all drew their own meanings from the process of deportation.

Some of the research for this chapter was done with a Fulbright Fellowship for research in Taiwan and Japan.

Terminology is important to this study, not least in regard to what to call the forced movement of Japanese citizens out of Taiwan. The possibilities in English are repatriation, which generally means the willing transfer of a national out of a foreign jurisdiction to their homeland, and deportation, which connotes forced expulsion from a place where one cannot legally reside to another territory but not necessarily to one's homeland.[1] Japanese scholars most commonly use the term *hikiageru*, which translates as both "to withdraw" and "to return home." Recent Chinese scholarship uses *qianfan* or *qiansong*, both of which carry a sense of sending someone back to a place. These Japanese and Chinese terms all mean "to repatriate" and thus they indicate a sort of reunion between a person (or persons) and a place, although in Japanese there is a greater sense that the person (or people) involved moved of their own volition. However, "repatriation" is a problematic term for the simple fact that perhaps as many as half of the Japanese who left Taiwan after 1945 had been born and/or lived much of their lives there.[2] The term that appears most frequently in the Japanese language sources from 1945 to 1947, and occasionally in Chinese sources, is *kansō/huansong*, which also contains the idea of return but more in the sense of giving back something that belongs to someone else. Thus, in context, it seems to have meant that China was forcibly returning to Japan a collection of misplaced people. Most contemporary Chinese sources used *qiansong*, which can mean to banish or send away, in addition to repatriate. In combination, these meanings suggest that "deportation" is a more appropriate term than repatriation to discuss the transfer of Japanese citizens out of Taiwan, where they had no legal basis to remain, and into Japan's diminished boundaries.

This study sheds light on how the Japanese, Chinese, and Taiwanese developed separate meanings for this major demographic shift and on how those interpretations affected relations between these three broad groups in the context of postwar Taiwan. I will pay particular attention to those Japanese and Ryukyuans who remained after the majority had been deported, those who were "kept behind" (*liuyong/ryūyō*) to aid in reconstruction, because their presence and experience altered the meanings of deportation and influenced the struggle for imagined and physical space after the ending of Japanese colonial rule.

The context and practice of deportation

Japanese residents of Taiwan, together with those in Japan's home islands and throughout the empire, greeted the Shōwa emperor's declaration of surrender with wonder, shock, and desperation. One Japanese settler in the port city of Kīrun (Jilong) later recalled the complex responses of those around him: "I understood that the war was over ... Soon, people dispersed, then gradually they began to sigh with grief, then tears began to fall, and it turned into an angry roar. At the same time, a feeling of relief came over us as from that point on there were no more air raids" (Dawley 2006: 293). Another Japanese settler, a high school student serving in a military brigade outside of Taihoku (Taipei), wrote in his diary on that day, "I don't understand anything. I cannot write anything. Whether it is true, or if it is a deception, what is true is that it is a disaster" (Itō 1982: 30). The Japanese in Taiwan knew that their status had changed, and some almost immediately felt anxiety over how Taiwanese and Chinese might treat them, but they did not know what would become of them. Most Japanese settlers wished to remain in what they regarded as home (Zeng 2005: 45, 48).

The majority of the island's population, the Taiwanese, shared the sense of astonishment that the war had ended with Japan's defeat and were aware that the emperor's announcement meant that they would no longer be under Japanese control. Those with close ties to the colonial regime experienced feelings of concern that were similar to those of their Japanese associates, but, as the initial shock faded, most Taiwanese saw the war's end as the dawn of a brighter era (Zeng 2005: 34–5). Wu Zhuoliu described the reaction in Taihoku—soon to be Taipei again—as one of almost delirious celebration:

> The whole city seethed with excitement—long-hidden lanterns, garlands, and silken banners were brought out, firecrackers exploded endlessly, and Taipei was transformed into a whirlpool of color and noise ... Six million islanders fervently hoped to turn their home into an even finer paradise than it had been in Japanese times. (Wu 2002: 167–8)

We can safely dismiss his claim of the unity of purpose of 6 million Hoklo, Hakka, and Austronesian residents of Taiwan as hyperbole, but the excitement in Taiwan was undeniable.

The Nationalist Chinese were prepared for Japan's surrender and, although the celebrations in Chongqing began even before August 15, the Chinese government's reaction was more measured than that of the Taiwanese people. Chiang Kai-shek had demanded and received the promise from Franklin Roosevelt and Winston Churchill that Taiwan would be made a part of the Republic of China (ROC), and his government had drawn up a basic plan for the takeover in late 1944. Perhaps most important of the main principles in the "Draft Outline for the Takeover of Taiwan" (*Taiwan jieguan jihua gangyao cao'an*), at least in regard to the residents from Japan, was the determination to "eradicate the influence of the enemy" ("Taiwan jieguan" 2000: 107, 115). This document, which was submitted by the ROC's Taiwan Investigation Committee in October 1944 and promulgated as legal orders in March 1945 for the coming takeover of Taiwan, made no specific mention of an intention to deport the Japanese. However, that action was likely in the minds of those responsible as they prepared to establish formal control over the island. The preparations to fundamentally change Taiwan, carried out under the direction of the presumptive Civil Administrator, Chen Yi, took on a more concrete form following the August surrender. These three basic attitudes—Japanese anxiety and desire to remain, Taiwanese eagerness for the new era, and Chinese determination to transform the island—determined the context for developments during the late summer and early fall.

Taiwan entered the immediate postwar period with severe damage to its economy and infrastructure and without a strong administrative structure. Wartime requisitioning left the island with serious shortages of food and other necessities, while aerial bombing had devastated parts of the island. Although there had been relatively low loss of life among civilians, the air war heavily damaged the harbors and transportation network (Wu 2002: 162–5; Phillips 2003: 65).[3] The Taiwan Government-General remained, but it took little initiative to resolve these and other problems. The colonial security forces maintained public order, and Governor-General Andō Rikichi wrote descriptive reports of conditions in Taiwan, but his government kept a low profile.[4] The limited role played by the Government-General created space for the Taiwanese to organize themselves and take responsibility for managing the society. The tremendous energy with which the Taiwanese prepared for the arrival of the Nationalists, established Three People's Principles Youth Corps to promote learning about China and provide a foundation for mass mobilization, studied the new national language, restored some of the religious activities and other customs that had been suppressed during the war, and pursued an expanded role in the governance of their island has already been well documented (Kerr 1965: 62ff; Wu 2002: 168ff; Phillips 2003: 40–63; Zeng 2005: 72–7).

The Taiwanese celebrated their liberation from Japanese rule, but they did not engage in widespread acts of revenge nor did they immediately push for the removal of Japanese settlers. They quickly seized or attempted to occupy property that they claimed, not always with justification, the colonial state or settlers had unfairly obtained in the preceding decades (Phillips 2003: 42–3). Wu Zhuoliu was not alone in his exultation that Japan's leaders had both failed in their efforts to transform the Taiwanese and suffered military defeat as well (Wu 2002: 169). During these high-spirited days, numerous incidents of theft and violence broke out around the island, at least some of which were interpreted, then and later, as evidence of emerging Chinese nationalism or acts of revenge against the Japanese colonialists and their Indigenous allies. However, Douglas Fix, in a recent analysis of several hundred reported cases during September and October 1945, argues that theft and violence were primarily a reaction against harsh wartime requisitioning practices and, therefore, not expressly anti-Japanese acts (Fix 2006: 350). While Taiwanese people of all classes sought relief and some redress from the previous era, the departure of the Japanese was not foremost in their minds during the late summer and early autumn.

The arrival of Chen Yi, along with significant numbers of Chinese troops and civilians, dramatically altered the context in Taiwan. Following the formal acceptance of surrender on October 25, in a statement broadcast across the island, Chen framed Taiwan's Retrocession to China as the completion of the long revolutionary movement of Chinese people begun by Sun Yat-sen and finished by Chiang Kai-shek (Zeng 2005: 280). Accentuating the fact that the Nationalists envisioned themselves as a group destined to remake the island was the serialized publication of Chiang's 1943 treatise, *China's Destiny*, in the pages of the newspaper *Minbao* throughout October–November 1945.[5] Soon before Chen's arrival, the paper published a passage that interpreted Taiwan's history as a territory that was opened by Han Chinese, lost to European empires and then reclaimed by the seventeenth-century erstwhile Ming loyalist Koxinga ("Zhongguo zhi" 1945: 1). The clear implication was that Chen Yi was a modern version of Zheng, recovering Taiwan from another imperial power.

After Chen arrived, he issued directives covering such matters as the replacement of the Government-General by ROC authorities, the demobilization and removal of over 200,000 Japanese soldiers (these *Rifu*—Japanese prisoners—were separate from the Overseas Japanese), and the expropriation of Japanese public and private assets. Chen's initial decrees did not address the ultimate country of residence for the over 300,000 Japanese and Ryukyuan civilians in Taiwan. Up to that time, the only public pronouncements regarding Japanese civilians were Chiang's Order #1, which mandated that they remain in place until Chinese authorities arrived (Zeng 2005: 268–73), and a widely publicized statement by Chiang that "the military of Japan is our enemy, the people of Japan are not" (Watt 2009: 45).

With no clear sense of whether or not they would be allowed to remain in Taiwan, the Japanese entered a period of limbo. The new rulers officially designated them as Overseas Japanese or Ryukyuans, probably to correspond to the Nationalists' understanding of the Overseas Chinese (*Huaqiao*) as a group fundamentally tied to its ancestral homeland (Watt 2009: 48).[6] More destabilizing was Chen's decision to remove Japanese bureaucrats and police officers from their posts. Without a regular source of income, Japanese citizens faced unaccustomed economic hardships. Some demobilized soldiers responded to their loss of military status by turning to crime, and there were occasional reports of violent acts by civilians as well ("Riren xuesheng" 1945: 1; "Rongzhuang" 1945: 2). Accounts of severe shortages of food, housing, and jobs in Japan had begun to reach those in Taiwan, which must have made the possibility of remaining in Taiwan seem more attractive to some. Zeng Jianmin cites a survey conducted by former Government-General officials in early November, which found that 180,000 Japanese civilians wished to move to Japan, while 140,000 wished to stay (Zeng 2005: 195). While it is unlikely that the survey in fact consulted the vast majority of Japanese throughout the island, it, nevertheless, appears that the anxieties of the immediate postwar period in Taiwan had convinced many that moving to Japan was the preferable option. The experience of familial separation, lack of employment, and, for some, life in holding camps had taken its toll (Satō 1982: 85–6).

Finally, in December, the Civil Administration of Taiwan announced its policy on the fate of Japanese citizens: all non-Chinese nationals were to be deported as quickly as possible. There would be no analog of what took place in 1895, when all residents of Taiwan were granted two years in which to decide if they wished to remain in Japan's colony or move to China. The transfer of demobilized soldiers to Japan began almost immediately, and an order for the deportation of civilians was drafted and promulgated in January 1946. Implementing the decision to remove all Japanese citizens from their former colony required a major investment of human and other resources to achieve that goal. It also set in motion, or perhaps accelerated, interactions that would influence how the Japanese defined their role in postwar Taiwan and their relations with Taiwanese and Chinese.

From late 1945 through early 1946, the situation in Taiwan and elsewhere in East Asia evolved in ways that had profound implications for deportation. Across the Taiwan Straits, the escalating civil war between Nationalists and Communists demanded huge amounts of the limited resources available, which produced shortages of daily necessities in Taiwan throughout 1946. The Japanese government was similarly distracted by domestic reconstruction, and the needs of its citizens in Taiwan were not a top priority. Rising tensions between mainlanders and Taiwanese had a much more immediate impact on the deportation process. The collapse of Taiwan's economy, disputes over the ownership and distribution of former Japanese assets, and increasingly strident disagreements over who would have a voice in the governance of Taiwan combined to produce a highly volatile atmosphere. The growing conflict between *waishengren* and *benshengren* was often framed in terms of a lingering Japanese influence. The former group used what they perceived as the stain of prolonged contact with the Japanese to suppress the latter, who in turn drew upon their experiences of the preceding five decades to differentiate themselves from the Chinese and critique their rule.

In contrast to the complexities of the simmering dispute, the logistical arrangements for deportation were relatively simple and straightforward. On December 30, 1945, the Taiwan Civil Administration established the Overseas Japanese Management Committee (*Riqiao guanli weiyuanhui*; hereafter, OJMC), under the leadership of Zhou Yi'e, a Nationalist official and associate of Chen Yi's from the wartime Fujian provincial administration. The OJMC held responsibility for all aspects of the deportation process, and it spent the first part of the year surveying the Japanese population. It found that there were roughly 350,000 Japanese civilian nationals in Taiwan, including the Ryukyuans. With this information, the OJMC laid out a plan for three waves of deportation. The vast majority would be sent out from March 1 to April 30; roughly 30,000 would go in the last months of 1946; and 3,500 would be deported in the spring of 1947 (Zeng 2005: 206–7).[7] The reasons for this phased removal will be explored below, but, simply put, Chen Yi needed the services of some of these Japanese.

The OJMC coordinated with the office of the Supreme Commander of the Allied Powers (SCAP) and the Japanese government to arrange transport for both civilians and the remaining military personnel. Most of the vessels used belonged to the United States, and the Japanese provided a number of military and commercial ships that were under US control (Kawahara 1997: Vol. 1, 4). According to a *Minbao* article, at set times people assembled at major urban train stations for transit to one of the two embarkation points, the port cities of Jilong and Gaoxiong, from which they boarded ships and departed ("Diyipi" 1946: 2). The deportation process ran smoothly in Taiwan, unlike in Manchuria, Korea, and Siberia, where chaos and hardship prevailed. Deportees from Manchuria faced a bitter winter, severe shortages of food and other supplies, and harsh treatment from some of the victorious Chinese. By one estimate, 179,000 civilians and 66,000 military personnel perished (Dower 2000: 50; Watt 2005: 243–54). There were fewer problems in Korea, but the one million Japanese soldiers and civilians stranded in Siberia suffered through forced labor, subsistence living, and psychological manipulation before eventually being sent to Japan (Watt 2009: 44, 126–31). In contrast, from the end of February to the end of May, the vast majority of Japanese left Taiwan and arrived in Japan almost without incident.

Although the first wave of deportation encountered no major difficulties, a number of factors made it noteworthy. One was the salience of the distinction between Overseas Japanese and Overseas Ryukyuans. The latter group had gone to Taiwan throughout the period of Japanese rule, with a significant influx following the brutal battle for Okinawa; in early 1946 some 15,000 were present. As noted above, it was the Nationalists who drew the official distinction between Japanese and Ryukyuans. However, it is likely that SCAP played a hand in this, given that the United States planned to keep Okinawa administratively separate from the rest of Japan. Moreover, the Overseas Japanese would likely have supported the differentiation, since the incorporation of natives of Okinawa into the Japanese family was far from complete (Christy 1997: 121–49). Whatever the reason, deportation officials ordered the Overseas Ryukyuans to construct deportation camps and serve as porters for the Overseas Japanese. The Ryukyuans began to depart later than did the other Japanese, in part because of their functional roles (Kawahara 1997: Vol. 1, 7). Thus deportation reinforced divisions within the larger body of the Japanese citizenry.

Both the Japanese and Taiwanese experienced complex emotional responses to the first wave of departures. By the time Chen Yi announced his intention to deport all non-Chinese citizens, most Japanese had begun to favor transfer to Japanese soil. However, many of them did not leave easily or abandon their sense of being from the island. Demobilized soldiers constituted the bulk of what came to be called the "Japanese residue" (*canyu Riqiao/zanyo Nikkyō*), which consisted of a small collection of prisoners, smugglers, orphans, spouses of Taiwanese, and the mentally and physically ill. Many of them decided that they had better prospects in Taiwan than they did in Japan and so did all they could to remain (Zeng 2005: 198–9, 207; Dawley 2006: 287; Watt 2009: 47).[8] On the night before his departure, one deportee met with three of his school friends, two of them Taiwanese, and together they sang a portion of their dormitory song, a verse called "the separation song (*betsuri no uta*)" (Itō 1982: 31). In contrast, a deportee later recalled the words of one of his fellow passengers as they departed Jilong harbor: "As for Taiwan, who cares? It's not a question of what [will happen to Taiwan]. We are saying goodbye to the Taiwan of the Taiwanese now, right? We should be thankful. Good riddance!" However, at least in retrospect, this deportee disagreed with his shipmate's words and saw them as those of a spoiled child or someone who had been embittered by the recent tumultuous changes (Aki 1982: 20). Some Taiwanese also experienced ambivalence as the Japanese left and the mainlanders arrived in greater numbers. Wu Zhuoliu, who celebrated the end of the Japanese presence in Taiwan, pitied the departing Japanese when he saw them selling their last possessions to greedy Chinese, for whom he felt only disgust. He also did not shun his Japanese friends and even took over the apartment of one when she left (Wu 2002: 211).

Wu's reaction hints at the effect that the removal of the Japanese from Taiwan had on the lives of the deportees. Shortly after the war ended, life for Japanese citizens resumed many of its daily routines. Children attended school, adults returned to work, Buddhist temples remained open for use, and many people stayed in their homes. However, once Chen issued the order for deportation, the practicalities of life drastically changed. The regulations for Japanese deportees throughout Chinese territory allowed each person to carry only two pieces of luggage and 1,000 yen and prohibited Japanese from taking gold, silver, and other items of value. A combination of the limitations on what could be taken and the need to acquire money in order to survive during the winter meant that many Japanese residents spent parts of their last days in Taiwan sitting by the side of the road selling their possessions. These settlers-turned-foreigners did not look forward to their arrival in Japan, where the small amount of money they carried would barely support them. Living on the margins like this was a new condition for the over 300,000 people who shared it.

Marriages between Japanese and Taiwanese, and their offspring, posed a particular problem for both categorization and deportation. Although these unions had not been common, they had occurred and had to be considered when determining citizenship and residency. When intermarriage had finally been legalized in Taiwan in 1933, it had been possible for either member of the union to join the household registration of the other—thus for the Taiwanese to become legally Japanese and vice versa (Tai 2014: 115–16). Under Chinese Nationalist rule, however, the status of these individuals had to be clarified. For spouses, Chen Yi's administration issued a straightforward determination meant to reward Chinese loyalties and punish allegiance to the defeated Japanese. If a Japanese person had married a Taiwanese before the end of the war, they could apply for and receive Chinese citizenship and remain. However, if the Taiwanese spouse adopted Japanese citizenship, then both husband and wife would have to leave Taiwan. The status of children was primarily tied to the citizenship of the mother; if the mother was Taiwanese, then the child automatically gained ROC citizenship, but if the father was Taiwanese, then the child had to apply. In cases where a Taiwanese woman chose to take Japanese citizenship, her child lost the right to become a Chinese national (Dawley 2006: 287–8). The distinction between the Taiwanese and Taiwanese who assumed Japanese citizenship indicates that the Nationalists established different categories of *benshengren*, based upon the degree to which those provincials had been tainted through their association with the Japanese. Those who had married and created offspring with the Japanese could still become Chinese, but those who chose Japanese citizenship could not be reformed and had to leave. These themes of pollution and retribution would recur in different ways as the deportation process continued into 1947.

By the end of April, only a relative handful of Japanese and Ryukyuan people resided in Taiwan, and they did so at the behest of the civilian authorities. Chen Yi and the others responsible for the takeover and administration of the island recognized that they could not achieve their goals of reconstruction and transformation alone. With the central government concentrating on the massive tasks of rebuilding and fighting the Communists on the mainland, the provincial government received limited aid and supervision from above. Faced with reconstruction, administering the government, managing enterprises, and keeping the Taiwanese in check, the Nationalist authorities turned to a select number of Japanese citizens to help with a range of technical and bureaucratic functions. At a press conference in March 1946, Zhou Yi'e stated that about 7,000 Japanese, all of them technicians, would be kept behind along with their families, for a total of about 35,000 persons ("Liu Tai" 1946: 2). In reality, those who stayed included more than just individuals with technical skills. While the Ryukyuans engaged in construction, some Japanese continued to staff local governments, captain ships, work as clerks and managers for various companies, or labor at shipyards (Kawahara 1997: Vol. 8, 56–7, 60–3, 104–12, 138–40). The Nationalist Chinese, having first named the categories of Overseas Japanese and Ryukyuans, had now created subsets of those groups.

Chen Yi and his associates needed to ensure that the Japanese citizens still in residence were well controlled. However, few of the officials in charge spoke Japanese—Chen himself was an exception—and they had other matters to attend to. Therefore, they relied upon the kept-behind Japanese and Ryukyuans to oversee themselves. The OJMC turned to a team of eleven Japanese, led by a former official with the Taiwan Government-General named Hayami Kunihiko, both to serve as an intermediary between itself and the Japanese and to govern the kept-behind population. These individuals held the title of Mediator (*sewayaku*), and together they made up a body called the Overseas Japanese in Taiwan Assistance Society (*Ryū Tai Nikkyō gojokai*; hereafter, OJAS).[9] As the first wave of deportation wound down, the OJAS called on all remaining Japanese to register with the organization ("Nikkyō ryū" 1946: 2; "Zanryū Nikkyō" 1946: 1). The Okinawan Provincials Association (*Okinawajin dōkyōkai*; hereafter OPA), a society that existed during the prewar period, served a similar function for the kept-behind Ryukyuans. The central office of the OPA coordinated with both the OJMC and US officials in Taiwan, and it posted representatives to the departure points to construct and manage temporary lodging for deportees as well as organize the ultimate deportation of their coprovincials (Kawahira 1982: 67–70).[10] The OJAS and OPA kept track of the professional activities of all people under their supervision, notified them of directives from the OJMC, and oversaw arrangements during phases two and three of deportation. Whereas the Nationalists had been in charge of deporting the bulk of Japanese citizens, the kept-behind bore primary responsibility for removing themselves once they were ordered to do so.

Hayami Kunihiko worked diligently in his role. In addition to receiving directives from the OJMC and passing them on to the remaining Japanese, he sent numerous reports to the Tokyo government and advocated on behalf of those Japanese with the Chinese officials. For example, during the summer of 1946, Hayami requested that Zhou Yi'e relax the restrictions on how much money Japanese could bring out of Taiwan. He said that the figure of 1,000 yen had been reasonable for the first wave of deportees, because at that time monthly living expenses in Japanese cities were 300 yen for a family. Since then, however, the cost of living had tripled, which meant that when the kept-behind were finally deported, they would face tremendous hardships. Furthermore, he argued, these Japanese had been retained at China's (*kikoku*) request to assist with Taiwan's reconstruction and therefore should be given special consideration (Kawahara 1997: Vol. 2, 240–2). On other occasions, in the face of rising prices, he asked that the Japanese be allowed to either recover some of the property expropriated from them or rent property they still owned, in order to cover their daily needs and educational expenses. He placed particular emphasis on any bank accounts that had been seized but not yet disbursed (Kawahara 1997: Vol. 2, 97–100). In the absence of evidence that existing policies were changed in response to Hayami's efforts, it seems that he had little effect. Nonetheless, he and his fellow mediators consistently advocated for Japanese interests.

Japanese and Ryukyuan children attended classes for as long as they remained in Taiwan. They went to Japanese-run schools and received instruction from Japanese teachers. In fact, their ongoing education proved to be a matter of concern for the OJAS the members of which worried that these children would be at a disadvantage in entering school when they got to Japan. In late September 1946, while preparations were underway for the second wave of deportation, Hayami Kunihiko sent a notice to all of the mediators, informing them that Japanese pupils needed to obtain certification from their current schools in order to transfer to institutions in the home islands. The requisite documentation included name and date of birth of the pupil, name of school and grade level, and a full transcript for every year of school attended (Kawahara 1997: Vol. 2, 405–7). Over a year later, after all of the schools had been shut down and the teachers sent home, Hayami continued to worry about the education of those few children who remained. He informed his superiors at the office of the Taiwan Government-General in Tokyo that he had established an office for Overseas Japanese education in Taiwan that was setting up elementary and middle schools in Taipei. The schools were to instruct pupils in Japanese language, Japanese history, civics, English, Chinese, math, sciences, household management, and physical education (Kawahara 1997: Vol. 7, 193–7). Most of these subjects were necessary to ensure that the children would be able to transfer into Japanese schools and society with relative ease once their families departed Taiwan. The Chinese-language classes, however, must have been intended to help the students function in their current environment.

In spite of these intermediary and advocacy functions, the primary responsibility of the OJAS and OPA was to facilitate the removal of Japanese citizens from Chinese territory. When the order came to begin the second phase of deportation in October 1946, Hayami worked to ensure that it proceeded smoothly, with limited contact between the deportees and other residents of Taiwan. Ostensibly the OJMC was in charge, but the Japanese and Ryukyuan representatives did most of the actual planning and practical work. Once Japanese citizens received an order to depart, they gathered their allowance of baggage and moved to either Jilong or Gaoxiong. Upon arrival, they went quickly to the accommodations prepared by the Ryukyuans where they were sequestered for, ideally, a few days. The on-site members of the OJAS and OPA, under the supervision of local government officials, searched deportees' luggage, conducted medical quarantine procedures, and provided food while they were in port. The process of quarantine serves as a very apt metaphor, at least from the Nationalist Chinese perspective. Deportees were strictly confined, much like carriers of a contagious disease, so that they could not escape and infect others (Dawley 2006: 289). From the Japanese perspective, the relatively clinical, regimented nature of the process may well have been designed to limit the pain of deportation. Strictly separated from their Taiwanese home even before they left it, and powerless in the face of official mandates, the Overseas Japanese were likely desensitized by the process.

In practice, the second wave ran much less smoothly than did the first. The Chinese government was required to provide transport ships for the second wave, but it only designated one vessel—an old Japanese cargo ship that had been sunk in Jilong harbor during the US aerial bombardment and then repaired for deportation—which was insufficient for the task. As a result, a number of deportees spent up to a month in the Jilong quarantine zone, until SCAP assigned more Japanese ships to provide transport (Kawahara 1997: Vol. 1, 9–11). Two factors delayed the removal of the Overseas Ryukyuans. During the spring, SCAP had ordered a halt to the transfer of people to Okinawa, because the territory had been so severely devastated during the war that it could not support any additional residents. This order held the Ryukyuans in place until conditions changed (Kerr 1965: 149–50). Furthermore, the practice of having Ryukyuans carry out much of the labor associated with deportation—construction, cooking, and loading ships—meant that they could not leave until after the Japanese did. Nevertheless, by the end of December, the majority of the kept-behind Japanese citizens had been removed from Taiwan. According to the plan laid out in January, the final wave would take place in April 1947.

The explosive February 28th Incident did not dramatically alter that timetable, but the remaining Japanese paid close attention to how the uprising and its suppression affected them. Hayami Kunihiko spent much of his time in March and April gathering information from a variety of sources and reporting his findings to the office of the Government-General in Tokyo. The kept-behind Japanese were peripheral to those events, for February 28th was the result of rising Taiwanese discontent with Nationalist rule and growing Nationalist frustration with Taiwanese dissent. Nevertheless, the Japanese got drawn into the storm because the Chinese regime in particular attempted to use the Japanese presence and perceived influence (a year and a half after surrender!) to advance its efforts to transform Retrocession-era Taiwan.

During the initial uprising and the subsequent brutal crackdown, the remaining Japanese experienced the February 28th Incident as a combination of stringent restrictions, confusion, occasional attacks, and mounting criticism from the Nationalist authorities. On February 28, Hayami and the other mediators received and distributed instructions to leave work early and return home, and the following day the OJMC informed them that all Japanese citizens were to remain inside. Even after Chen Yi briefly lifted martial law on March 2, the Japanese were told not to interact with the Taiwanese, a restriction the government restated with greater intensity a week later. In the chaotic first days of the crackdown, Hayami met frequently with the OJMC to discuss incidents that had occurred involving Japanese, such as a professor at National Taiwan University who had reportedly provoked his students to rise up. The OJMC ordered the OJAS to inform the Japanese that they must produce proof of residence and that their homes would be searched for insurgents. Hayami received a number of reports from his staff around the island that Japanese people might have been targeted by the violence, while other rumors said that they had promoted it, but no one was certain what had happened. By March 19, the OJAS began telling the Japanese that they could return to work if they chose, and an official announcement to that effect came a few days later (Kawahara 1997: Vol. 4, 250–8).

The reports of Japanese involvement in the uprising bear further examination. In one communication to Tokyo, Hayami included a translation of an article from the *Zhonghua ribao* of March 27 that addressed purported Japanese actions and the Japanese presence more generally. According to the article, the Japanese had not suffered from violence during the Incident but instead had walked the streets freely. Nevertheless, when mobs attacked Nationalist troops in Taizhong, Gaoxiong, and Jiayi, a number of Japanese were among the insurgents, in some cases issuing commands to the crowd. The newspaper investigated these cases and found that in spite of delusional claims by the insurgents that "the Japanese did not attack," the Japanese had engaged in plots and conspiracies (Kawahara 1997: Vol. 5, 69–70).[11] This report came ten days after Hayami had petitioned the OJMC to correct the misunderstanding that Japanese had provoked or supported the uprising by issuing a statement that the kept-behind Japanese should be trusted (Kawahara 1997: Vol. 4, 255). His entreaties clearly had no effect. Two days after the newspaper report was published, ROC minister of national defense Bai Chongxi issued his study of the main causes behind the Incident, emphasizing that Japanese colonial education had taught the Taiwanese to dislike the Chinese and that the Japanese had supported "dangerous" elements during the war.[12] Bai's claims and the reported incidents served as convenient rationales for the Nationalists' main goal of consolidating their hold over Taiwan.

By the end of March, Hayami gathered more definitive reports on how the incident had affected the Japanese, and it turned out that they had been almost completely untouched. One Japanese, a man named Kimura Toshio who had worked for the OJMC, had died; property belonging to eleven staff members at the Jinguashi coal mines had been damaged; in Gaoxiong, a number of Japanese had been ordered to take refuge on March 6, and their hiding place had subsequently been attacked, but no one was hurt; and here and there around the island, a number of Japanese and/ or their property had experienced violence (Kawahara 1997: Vol. 5, 179–80). There may have been other incidents, but those were the ones that Hayami mentioned in the last of his fourteen reports to Tokyo. In spite of the fact that the Japanese had suffered only mildly, and may not have been involved in the uprising, the Taiwan Civil Administration decided that every last Japanese would be deported during the upcoming third phase (Kawahara 1997: Vol. 4, 258).[13] One important result of the February 28th Incident was the urgency it contributed to the Chinese sense that all remnants of the colonial past had to be removed.

The meanings of deportation

The preceding narrative offers some hints as to how the Japanese, Chinese, and Taiwanese interpreted or made use of deportation, but it remains to explore those meanings more fully. The former Japanese colonial settlers did not simply see the process as the mechanism by which they were removed from their homes but also used it to redefine their relationships with Taiwan, the Taiwanese, and the Nationalist Chinese. These last viewed deportation as a central part of their plan to transform and re-Sinicize the island, but they also used the multiple phases of the process to pursue the goals of reconstruction and control. Some Taiwanese saw the removal of the colonizers as an opportunity to take on a higher profile in the island's politics and economy and as a means to carry out their struggle with the new rulers—the neocolonizers—for self-control in Taiwan. These different meanings intertwined with and reinforced each other from late 1945 through early 1947 and set in place understandings of the relations between these groups that have persisted to the present.

For the Japanese, deportation had three meanings, the first being that they now had a limited time in which to fulfill their role as benevolent colonizers and promote the development of Taiwan and its (non-Japanese) residents. This understanding applied to the kept-behind in particular, for they were there for the express purpose of rebuilding the island's physical and mental infrastructure. Hayami's reports clearly show that even though the Japanese were retained at the behest of the Chinese, they welcomed the opportunity to promote reconstruction. Hayami used their willingness to work for the Chinese in an effort to improve their financial situation, and the kept-behind worked on a range of important projects right up until the third phase. Japanese staff performed an impressive list of tasks for the Jilong Port Authority, including a thorough survey of the damage sustained by the port facilities during the war, a plan for the renovation of those facilities, and some of the actual work to fulfill that plan (Kawahara 1997: Vol. 10, 111–16). These postwar activities were an almost exact replication of the massive task of port construction completed in the early years of Japanese colonial rule (Takekoshi 1907: 261–2; Dawley 2006: 43–4), although now the Japanese technicians and laborers worked for a foreign government. At a more personal level, departing Japanese tried to aid their Taiwanese acquaintances as best they could. When Wu Zhuoliu moved into the home of his friend, a Miss Kaku, the exchange occurred largely because the Japanese woman insisted that he take the house (Wu 2002: 211–12). This transfer could be interpreted as the woman's attempt to prevent the house from falling into Chinese hands, but it is more likely that she saw it as a final act of generosity. The chance to rebuild Taiwan after the wartime destruction might have imparted to the deportees, particularly the kept-behind Japanese and Ryukyuans, a sense that they had performed a service for their former colony. Certainly, Hayami's attention to the Japanese reconstruction work in his reports reflects an experience that would not have resonated with home-island Japanese, who sought to distance themselves from Japan's colonial expansion.

On a second level, Japanese now saw themselves as a diminished people. This vision was not the same as the narrative of victimization with which many Japanese have come to remember World War II but instead was specific to the experience of the former colonial settlers.[14] Having long been the dominant group, deportation forced Japanese citizens into a dependent role. Once most of them lost their jobs, they became reliant on the Chinese government and US authorities for relief supplies, on Taiwanese friends for assistance, and on whoever would buy their possessions for money needed to survive. Although still benevolent colonizers, they were no longer superior. Humbled by this experience, they lost their view of Taiwan as a place from which they could extract wealth and over which they could assert dominance. This embittered some, like the deportee quoted above who was eager to leave "the Taiwan of the Taiwanese," but the singularly smooth process of deportation out of Taiwan suggests that the Japanese there accepted the inevitability of their change of status with more equanimity than did those in Manchuria. In neither place did Japanese have the option to reject the new conditions, but those forced to leave Manchuria seem to have viewed it as a calamity, perhaps because most had become colonists at the height of imperialist expansion. The efficiency with which the Overseas Japanese and Ryukyuans removed themselves indicates that they were both ready to re-enter Japanese territory and, more importantly, acquiesced in the ending of their role as colonizers. With this loss of status came an awareness of commonality with those they had formerly colonized.

The third meaning of deportation for Japanese concerned their relationship with the Chinese, and Chinese culture more broadly. To the extent that Japanese settlers in Taiwan had thought about Chinese prior to 1937, it had been with an Orientalist outlook that framed the Chinese as a backward people to whom the Japanese would bring civilization (Tanaka 1993). The climate of the war years certainly could have instilled in them an intense hatred for the Chinese, but the relative ease of relations after the war suggests that the Japanese quickly overcame any ill will that they may have felt for their recent adversaries. The need to survive under Chinese control must have been a strong motivation to accommodate, and the new regime's reliance on Japanese assistance likely eased some of the wartime bitterness. In August 1946, the eleven mediators of the OJAS sent a message of thanks to the OJMC and its head, Zhou Yi'e. They expressed admiration for the generosity of the Chinese government, the fairness of the civil administration, and the strict discipline of the Nationalist troops. Many Taiwanese and others on the scene would have disagreed sharply with these characterizations, which were exaggerations expressed in a fawning tone. However, the specific set of interactions that these individuals engaged in with the Chinese lent some measure of truth to their statements. The letter singled out Zhou and the OJMC with particular praise for the success of the first wave of deportation and added the hope that the Japanese would receive similarly favorable treatment during the upcoming second wave (Kawahara 1997: Vol. 2, 372–4). The subtext here echoed Hayami's request for the restoration of assets to the kept-behind Japanese, but the first phase had, in fact, proceeded without incident or undue difficulties for most of the 300,000 Japanese citizens it involved. As an example of the rapid transfer of large numbers of people with limited resources, it was a success. The specific experience of deportation caused the Japanese in Taiwan to change their vision of the Chinese. Their belief in Japanese civilizational superiority may or may not have disappeared, but it was at the very least tempered by a sense that the Chinese were themselves benevolent and trustworthy.

Removal of the Japanese also held multiple layers of meaning for the Taiwanese and Chinese, both of which groups utilized it in their mutual struggle for control over who would govern in Taiwan. This battle played out in a number of ways, first in the reception and distribution (or lack thereof) of Japanese public and private assets. In preparation for the takeover of Taiwan, the Nationalist government issued a decree on October 15 that the Japanese had to report all of their assets, were forbidden from transferring anything to Taiwanese ownership, and had to recover anything that had changed hands after August 15 ("Riren gongsi" 1945: 1). In January 1946, following the takeover of publicly held property, Chen Yi set up the Japanese Asset Management Committee (*Richan chuli weiyuanhui*; hereafter, JAMC), which began to collect the savings accounts, real estate, and other capital assets of Japanese citizens and companies. By the end of April, it had seized some 9.5 billion yuan in bank and postal accounts, bonds, and housing and other physical property (Lai 1991: 71).

With the assets thus collected, the Taiwanese and Chinese began a process of contestation over how they would be distributed. Taiwanese citizens felt that they deserved a significant portion as redress for spending fifty years under Japanese rule. Instead, the Nationalist authorities made some of these properties available for purchase but retained most of them for use by the state. This decision caused considerable consternation among the Taiwanese, especially when they saw a significant quantity of good quality housing sitting empty. An editorial in *Minbao* carefully summarized the dispute, suggesting that, while government officials should be allowed to take over the housing formerly designated for colonial-era civil servants, privately owned dwellings should be made available to the general public. Many houses had been destroyed during the war, it continued, but the people's livelihood (*minsheng*) could be improved if the common people were allowed to move into the Japanese houses ("Shelun: Richan" 1946: 1). The reference to one of Sun Yat-sen's Three People's Principles was probably calculated to force the Nationalists to live up to their own stated ideals, but it had little effect. Taiwanese resentment over their lack of access to the formerly Japanese property continued unabated and was exacerbated by numerous cases in which individual *benshengren* owned property before August 15, 1945, but did not have enough documentation to satisfy the Chinese officials, and so were dispossessed ("Richan fangwu" 1946: 2; Lai et al. 1991: 72; Phillips 2003: 66).

The simmering conflict between mainlanders and islanders fundamentally revolved around the question of whether or not the Taiwanese had been tainted by their extended contact with the Japanese. The dispute over assets was just one manifestation of this deeper battle, which intensified just as the majority of Japanese were being deported. The initial excitement with which the Taiwanese greeted the defeat of Japan and the arrival of the Chinese government and military had faded by the spring of 1946 as discontent increased, particularly among elites (Phillips 2003: 64–73). However, rather than express their dissatisfaction as overtly as they would the following year, many Taiwanese tried to advance their interests by dissociating themselves from any purported Japanese influence. In the process, they incorporated a discourse that the Chinese had been using against them, perhaps in an effort to accommodate the views of the new rulers. As the first deportees were being sent out, *Minbao* published a bitter editorial farewell to them. Although the author(s) expressed some sympathy for those who had been born and raised in Taiwan, they took the opportunity to castigate the Japanese for being cruel militarists who had tried to "wipe away our Chinese culture" and wanted to "destroy our Chinese language" ("Shelun: Songgui" 1946: 1). Moreover, they insisted that they had never been enslaved, as the mainlanders suggested: "We can clearly see that the Japanese had the intention to 'enslave' Taiwanese (*benshengren*), but the Taiwanese continuously protected the last thread of their national/ethnic spirit (*minzu jingshen*), strongly resisted ... and did not accept the brainwashing of enslavement" ("Shelun: Taiwan" 1946: 1).

While it is possible that the authors of these articles had waited to express their true feelings until it was clear that the Japanese were leaving, an alternate explanation is more likely. Deportation meant that the most prominent example of Japanese rule of Taiwan—the Japanese themselves—would soon be gone. The editors of *Minbao*, who consistently advocated for Taiwanese involvement in the government of Taiwan, recognized that Taiwanese people could easily become the next target for de-Japanization. The "Draft Outline for the Takeover of Taiwan" aimed at the eradication of all Japanese influence regardless of where it existed, not simply in the form of Japanese settlers. In this light, the critical farewell to the deportees and the subsequent insistence that the Taiwanese had never been enslaved appear to be a preemptive defense against accusations of mental or spiritual pollution in order to improve these authors' and institutions' positions in Taiwan's new order.

The belief that such defensive actions were necessary was not misplaced, as became apparent during the crackdown on the February 28th uprising. Bai Chongxi singled out Japanese influence as one of the primary causes of the unrest, and rumors swirled that Japanese themselves had been behind at least some of the violence. The same article in *Zhonghua ribao* that had supposedly confirmed Japanese involvement took the opportunity to highlight differences between Chinese and Japanese people. The article insisted that the Chinese had acted with kindness, tolerance, and great humanity in the process of taking control of Taiwan, but the Japanese interpreted this treatment as cowardice and incompetence. Instead of helping the mainlanders when they came to Taiwan, the Japanese teachers had turned the Taiwanese against the Chinese. Moreover, the article alleged that the last of the deportees did little more than complain that they had not yet been allowed to leave (Kawahara 1997: Vol. 5, 70–3).

The timing of these comments suggests that the Chinese used the Japanese presence to justify their suppression of the February 28th Incident. The vast majority of Japanese had left almost a year earlier, and only a few thousands remained in the island. Although they filled key positions in some government and educational institutions, the direct influence of these kept-behind Japanese was heavily circumscribed. In spite of the effective removal of Japanese citizens, however, recent events had proven that there was significant resistance to Nationalist rule. To further assert their dominance over Taiwan, the Nationalists raised the specter of Japanese influence to launch a more aggressive campaign for transforming Taiwan. Nationalists were not targeting Japanese in this case—in fact, a handful of Japanese scholars continued to teach at National Taiwan University into the early 1950s (Kawahara 1997: Vol. 1, 12–13)—but rather were framing their battle against internal dissent in terms of spiritual pollution.

Conclusion: Deportation and triangular relations

The meanings that the Japanese, Chinese, and Taiwanese drew from the process of deportation dramatically affected their relations with each other. Overlaying these meanings was the simple fact that, with the transfer to Nationalist rule, Taiwanese and Japanese residents all needed to find ways to accommodate the new regime in order to improve their daily circumstances. The removal gave both the Taiwanese and Chinese a means to contest with each other over resources and conceptions of political order in Taiwan, without actually confronting one another directly. The Taiwanese people took advantage of the Japanese departure to insist that they had not themselves been Japanized, in the hopes that the Chinese would, therefore, be more willing to include them in the governance of Taiwan. When the Chinese defined Taiwanese resistance to their rule in terms of a lingering Japanese stain, they left open the possibility of curing the islanders of their illness. In other words, the Chinese saw that it was necessary to get rid of the Japanese people, in part to facilitate transforming the Taiwanese.

Deportation also influenced Japanese–Chinese and Japanese–Taiwanese relations. In the first case, it provided the entire context for interactions in postwar Taiwan, and as such it enabled a measure of resolution of some of the wartime animosities. As described by one kept-behind Japanese, he and his new Chinese colleagues first viewed each other with distrust, but after a year of working in the same office, they threw him a going-away party and saw him off when it came time to board his ship and depart (Inatomi 1982: 36–7). These sentiments represented, in a microcosm, the relatively swift improvement in relations between the ROC and Japan. In the second case, both the Japanese and Taiwanese found a measure of closure to their shared colonial era. Japanese sought ways to both reconstruct the war-torn island and make what recompense they could on an individual basis, hoping to be well remembered by the Taiwanese. On May 3, 1947, one of the last groups of third-wave deportees sailed out of Jilong. As their vessel exited through the mouth of the harbor, they passed groups of Taiwanese people, who had gathered on shore and on a boat in the water, waving small Japanese flags to bid them farewell (Satō 1982: 87–8).

Notes

1   Both deportation and repatriation in the context of postwar Asia, and particularly in Taiwan, have been little examined to date. The major study in English is Watt (2009). In Japanese, the main comprehensive study is Wakatsuki (1991); Taiwan is discussed on pages 88–95. Katō (2002) is a collection of primary sources. One Taiwanese study of the postwar years gives some attention to the removal of the Japanese; see Zeng (2005). Prominent studies of the postwar period in Taiwan and Japan briefly refer to the process. See Kerr (1965: 92–101 *passim*, 149–51); Lai, Myers, and Wou (1991: 63); Dower (2000: 48–58).

2   According to the last census of Taiwan in 1940, almost half of the Japanese
    population were aged 20 or under (145,188 out of 312,386 people), most of who were
    born or spent their formative years in the colony (Taiwan sheng 1946). Watt discusses
    how the Japanese became repatriates (*hikiagesha*) during the 1950s (2009: 13–15).
3   Peng Ming-min estimated the destruction in Jilong to be about 80 percent of the city
    (1972: 47).
4   This assessment is based on a brief survey of the documents collected in Su (2004).
5   Chiang's treatise appeared in thirty-two parts from around October 11 to
    November 14, with one section published almost every day on either the first or
    second page.
6   An article in *Minbao* from October 16 used the neutral term "Japanese nationals
    (*Riji renmin*)," but by early November the term "Overseas Japanese" was more
    common ("Riren gongsi" 1945: 1).
7   There is some disagreement over how many Japanese people remained in Taiwan
    in early 1946 and how many left during the first wave of deportation. Zeng, citing
    the survey conducted by the OJMC, says that there were 388,332 Overseas Japanese
    present and that 291,159 were scheduled to depart in the first wave (2005: 206).
    Watt, citing a different report from the OJMC, says that 453,913 were deported
    from March 2 to May 24, including very small numbers of Ryukyuans and Koreans
    (2009: 47). Kawahara, citing a 1977 report from Japan's Ministry of Health and
    Welfare, states that 284,105 people, including soldiers and bereaved family members,
    left between February 21 and April 29. Zeng's total figure is too high and may be a
    misprint, but his number for planned deportees matches up well with Kawahara's
    data. Watt's higher numbers can be explained by the longer time frame and the
    inclusion of more military personnel.
8   Reports had arrived in Taiwan about difficult conditions in Japan, so the recalcitrant
    former soldiers may have heard of the negative reception that home-island Japanese
    had been giving to returned military personnel (Dower 2000: 60).
9   The OJAS existed during the first wave but became much more active thereafter. For
    an earlier reference, see "Kikan Nikkyō" (1946: 1).
10 Author Kawahira Chōshin was a leading member of this association; he recalls
    meeting personally with both Zhou Yi'e and US Naval Attaché and Vice-Consul
    George Kerr.
11 The quote is in the original article, or at least the translation. It is difficult to assess
    the credibility of this report, which purported that Japanese aid to the Taiwanese
    resembled the assistance that some Japanese soldiers and officials gave to Vietnamese
    and Indonesian nationalists in their struggles against postwar restorationist regimes
    (Spector 2007: 129–30, 171–4, 179).
12 Phillips lists four causes: Japanese education, Japanese support of "dangerous" people,
    economic difficulties during the war, and the lack of opportunities for political
    participation by Taiwanese (2003: 85). Kerr adds three more reasons, including
    the presence of Communists, existing monopolies, and the incompetence of a few
    Chinese officials (1965: 315).
13 The last official deportation ship, carrying 239 deportees, arrived in the Japanese port
    of Sasebo on August 14, 1949 (Kawahara 1997: Vol. 1, 12–13).
14 See Dower on the "victim consciousness" prevalent among many Japanese people
    (2000: 119–20).

7

Ethnic Diversity, Two-Layered Colonization, and Complex Modern Taiwanese Attitudes toward Japan

Chih Huei Huang

Preface

Following the end of Japanese rule in 1945, Taiwan entered what should have been a postcolonial period of its history. In theory, after liberating themselves from the political control of their colonial overlords, citizens of a newly independent colony proceed to revive their freedom of independent discourse: intellectuals re-examine colonial texts, reinterpret history from the viewpoint of the colonized, heal the scars of colonization, and so on. The former European colonies that gained independence shortly after World War II went through—more or less—this process of "decolonization" (Moore-Gilbert 1997; Loomba 1998).

Over the past seventy years, however, Taiwan has followed a markedly different historical path. Although Taiwan began "de-Japanization" after Japan's defeat, it was not the colonized Taiwanese who led the movement. Those colonized Taiwanese did not start producing significant amounts of independent discourse until after the lifting of martial law in the late 1980s (as will be seen below), the same time that Taiwanese postcolonial research began to appear. But this wave of research, based mainly on literary sources, did not discuss what had occurred after Japanese colonization; rather, it fought to break free from the Republic of China (ROC) and the repressive national identity the Chinese had imposed (Chen 2003; Lu 2003).

At the end of the colonial period, Taiwan's population numbered less than 6 million. When the Pacific War ended, over 300,000 ethnic Japanese left the island that had been their home for nearly five decades. Soon after, 1.1 million Chinese soldiers and civilians poured into Taiwan from the mainland as a result of the Chinese Civil War. These Chinese soldiers and civilians, who before the outbreak of civil war had just finished fighting the Second Sino-Japanese War (1937–1945), had a "postwar" relationship with

This chapter was presented in longer form at the first Asia Future Conference: "Asia in the World—Potentials of Regional Cooperation" in Bangkok, Thailand, March 8–10, 2013. I would like to express my deepest gratitude to Nicholas Hawkins for his meticulous translation.

Japan and are thus unsuitable subjects for a discussion of "postcolonialism" in Taiwan. Local Taiwanese, however, who had just broken free from colonial rule as a result of Japan's defeat, were still constructing a "postcolonial" relationship with Japan. These two "Japans" coexisted within Taiwanese society for half a century. What attitudes toward Japan did the interactions of these views produce? This sociocultural phenomenon has received very little attention from academics, and postcolonial theories developed to explain former Western colonies do not explain it either.

In recent years, Taiwan has been described as a "Japanophilic" nation,[1] albeit one where contradictions and paradoxes abound. Japanese citizens of the prewar generation who visit Taiwan seem to find long-lost friends in their Taiwanese counterparts: a few words are all it takes for them to understand one another. Younger Japanese who come harboring a sense of postcolonial guilt are surprised at the warm reception they meet with from the Taiwanese and further perplexed to hear their praise for the actions of the colonial government.

Still more perplexed, in fact, are the first generations of the Taiwanese educated by the ROC. Their history textbooks taught them how the congenitally cruel Japanese slaughtered innocent Chinese and oppressed the people of Taiwan, but their parents (or grandparents) love Japanese culture and converse in Japanese with friends. They might recall sleeping on tatami mats in Japanese-style rooms as toddlers, but then they also recall hearing their parents talk about Japanese brutality toward the Chinese in the war.

Beginning in the 1990s, Japanese-style product advertisements, tatami rooms, and department stores began popping up all over Taiwan even as discussion of Japan-related issues in the media still provoked explosive emotional extremism. Controversy has persisted into the twenty-first century: Kobayashi Yoshinori's hot-selling manga *Taiwan-ron* (*On Taiwan*) provoked a war of words in Taiwan with its comments that the Japanese government never lied to Taiwanese "comfort women"; surprisingly, many Taiwanese agreed with this view (Huang 2001; Li 2002). Similarly, when well-intentioned Japanese gathered donations in 2006 to refurbish a Takasago Volunteer Units memorial in Taiwan, the ROC government forcibly removed it and filed a lawsuit because it opposed the idea of memorializing soldiers who fought for Japan (Huang 2009: A12). Events like these give rise to public controversy because they reveal the contradictions and conflicts that result from Taiwanese ethnic groups' very different attitudes toward Japan. How have these *postwar* and *postcolonial* relationships coexisted in the same society for the last seventy years?

The difficulty of research on Taiwanese attitudes toward Japan

Just two years after the end of World War II, an English-based system of foreign language instruction was instituted at Taiwanese universities; Japanese programs, by contrast, did not come into being until 1963. The private Chinese Culture University (*Zhongguo wenhua daxue*, founded in 1962 as Far East University [*Yuandong daxue*]) led the way by setting up a Japanese division under its Department of Oriental Languages and Literature in 1963. Thereafter, the policy was to allow one Japanese studies program to be established at a private university every three years: this was first introduced in Tamkang University in 1966, then in Fu Jen Catholic University in 1969 and Soochow University in 1972. Unable to create full Japanese departments, these schools had to resort to Japanese studies divisions set up under broader "Oriental languages and literature" departments. Then Japan severed diplomatic ties with the ROC in 1972, and the growth of Japanese studies came to an abrupt halt. Of the forty universities in Taiwan, only four private schools offered Japanese programs. Not until 1989 did a national public university (National Chengchi University) establish a Japanese-language division under its Oriental languages and literature department; by then, English departments had been around for forty-two years.

Once a public university had broken the taboo, Japanese programs proliferated rapidly: beginning in 1989, public and private universities established fourteen Japanese departments or divisions, and vocational and technical schools added fifty more. Once the restrictions of the Nationalists' martial law were gone, there was a rush to meet the demand (Cai 2003).

By 1945 overall primary school enrollment had reached 70 percent, a complete system of secondary and technical education was in place, and considerable numbers of Taiwanese had earned degrees from universities in Japan. By these standards, Taiwan probably had more potential as a center for Japanese studies than any other country outside of Japan. However, only a year after assuming control over Taiwan, the ROC government banned the publication, circulation, and use of Japanese newspapers, magazines, and books. Local intellectuals protested, but their objections went unheeded. After the February 28th Incident broke out in 1947, and the resulting KMT targeted killing of Japanese-educated Taiwanese intellectuals, there were no more debates on preserving the use of Japanese. The books on Japan published in Taiwan before martial law was lifted in 1987 were written by *waishengren* (provincial-outsider, i.e. mainlander) authors who took as their starting point the historical experience of the Chinese War of Resistance. Some, speaking as victors in the war, censured Japan, while others recalled the hardships of the war and the tremendous animosity between China and Japan; all, however, perpetuated wartime attitudes toward Japan.[2] Narratives like this dominated the Taiwanese book market for forty years, a phenomenon I have previously referred to as one of *substitution*—taking local Taiwanese ruminations on Japanese rule and replacing them with the discourse of an external group. No such phenomenon of substitution occurred in other former Japanese colonies.

Under KMT party-state rule between 1945 and 1987, historical research that did not meet the government's ideological needs—such as studies of the Chinese Civil War, the early PRC, or Japanese-era Taiwan—was roundly suppressed. The few writings on Taiwanese history that did emerge were penned by Chinese-born historians (Guo 1954), not the colonized Taiwanese who had experienced fifty years of Japanese rule. The fields of historical research and education tilted strongly toward Chinese history for at least forty years after the war. The first master's thesis on Taiwanese history did not appear until 1966; the first Ph.D. dissertation was submitted in 1982. Only 10 percent of history theses pertained to Taiwanese history, and the minority of those that dealt with the Japanese period concerned themselves chiefly with resistance movements (Peng 2002; Liu 2003: 67–78). The first academic society devoted to

Taiwanese history, the Taiwanese Historical Association, was not established until 1995. Looking at the publication of autobiographies in Taiwan, one finds a similar imbalance: *waishengren* autobiographies outnumbered those of Taiwanese by a ratio of 20:1 between 1945 and 1964 and 10:1 between 1945 and 1974, even though locals comprised at least 80 percent of the population (Wang 1996: 161–5).

Stung by their country's defeat in World War II, Japanese historians categorically repudiated Japan's colonial conduct and tended to place Taiwan at the margin of a Greater Chinese historical framework; as a result, little research on Taiwanese history has been undertaken in Japan (Kabayama 2003: 17–24). Also, due to the nature of the colonial relationship, many sources were scattered between Japan and Taiwan, making research difficult. Only after the loosening of speech restrictions in the 1980s were Taiwanese historical source materials organized and made available. Japanese research produced more results after the late 1980s, but by that time, sources had been lost and many members of the colonial generations had died.

Double-layered postcolonial structure and nonlinear ethnic relationships

A study of Taiwan's complicated postcolonial ethnic structure also requires a short historical treatment. As described in the earlier chapters in this volume, the hybrid culture and tense rivalries between the Taiwanese Hoklo, Hakka, and Austronesian Aborigines was complicated even further after the Treaty of Shimonoseki ceded Taiwan to Japan in 1895. A new group of migrants came from all over Japan to the newest territory of their empire. Their own customs and dialects differed, but the *naichijin* (Japanese nationals living in Taiwan) became a new ethnic category. In 1905, they numbered merely 50,000; by 1945 their ranks had swelled to more than 300,000, or 6 percent of the population, more than the Austronesians (3 percent) but less than the Hoklo (75 percent) and the Hakka (13 percent) (Nanpō 1944; Taiwan zongdu 1992). By the end of the colonial era, many second- and third-generation *naichijin* considered Taiwan as their home (Yan 2008: 173–217), but (as Dawley describes in Chapter 6) they were repatriated to Japan by mid-1947.

At the same moment an influx began of 1.1 million Chinese Nationalist soldiers and officials—refugees from many different mainland provinces who spoke very different Chinese languages and dialects and observed very different customs. But because they did have more in common with each other historically than with the Taiwanese, they became a new single ethnic group, the *waishengren*. These native citizens of the ROC had been taught for decades about their nation as a Republic of Five Races (Han Chinese, Manchurian, Mongolian, Chinese Muslim, and Tibetan) that combined to form a single national "Chinese people" (*Zhonghua minzu*). In postwar Taiwan, the ROC sought to instill this ideology of nationalism through the national education system. The Austronesians, whose different origins were most obvious, were a particular target: they were required to adopt Chinese-style names and accept the myth that they too were the descendants of Chinese civilization.

The myth of a single national race did not weaken until the end of martial law. One of the first challenges to it was the "Return Our Land" campaign launched in 1988 (one year after the end of martial law) by the Association for the Advancement of Aboriginal Rights, established four years earlier. Also in 1988, Hakka began to seek the restoration of their basic social and cultural rights. A year later, constitutional scholar Koh Se-kai proposed a new draft constitution centered around "cultural pluralism" to replace the five-race *Zhonghua minzu* with a system consisting of Taiwan's four major cultural groups: Hoklo, Hakka, Aborigines, and mainlanders (Koh 1991).

In the constitutional reforms that began in 1991, the Aborigines' official name was changed from *shanbao* (mountain comrades) to *Yuanzhumin* (Indigenous People). The change was momentous, for it signaled the ROC government's acceptance of the Austronesians' status as the original inhabitants of Taiwan. Once it was acknowledged that the *waishengren* were the last ethnic group to come to Taiwan, the *Zhonghua minzu* ideology lost its legitimacy. As each community campaigned to revitalize its language and culture, the notion of four major ethnic groups gradually became established in the central government and became widely accepted in Taiwanese society. With the rise in ethnic consciousness came an increase in academic research: the years since 1991 have seen the establishment of three colleges and thirteen departments of Hakka studies as well as fourteen Aboriginal Studies departments and research centers (Wang 2008: 20–9).

These shifts in Taiwanese ethnic identification and the corresponding re-evaluation of Taiwanese history are not all that different from historical experiences of decolonization in other parts of the world. The difference is, the target of decolonization was the distorted view of history and ethnicity imposed by another people after the first colonial overlords had already departed; considered from this perspective, the uniqueness of Taiwan's postcolonial experience is immediately apparent.

After martial law was lifted in 1987, oral accounts by former colonial subjects began to emerge, and oral and written narratives of the once-taboo February 28th Incident began to be published,[3] and personal histories written in Japanese began to appear. Emerging after four decades of suppression, these once colonized voices swept over the publishing world, their narratives mostly focusing on personal life experiences and comparing life under the Japanese with life under the KMT. Although the authors belonged to different professions, social classes, and genders, their accounts exhibit a high degree of similarity due to the historical experiences they shared. They were not men and women of letters nor were they scholars or researchers, but Japan was intertwined in their seemingly ordinary life experiences. If one wants to analyze Taiwanese attitudes toward Japan, these accounts are a good place to start.

In terms of genre, most of these personal experiences were written in Japanese as biographies, memoirs, poems, journal entries, or collections of testimony. Most were self-published at the author's own expense; only a few were formally published by publishing companies. Some were published in Japan, others in Taiwan; even today they continue to emerge.[4] One such genre was the body of short poems written by former Taiwanese colonial subjects. Impossible to publish in Taiwan, these poems circulated among poetry aficionados in Taiwan for many years before finally being published in Japan beginning in 1994 (where they were dubbed the "*Taiwan Man'yōshū*"), attracting widespread attention in Japanese poetry circles. After martial law ended, Taiwanese *senryū* poets formed a poetry society in 1990 to satirize current events and look back on past experiences with their haiku-like three-line ironic poems. Many educated by the Japanese through high school and beyond could now join poetry societies to study, giving voice to their inner emotions with their succinct verses. Naturally, Japan was an important theme of their poems, which represent attitudes toward Japan held by ordinary Taiwanese (Huang 2003a: 115–46).

If one relies only on personal (or ethnic group) memories and perceptions, there is the problem of the imprecision and fluidity of memory: these must be read in combination with the research on Japan, Taiwanese history, and ethnic relations discussed above to truly understand the causes and effects of events. As if by some tacit agreement, these four types of knowledge all accumulated at an amazing rate after the end of martial law. This sudden liberation was significant not only for the former colonial subjects but also for the many rank-and-file *waishengren* who also suffered during the White Terror, for now their records of events like the Protect Diaoyutai movement (*bao Diao yundong*) could be published and discussed openly.[5] As though to prove that the shackles of the second colonialization had finally been shattered, every action of the former colonial overlords was spread out in the sunlight to be scrutinized. Colonialism's influence extended not only to the colonized Taiwanese but also to the Japanese *naichijin* who came to Taiwan in the first half of the twentieth century and the *waishengren* who arrived after they left. The relationship between these two groups combined with their separate relationships with local Taiwanese groups to form an even more complex spectrum of attitudes toward Japan (Huang 1989; Huang 2006a: 51–75, 2006b). Multiple layers of historical experience have mixed with multilateral ethnic interactions to form a nonlinear, asymmetrical, continually evolving relationship structure.

Changes before and after February 28th: Transformation, comparison, and resistance

Reading through the memoirs and other autobiographical writings of former colonial subjects over the last twenty years, one notices an obvious common characteristic: in order to resist the discrimination and oppression imposed by an alien people (the Japanese), intellectuals originally held out hope for the ROC on the mainland, but all that changed dramatically after the February 28th Incident. It was not only the victims and their families who were transformed but intellectuals and ordinary people as well, especially the Hoklo.

Although this transformation is discussed mainly in literature, there is no lack of more concrete historical evidence. For instance, in the diaries of Yang Jizhen (1911–1990), written in Japanese over four decades beginning in 1944, one can get a look at it. Born in a small town in central Taiwan, Yang developed a deep dissatisfaction with Japanese discrimination during his time at school. Later, as a student at Japan's Waseda University, he and other Taiwanese students often contemplated how to change the status of the colonized Taiwanese population. After he graduated with outstanding grades, he took a job as a technician in Manchukuo, hoping to be nearer to the ancestral home of his heart. To his dismay, after the war, "When I returned to Taiwan in May 1946, the Taiwan I saw was completely different from the one I used to live in. There was no difference between Chen Yi's absolute power and the colonial power formerly held by the Japanese—in fact, [Chen's] power was even more barbaric, ignorant, unenlightened and unfair. The people of Taiwan live in secret discontent." He then added, "Only now do I begin to reflect critically on the dream of my ancestral homeland I had pursued so desperately" (Huang and Xu 2007: 693).

The inward confessions of these lines reveal the deep disappointment that comes when high expectations go unfulfilled. There was now something to compare Japanese colonial rule with. This mind-set of comparison was mentioned by Ong Iok-tek (1924–1985) in 1960:

> Most of the 10 million Taiwanese of today have lived through two different eras, which they compare when considering anything. It's just like how when we move to a new place, we compare the new house to the old; it's human nature. However, if the result of the comparison is that the Japanese era was better, that's a really serious problem .... Actually, the Taiwanese themselves never dreamed that things would get so bad that they would be forced to compare them with how they used to be. (Ong 1970: 103–4)

After February 28th, a few Taiwanese fled overseas to escape arrest and execution at the hands of the new government. Ong and Shi Ming are two examples; the latter was originally discontented with Japanese colonial rule and hoped to travel to the "ancestral country" to seek strength to resist Japan. Later, having suffered the disillusionment of his expectations being turned to despair, he thought that KMT rule was a more arbitrary and exploitative form of foreign rule than Japan's had been, so he campaigned for Taiwanese independence from his new home in Japan, not returning to Taiwan until the 1990s (Shi 1994). Another path was followed by Taiwanese communists like Xie Xuehong, who fled to the Chinese mainland after the failure of February 28th, hoping to use China's strength to liberate Taiwan from KMT rule. However, these were choices that could be made by a very few individuals. The great majority of Taiwanese intellectuals who, like Yang Jizhen, stayed in Taiwan tried contesting local elections in the 1950s and cooperating with the faction of *waishengren* opposed to Chiang Kai-shek's dictatorship, but their efforts failed. The following decade saw *waishengren* liberals like Lei Zhen and Yin Haiguang suppressed by the powerful party-state machine. Yang finally chose to relocate to the United States, where he fought for the establishment of an independent new nation, even considering cooperating with the CCP to escape unreasonable ROC rule.

What methods of resistance were available for the much larger number of Taiwanese unable to emigrate or throw themselves into politics? The KMT's high-handed campaign of "de-Japanization" disparaged Japanese education as "slave education" (*nuhua jiaoyu*), robbed intellectuals of their main language of communication, and stigmatized the high level of educational and cultural capital the Taiwanese had worked so hard to achieve. After February 28th, Japanese songs, movies, and other media remained banned, and even native Taiwanese songs and movies were suppressed. As a result, Japanese disappeared from the public sphere (except in Aboriginal areas), but it survived in private in families, clubs, friends, and journals, eventually re-emerging into the open with the tidal wave of poetry, journals, novels, and other writings that gushed forth following the end of martial law.

From these texts one can observe a unique form of resistance: the same people who had been unwilling to learn Japanese as colonial subjects studied the language with enthusiasm once it had been forbidden by the KMT, an attitude expressed in spirited *senryū* such as Gao Shousou's "Never have I studied Japanese so hard as—after the war" and Li Zhuoyu's "Reject Mandarin until the end of my days: let this be my vow." Speaking only Japanese and one's native dialect, like Hoklo, became a way to proclaim one's distinct identity (Huang 2003a: 129–31).

On a spiritual plane, many Taiwanese found the "Japanese spirit" (*Yamato-damashii*) which had been instilled in them during the colonial period—particularly during mobilization for the war—more persuasive than Sun Yat-sen's Three Principles of the People so widely promoted by the KMT. That spirit helped them overcome life's adversities and embodied the spiritual values these people hoped to pass on to their children (Hirano 2008: 235). In his memoirs, Cai Kuncan opined, "The Japanese spirit embodies hard work, integrity, keeping one's word, and other virtues" in contrast with its opposite, the "Chinese style" (Cai 2001: 240, 243). One can see the importance of *Yamato-damashii* to the so-called "Nihongo generation" of Taiwanese who insisted on using Japanese in their daily lives. But were they really Japanese, or were they willing to become Japanese? This is a deeply misunderstood question in the postwar ethnic relations of Taiwan.

"I was a Japanese until I turned 22," said former ROC president Lee Teng-hui, for example (Shiba 1994); "Taiwan is my ancestral land; Japan is my motherland" (Ke 2005), said another; "I'm a sushi-eating, *enka*-singing Japanese—or so I seem, anyway," added a third. The new hybrid culture that grew up during the colonial period belonged neither entirely to Japan nor to old Taiwan; one could say it was both, a phenomenon of dual identity that can be seen everywhere in the world where colonialism once flourished. However, because this dual identity was suppressed under a new regime, it went through a process of transformation, comparison, and resistance, developing into a peculiar expression of self-identity.

In addition, because Japanese was the best linguistic tool the Taiwanese had to express themselves, it was easily misunderstood or maliciously distorted, on one hand by the *waishengren* (as seen in two poems by Wang Jinyi: "All I did was show a little Japanese-style politeness, yet I was called 'Japanese devil'" and "As soon as he heard me humming a Japanese tune, he called me a 'natural-born slave'"), on the other by the Japanese themselves (some referred contemptuously to their reciting of Japanese poetry as "living off Japanese feces"), and even by their own children who, having been educated after the war, lacked understanding of history and the Japanese language (Wang Jinyi, quoted in Huang 2003a: 126, 133, 141). Reading their words for myself, I have come to believe that after undergoing a process of transformation and comparison, these Taiwanese came to a remarkably subtle and balanced interpretation of the Japan of the past, as evidenced by this *senryū* of Li Zhuoyu's: "Let us destroy all past attachments and hatreds/And start over again." Faced with the reality of Japan's departure, they overcame the grievances and sorrows of colonization and used sarcasm to criticize the postwar Japanese government, as seen in Li's *senryū*, "The country on earth most satisfying to abuse/Is Japan" and "To be betrayed and, before that, abandoned: the history of Taiwan" (Imagawa 2006). Some even published books in Japan castigating postwar Japanese policy, "instructing" a younger generation of Japanese from their high position as "elders" (*senpai*).[6] Perspectives like this, refracted through the prisms of a dual colonial history and complex ethnic relations, require a new methodology to be fully understood.

The allure of Chinese nationalism: Original homeland, "half-mountain people," and the left wing

China's early-twentieth-century anti-Manchu and anti-Japanese nationalism had little to do with Taiwan. Some Taiwanese intellectuals, however, did see Chinese nationalism as a force they could rely on to resist imperial Japanese colonization and assimilation. The attraction was especially strong for the Hakka, who had always been more mindful of their *yuanxiang* (original homeland). After the end of World War II, the Hakka were pulled in one direction by their idea of their *yuanxiang* in China and in the other direction by the Japanese colonial assimilation they had experienced together with the Hoklo, which led them to identify themselves as Taiwanese (*benshengren*). Postwar historical research generally interprets the conflict with the newly arrived mainlanders as a form of *shengji maodun* (friction between people of different provincial origins), but this point of view completely ignores the differences between the Hoklo and the Hakka.

That the Hakka survived for hundreds of years in Taiwan without being assimilated by the Hoklo, who greatly outnumbered them, attests to the cultural resilience of the former. Recent scholarship on Hakka social and political history has shown that proportionally fewer Hakka were victims of the February 28th Incident because their population was concentrated in agricultural areas, whereas the cities where most of the killing took place were populated mainly by the Hoklo; in fact, some *waishengren* fleeing from angry Taiwanese took refuge in Hakka villages. However, during the White Terror and "village cleanup" that followed, rural Hakka left-wing sympathizers were killed in greater proportion than the Hoklo (Xiao and Huang 2001: 398–9).

From a cultural perspective—language, ancestor worship, education for imperial examinations, and so on—the Hakka placed greater emphasis on the idea of China in their imagination of nationality. For example, although Dai Guohui (1931–2001) also fiercely criticized the Chiangs' rule during martial law, he took exception to Taiwanese independence advocates like Ong Iok-tek and Shi Ming:

> The fathers of the Taiwan independence movement … the notion of a Taiwanese race that they advocate—that the Taiwanese have developed into a people separate from the Chinese, and the self-determination they demand on that basis, is a fiction that has collapsed of its own accord … [I hope] the "quasi-border" of the

Taiwan Strait may open soon and the people of both sides may become the sort of "Chinese people" anticipated by Nixon. All Chinese—whether on the left or on the right, on the mainland or on an island—are compatriots. (Dai 1989: 179, 228)

In the same book, Dai mentions the February 28th Incident, which he experienced, and expresses sympathy for his *waishengren* "compatriots" persecuted by the Hoklo, who in his view had been aggressors no different from the Japanese (1989: 107–8).

Hakka author Wu Zhuoliu's autobiographical works also demonstrate his own unique attachments to China and interpretation of February 28th. Born in 1900, Wu was thoroughly Japanese-educated, but influenced by his grandfather's stories of Chinese culture, he worked to resist Japanese assimilation and spent time in Nanjing during World War II. February 28th marked the beginning of his disappointment with his ancestral home, however. With a reporter's keen powers of observation, he criticized the role played in the incident by so-called "half-mountain people" (*banshanren*): Taiwanese (both Hoklo and Hakka) who, dissatisfied with Japanese colonial rule, had gone to China (metonymized as the "mountain," Tangshan) to seek assistance. After the war, many returned to Taiwan with the KMT and became part of the ruling class. Wu explicitly rebuked them for assisting the government to hunt down local intellectuals during their 1947 assault. (Knowing the danger of making such thoughts public, however, he requested that his words not be published until ten years after his death [Matsuda 2006; Ren 2008].) While some Taiwanese (Hoklo and Hakka alike) kept their faith in "China" despite the turmoil of the February 28th Incident, many others felt betrayed by their new compatriots and were alienated from any sustainable Chinese nationalism. These two psychological courses differed immensely; their ideas of nation-building were irreconcilably different, and the differences are reflected in their attitudes toward Japan.

The Hakka, in particular, had to find a way to survive as a minority caught between two more powerful groups, the Hoklo and the *waishengren*. In terms of cultural consciousness, their ideas of *yuanxiang* and *zuguo* (motherland) were closer to those of the mainlanders. At the same time, they also feared Hoklo chauvinism in the Taiwanese independence movement. Their memories of the early colonial period stressed their armed anti-Japanese resistance, while the Hoklo, by contrast, tended to stress Japan's later efforts to modernize Taiwan and their experiences fighting alongside the Japanese in the war, and often in their memoirs they viewed Japan as their motherland (Cai 2001; Ke 2005). However, as one Hakka researcher put it,

At present there are two versions of Taiwanese history: one that portrays Chinese culture as the root of Taiwanese culture, and one that ostensibly focuses on Taiwanese culture but is actually narrated from a Hoklo point of view. Neither version acknowledges that Taiwanese culture also includes the Pingpuzu (plains Aborigines, largely assimilated or driven into the mountains by Chinese settlers), Aborigines and Hakka. (Xiao and Huang 2001: 632)

The Hakka are often ignored by being lumped under the vague heading of "Taiwanese," even though their experiences, loyalties, and ideals have differed greatly from those of the Hoklo majority which has been able to more successfully define the "Taiwanese" experience.

Tribal village meets nation-state: Aborigines, Japan, and the Republic of China

Taiwan's ethnic groups have never been equally represented: some are enormously outnumbered by others. In terms of population size, the Austronesian Aborigines are the smallest group. However, with nearly twenty tribes, the Aborigines are extremely diverse, and the area of their traditional lands comprises over half of Taiwan. While some tribes number in the hundreds, others number in the tens of thousands, and their languages, cultures, living spaces, and social organizations also differ greatly. This complex combination of factors complicates outsiders' efforts to understand Aboriginal history and identity.

As described in earlier chapters of this volume, the first efforts to comprehensively study these diverse, complex Aboriginal peoples of tremendous vitality who had no written language came from the Japanese government, whose quest to alter their way of life and incorporate them into a modern nation-state began in the late nineteenth century. Before interacting with Taiwan's Aborigines, Japan had expanded its national control over the Ainu of Hokkaido and the indigenous Ryukyuan peoples after centuries of contact with southwestern and northeastern natives. By contrast, a significant number of Aborigines of Taiwan were incorporated into the empire over a very short time, a colossal project completed at a huge price.

The Aborigines encountered the Japanese under very different circumstances than the Hoklo and Hakka had. How to claim sovereignty over them under international law was a question that vexed Japan. The Japanese eventually adopted a deliberately ambiguous approach, treating the Aborigines as a rebellious group that had never accepted Qing imperial authority; since Japan had inherited Taiwan from the Qing, the new government had a duty to "put down" rebellions whenever they occurred. The Japanese knew, however, that this was not a valid legal interpretation, so they proceeded gradually, prioritizing appeasement over force—at least in many cases where access to valuable natural resources were not being obstructed. Whenever an Aboriginal group agreed to accept Japanese rule, a *kijunshiki* "allegiance ceremony" would be arranged to announce the new addition to the empire.

The *kijunshiki* were designed for the participation of individual villages or districts. The Aborigines saw the ceremonies as "reconciliations": some tribes gave up their weapons after being defeated in battle, while others used peaceful negotiations to obtain favorable terms. The Japanese official *Records of Aborigine Administration* (*Riban shikō*, 1895–1926)[7] mention over seventy such ceremonies, mostly in the north. Camphor trees could be found in abundance throughout the Atayal tribe's mountainous territory in central and northern Taiwan, and the Japanese, anxious to harvest valuable camphor, met fierce resistance when they pushed to establish a line of outposts called the *aiyusen* that effectively shrank the Aborigines' territory. During this period (1896–1920), some 151 battles or skirmishes were fought between the Japanese and Aboriginal groups, most in Atayal territory. In many other areas, however, tribal leaders negotiated for peace, and no record of *kijunshiki* exists.[8] After the largest offensive, the Taroko Battle, ended in 1914, Japan declared victory in its five-year campaign against the Aborigines. However, it had come at great cost. Japan settled on the name of *banchi* (savage land) for Aboriginal territory and used police officers to rule it in a manner distinct from the way the plains were governed.

During the Japanese era, police officers and their families were essentially the only Japanese to travel deep into Aborigine territory. Beginning in 1910 or so, Japanese farmers and fishermen began immigrating to the Karenkō (Hualian)—Taitō (Taidong) coast, settling in an arc of nearly twenty villages, of which Yoshino (with a population of 1,500) was the largest. Other Japanese who bought land on the east coast lived more or less in isolation.[9] Thus the Aborigines of the east had a greater variety of interactions with the Japanese; some even acquired agricultural or fishing skills from them. Most Aborigines, however, called the mountains home, and the police officers there were surrounded by Indigenous villagers with few or no Japanese to keep them company.

By the 1930s, there were 5,000 policemen in Aborigine territory, about as many as there were on the plains. Of course, the population of the plains was much greater, so the ratio of police to locals was far higher in Aboriginal areas. Leo Ching has written that "the role of the police in the aboriginal territory was to instill awe and dread of imperial authority" (2001: 136). In fact, half of the police officers in the Aboriginal areas were *keishu*, a low rank that existed only in those areas; they functioned as assistants to the other officers. Japanese nationals accounted for only a minority of *keishu* in the 1930s; the rest were split evenly between Taiwanese islanders and Aborigines; later still, village *seinendan* or youth groups assisted the police (Ishimaru 2008). Besides their military and law enforcement responsibilities, the police were involved in everything from judicial administration, education, and social guidance to public health and economic development, and they even helped mediate disputes over hunting grounds; meanwhile, their wives taught things like etiquette and sewing. This work was also uniquely dangerous; from 1904 to 1929 more than 2,600 police officers or their family members were killed by resisting tribes, compared to 1,400 civilians. Even the Aborigine Administration (*riban*) authorities admitted that "serving in such dangerous areas where fighting might break out at any time is a duty not found in other parts of the empire" (Yagashiro 2008: 519, 808 10).

In the mid-1920s, headhunting incidents gradually ceased as the Atayal tribes of the Central Mountains, particularly the Eight *She* (Aboriginal villages) of Hokusei (Beishi), submitted to Japanese authority. The colonial government then turned to economic development, road building, and education (Dali 2001), as *riban* officials began to describe these special subjects as "unsullied," "lovable," and "childlike" instead of "dim-witted, violent and cruel" (Yamaji 2004: 100). The electric fence along the *aiyusen* in the northern and central mountains was removed; it had been installed as a deterrent to resisting tribes, but a third of those killed by accidental contact with it were police officers.[10] It was because tensions had finally subsided that the Musha Incident, a violent rebellion by Seediq tribesmen in 1930, came as such a shock to *riban* authorities. In the aftermath of the incident, Governor-General Ishizuka Eizō, his administrative chief, the head of Taichū Prefecture (where the incident occurred), and the police chief all assumed responsibility and resigned, provoking a thorough re-evaluation of *riban* policy.

In the new *riban* policy announced by new Governor-General Ōta Masahiro, special emphasis was placed on appointing "sober, level-headed" officers to Aboriginal areas, where they would remain in their given areas and win the trust of the Aborigines by means of a "human-centered" approach. The officers were also expected to learn the local tribe's language, understand its unique psychology, and take its culture and customs seriously, and avoid the use of violence. These were all major changes. The new *riban* policies were printed and distributed as a handbook, which the police officers dubbed the "*riban* constitution." Based on the officers' subsequent treatment of the Aborigines, scholars agree that the new policy was faithfully carried out (Kondō 1993: 6–11). The memoirs of Dali Kakei, a descendant of the chiefs of the Eight *She* of Beishi, attest to the image of hardworking, enlightened police officers (Dali 2001: 130–57).[11] The new "gentle" policy lasted until 1939.

Following its declaration of war against China, Japan launched its "national spirit general mobilization movement" in 1937 and passed the National General Mobilization Law the following year. In keeping with the new policy, Japan once again began appointing military governor-generals to Taiwan and announced the beginning of the *kōminka* (imperialization) movement. *Riban* officials did not come up with a policy response until a plenary meeting in March 1939, by which point large numbers of police officers in Aboriginal areas were being recalled to Japan for military service. At the meeting, it was decided to develop the Aborigines into "benevolent self-ruling citizens" and introduce them to a new way of living. This included many modern notions such as using mosquito nets, toilets, and bathrooms, introducing more Japanese-style clothing, cultivating "national spirit," and training to become subjects of the emperor—in other words, accelerated Japanization to meet the needs of the wartime system.

Having grown up under the softened policy of the 1920s and the "gentle" policy of the 1930s, a new generation of Aborigines came of age as Japan was mobilizing for battle. These young Aborigine men surprised their Japanese officials with their thirst for battle and eagerness to prove their loyalty to the nation, and the exploits of the native "Takasago Volunteers" (*Takasago giyūtai*) became legendary. In a mere fifty years, the colonists had won the heartfelt loyalty of a significant number of the ethnic minorities they ruled. On the battlefields of the south Pacific, Aborigine soldiers saved the lives of many Japanese, and this experience of being brothers-in-arms left a mark on that generation's attitudes toward Japan that endured long after war's end.

A generation that included Japanese-literate Aborigines had recently appeared; beginning in the 1930s, many started submitting articles in publications like *Riban no tomo* ("Aborigine Administrators' Companion," 1932–1943). From these submissions, one can see how fervently many Aborigines strove to be outstanding Japanese citizens and to cleanse themselves of the "savage" stigma. After the war, a few Aborigine elites left memoirs, letters, and diaries which, together with oral interviews, court testimony, and reportage, comprise a treasure trove of written information on, among other things, their attitudes toward Japan. There were no differences apparent between elite men of different tribes, but there is a lack of material from the nonelite as well as women, which might explain the overwhelming impression that a whole generation of Aborigines indeed became loyal subjects.[12]

From these texts and fieldwork, I have observed that due to their innate respect for fighting spirit and strict distinctions among social classes, the Aborigines, compared to the plains people, felt it easier to adapt psychologically to wartime mobilization. Many Hoklo and Hakka youth of the same generation also exhibited devotion to "Japanese spirit" (Zheng 1998), but others went through a psychological transformation, as embodied in this Japanese poem by Hoklo Huang Delong: "I recall I hated Japan when I was a Japanese soldier/But now I write this poem as a Japanophile/What a marvelous thing!" (Huang 2003a: 131). The Aborigines' psychological transformation, by contrast, came before the war; for example, Walis Piho, a descendant of the Musha rebels, recalled, "At that time, I had forgotten the Musha Incident, forgotten my father; all I thought about was how to show loyalty to the country" (Hayashi 1998). The greatest difference was that the Aborigines had no notion of a *yuanxiang* or *zuguo* in China—Taiwan was the only home they had ever had, and Japan was their first country; they did not hesitate because they had no other choice.

When the Aborigines who had fought as Japanese soldiers returned to Taiwan and saw the Chinese troops on the island, the shock of the realization that their "country" had changed hands was much greater for them than for their counterparts on the plains. Did Japan have the right under international law to do what it did by signing the Treaty of San Francisco—give up the people and land over which it had assumed sovereignty via *kijunshiki*—without telling them? From many Aborigines' perspectives, the new rulers were handed complete authority over Taiwan's native peoples without having to pay the smallest part of the price of blood and treasure the Japanese had sacrificed to win it.

Under the Japanese, the leading members of the Tsou and Atayal tribes had already grasped the idea of self-rule, and like the plainsmen they were jailed or executed for demanding it in the February 28th Incident. Thus they concealed their self-identification as educated Japanese citizens and the affection they had developed for the Japanese from fighting together in the war until they were able to voice these sentiments to Japanese people (or Japanese speakers) who visited their mountains in the late 1980s. Also, because the new "national language" of Chinese took time to permeate mountain villages, using it to conduct village affairs was infeasible; Japanese remained the lingua franca for some areas until the 1990s, and a new Creole or mixed language developed (Tsuchida 2008: 159–72). Despite never having received a Japanese education, many of the next generation of Aborigines learned Japanese from hearing it spoken at home and in public meetings; however, this did not occur among the Hoklo or the Hakka.

With the arrival of the *waishengren*, ethnic relations among the Aborigines changed. The Chinese chauvinism endemic among many *waishengren* did not take into account the cultural differences of the Aborigines and indeed forced them to adopt Chinese names. Also, the government gave Aboriginal land to newly arrived ROC soldiers to farm. In 1955, *waishengren* comprised 1.1 percent of the population in Aboriginal mountain areas; this increased to 4.9 percent ten years later (Li 1970: 80–1). Due to the large number of former soldiers among the *waishengren*, the male–female ratio among them in 1956 was 4:1; hence, intermarriage with all of Taiwan's ethnic groups was inevitable. During the early 1950s, the government had forbidden low-ranking soldiers to marry; after the ban was lifted, many of these soldiers married young Aborigine women.

In the postwar curriculum put together by the *waishengren*, events like the Musha (Wushe) Incident were used to portray the Aborigines as models of resistance against the Japanese; no mention was made of their friendly relations with the Japanese after that. Mona Ludaw, the instigator of Musha, was honored with a place in the national Martyr's Shrine, while the Aborigines who had lost their lives on the battlefields for Japan were forgotten (Huang 2006b).

The recoil of Chinese nationalism: New and old hatreds, threats foreign and domestic, and the entanglement of three "postwars"

Compared with Hoklo, Hakka, and Aboriginal perspectives of Japan, the views of the *waishengren* were shaped by completely different experiences.

According to historians' estimates, during eight years of war between China and Japan, the ROC army suffered in excess of 3 million casualties, including 1 million dead, not to mention the incalculable economic losses. Prices soared, and hyperinflation nearly destroyed the nation's finances (Li 1995: 22–5). Yet Chiang Kai-shek refused to seek reparations from Japan, to the great amazement and relief of the Japanese. Recent research indicates that although Chiang advocated leniency toward Japan, he never intended to refuse reparations; his hand was forced, however, by his fear that once the mainland had been lost, the United States and Japan would recognize Communist China (Z. Huang 2009). Thus, in the Sino-Japanese Treaty of 1952, the ROC expressed "magnanimity and friendship toward the people of Japan," vowing to "repay enmity with virtue" (*yi de bao yuan*) in its postwar relations with Japan (Nagano and Kondō 1999: 160). This conspicuously generous position was in spite of the fact that the government, having just lost the mainland and fled to Taiwan, desperately needed financial and material assistance. Refusing reparations clearly was not in the immediate interests of the government or the people. After China's first victory in a century of humiliations, the psychological foundation for "magnanimity and friendship" did not exist; the people's accumulated suffering was too great. Chiang's choice to "repay enmity with virtue" (and, conveniently, to advertise its charity toward Japan to the world) is important in calculating how the postwar was experienced in Taiwan. In return, Japan showed its support by sending officers to train Nationalist forces to fight their Civil War against the Communists, supporting the right of Chiang Kai-shek and his regime to rule Taiwan and allowing the KMT to take possession of all its assets on the island.

With or without a foundation, this so-called "gratitude diplomacy" (*ongi gaikō*) endured for two decades before changing dramatically in the 1970s. First, when the United States elected to give control of the Ryukyus back to Japan, it planned to transfer the Diaoyutai Islands, abundant in fish and oil deposits, as well. This offended the patriotic sentiments of students from Taiwan and Hong Kong studying in the United States, who joined together to organize large-scale street protests to "protect Diaoyutai." The movement was fueled by high-octane Chinese nationalism: ranks of students from all over China and Taiwan shouted slogans like, "Down with Japanese militarism! Stand up, people of China! The Chinese people do not surrender!" (Lin 2001: 5, 519). The overseas students' patriotic enthusiasm spread across the Pacific to the ROC, unleashing a tide of student movements the likes of which the martial law-era the ROC had never seen, as well as a debate on Chinese nationalism.

Next, in September 1972, Japan established diplomatic relations with the People's Republic of China and cut formal diplomatic ties with the ROC, marking an end to twenty years of "gratitude diplomacy." The break happened to occur right after the Protect Diaoyutai movement (1970–1972) and the United Nations' expulsion of the ROC (October 1971). Not only did the beleaguered KMT government have harsh words for Japan's "rank ingratitude" but the people also demonstrated in protest. Students and professors issued a proclamation that was published in the *United Daily News* of September 30:

> This treacherous, despicable treatment of the Chinese people is infuriating; if this is not unendurable, nothing is. We cannot hold back our accumulated animosity any longer. The tears of the eight-year War of Resistance have not yet dried, and already Japan sees profit and forgets justice, just like before. It is not only a galling humiliation to our country, but a provocation toward the sons and daughters of China as well.

They called on the people to take revenge by refusing to deal with Japanese businesses, watch Japanese films, listen to Japanese music, or eat Japanese food. Although these actions failed to present a real threat to Japanese interests, the sense of "galling humiliation" and "rank ingratitude" burned deeply into the hearts of the Protect Diaoyutai generation.

The intellectuals of the Protect Diaoyutai movement were the first generation in Taiwan to be born and educated under the ROC. Although the *waishengren* enjoyed relatively greater access to educational resources, they were not a majority. However, as one participant in the overseas movement put it:

> Antipathy for Japan was the main impetus for the Protect Diaoyutai movement … Those who participated were mainly Taiwan mainlanders and Hong Kong students; very few were local Taiwanese. In my own experience I found that although the Taiwanese students had all kinds of reasons for not taking part, the main one was a lack of hatred for Japan. If they did participate in the movement, they did so either because they opposed the KMT or because they were attracted to socialism. (Shui 2001: 716)

The Protect Diaoyutai movement in Taiwan was led mainly by *waishengren*. There were a few local Taiwanese who defended Chinese nationalism as fervently as the *waishengren*: "Nationalism is sincere love for one's comrades, a sense of belonging to one body. We want to unify China; what weapon could be more powerful than that?"[13] However, the locals were much less involved in political activity; one Chinese student from Korea observed that "the local classmates were still deeply caught up in the tragedy of the February 28th Incident and the White Terror: 'Stay out of politics' was the guiding principle their parents drilled into them at every opportunity" (Xu 2001: 732).

From the above, it is apparent that despite the Chinese Cultural Renaissance Movement and *Zhonghua minzu*-oriented education, attitudes toward Japan still differed by ethnic group. The passionately nationalistic *waishengren* youth linked the Protect Diaoyutai movement with the May Fourth movement of the early republic, and they saw it as their duty to assume the mantle of "5000 years of history and culture, 130 years of national calamity and more than 20 years of exile" (Mao 2001: 519); this differed substantially from the historical experience of the local ethnic groups under the Japanese.

In fact, the Chinese nationalism the KMT government worked so hard to establish was a double-edged sword that, if used carelessly, could cut the hand that wielded it. In Taiwan, nationalism served to bring together and eliminate dissent among separate ethnic groups with differing views of Japan. Identifying with the Chinese who had triumphed in the eight-year War of Resistance against Japan was much more attractive to young people than identifying with the Taiwanese who had been in bondage for fifty years. Filled with naïve youthful enthusiasm, they were willing to devote themselves to the noble mission to liberate the suffering comrades on the mainland. Moreover, nationalism healed the rifts among the *waishengren* caused by the White Terror and the suppression of opposition parties.

Overseas, however, rampant anti-Japanese nationalistic sentiment greatly damaged the ROC's reputation. Students saw the ROC government as weak and indecisive; to them, unifying China was the only way to grow strong enough to resist Japan. Thus some even resolved to accept the PRC as the sole legitimate government of China and, in the fervent hope that the Cultural Revolution would bring hope for China, rushed to visit the mainland. Once it realized the surge of nationalism had gotten dangerously out of control, the ROC government started clamping down on the students and teachers most active in the Protect Diaoyutai movement (Wang 1996: 364).

From the discussions above we see that the ROC government had to walk a tightrope between reining in domestic attitudes toward Japan and responding to the threat posed by the movement to unify China. Having lost the trump card of "gratitude diplomacy," the ROC responded to subsequent events in Japan—the history textbooks controversy, the prime minister's visits to the Yasukuni Shrine, and so on—the same way the PRC did, only without the authority or strength to speak for all of China.

As for the millions who had followed the KMT government to Taiwan, every international blow to the legitimacy of the ROC version of Chinese nationalism increased their sense of crisis. One second-generation mainlander, drawing on the experiences of his family, put it this way:

The formation of the *waishengren* identity was tied closely to early modern Chinese history. In terms of ideology, *waishengren* were limited to the KMT view of history whether they agreed with it or not; in terms of destiny, because of the continuation of the civil war and the pressure of Taiwanese separatism, the *waishengren* became a kind of nebulous collective. Their common experience— of ushering in a new era, resisting foreign intrusion, enduring crushing defeat, migrating on a massive scale (a kind of KMT or *waishengren* version of the Long March), and then surviving threats domestic and foreign—has molded a strong and deep sense of identity and history that probably exceeds that of most other ethnic groups in China and Taiwan alike. (Yang 2008: 97–8)

Thus, the discouragement and frustration with which the *waishengren* perceived Japan were deeper and more complex than just having been "victims of aggression" during the war.

On the other hand, the three native Taiwanese ethnic groups now living in the ROC had taken part in the Pacific War as Japanese subjects. Yet the governments of both Japan and the ROC for decades avoided the duty to seriously handle the war's legacy, including the issues of pay owed to soldiers and compensation for the families of the fallen, not to mention comforting the souls of the deceased. Instead, the task of negotiating with Japan for compensation and closure fell on private citizens. Recent incidents such as Taiwan Solidarity Union chairman Shu Chin-chiang's 2005 visit to the Yasukuni Shrine and the 2006 forced removal of the Takasago Volunteers memorial in the Atayal town of Wulai are part of the postwar legacy that needs to be addressed. It is clear that Taiwanese society is still entangled in three "postwars," unable to resolve them and move on to the next stage of history.

Complex relationships resulting from the interweaving of ethnicity and history

In Taiwan, attitudes toward Japan have not developed in a regular, proportional, linear way, as they have in the United States, China, and Korea. When multiple ethnic groups live through multiple historical eras, these various elements influence each other in convoluted ways to produce a multilayered, nonlinear path of development, very much like a complex system. The notion of "complex systems" has developed over the last twenty years or so in the fields of information technology and natural science as a way of understanding nonlinear, diverse, and interconnected natural and human phenomena. This model can be applied to the present subject as well. Taiwanese attitudes toward Japan exhibit characteristics of a complex system: the fractious combination of similar yet distinct ethnic groups, interactions between different generations, and the multiple layers of issues have intertwined and accumulated to the extent that it is hard to untangle them all. The interactions within the system display fragility, unpredictability, contradictions, and chaotic tendencies. Using the notion of complex systems to analyze Taiwanese attitudes toward Japan helps us sort out the various layers and horizontal links.

As discussed above, attitudes toward Japan are a product of accumulated historical experience, but Taiwan's ethnic groups were separated into different areas on the island and had different relationships with one another in different historical periods, so their historical experiences differ. In this complex system, ethnicity is the most important factor in determining attitudes toward Japan. This includes four ethnic communities in modern Taiwan: the Aborigines, Hoklo, Hakka, and *waishengren*. Ethnicity is the primary determinant of historical experience, language, area of residence, livelihood, religious life, and cultural tradition. The system is open and unstable, for each ethnicity can be further divided into subgroups. The relationships among these ethnic groups over a century of turbulent history can be divided into at least two distinct types: (a) the colonizer and colonized and (b) adversaries and allies. Type (a) includes two "postcolonial" relationships resulting from two different colonial periods and type (b) can be divided into six types of "postwar" relationships resulting from six episodes of sustained violence.

(a) Relations between the colonized and colonizer: Between 1895 and 1945, the colonizers were the Japanese and the colonized were the Hoklo, Hakka, and Aborigines. Then, between 1945 and 1987, the colonizers were now the *waishengren*, and the colonized were the Hoklo, Hakka, and Aborigines. There were various types of relations between the colonizer and colonized: the most often discussed is that of resistance by the colonized. In a multiethnic society like Taiwan, resistance was often not simply one side versus another but a triangular tug-of-war. Under the Japanese, the colonized could invoke the strength of the ROC to resist their colonial overlords. Under KMT-imposed martial law, however, the colonized used the spiritual strength they had acquired under the Japanese to resist the ROC's colonial rule.

Also, "postcolonial" relations should have developed immediately following the end of Japanese rule, but before that could happen in Taiwan, a second colonial era under the ROC had begun. Thus, when the government was no longer controlled by the *waishengren*, those who had lived under the Japanese as well entered into a doubly postcolonial era.

(b) Relations between antagonists or allies: Over more than a century, Taiwan's four major ethnic groups have participated in six large-scale conflicts and wars, namely: (1) Japan's initial conquest of Taiwan and the attending armed resistance (1895–1915), (2) the Japanese campaigns against the Aborigines (1896–1920), (3) the Sino-Japanese War (1937–1945), (4) the Pacific War (1941–1945), (5) the February 28th Incident and its aftermath (1947), and (6) the Chinese Civil War (1946–1949). The first four took place during the Japanese era, and the last two during the early years of KMT rule. Different wars were fought between different enemies, which meant that today's enemy might very well be tomorrow's ally. For example, the Japanese and the three Taiwanese ethnic groups were enemies in the early colonial era but fought on the same side in the Pacific War. Likewise, the native Taiwanese groups under the ROC rule were pulled into war against the Communists, with whom they had hitherto had no quarrel. The fact that armed conflict took place in the framework of colonialism further complicated ethnic relations.

For the past 120 years, Taiwanese history has been closely tied to two countries, China and Japan. And during that period, China and Japan have each gone through multiple stages of rapid historical change. The Qing Dynasty, the ROC, and the PRC are three totally different polities; the same holds true for the Meiji, Taishō, and Shōwa imperial polities and postwar Japan. Japan's rule of Taiwan also went through three very different stages. Because Taiwanese attitudes toward Japan developed in the context of these multiple rapid historical changes, they exhibit the diversities we see today.

To distinguish the different attitudes toward Japan found in Taiwanese society, the first factor to look at should be ethnicity. Since different groups did not share the same past, that makes the historical experiences of Taiwan's ethnic groups display nonlinear patterns of antagonism and cooperation. This is further complicated by the fact that there are over ten tribes of Aborigines, the *waishengren* came from all over China, the Japanese came from all over Japan, and Taiwan's Hoklo and Hakka originated from different homelands and clans. Ethnicity, even though enlarged by many subgroups, can still be refracted into the postwar relationship as to view Japan from the angle of a foe and the quite ambivalent postcolonial relationship.

The second most important factor is generation. Each generation's attitudes toward Japan were shaped by its education in school, at home, and through the mass media. Intermarriage between different ethnic groups gave rise to conflicting views of Japan within families, especially in the second and third generations, which have been affected greatly by the appeal of Japanese popular culture.

The third factor is governed by socioeconomic background: commercial interests, political factions, and the like also affected attitudes toward Japan, creating an open, interacting complex system. And this all in turn has been affected by the re-emergence of China as a superpower; the PRC's insatiable demand on capital and human resources has drastically changed the political and socioeconomic balance in the Asian Pacific—and this sensation inevitably has affected Taiwanese attitudes toward Japan.

After the end of Japanese colonial rule in 1945, Taiwan's society should have entered the historical phase of decolonization. However, the reality was different. Native Taiwanese (ethnic Hoklo, Hakka, and Taiwan Indigenous Peoples), that is, the previously colonized inhabitants, began to seriously take stock of the historical legacy of Japanese colonial rule, but this reflective evaluation appeared in a significant way only after 1987. This pivotal moment marked the end of the KMT's forty year period of martial law; only then could various "postwar" and "postcolonial" attitudes toward Japan be displayed equally among Taiwan's ethnic groups.

As seen above, these two incompatible categories can be subdivided into multiple intertwining subcategories that make them difficult to figure out. So, is Taiwan "Japanophilic" or "Japanophobic"? Are its people resistors or collaborators? Due to the complex nonlinear relationships among the island's ethnic groups, attempting to understand them with the inductive methods of traditional behavioral science is not a trivial exercise. This chapter has endeavored to shed light on Taiwanese attitudes toward Japan with an analysis of the two most important factors that have shaped them: history and ethnicity, as the accumulated influence interwoven by these factors produced so-called complex systemic entanglements. It is my hope that this analysis will help readers gain a different angle than simple stereotypes of "Japanophilic" or "Japanophobic" belief and a better understanding of Taiwan's uniquely abundant, multilayered social and cultural dynamics.

Notes

1   See, for example, Okada (1997, 2009).
2   Of the twelve books I have collected, only one fails to fit this pattern; see Huang (2006b: 156–8).
3   Ruan (1992) was the first book to break the taboo; after its publication, many other collections of interviews appeared, providing valuable historical testimony.
4   I previously have used these colonial texts that began to emerge in the 1990s in conjunction with anthropology-style fieldwork (Huang 2001: 222–50, 2003b: 296–314).
5   The "White Terror" refers to the period of martial law and anti-communist laws in Taiwan (1949–1992), during which thousands of people, including *waishengren*, were imprisoned or killed for their political views and opposition to Chiang Kai-shek's totalitarianism on the pretext of being Communist agents. The Protect Diaoyutai movement refers to a series of protests in 1970–1974 by students in Taiwan, Overseas Chinese, and Hong Kong people against Japanese claims of sovereignty over an archipelago known in Japanese as the Senkaku Islands.
6   The third type of text discussed in Huang (2006b) particularly reflects Lee Teng-hui's influences from Japanese culture.
7   More literally "savage administration" or "savage policy."
8   For example, there is no record of incidents or battles with the Tsou and Puyuma. The number 151 comes from my own calculations. For a table of Japanese battles with the Aborigines, see Yagashiro (2008: 796–805).
9   A total of 888 people had migrated to the eleven Japanese sugar cane villages in the Taidong area by the 1920s; a decade later, only 171 remained (Yamaguchi 2007: 217–53).
10   Between 1916 and 1926, there were twenty-seven people who died as a result of accidental contact with the electric fence; ten were Japanese policemen (*Riban shikō* 1918–1938, editions 1–5).
11   "If anyone tries to purposely distort the facts by saying the Japanese made no positive contributions to the Eight Tribes of Beishi," wrote Dali Kakei, "his words will be utterly unconvincing."
12   Yanagimoto (2000) is a work of literary reportage, presenting cases of war crimes against women.
13   See the debate between Huang Daolin and Mu Gu (Sun Qingyu) in Wang (1996: 388).

8

Oh Sadaharu/Wang Zhenzhi and the Possibility of Chineseness in 1960s Taiwan

Andrew D. Morris

Baseball king Oh Sadaharu is respected for his everlasting loyalty, bravery, and his patriotism while never giving up his individual identity, and he has moved all of the Japanese people ... One could say that Oh's patriotic spirit, the cultural and life spirit that courses through the veins of the Chinese people, has been passed on to the Japanese people.

Marginalia in the Taiwan National Central Library copy of
Oh Sadaharu: Returning Home after a Century (2005)

Oh Sadaharu (or in Chinese, Wang Zhenzhi), who hit 868 home runs and played first base for the Yomiuri Giants from 1959 to 1980, was the finest player in Japanese baseball history. The son of a Chinese father, Wang Shifu (Oh Shifuku), who had immigrated from Zhejiang Province as a young man in 1925, and a Japanese mother, Tōzumi Tomi, a native of Toyama Prefecture, Oh's ethnic background had a distinct impact on his baseball career, his life, and his image in Japan and abroad.

An icon in Japan (as well as a cult figure among American baseball fans), Oh also became by the mid-1960s the most memorable, influential, and complicated connection between Taiwan and Japan. The two decades since the departure of the former colonial masters had been a time of fundamentally and officially denigrating and/or erasing the history of Japan's fifty-year rule. Chiang Kai-shek's famous postwar proclamation of "repaying enmity with virtue" aside, his Republic of China (ROC) quickly embarked on a full program of "motherlandification" (*zuguohua*): outlawing the use of Japanese language and the consumption of Japanese culture, erasing and/or Sinicizing all spatial and architectural traces of Japanese rule, supporting an intense educational and cultural infusion of Sun Yat-sen's Three People's Principles as a means

This chapter expands on a short section of my book on the history of baseball in Taiwan (2010: 72–6). The author would like to thank the Republic of China Ministry of Education, the Fulbright Scholar Program, the Institute of Taiwan History, Academia Sinica, and the Cal Poly College of Liberal Arts for their support of this research.

of defeating (in the words of one provincial education committee) "the extremely deep poison of Japanese rule," and indiscriminately slandering all Taiwanese who lived through the Japanese era as mere "slaves" of their former masters (Yang 1993: 80–7; Chen 2001: 189–96; Y. Huang 2006: 312–26; Allen 2012).

The persona of Oh—and the Chinese "Wang" he became in official ROC culture— transcended this ethnopolitical history of Taiwanese–mainlander–Japanese suspicion and resentment. Since the mid-1960s, Oh has been a hero in Taiwan, truly beloved by Taiwanese and mainlanders. Oh's brilliant accomplishments and gentle, cultured manner have been praised by men and women, adults and children, and baseball fans and plain old nationalists, and he seems to have signified something different yet equally powerful for each of these constituencies.

During the summer of 2011, upon borrowing the 2005 Chinese translation of Suzuki Hiroshi's biography of Oh and his father[1] from the National Central Library in Taipei, I noticed a small stack of 8-centimeter-square yellow Post-it notes inside the book's front cover. There, a reader had taken the time to record (and leave for others to ponder) his reflections on Oh's magnificence, his ethnic identity, and its implications for Taiwanese/mainlander ethnic tensions in Taiwan. I should not give this armchair cultural critic too much credit for clarity of argument; in just six adhesive notes he careens from comparisons of a moral, free, and democratic ROC to the "waste of time of 40 years of struggle" in the People's Republic of China (PRC) to apocryphal tales of Chinese bravery under fire during World War II to very particular and cheap smears against former ROC education minister Du Zhengsheng. However, the reader is definitely struck by the passion that Oh stirred in the hearts of Taiwan observers more than a quarter century after his last triumphant home run with the far-off but ever-present Yomiuri Giants and by Oh's power to represent important ideological positions in all sorts of ethnopolitical debates.

As he ascended to superstardom with the Yomiuri Giants, Oh became, in the eyes of the Chinese Nationalist Party (KMT) and their largely mainlander constituency, an Overseas Chinese idol who had triumphed over Japanese discrimination; at the very same time in the eyes of many Taiwanese people, he was clearly a former-fellow subject of the Japanese empire who had triumphed *over* and *despite* his Chinese heritage.

Learning to be Chinese in Japan

Oh's legend and popularity in Taiwan and his attachment to the ROC have led many to incorrectly refer to Oh as a Taiwanese national; this is not the case. Oh was born in Japan in 1940 and always felt growing up that he was indeed "more Japanese than the Japanese" (Suzuki 2005: 155). Part of the Chinese myth of Wang/Oh regards his father's lifelong yearning for his Zhejiang homeland and his constant talk of going back to China; his early, very specific, and oft-discussed plan for his sons was to have Sadaharu become an electrical engineer and his older brother Tetsujō (Tiecheng) a doctor, and in this way finally become of use to their Chinese motherland (Oh 1981: 144). The younger Oh was clearly conscious of his Chinese heritage, but it seems to have felt very distant; he later said that he always felt his "Chinese half had been totally Japanized" (Suzuki 2005: 156).

This matter was settled for young Sadaharu in 1957, during his 11th-grade year at Waseda Business High School (*Waseda jitsugyō gakkō*). As a starting pitcher and cleanup hitter, he led his team to the championship of the prestigious National High School Baseball Invitational Tournament (or Spring *Kōshien*) for the first time and was honored by being selected by his teammates to receive the championship plaque.[2] However, just five months later, the young star learned that there was more to his ethnic/national identity than just his own formulation. When his standout team qualified for the baseball competition of the prestigious Kokutai National Sports Festival of Japan (*Kokumin taiiku taikai*) to be held in Shizuoka, Oh was told that he could not compete for the painfully simple reason that he was not a Japanese citizen.

This decision to exclude from Kokutai one of Japan's very finest athletes was newsworthy; for two days the *Yomiuri shimbun* reported on the Waseda Parents Association's attempts to gain an exemption from this harsh rule by meeting with the distinguished Matsunaga Tō, minister of education, Kokutai honorary chairman, and Waseda alumnus (Suzuki 2005: 88). When these negotiations failed, Oh's teammates gallantly offered to refuse to participate in the tournament at all until Sadaharu's father pleaded with them to go forward. (They also insisted that Sadaharu join the opening ceremony parade with them, although after that he could only wear his jersey in the stands and watch [Oh and Falkner 1984: 55–7].)

These young men, many of whose fathers likely fought in China in World War II, exhibited an admirable humanity that must have been truly meaningful to young Oh. But the traumatic way that his identity (read Wang) was defined for him so forcefully, and in such an exclusionary manner, still has implications for him and his family almost six decades later. To this day, Oh has never taken Japanese citizenship and (as Wang) carries a passport of the ROC—of course, the government that ruled China when his father left the mountains of southern Zhejiang for Japan in 1925 but since 1949 has ruled only Taiwan. And even in Japan, he romanizes his own name not as "Sadaharu Oh" but as "C. C. Wang" or "Chen-Chu Wang" (Wetherall 1981: 411n51; Suzuki 2005: 152).

It seems clear that from this moment he developed a clear resolution to embrace a Chinese identity, or at least a non-Japanese identity, even if it took him some twenty-four years to be able to discuss it publicly. His 1976 autobiography did not mention the incident. His 1981 memoir did but in very brief and unemotional fashion, and then only with the following vague statement as cover for any perceived lack of patriotism: "When I hear the terms 'China,' 'Japan,' and 'motherland' (*sokoku*), my eyes moisten and hot feelings cannot help but gush forth from my mind and heart . . . . The word 'motherland,' and the words 'China' and 'Japan,' are beautiful words" (Oh 1981: 140). Only in his 1984 English-language autobiography did he seem to feel able to explain his true feelings about this de-/re-nationalizing moment:

> To say I was hurt and confused means almost nothing. I was more hurt than
> I have ever been in my life. My confusion was even deeper. How could this

happen to *me, who was a Japanese*! My father was Chinese, and I was his son,
that was true, but I had grown up as a Japanese ... I came to an understanding:
"Hey! They're damn right, I'm *not* Japanese!" Of course ... I vowed then and
there to make sure that at least I would keep my feelings to myself. (Oh and
Falkner 1984: 54–5)

Oh was soon to learn that keeping silent about this issue would not end the
discrimination that he faced even as a star athlete. Takahashi Dairiku, a 1960s
Giants beat reporter, remembered Oh's self-consciousness about his biracial identity.
In 1962, the year of his first home run title, the handsome all-star agonized to his
hitting coach that he might easily be identified as half-Chinese by strangers on
the Tokyo streetcars. Unfortunately, his self-pity was not unprovoked; even after
establishing himself as the finest (part-)Japanese player ever, he still had to endure
cruel racist chants by fans of opposing teams. In 1969, after a hard night of abuse
from the Chunichi Dragons fans of Nagoya, this superstar could only ask Takahashi,
"Am I really so strange?" (Suzuki 2005: 157–8). All this evidence suggests that as
an accomplished but still frustrated young man, Oh was as open as ever to a new
formulation of his ethnic identity: if everyone else saw him as Chinese, could he see
himself in this way?

Coming home (*sic*): A world Chinese

The year 1964 was Oh's sixth season with the Giants. By that time, he had helped
deliver two Japan Series championships and led the Central League in thirteen
statistical categories during the 1962–1963 seasons. As familiar as Taiwanese fans of
Japanese baseball would have been with Oh's achievements, however, he had never
even been mentioned once in Taiwan's official *United Daily News* until an April piece
celebrating Japanese youth's seemingly unanimous affection for the player they called
"Wang-Chang" (*sic*) appeared. In case this endorsement seemed troubling to Chinese
Nationalist readers still suspicious of Japan, the ideologically conscious reporter was
quick to praise Oh's Chinese virtues and to cite actress Awashima Chikage's observation
that Oh was "not just a Japanese Chinese but a world Chinese." (The author also, for
the benefit of the paper's many Taiwan mainlander readers, who were still unfamiliar
with the Japanese-seeming game of baseball, had to explain what a home run was.)
(Sima 1964: 2) As Oh dominated the baseball world that summer, winning his third
home run crown (setting a Japanese season record with fifty-five) and his first of nine
MVP awards, official ROC media began to pay more attention to the 24-year-old
titan with Chinese blood coursing through his heroic veins. One development that
began framing Oh as a straight and upstanding Wang was the September report that
he hoped within two or three years to marry a "female Chinese compatriot" ("Lü Ri
Huaqiao" 1964: 2).

In March 1965, the ROC government directly reached out to Oh by naming him
a winner of the annual Outstanding Overseas Chinese Youth Award ("Tianya hechu"
1965: 3). At the end of that year, the 25-year-old Oh made a celebrated and successful

(if erroneously termed) "return to his motherland" (*fan zuguo*) as Wang when he visited Taiwan for the first time—as KMT media put it, in order to "give tribute to the great President Chiang [Kai-shek]" ("Qiuwang zhi" 1965: 3; "Bangqiu wang" 1965).

Oh/Wang's eight days in Taiwan were a time of both great excitement and tension. His status as a hero of the Japanese baseball world was thrilling to native Taiwanese people who followed the game and who remembered keenly the importance of baseball during the colonial period. The former colonial rulers were long gone, but the Japanese influence on baseball was still strong. Literally every baseball coach in Taiwan for the next three decades was an alumnus of colonial rule; the majority of them saw this work as continuing the culture and way of life that they had learned for decades as Japanese subjects. Also, it was extremely common for Taiwanese baseball fans to have access to newspaper reports and magazines that were sent to Free China by their teachers, neighbors, and friends who had returned to Japan (Morris 2010: 65–72, 77).

At the same time, Oh's instant cache as (a son of) a fellow Chinese sojourner strongly appealed to Taiwan's mainlander population, even if they seemed to have extremely little knowledge about the game. After two decades in Taiwan, these emigres shared a keen sense of their isolation from their true Chinese homeland (Fan 2011: 59–62), at the same time that they saw themselves as the guardians of an authentic Chinese culture unsullied by the vulgarities and ravages of Maoism. What Stéphane Corcuff calls their "ambiguous sentiment of exile" (2011: 40–1)—their certainty that they represented an ideologically "real China" despite and because of their separation from a geographic China—primed this group to receive a Chinese-but-not-quite Superman like Oh, whose solid Zhejiang heritage and near ignorance of Chinese culture and language could be molded into an image of ROC greatness on the world stage.

The newly crowned MVP of Japanese baseball arrived at Taipei's Songshan Airport on December 4 to great fanfare. One of the distinct highlights of the official welcome, according to media reports, seems to have been the presentation of a wreath of flowers to Oh by Chang Mei-Yao, the beautiful Taiwanese movie star known as "Jade Maiden of the Treasure Island" (*baodao yunü*). Indeed, this detail was highly anticipated; its planning and background was the subject of a mid-length article on page 3 of that morning's *United Daily News* ("Meiren ru yu" 1965: 3).

The 24-year-old Chang, a native of Puli in central Taiwan, had been recruited into the official welcoming party by the leaders of the Japan-based [Baseball] Player Wang Zhenzhi Overseas Chinese Fan Club (*Wang Zhenzhi xuanshou Huaqiao houyuanhui*). The KMT-associated attachés and journalists who organized this extremely official "fan club" had taken it on themselves to accomplish an important mission—getting this Chinese baseball star out of his five-year relationship with Japanese girlfriend Koyae Kyoko and getting him engaged to a good Chinese wife (Suzuki 2005: 124–5). Such a virtuous maiden could help transform Oh into much more of a Wang and reclaim even more convincingly this son of a sojourner as a world-famous champion of the ROC regime.

The beautiful Chang did not disappoint in her performance. Four articles on page 3 of the next day's *United Daily News* were dedicated to Chang's warm welcome of Oh—from the way that her hand lingered on Oh's chest as she put the flowers around Oh's neck (Li 1965: 3), to the two hours and twenty minutes she spent seated next to Oh at dinner and a subsequent musical performance ("Keguan dui" 1965: 3), to a cruelly hopeful but probably inaccurate report that Oh's girlfriend Koyae recently had become engaged to another man ("Huiguo xinqing" 1965: 3). Labeling Oh and Chang "the man and woman of the moment," official media outlets like the *UDN* placed sizable bets that Oh's short trip "home" could be transformed into something much more significant. These details, however, also reveal much about the masculinist and heteronormative framing of the Oh/Wang narrative in Taiwan. The "motherland" welcoming Oh was meant to be a world designed by Chinese men, where female influence was important in the way it could be deployed strategically to help Baseball King Oh become Paterfamilias Wang. Few women ever entered into the Oh/Wang narrative—only Koyae and Chang as love interests and potential mothers of his future Chinese progeny, his mother Tōzumi as object of filial devotion, plus (soon) a special cameo by ROC First Lady Soong May-ling as moralizing matchmaker extraordinaire. The proper nationalizing orientation of this visit left little room for challenges to these masculinist assumptions.

Another issue at the heart of Oh's identity as Wang, long-lost son of the Republic, was addressed during his first day in Taiwan. Liu Tianlu, vice president of Oh's official ROC "fan club" and leader of Oh's entourage in Taiwan, made a dramatic and palpably defensive announcement to the press on the star's arrival. Lest anyone doubt his client's singular devotion to his fellow exiles in Taiwan, Lu described the Wang who resided in the heart of Oh: a "good and aware youth who loved his (*sic*) country [i.e. the ROC on Taiwan]," who had heroically, "resolutely refused the [PRC] commie bandits' shameless seduction" and invitations to visit the mainland ("Chicheng qiuchang" 1965: 3; "Jianju fu" 1965: 3). As explained below, anti-communism was an important element of how this glorious "return" was understood in Taiwan. This was not only for public consumption; KMT agents even took care to investigate the Japanese reporters who visited Taiwan with Oh—and even their families—in order to make sure that none of them harbored communist sympathies that could ruin the visit![3] In particular, though, Oh's rejection of the Chinese Communist Party's (CCP) efforts to lure Oh to their side of the China–Taiwan standoff and turn him into *their* Wang would remain an important part of the Oh/Wang persona in Taiwan for decades.

Oh's biographer Suzuki Hiroshi has examined the origins of this narrative of Oh's repudiation of the CCP's "seduction" and has identified a fairly innocent story as the only incident to which Liu could have been referring. In 1957, as the high school prodigy described above, Oh was interviewed alongside his father at their modest restaurant by a reporter from the *Tokyo Overseas Chinese Association Bulletin* (*Dongjing Huaqiao huibao*), the official publication of the body that organized Chinese Tokyoites' loyalties under PRC auspices. The reporter asked young Oh, "In the future would you want to return (*sic*) to the motherland and help develop the Chinese baseball world?" The polite 17-year-old, sounding both aware of his father's strong patriotism and also wary of signing up for anything too strange or distracting (the Communist Chinese baseball world?!), answered vaguely, "After I graduate from college I would like to return (*sic*) to China" (Suzuki 2005: 120).

Few overhearing this noodle-shop banter in 1957 would have termed this encounter "communist seduction." However, recasting this event in this way seemed to be necessary for two reasons. The first was simply that Japanese slugger Oh seemed to become a much more believable Chinese patriot Wang if he had some anti-communist accomplishment to advertise in Nationalist Taiwan. The second was perhaps more compelling: Oh's father Wang Shifu's patriotism toward the Chinese motherland was much more oriented toward the PRC, which ruled the mainland where he had actually grown up and lived for more than twenty years, than toward the ROC, which now could extend authority only over Taiwan, some 3 percent of the territorial "China" they claimed to represent. By the time of Oh's first visit to Taiwan, his father had returned to his home in Qingtian County, Zhejiang, three times, taking advantage of the liberalizing postfamine moment of 1962–1965 to take funds home to help pay for the electrification of his hometown (Suzuki 2005: 175). The senior Wang would eventually make a total of six trips to the PRC and was very open and honest about his preference for the PRC and a real China over the ROC's hopeless imagined sovereignty over the mainland (Suzuki 2005: 148–9). Indeed, when Oh and the Giants conducted spring training in Taizhong during February 1968, his mother joined the trip with a dozen members of the ROC's official Oh Fan Club. However, Oh's father did not make the trip—a decision directly related to the explicit PRC affiliation of his beloved Tokyo Overseas Chinese Association ("Quan Riben" 1968: 6; Suzuki 2005: 132–3).

The official Nationalist narrative of Oh as Wang the Chinese hero drew heavily on images of him as filial son. This trope was a crucial part of the official KMT discourse for decades—the Central Motion Pictures Company 1989 biopic on Oh was titled *Honor Thy Father* (and in Chinese, *Gan'en suiyue*, literally "Years of Gratitude") (He 1989). However, this element of the Oh-as-Wang narrative was directly contradicted by the equally strong emphasis on Oh's anti-communist outlook described above. Indeed, the Nationalist party-state that reified Confucian thought and conduct as part of their claim to sovereignty in China—and the constituents of which indeed bore very close personal witness to the tragedy of family divided by the Nationalist–Communist civil war—seemed very purposefully to use anti-communism as a wedge between Oh and his PRC-leaning father.[4] Biographer Suzuki has positioned this contradiction between loyalty to father and to "country" as one way of seeing Oh's Chinese-Japanese life as a "tragic" one: Oh's sports fame and newly discovered identity as ROC patriot and his father's decades of exile and pain pulling in opposite directions and ultimately forcing many difficult choices on both men (Suzuki 2005: 171–4). Even without this recourse to literary tropes, however, we can still see clearly how serious the ROC media and mythmakers were with this precious Chinese-Japanese resource. Oh's biography, skills, bearing, and looks presented the Nationalists with an opportunity to claim international mastery in a very important cultural realm.

Oh's eight days back "home" in the ROC were meant to posit a unique Nationalist Chineseness shared by Oh and his hosts in Taiwan. This comes through perhaps most vividly in the official "Baseball King Wang Zhenzhi in the Motherland" newsreel compiled and released by the Government Information Office. Starting with Oh's welcome by the beautiful Chang Mei-Yao and the airport press conference celebrating his imagined conquest over Communist duplicity, the newsreel shows us patriotic Wang's trip the next day to the Sun Yat-sen Museum to look at antique Chinese relics and then to Taipei County to lay a wreath for the late ROC Premier and Vice President Chen Cheng. Oh's much-anticipated hitting demonstration at Taipei Municipal Stadium delayed, Wang was taken instead to the offices of the ROC Baseball Association to present an autographed bat to association head Xie Dongmin.[5] This proved an uncomfortable event when Xie showed his utter unfamiliarity with the bat, which he clearly had no idea how to hold. Xie's fumbling and his pathetic attempt at a swing—screened throughout Taiwan on the official newsreel—visibly embarrassed his celebrated guest, who no doubt at that moment was feeling much more Oh than Wang ("Bangqiu wang" 1965).

Oh spent December 6 learning about the ROC's many Air Force martyrs, witnessing for the first time his "homeland's" scenery and visiting the Presidential Palace and the Foreign Ministry ("Bangqiu wang" 1965; "Qiuwang zhi" 1965: 3). He also had to continue to address both the published reports that he was in Taiwan to find a girlfriend and the nature of his new relationship with movie star Chang ("Huiguo xinqing" 1965: 3). It is revealing that the Nationalist media became so obsessive about these points where sexuality and masculinity would be crucial in establishing Oh's emerging identity as a thoroughly Chinese Wang.

Loyal KMT reporters were not the only ones asking Oh about his marriage plans and prospects of fathering a line of Nationalist sluggers for the glory of the ROC. KMT secretary-general Gu Fengxiang, when he met Oh, made sure to pry into his love life as though it were any of the party's business. One of the highlights of Oh's visit was supposed to be his audience with President Chiang Kai-shek on December 10; however, even during his twenty-minute chat with this great anti-communist titan, Oh still had to fend off First Lady Soong May-ling's offers to help "introduce a wife" to him (Suzuki 2005: 125). It becomes tempting to wonder if the Nationalists' policy of "motherlandifying" Oh into Wang actually helped him understand the limits of his Chinese identity. Biographer Suzuki has Oh standing up to the busybodies of his "Fan Club" and telling them that he had to refuse their offers in this department, insisting that he wanted to marry a woman who would concentrate on family, and not a movie star. And indeed, it only took Oh twenty-six days after leaving Taiwan to announce his engagement to long-time girlfriend Koyae Kyoko at a press conference in Tokyo's Hotel New Otani on January 6, 1966 (Suzuki 2005: 125–6).[6]

On his fourth day in Taiwan, however, Oh finally was able to get back to some baseball. On December 7, more than 30,000 fans showed up to watch him put on the free hitting demonstration that was postponed on the 5th. Taipei Municipal Stadium, built to accommodate at the very most 20,000, got rowdy as the spectators waited for Oh to arrive. While their hero was trying to get out of the long lunch banquet held in his honor by Work Groups #3 and #5 of the KMT Central Party

Headquarters, impatient and uncomfortable fans started spilling onto the field and brawling. Police had cleared most of these battles when Oh arrived and, in his street clothes, began demonstrating the one-legged "scarecrow" hitting style that he had mastered (see Figure 8.1). The rough atmosphere continued, with fans cursing the photographers who were crowding home plate and blocking their view, as well as the intimidated ROC Air Force pitcher who missed Oh's relaxed strike zone with his first ten pitches. Oh took forty swings in all, and provided (Japanese-language) narration about the elements of his famous swing. The event could only have seemed more appropriate in Japanese, representing—along with the crowd and violence— another element of this rare and exciting escape from Nationalist orthodoxy in the capital city ("Bangqiu wang" 1965; "Qiuwang zhi" 1965: 3; Suzuki 2005: 121–2). Oh's hosts made sure to nationalize the tone of the day, though. After watching the game between the Air Force and 10th Credit Union teams, Oh was whisked off to tours of the Taiwan Film Production Studios and the Government Information Office, which held another banquet for him, and then to meet Chiang Ching-kuo, son of President Chiang and head of Taiwan's secret police and the China Youth Anti-Communist National Salvation Corps (*Zhongguo qingnian fangong jiuguotuan*). Oh spoke in Japanese again at this meeting, his remarks translated by an official interpreter, before receiving a medal from Chiang.

These honors were not easily won, however; Oh's hosts in Taiwan were ruthless in their motherlandifying scheduling. On December 9, for example, Oh spent a day in and around Taizhong, the self-described "City of Culture," observing the proceedings

Figure 8.1 Oh Sadaharu puts on hitting demonstration at Taipei Municipal Stadium, December 7, 1965. Photo by Pan Yuekang, used with permission of Central News Agency (*Zhongyang tongxunshe*, Taiwan).

at the provincial assembly and being guided through the Chinese garden outside, visiting the provincial government inland at Zhongxing, taking in lectures on Taiwan's geology and models of its modern infrastructure, and finally putting on another hitting demonstration at the Taizhong Stadium (after speaking to the crowd, 23,000 strong and "so packed as to be watertight," through an interpreter). It could have been worse, however; after Oh left, newspapers told of the fury and hurt feelings among leaders of the Ningbo Natives' Association who, on the basis of their hailing from the same part of China as Oh's father, also felt owed a banquet with the star. (Their two hours of Oh's time was instead granted to Japan's ambassador to the ROC.) ("Bangqiu wang" 1965; Jian 1965: 2; "Qiuwang zhi" 1965: 3; Suzuki 2005: 122)

The official preoccupation with Oh/Wang says much about Nationalist attitudes toward baseball, a game that was still very foreign to almost any mainlander in Taiwan. The Nationalist party-state had long championed modern sports as a way of cultivating a unified, fit, and dutiful citizenry, but their focus was largely on soccer, basketball (the co-"national games" of China dating back to the 1930s) and the typical lineup of Olympic sports (Morris 2004: 120–242). Oh's visit did not seem to "raise the profile" of baseball at all—the game was already part of the lifeblood of Taiwanese culture, and general Nationalist attention to the game did not seem to deepen at all. For example, Oh's visit to Taiwan totally overshadowed the ROC's participation in the 6th Asian Baseball Championships in Manila, which took place the same week. On December 4, when Oh's itinerary in Taiwan merited a 1,194-word story in the government's *United Daily News*, the opening of Asia's biggest biennial competition got eighty-two words in the same paper ("Yazhou bangqiusai, jin" 1965: 2). Even with a win over eventual champions Japan, the ROC national baseball team had to share billing with news of the return of the national cycling team from their competition in Manila, receiving (in column space) much less than half as much as the piece on Oh's love life two days earlier ("Yazhou bangqiusai, wo" 1965: 2; Zhao 1965: 3). In all, the first fifteen days of December saw the *United Daily News* publish thirty-five articles on Oh's eight days in Taiwan and nine very short articles on the ten-day Asian Championships, a fair measure of how unimportant this still-Japanese game seemed to the ruling mainlanders unless it could directly reify mythologies of Chineseness in Nationalist Taiwan.

It is hard to know exactly how Oh's visit helped his understanding of his Chinese identity. There were moments when he seemed to warm to his role as Wang. Raised on tales of President Chiang Kai-shek's virtues, Oh seems to have been truly honored at the chance to meet the leader of Free China. But Chiang made his guest again end up feeling much more Oh than Wang when he asked Japan's finest baseball player if he would be "moving back to the motherland"! His gentle scolding of Oh for not being able to speak Mandarin probably only illuminated further the limits of this Tokyo native's ability to ever really be "Chinese." (Oh assured Chiang that he would be sure to work on his Mandarin Chinese before his next return to Taiwan. He never did, even though his wife Kyoko devoted many years to learning Chinese and always hired Mandarin tutors for their three daughters!) ("Zongtong gao" 1965: 2; Suzuki 2005: 123, 129–30)

Oh's reluctance to learn to speak Chinese, however, was not due to any lack of loyalty to his inherited "homeland." His commitment to ROC citizenship was the source of much inconvenience as this budding star found new opportunities to travel around the world, his ROC passport meaning little in many countries that recognized the PRC. Even travel between Japan and Taiwan was difficult; his status as an Overseas Chinese required special immigration procedures in Taipei, while his status as a "foreigner" meant that he had to be fingerprinted every time he returned to Japan (Suzuki 2005: 152–3). Oh's insistence on keeping ROC citizenship—as opposed to Japanese and PRC citizenship, both of which were offered to Oh many times, and the latter of which his father eventually accepted (Zeng and Yu 2004: 136)—for the last four decades does indicate the loyalty and regard he came to feel for the people and government of Taiwan and the gratitude he felt for their warm support and long-lasting interest in his career.

Oh-chan, mangy cur: Nationality and tragedy

Oh returned to Taiwan twice more in the 1960s. His second visit was on the occasion of his honeymoon with Koyae, after a sensational Meiji Jingu Shrine wedding on December 1, 1966 (Suzuki 2005: 127–8). The first reports of this Taiwan honeymoon brought two very welcome pieces of news as the KMT's traditionalist and anti-communist Chinese Cultural Renaissance Movement (*Zhonghua wenhua fuxing yundong*) got under way in November. Nationalist newspapers were ecstatic to report that Oh's new wife was actually adopting ROC citizenship under the Sinified name Wang Gongzi ("Bangqiu zhi wang" 1966: 3; "Riben xiaojie" 1966: 3). Even more exciting was the news that this honeymoon was the result of yet one more heroic refusal of Communist seduction; the PRC's offer to Oh's father to host the newly married Wangs—amazingly, as the Great Proletarian Cultural Revolution was raging there—was "strictly refused" by the newly (ROC) Chinese baseball great ("Wang Zhenzhi xia" 1966: 3).

Good sports, the couple took time out of their busy schedule at beautiful Sun Moon Lake to appear at a nearby baseball game between Taiwan Cooperative Bank and Japan Oil, and then to visit President Chiang and his wife Soong May-ling at their Blue Jade Mansion mountain villa (built by the Japanese in 1916) ("Hanbilou" 1966: 2; "Wang Zhenzhi jin" 1966: 3). Records of this presidential audience reveal another round of scolding from the Generalissimo and Madame Soong over Oh's inability to speak Chinese, although Kyoko/Gongzi saved significant face by telling their hosts that she hoped to live in Taiwan forever. The *Profundity News* reported on a touching moment during this audience, when the visitors stood up to bow to Chiang and Soong when they mentioned their upcoming fortieth wedding anniversary. There was also a somewhat crass one on their exit, though, when the president presented Oh and Koyae with two coins commemorating his eightieth birthday and offered to pay for their hotel stay ("Jiang zongtong" 1966).

Oh tried his new bride's patience a bit further when this event was followed by meetings with the vice president, the minister of education, and the leader of the China Youth Anti-Communist National Salvation Corps (Suzuki 2005: 130). Just when they thought they were finished with this leg of the honeymoon and could leave for Honolulu, the couple got stuck in the Taipei airport after Oh left his passport with his Japanese-Chinese guide. Reporters got a piece of Oh again, and he told politely of his affection for Taiwan's food and friendly spirit, and promised (again) that he would soon get around to studying Chinese with his wife ("Nanwang zuguo" 1966: 3).

Just over one year later, Oh's third trip to his new "homeland" was even more momentous for the Taiwanese baseball world. In February 1968, his Yomiuri Giants team, three championships into their "V9" decade of dominance, carried out their spring training in Taizhong. Eager to impress their world-famous guests, Taiwan's provincial government quickly renovated the Taizhong Municipal Stadium for the training session (Zeng and Yu 2004: 139). Six young standout players from the Provincial Physical Education College, whose campus backs up against the stadium, were allowed to train with these gods, who they actually found "affable, genial and easy to approach" ("Tizhuan" 1968: 6). An 8 mm film made by baseball player/artist Chen Yanchuan of Oh and his teammate Nagashima Shigeo taking batting practice circulated for years in pre-TV baseball circles in Miaoli (Xie 2005).

It was on this occasion when Oh made a remark that has encouraged historian Zeng Wencheng to call the baseball star "the great tragic figure of his age" (Suzuki 2005: preface 3–4). Oh was socializing with the Japanese wife of Cai Bingchang, a 1950s pitching star from Jiayi, when she asked about his nationality. "I don't plan to take Japanese citizenship," Oh answered sadly, "and it is a good thing I don't have a son" (Suzuki 2005: 160). (His three daughters could someday achieve Japanese citizenship through marriage, but his choice to keep ROC citizenship would restrict a son to this one option.) If Oh went above and beyond the call of Confucian duty with his filial and reverent treatment of his parents, his relief at not fulfilling another Chinese imperative—producing a son—strikes Zeng and biographer Suzuki as a sign of the cruelest punishment of his principled stand.

Even as the all-time home run champion of the world, Oh faced racist insults and humiliations in Japan that may have required him to respond via an inner iron Wang. The day after Oh broke Henry Aaron's world record with his 756th career home run in September 1977, Prime Minister Fukuda Takeo presented him with the first-ever People's Honor Award (*Kokumin eiyoshō*). However, Fukuda immediately and unbelievably "was criticized by those who felt that a foreigner should not receive such an award" (Wetherall 1981: 411n51). And even after Oh's playing career was over, when he managed the Giants from 1981 to 1988, he still had to contend with players more loyal to his longtime teammate/rival Nagashima and his "pure-blooded Japanese aura." Even the team captain at that time, Nakahata Kiyoshi, a loyal "Nagashima man," would behind Oh's back refer to his manager as "*wan-kō*," a pun on his Chinese surname Wang and also on his uniform number 1, but also a slur that can be translated as "mongrel" or "mangy cur" (Cromartie with Whiting 1991:

122, 124; Whiting 2008). It is perhaps for reasons like this that, in 1997, when Oh was listed as a "famous Japanese" by the national New History Textbook Committee, Oh angrily insisted they take his name out: "I am not Japanese and I have no place in Japanese historical education!" (Suzuki 2005: 159)

Years of gratitude: Beyond Oh's playing career

On August 31, 1977, Oh tied Aaron with the 755th home run of his career. The conservative Nationalist scold who authored *United Daily News*' "In Black and White" column—and who for years was reliable in his disdain for the Japanese remnant of baseball—in a terse editorial gave Oh credit for the gratitude he showed his parents and for the example he could serve for the youth of society: "too many of whom forget their ancestors, who find some small achievement and forget where they come from, who surely will never succeed or accomplish anything meaningful" ("'Heibaiji'" 1977: 3). The day after tying Aaron's mark, Oh was able to meet with the teenage heroes of Taiwan's world champion LLB Senior League and Big League squads during a Tokyo layover. He congratulated the young men for what they had sacrificed and accomplished as a team. KMT oldtimer Ma Shuli, in the luncheon as the ROC's de facto ambassador, was more to the point, praising Oh's slugging efforts as representing "the spirit that is the best means of rescuing our 800 million mainland compatriots [living under communism] and retaking the rivers and mountains of the mainland" (Yu 1977: 3). For all of Oh's loyalty to the ROC and his gratitude for the support of the people of Taiwan, he most likely never could have been Wang enough to understand this kind of hyperbolic and archaic discourse.

Since the end of his playing career, Oh has continued to play an important role in the development of baseball in Taiwan, offering moral and technical support and helping standout players sign with Japanese teams. For all of this effort, however, Oh is probably still much better known in Taiwan for the ideological weight of his legacy—for some, again, the Chinese champion triumphing against Japanese discrimination, or, for others, a fellow Japanese subject escaping the shackles of his Chinese ancestry.

In the very last years of KMT one-party rule on Taiwan, Oh emerged once again as one of the great heroes of these besieged authoritarians. After a summer where Oh's mother's memoirs were serialized over seventy-nine days in *Minshengbao*, an official Nationalist tabloid-style newspaper (Oh 1985), plans were unveiled in 1985 for one of Taiwan's state film studios to make a movie based on Oh's life. *Honor Thy Father*—the title an obvious reference to the imagined uniquely Chinese value of filial piety—was meant to stake claim to a firm moral ground for the KMT as it continued to be embarrassed by the successful mainland reforms of the PRC and the steps toward legitimacy by Taiwan's illegal opposition movement. Publicity for the film even dipped into that old reservoir of anti-communist heroism with the *United Daily News*' claim that the star (as Wang) had "harshly refused" PRC and even Japanese bids to make an Oh biopic ("Junju Zhonggong" 1985: 9).

The film, eventually released in 1989 by the state's Central Motion Pictures Company, attempted to finally set down a strong case for the slugger to be understood as a Chinese hero who triumphed over the blatant discrimination suffered by Oh, his father, and his brother in Japan. *Honor Thy Father* features one virtuous Japanese character, his personal batting coach Arakawa Hiroshi, who works continuously with Oh and even learns to make a fine plate of Chinese noodles in the process. But the rest of the "Japanese" cast exist as simply a faceless backdrop of haters, worshipping fans, or haters-turned-worshipping fans. The Nationalist judgment, made here just at the historical moment that the party's "Chinese" character was being finally exposed as illegitimate, was clear: Oh's place in history was as a wise and humble hero of the Chinese race.

This identity has been challenged in recent years by explicitly (if not gratuitously) Taiwanese politicians fond of Oh's Japanese heritage, and then again by Nationalist loyalists invested in Oh as a "Chinese" hero. This has placed Oh in the middle of Taiwan's recent explicit repoliticization of baseball, as he has been the conspicuous guest of pandering politicians all across the blue–green spectrum since 1999. In 2001, during President Chen Shui-bian's first eight months in office, he awarded Oh with a 3rd-Class Presidential Order of the Brilliant Star and named him ROC Ambassador without Portfolio ("Sadaharu Oh named" 2001). Not to be outdone, though, Taipei's KMT mayor Ma Ying-jeou threw out the first pitch at a home game for the Oh-managed Fukuoka Hawks ("Taipei mayor" 2001). His party also teamed with the explicitly pro-unificationist People First Party (*Qinmindang*) in hosting Oh's Hawks in Taiwan in 2003, and made news by not inviting President Chen to sit in the VIP seats ("Baseball strikes" 2003: 2).

Two years later, President Chen was in trouble again after his Democratic Progressive Party's disastrous showing in the 2005 local elections. Chen quickly played one of his few remaining trumps, making an ostentatious show of welcoming Oh to Taiwan (Lin 2005). Ma had to wait four more years to top Chen and reclaim Oh as Wang for the Nationalists, but in February 2009, now as ROC president, he conferred the Order of Brilliant Star with Grand Cordon (*Erdeng jingxing xunzhang [dashou]*) on Oh in Taipei. Ma had to have been satisfied when Oh said that this was "the greatest honor of his life" ("President confers" 2009).

Oh has been a rare figure, able as one of the most famous Japanese and Chinese people in the world to inspire Taiwanese and Chinese people of almost all backgrounds and ideologies. The crass political pulls—toward the "Chineseness" of the Nationalist Party or toward the Taiwanese appreciation of Japan as fetishized by the Democratic Progressive Party—will likely last the rest of his life, just as his obvious dignity and humility will likely allow him to personally transcend these short-term political considerations.

In 2012, almost half a century after Oh Sadaharu was instantly made into such an iconic figure in Taiwan, another faraway star instantly captured the attentions and affections of the Taiwanese sporting public. The then-New York Knick point guard Jeremy Lin (Lin Shuhao), the Taiwanese-American Harvard graduate who sparked the NBA's "Linsanity" sensation with his out-of-nowhere successes in February 2012, was the focus of an even greater media storm in his parents' home country of Taiwan. While Lin has more of a clear ancestral and cultural connection to Taiwan than did Oh in the 1960s, the general outlines of the phenomenon are the same; as Soochow University political scientist Liu Bi-rong told the Associated Press, "Jeremy Lin may not consider himself a Taiwanese, and his success has had nothing to do with Taiwan, but Taiwanese regard him as one of their own" (Ghosh 2012).[7] And the story even has a similar "China wants him too" angle as well; Taiwan's Central News Agency reported in 2011 that Lin had been approached by the PRC to join their national team for that year's FIBA Asia Championship.[8]

Lin's career arc will not be the same as Oh's; he will not dominate the NBA or be remembered as the best ever. And despite the unpleasant intimations of anti-Asian racism that he has faced, his life in the United States will not be defined, as was Oh's, by institutionalized racial and national discrimination. Lin has a freedom that Oh never had to craft and articulate his own ethnocultural identity. Basketball culture in 2010s Taiwan, despite the game's clear historical roots in American culture, carries nothing of the transgressive thrill that defined 1960s baseball culture as Taiwanese diehards propagated this Japanese game under KMT rule. One wonders if in 2060 Lin could be as universally loved and esteemed as Oh is today after half a century of his life as Wang in Taiwan.

However, Lin's instant yet familiar fame in Taiwan reminds us of the vulnerabilities, tensions, outward orientation, desires, and fears that still define life on the Beautiful Island: their status as a nation vis-à-vis Japan, the United States, and China, Taiwanese/mainlander ethnic politics, and the idealized importance of sport in Taiwanese/Chinese culture at the same time that these elite athletes could only have thrived outside of Taiwan. These routine if still significant gestures to Japanese and American culture, as much as ever, help to define the limits of Chineseness in the Nationalist-ruled former colony.

Oh Sadaharu's career in Taiwan as Wang Zhenzhi helps illuminate the complicated nexus of Taiwanese, Chinese, and Japanese culture and identity that churned in 1960s and 1970s Taiwan. The Taiwanese majority loved Oh/Wang because he fit the narrative of Japanese modernity and progress that they believed defined their island's twentieth century. The Japanese game of baseball had allowed the handsome Oh to rise from the kitchen of his father's modest noodle shop, in the way that many of them imagined a half-century of Japanese rule to have lifted Taiwan from a limbo of Chinese neglect. At the same time, Taiwan's recent mainland Chinese immigrants, convinced of the righteousness of KMT rule and of their continued victimization by Japanese and Chinese Communist enemies, were thrilled by the visible triumphs of the Chinese superstar Wang. Oh/Wang's fundamental dignity, humility, and kindness worked to soothe many of East Asia's twentieth-century traumas as Taiwanese and Chinese residents struggled over the meanings and future of the island. Taiwan was Japanese no more, but the king of baseball's long reign as a unanimous hero and role model for colonial nostalgist and anti-communist alike provided a rare instance of cultural concord during more than two decades of Chinese Nationalist one-party rule.

Notes

1   Suzuki (2005); this book is a translation of Suzuki (2002). One notes that the title of the Chinese translation—for all of the "Chinese culture/filial piety" discourse that revolves around Oh's persona in Taiwan—is the one that does not mention his father.

2   Oh also set a record for the tournament (*Senbatsu kōtō gakkō yakyū taikai*) by pitching thirty-four consecutive innings without giving up an earned run.

3   On the other hand, these Japanese reporters accompanying Oh to Taiwan were also interviewed as important figures in their own right (Suzuki 2005: 123, 119).

4   In 1973, official ROC media reported that Oh's father had sent money to his nephew in the PRC, only to have it confiscated. Mr. Wang went as far as to publish an article in the *Tokyo Overseas Chinese Association Bulletin* attacking the ROC-supported *Liberty News* (*Ziyou xinwen*) for misrepresenting what was actually just a delay; *Liberty News* was headed by Zhang Hexiang, also head of the official ROC Oh Overseas Fan Club (Suzuki 2005: 147–8).

5   Xie was a native Taiwanese who had lived in Nationalist China for twenty years, studying, working in journalism, and eventually taking a crucial role in wartime propaganda and political work. Figures like Xie—known to Taiwanese as "half-mountain people" (*banshanren*, for their loyalties to the mainland KMT regime)—seemed to appear to the Nationalists inherently more reliable in handling the dangerous "Japanese" realm of baseball, despite the fact that their extended tenure in China would mean by definition real unfamiliarity with the game. As a measure of the esteem with which he was held within the KMT, in 1972 Xie would be named governor of Taiwan Province and in 1978 vice president of the Republic of China (Morris 2010: 58–9).

6   The KMT's *United Daily News* reacted with distinctly sour grapes, accusing Oh of explicitly disregarding his father's wishes and misleading the gossips and bores who had harassed him about his personal life during his Taiwan visit ("Fujia qian" 1966: 3).

7   Thanks to Kenneth Cohen for helping me think about the connection between these two honorary Taiwanese icons.

8   This request was made on the basis of Lin's maternal grandmother having been born in Zhejiang (also Oh's father's home province) ("Lin considering" 2011).

9

Haunted Island: Reflections on the Japanese Colonial Era in Taiwanese Cinema

Corrado Neri

The colony

The year 1895 was a pivotal year for the history of Asia and the history of arts: while in France the first public projection of the "cinématographe" was going to change forever the notions of realism and narration, the Treaty of Shimonoseki sealed Taiwan's fate of becoming the first Japanese colony. The cinema is stammering, groping, and hesitating, but soon turns out to be a powerful weapon of propaganda and indoctrination. At the same time, the films are incredible windows opened to the world: for the Taiwanese, they represent the opportunity to discover both the "Western" and the Japanese civilization—the two cultures that are starting to reshape the island, its identity, its politics, and its everyday life, as well. Stimulated by the Japanese government, Taihoku becomes a modern capital, equipped with movie halls—as well as theaters, dance halls, modern transports, and electric lights.

Yet, the local cinematographic production stays underdeveloped. Perhaps because of its mostly decentralized geographical position, Taiwan will never become the center of cinematographic production as can be said about Manchuria—the predominant source of cross-border pan-Asian imagery. This does not prevent the colonial government from supporting the distribution and projection of Japanese films, as well as the typical aspects of the Japanese cinematographic culture, like *benshi* and *rensageki*, for example, in Taiwan. The term *benshi* refers to a person who sits near the screen in the dark auditorium, reads and translates the subtitles interpreting their content, explains the history of the film, comments on the images, and, in a postmodern manner far ahead of its time, also talks about the means of production, the camera, the ways the films were made, and the actors who play in them. A *benshi* can become a star, with his name listed on the posters in fonts larger than the names of the actors; yet, although the profession seemed destined to vanish, we can still find artists who perform this art in the cultural manifestations linked to the silent film. *Rensageki* is another hybrid form which brings live performance and the "true" cinema together: the actors play out the scenes of the film in front of the camera that records it, and afterwards during the projection, they are on the scene giving voice to their characters and connecting the sequences (Baskett 2008). Even though the import of Japanese films is very significant, many works keep arriving from China until the 1930s, tolerated by the colonial administration. The influence of the Chinese civilization on Taiwanese intelligentsia is still very strong, although a bit washed-out at the beginning of the twentieth century. The 1920s are a liberal and cosmopolitan period, at least for the elite who can travel relatively freely, and have the means to enjoy the exuberance of the urban and cultural life, while taking advantage of the seemingly infallible economic expansion.

For the Japanese producers, Taiwan is a perfect place for films like *The Braves of Mount Ali* (*Arisan no kyōji*, dir. Tasaka 1927), aimed both at the internal Japanese market and the utopian pan-Asian market. As Wafa Ghermani explains,

> For the Japanese, the films made in Taiwan were the means to let city residents and the locals discover the new colony, with its wild side (the aboriginals) and the benefits of colonization. The fiction films, produced with the Taiwanese financial contributions, but made by the Japanese crew, were always under close surveillance. (2009a: 21)

The descriptions of Taiwan are at the same time orientalist and exotic—the land of savages, mysterious rituals, tribal dances, and diseases caused by the tropical climate. Moreover, the films are also suitable means of propaganda focusing on the creation of an Asian community guided by Japan, the source of civilization. Japan represents itself as a shield against Western invasion, wishing to be a modern industrialized country, and—as the newsreels, vastly spreading in schools and public places in the motherland, as well as in the colonies, testify—it is the only Asian country whose military defeated a Western country (Russia during their 1904–1905 war). Many educational films are made in 16 mm format—and shot in Japanese. These films are unfortunately lost; according to the descriptions in the written sources, these were geographic or animal documentaries about the "intact" nature of the island, the ethnographic films about the traditions of its inhabitants, as well as reports about the activities of the Japanese government in Taiwan. Many descriptions are ideologically marked by evocating the benefits of Japanization: industrial development, modernity of the cosmopolitan life of Taihoku, and so on. The colonizer is portrayed as benevolent and paternalistic: educators, doctors, police officers, and soldiers exert their authority firmly and righteously, assisted by the cooperation of local inhabitants.

Yet, the situation changes in the 1930s, as the tension between Japan and China intensifies. After the Manchuria Incident of 1931 and the 1932 bombing of Shanghai, the majority of films made in the Republic of China are more and more openly anti-Japanese. Japanese censorship operates on two fronts: eliminating conflicting images likely to link Taiwan to the mainland and creating new ones that serve the political agenda now leaning toward ultra-nationalism. From the 1930s on, the Japanese propaganda becomes more powerful and aims at making its colonies part of the empire, suppressing the local identities and idealizing the civilizing role of Japan. Local languages are forbidden in public places, classes at schools are taught in Japanese, the altar for worshiping *kamis* is placed in homes, and members of the elite have to adopt a Japanese name. This politics called *kōminka* is officially imposed in Taiwan in 1937, when the conflicts with China escalate, introducing the "imperialization" of colonial subjects, their forced assimilation within the Greater East Asia Co-Prosperity Sphere. Still marked by a strong anti-Western sentiment, the government demands the subjects of the emperor to enroll in the army and fight for Japan, awarding them the right to die for the ruler. One of the most frequent themes in Taiwanese literature (written in Japanese and Chinese language) is this desire, contradictory and unfulfilled, to become a "true" Japanese, the loyal subject of the emperor.[1] The cinema is used, along with science, as a weapon of propaganda and education. In 1941, the Taiwanese Cinematographic Association (*Eiga kyōkai*) joins the Taiwanese Educational Society (*Kyōikukai*), which was founded by the government to promote Japanese culture in Taiwan: cinema, like all other forms of expression, cannot ignore World War II anymore. During the 1930s, the Taiwanese students are shown the most famous places in Japan, they learn the national anthem, watch the cherry blossoms—and thereby already begins to spread the aestheticization of death in battle which will become the leitmotiv of the recruitment imposed during the last years of the Pacific War (Ohnuki-Thierney 2002). *Pirates of the Seas* (*Umi no gōzoku*, dir. Arai 1942), for example, is set in the seventeenth century and tells the story of the Asian battle (the Japanese based in Taiwan) against the Dutch for the supremacy over the seas.

Sayon's Bell (*Sayon no kane*, dir. Shimizu 1943) is probably the most representative film, showing the efforts of militarization and Japanization. It is supposedly inspired by a true story, according to the propaganda. Sayon, a young Indigenous girl, is especially attached to her teacher, educated in Japan, who is leaving to go to war against China. Sayon supports him, and accompanies him in the pouring rain; yet, after shouting the last "Banzai!" she falls into the river and drowns. The imperial government erects a bell in the young girl's native village to honor the spirit and the devotion of the martyr. The idealistic representation of the Pax Nipponica is obvious: everyone—including the villagers—speaks Japanese flawlessly. All of the big symbols of the imperialist culture are there: Japan is manly and warlike (that is the place where one learns to fight), and the colony is feminine and in need of protection. The role of Sayon, the ideal colonial subject, is played by Yamaguchi Yoshiko, aka Li Xianglan/Ri Koran.[2] In the film *Sayon's Bell* peasant values (solidarity, the central importance of the community and the family) are particularly emphasized. The villagers, although perfectly mastering the language of the colonizer, are represented performing their strange apotropaic and primitive dances. The gaze of the camera records, in a documentary manner, the primitive traditions of the locals—their clothes in high colors, the stubbornly highlighted lack of shoes, and the distant awe exhibited during the flag-raising ceremony. This film is dedicated to the patriotism and civilized transformation of the loyal subjects, to the regional government and to the devoted police officers.

Sayon's Bell was evoked/parodied decades later in *Island Etude* (*Lianxi qu*, dir. Chen 2006), a film that tells the story of a young man who travels around Taiwan on a bicycle, describes the people he meets on his journey, and offers a dreamlike episode evoking this chapter of Japanese legacy. First, the young protagonist stops to look at a group of tourists who are admiring the bell of Sayon, while listening to the explanations of their guide. Then, without interruption, a dreamlike sequence unfolds: asleep, the main actor dreams of a remake of the episode of the film from 1943. Illuminated by the bluish beams of light, a young girl accompanies the soldiers going to the front; the atmosphere remains serene, seductive, and mysterious. We are far from the portrait of the Japanese soldier as a sadistic stereotype like the ones we could see in the propaganda films of the 1950s and 1960s. More and more frequently, the Japanese colonization is represented, in the 1990s and 2000s, like a politics that left a positive cultural heritage; this contributed to reinforcing an assumed originality of the Taiwanese identity (precisely mixed and multicultural) as opposed to continental China—more and more influential in Asia and in general in the global geopolitical arena on the economic front and, subsequently, on the cultural front.

In 2008, the National Museum of Taiwan History, located in Tainan, restored and published in DVD format a series of documentaries made by the Japanese during the colonial era. Even though the discourse of fiction films often represents Taiwan as a barbaric and backward society, these documentaries show, on the contrary, a modernized, rich, and multicultural colony. The colonial administration is proud to lead the countries that fall under its control out of "savagery" and underdevelopment in which they were immersed previously under Chinese/Manchu rule, claiming the duty to protect them from the influence of Western imperialism. Just like the much hated and resented Western powers did in their colonies, the Japanese shaped the industrial development and ways of communication, and established banks and post offices. The propaganda documentaries, rarely seen today, are mostly about convincing the subjects of the emperor (whether in Taiwan or in Japan) of the benefits of the colonization. *Southward Expansion into Taiwan* (*Nanshin Taiwan* 1935) outlines a tour of the island and revises the regime's technological achievements, especially dwelling on the modernization of industry and urbanism. The focus is also on the ancient and abandoned tradition of the binding of women's feet, emphasizing the evolution in customs—but also taking care to feature the local beauties and the legitimizing colonial phenomenon of cultural blending, with girls in *qipao* and ladies in *kimono* all walking down the street. In the first part of the film, an off-screen voice declares the following:

> Because of population growth, Japan has exhausted its natural resources... we need to create a defense line in the South, and Taiwan is right there... Formosa is an important base for the expansion of the Empire towards the south. Therefore, we need to understand contemporary Taiwan in details. It is a rich island, bathed in sunlight and warmth, a source of wealth for Japan... a dream island in the south... Earlier, Taiwan had been regarded by the Qing Government as a wasteland with uncivilized inhabitants. But through the assimilation process the Japanese Government has succeeded in turning them into loyal subjects of the Empire.

Other documentaries, like *Tainan Prefecture Civilian Dojo* (*Tainan-shū Kokumin dōjō* 1943), for example, are about the proto-military training of the Taiwanese youth.

Guided by severe Japanese discipline, the young Taiwanese spend an obligatory period in the barracks where they learn to march, handle weapons, pray to the *kamis*, honor the emperor, and endure the physical tests their trainers impose, such as taking a bath in the river we imagine to be frozen, involving in forced marches, and waking up at dawn. The young men also learn the language and lodestar principles of Japanese civilization. The last sequence, particularly impressive, shows the graduation ceremony. The young Taiwanese, impeccably lined in rows, salute the Japanese flag and pledge allegiance to the emperor:

> These subjects are taking the oath to devote themselves to the sacred imperial war. Their devotion is evident in the ceremony: "I solemnly swear to offer my entire life to the Emperor; I am ready to sacrifice it for the great cause of establishing the Great Japanese Empire. I swear to undertake the meditation exercises, not to let my spirit wander, but to continually search for the knowledge of the world. After I quit the *dojo*, I will do my best to eradicate all the distracting thoughts in order to pursue my quest for knowledge."

Subsequently, they become the true "subjects of the Empire": stepping out of savagery, renouncing the status of the "primitive," entering the aristocracy of the imperial civilization. The 2008 restoration of these documentaries by the National Museum of Taiwan History reminds us that the colonial past is no longer suppressed—on the contrary, officially and scientifically debated in the public arena and even commodified into sophisticated souvenirs and novelties.

The great masters revise the story

After 1945, Taiwan "goes back" to China, even if, as we know, this was an ambiguous "return": the Qing dynasty that ceded the island to Japan does not exist anymore. Taiwan "returns" to its motherland, but the artificiality of expressing themselves in the official Japanese language (in the Taiwanese context) is replaced by the inauthenticity of expressing themselves in Mandarin. The key terms for understanding the cultural politics of Taiwan are "exile," "remembrance," and the "orphan syndrome." Exile is immediately associated with the separation from the motherland—and soon enough from the international community which recognizes the PRC as the rightful "China." Cultural memory is equally related to the land of the ancestors, where the tombs of the forefathers and the remains of the glorious historical past are located. As for the "orphan syndrome" (see Ma 2009), we can ask the following question: Do the Taiwanese feel more like the orphans of China or of Japan?

Taiwan certainly goes through social and political changes that bring it closer to a contemporary democratic system—an ideology that had already penetrated the Taiwanese collective imagination during the "Taishō democracy" era. Taiwan adopts a democratic system during the 1990s with universal suffrage elections and the birth of several political parties. Non-Manichean narratives of Japanese domination start to spread from the 1990s; there are mentions of violence and deception of the colonial yoke, but at the same time, some films now also depict a nostalgic portrait of the remarkable figures of the Japanese administration, of the technical progress introduced by the colonizers, and the relationships of love or affections created between the two ethnic groups. See, for example, the very influential *The Puppetmaster* (*Xi meng rensheng*, dir. Hou 1993), where we can find both of these aspects as interconnected and complementary. One sequence shows the Japanese superintendents asking the male population to cut off their queue—a distinctive sign of identity and belonging to the Qing dynasty. The other episodes evoke how the master of puppets (the protagonist Li Tianlu) was able to survive during the war, that is, modifying his repertoire: discarding the traditional stories of the emperors, warriors, and concubines, and introducing the stories of heroic imperial soldiers who fight in the Pacific and die for the glory of Japan (in these episodes a change regarding language also takes place: Taiwanese is out and Japanese takes over). In the same film, upon evoking the departure of the colonizers, Hou films the sequences portraying the students in tears saying goodbye to their beloved Japanese professors.

In *A Borrowed Life* (*Duosang*, dir. Wu 1994), an autobiographic story of one of the main Taiwanese intellectuals (a screenwriter, novelist, and film director), the son has to confront his father who claims he belongs to the Japanese culture, calling himself *Duosang*, which is the Taiwanese (phonetic) version of the Japanese *otōsan* (father). The father suffers after the end of the colonial period and does not accept the "restoration" of Chinese governance; tragically, this shift makes him no longer attuned to the contemporary society or in unity with his children. This movie helps the contemporary public to develop a more nuanced view of history and its influence on lower-class workers, developing a complex discourse of intertwined emotions. The public can hardly relate to the stubborn, macho/patriarchal father figure, yet in the film a deep affection clearly transpires for the hard-working, silent, and frustrated *Otōsan*. It is hard to emit a clear-cut judgment (both on the nostalgia of the main protagonist and the lack of comprehension shown by his "modern" daughter, imbued with Chinese Nationalist education); it is precisely this ambiguity that gives its relevance to *A Borrowed Life* (Chen 2008). If we consider that Wu is one of the most famous and influent voice of an "authentic" Taiwanese culture, this film resonates with further implications in the definition of a shifting "identity"—both personal and national.

Besides the contradictions related to different readings of history, it is particularly clear, in this film, that speaking about the heritage of Japanese domination means to speak about Taiwanese identity itself, notably in contrast with Mainland China. As Lu Tonglin has convincingly demonstrated,

> Instead of serving as an external other against which national identity could be defined, colonial Japan offers a counterpoint to mainland China in the reformulation of Taiwanese identity, after four decades of the Nationalist Party's China-centered ideology, and Communist China's military threat of the 1990s. (Lu 2011: 765)

The sympathetic description of Japanese culture is unique in Taiwan—compared to other former colonies. This is to be drawn to the confrontation with China but also, again following Lu Tonglin, to the Nationalist imposition of the four-decade-long martial law. Lu argues thus:

> If nostalgia for the Japanese colonial period has a broader retrospective appeal among the Taiwanese of Duosang's generation than it has historically, ironically, this has more to do with the Nationalists' accusation of Taiwanese "enslavement" at the initial stage of their power than with the success of *kōminka*, which was largely limited to the educated upper class. This partly explains why Taiwan is the only former colony in which this nostalgia is publicly professed. (Lu 2011: 767)

Duosang—and his generation—has been disempowered by the arrival of the Guomindang: his Japanese education became suddenly useless (or suspicious), and his poor Mandarin skills made him redundant in the ROC era. Drawing a parallel—proposed by Wu himself—between his father and former president Lee Teng-hui, Lu argues that nostalgic representation of Japan is more than a deconstruction of nationalism or a cultural relativism. It is used instead as the image of the (missing) Other/Father in opposition to the pre-1987 (martial law-era) Nationalist Party and/or to the contemporary menacing political, economic, and cultural hegemony of China, an image of postideological consumerism as well as a politicization that declines different definition of local identities.

Viva Tonal: The musical memory

Numerous other texts recall the Japanese cultural heritage with sympathy and nostalgia. Several contemporary Taiwanese films show a problematic and ambiguous relationship with Japan, at the same time marked by nostalgia, reverie, and regret for the departure of the ancient colonizer. The documentary *Viva Tonal, the Dance Age* (*Tiaowu shidai*, dir. Chien and Kuo 2003) recounts the story about the spread of gramophones in Taiwan under occupation in the 1930s–1940s. The interviewees, old pop music stars, express themselves in a mixture of Mandarin, Taiwanese, and Japanese language; and often sing in the language of the former occupant, the language of their artistic glory, the language of the golden age of Taiwanese popular culture at the beginning of modernity. *Viva Tonal* was supported by the government and press and brought to public attention by former ROC president Lee Teng-hui (the DVD collector's edition booklet features an appraising article by Lee). Can we say then that the Taiwanese represent themselves as deprived of a voice, or that this film—which was a big success, and was shown in cinemas for months, and then broadcast on TV and even available in video and book stores—indicates a deprivation of voice? Or yet, does it portray the pleasure of speaking in a borrowed—and really fascinating—voice of the old colonizer? Aren't we facing a symbol of the specific Taiwanese identity (a hypothetical concept) which is erased in the name of the victorious and lamented model of the old occupier? In any case, the mixture of languages and cultures cited above relies, all in all, on a very positive vision of the colonial period. Even when they do not sing in Japanese, the aesthetic model comes straight from the Tokyoite craze of that period, about the popular culture (mainstream?) of the Western model, but reviewed and adapted to the Asian context.

The paradigms of love

We have already mentioned the quotation from *Sayon's Bell* (1943) in a sequence of *Island Etude* (2006). This film gives us the opportunity to evaluate the presence and persistence of a love paradigm between the two countries. Paradoxically, we could even say that Japan—as a social body, the myth of pan-Asian (post)modernity—stays (or imposes itself again as) the object of desire and nostalgia. These contemporary representations tackle different themes which express various modalities of the relationship to the other, where the other—Japan—ignites passions and often introduces new ways to love, and to relate to sexuality and love. More and more often Taiwan demonstrates the necessity to come back to its colonial history to find a solution for its isolation and make up for its losses; the nationalist (Japanese) and ideological (imperialist) approach of the colonial period was suppressed but resurges again.

In the first place, it is remarkable that in the two very recent films *Miao Miao* (dir. Cheng 2008) and *Somewhere I Have Never Travelled (Dai wo qu yuanfang,* dir. Fu 2009), a Japanese character is the trigger of the protagonist's awareness of his or her homosexuality (a young girl in the first, and a boy in the second film). The otherness arouses desire. The stranger, the one who is in transit, suggests the paths that were not explored before the encounter. If we adopt a political reading, we can equally observe the re-evaluation of a colonial relationship in these texts, a relationship which, in spite of the corrupt practices the Taiwanese were subjected to, shaped a kind of individual consciousness and a new relationship to the other which, in addition, moves away from China.

Love (with several parental/incestuous connotations) is inevitably reactivated in the relations of Taiwanese and Japanese characters who meet each other in these movies (we will visit later *Cape No. 7*); the search for a paternal figure who can confirm an identity implies a declaration of love, embodied in a pan-Asian relationship where Taiwan imagines the ancient colonizer as a lover, model, and passion. There are even several films that use the Japanese body as an erotic element. In *Invitation Only (Jueming paidui,* dir. Ko 2009) and *The Wayward Cloud (Tianbian yi duo yun,* dir. Tsai 2005), for example, Japanese AV actresses (Maria Ozawa and Yozakura Sumomo, respectively) are asked to show what Taiwanese actresses cannot or do not want to show. *The Wayward Cloud* is a porno-musical which plays with the codes of the cinema of the absurd to point out to the mechanization of desire in the contemporary society: the insatiable thirst for love and feelings that are temporarily relieved with the capitalist consumption of erotic representation. *Invitation Only* is the first Taiwanese attempt at a true "slasher" film, where the first girl who breaks the chastity taboo automatically becomes the first victim of the sadistic killer. Respecting the rules of the genre, the first victim of *Invitation Only*, Ozawa, is the first (and the only) girl to show her private parts "shamelessly." In *Invitation Only* and *The Wayward Cloud*, the naked bodies of the actresses are exclusively Japanese. On the one hand, this simply reveals the Taiwanese interest (and more generally that of East Asia) for the very developed Japanese porn industry, particularly vivacious, and which, even if it has to juggle with the old codes of censorship, can allow itself to cross the borders of representability, impossible in other Asian countries. On the other hand, in the systematic use of the eroticized Japanese body in the Taiwanese movies, we can equally observe a sort of macho revenge that uses the feminine body of the ancient colonizer finally disposable as a sex tool. Or, in a Freudian manner, Japan is the fetishized body that legitimates an erotic passion otherwise (hypocritically) suppressed. Pornography is accepted if performed outside of its symbolical limits, coming from the outside—a representation that does not compromise the innocence and purity (of course, imaginary) of the national body. In any case, what is at stake here is a "ghostly" presence, a symbolical substitution of the suppressed elements of (the representation of) sexuality—displaced toward the available and visible body of the Japanese actresses.

We can suggest a meta-cinematographic reading, in which the presence of a Japanese actress is an allegory of the call for authority of the emblematic Japanese tradition. The choice of transferring and reducing the erotic impulses to a Japanese female actress indicates a strategy of legitimization on the part of the Taiwanese cinematographic industry, which has been in crisis for about fifteen years. The role of the young Japanese girl is used not only to break certain sexual taboos but also as tactics to demand a figure of paternal reference, Ozawa's ghostly presence remaining an allegoric sacrifice asking for blessing in the future production of Taiwanese film.

Parenthesis: Taiwan in Japan

We will make a small digression about *Café Lumière* (*Kafei shiguang*), Hou Hsiao-hsien's (2003) tribute to Ozu Yasujiro. Invited to shoot a film in Tokyo to commemorate the 100th anniversary of Ozu's birth in 2003, the master of the Taiwanese cinema creates a story about a young Japanese girl who is impregnated by her Taiwanese lover (who is never shown); the baby's body indicates the hidden presence of Taiwan in the most everyday aspects of the contemporary Japanese life—the guilt and the need to get the old passion back, at the same time. Moreover, the young protagonist makes some inquiries about the Taiwanese composer Jiang Wenye, who worked in 1930s Tokyo as Kō Bunya and represented Japan in the Art Competition of the 1936 Berlin Olympics with his "Formosan Dance" (*Taiwan bukyoku*). We can here comment on Hou's hypothesis, inviting us to think about the underground influence of Taiwanese culture on Japan. Actually, connecting these two symbols of persistence and intimate alliance between the two countries (the baby of the Taiwanese father and the Taiwanese artist who works in Tokyo) to a presence of a very peculiar anachronism (which we will discuss in an instant), we can interpret the idea of the cultural transits. The relations between the two countries are less unidirectional than we are often inclined to believe. In fact, we have a tendency to describe the influence of the Japanese culture on Taiwan but we usually neglect to examine the relationship the other way around. The musician figure casts doubts on the dialogue between the two countries, on the possibility of the ongoing presence of cultures of the formerly colonized country in contemporary Japan. Furthermore, in an ambiguous ellipsis—asking the audience to actively engage in the interpretation of the film—Hou raises yet another suspicion. The young girl offers a souvenir from Taiwan to her boyfriend—a watch commemorating the 116th anniversary of the railway inauguration in Taiwan. As Shota Ogawa affirms, this means that the aforementioned railway track was built in 1887, eight years before the arrival of the Japanese on the island:

> The eight-year lapse between the railway opening and the Japanese colonization of Taiwan demands us to reconsider the oft-made association between Taiwan's colonial history and technology and institutions of modernity … Through the eight-year lapse between 1887 and 1895, Hou questions a closed notion of history as a linear progression formed by a series of causal effect relations and demands an understanding of cinema as a modern institution that ambivalently empowers the state as well as the masses … *Café Lumière* quietly but evocatively imbues the contemporary images of Tokyo with the traces of multicultural reality on which both Japan and Taiwan are founded. (Ogawa 2009: 165)

This interpretation of history modifies the relationship between Japan and Taiwan. The two chronologies intertwine and stay penetrable and porous. Hou suggests an overlapping of the history of two countries; he does not assume the role of a historian, but of an artist, who goes on questioning and suggesting, rather than demonstrating. Inspired by the vision of *Café Lumière*, the audience can begin to investigate history and observe that, even though Japan kept the predominant role in this relationship, Taiwan in fact had a very visible influence on the social and cultural history of Japan.

Conclusion

The trend of "reconciliation"[3] is a major current in Taiwan since the end of the 2000s. *Blue Brave: The Legend of Formosa in 1895* (*1895*, dir. Hung 2008) evokes the Taiwanese Hakka resistance to the Japanese troops who arrive in 1895 to claim their first colony and their subsequent efforts to fight for the independence of their new Republic of Taiwan. It predictably glorifies the deeds of the warriors, but the only off-screen voice—which allows us to enter the intimacy of the first person—is Japanese, incarnated here in the historical figure of a writer, Mori Ōgai, who was sent off to Taiwan to be an army doctor. During the entire movie, the only voice that we hear in the first person is exclusively Japanese. That is, the only subject who truly can express himself is Japanese. Even though Taiwanese characters make conversation throughout the entire movie, the character of Mori Ōgai is the only one to express his individuality via the intimacy of a diary, and with pacifistic and profoundly humanistic comments. In the final sequence, he is the only one who has the privilege and the right to speak, and to regret the war, exclaiming with regard to the victory of the Japanese repression over the local resistance, "there is nothing to be proud of in a victory; there should be a funeral march instead of a celebration." Although he certainly does not represent democracy, Mori Ōgai might as well be the voice of individuality with which the Taiwanese characters are never able to speak.

But why don't the Taiwanese speak in this film, which after all is supposed to represent them and portray their fight for independence? More precisely, they do talk, but only through dialogue; the only one to have the privilege to engage in a monologue, and thereby express the individual emotions and thoughts, under the projector, without sharing the scene with anyone, is the Japanese intellectual. In a discussion about this subject, Professor Chiang Shu-Chen maintains that this gives the audience the unique opportunity to identify with Mori Ōgai's implicitly pacifistic character (personal communication, June 2010). To pin down the accuracy of this representation of the writer is a particular difficult task, since Mori Ōgai was a greatly influential writer as well as a public/official figure. The contradiction of being an army officer and a Westernized humanistic intellectual compels Lorenzo Costantini, who depicts Mori as a libertarian and a "paternalist and illuminated conservative" (1994). Mori defended the freedom of press when, at the end of Meiji, repression and censorship were increasing; but he always was a strong upholder of Confucian traditional values and morality; he criticized despotism but also praised the imperial army for its discipline, values, and spirit of sacrifice; he contributed to modernizing and Occidentalizing Japanese literature but ended his literary career rewriting stories of feudal Japan; he was a rational intellectual influenced by Western philosophy, but at the same time defended the Confucian, socially relevant figure of the intellectual.

Mori's characterization in *1895* could be accurate but mainly it is embedded in the contemporary reconciliation strategy that, in my view, tends to "shift" Taiwan away from China and toward Japan. This agenda is by no means accepted by all Taiwanese; still, the examples here have a telling frequency to portray the Japanese invaders in a civilized, positive way—an impossibility in PRC filmography. Mori depicts the ideal modern and independent intellectual, still moved by "traditional" aesthetics but committed to a benevolent colonial position. Which begs the question: why use a Japanese character as an instrument of engaging the public in the story? And why give him explicitly this aura of wisdom and exemplary nature? Is the Taiwanese public supposed to identify more easily with a Japanese intellectual, rather than a Hakka militant?

Cape No. 7 (*Haijiao qi hao*, dir. Wei 2008), tells a twofold love story in chiasmus. In the narrative a Taiwanese rock musician falls in love with a Japanese girl; in flashback sequences the love story depicts a Japanese teacher, who has to leave Taiwan in 1945, leaving behind a young Taiwanese woman in mourning. The film is punctuated by the unsent letters of the young man, who—*again*—is the only one to talk in first person, in an intense and poetic monologue. As in *Blue Brave*, this Japanese protagonist is the only one who has the right to speak, the right to represent his individuality, and the power to "start a speech." The voice heard in the beginning and in the end of the film (under the flag of Retrocession[4]) is not a "free" or "freed" voice of the Taiwanese people but a romantic, imperialist, seductive, and idealistic voice of Japan. We should also mention the sequence that marks the culmination of the love story at present: the young Taiwanese singer finally decides to reveal his feelings for the Japanese girl, and whisper to her on the beach at sunset: "stay, or otherwise I'll come with you." If we read this episode from a "political" perspective, in which the Taiwanese boy allegorizes Taiwan and the Japanese girl represents Japan, we can hear a cry advocating the comeback of a poor orphan under the Japanese domination. If we overlook the "sentimental" character of this mainstream film, we can easily find a political parable that suggests an overdetermination of feelings, as if these individuals were obliged to reactivate their colonized/colonizer relationship, and to do it with passion. What is in question here—is this the reactivation of a new love relationship or a parental one?

Cape No. 7 was the most successful Taiwanese film ever. The "avatar" of the local production is a voice that does not express itself either in Mandarin or in Taiwanese but quite obviously in Japanese. Isn't the idea of the Taiwanese individual—also, of course, as a reaction to the fear of the PRC superpower which threatens to swallow it up in its one-party system—more and more oriented toward the Pacific, and consequently toward Japan? The Taiwanese citizen/subject is increasingly imagined without a voice, deprived of voice, or more accurately, as the orphan of Japanese expression, of authenticity, poetry, and power of the Japanese language. This attempt to redefine national identity is a compromise between the search for the roots and the need for independence: in any case, it is a centrifugal force aiming to move the Taiwanese identity away from China, and consequently, to draw it closer to Japan. It is important to underline that *Cape No. 7* has not been an isolated case; Wei Te-sheng continued to explore the history of Taiwan with *Warriors of the Rainbow: Seediq Bale* (*Saideke Balai*, dir. Wei 2011) and *KANO* (prod. Wei; dir. Umin 2014). *Warriors* is set in 1930 during the bloody Seediq-led Musha uprising against the Japanese; while the colonial power suppresses the revolt, the winning general shows great respect for the Aboriginal adversary. he is surprised to find on a lost island in the middle of the Pacific the long-lost spirit of Bushidō. Set months later in 1931, *KANO* is a baseball drama that features an ethnically mixed high school team (Japanese-Taiwanese-Aboriginal) that, under the inflexible but inspiring coaching of a Japanese retired champion, manages to represent Taiwan at the Kōshien championships in the home islands. They will not win, but will earn the respect of the spectators (who overcome their initial prejudices) by displaying a true sporting spirit—competition, self-surpassing, honor. The final sequence is a reverse shot of the beginning of *Cape No. 7*, showing the team on the boat coming "home" to Taiwan after having earned the admiration of the Japanese motherland. *KANO,* a commercial success, also already has shaped the public debate—even if the director and producers refrain from giving overtly political interpretation— over Taiwan's Japanese and Chinese heritage.

For Taiwan—a sovereign nation with great resources but still diplomatically isolated and constantly threatened by the rise of the PRC—Japan could represent a guide or, in any case, an image of power to which it is ideologically, politically, and socially attached, or so these movies seem to suggest. It has to be indicated that Taiwan is a plurivocal place where not everyone shares this craze for Japan I have just reported; other voices, on the contrary, revive the memory of the injustices suffered during the colonial era. What seems interesting to analyze here is this particular form of representation, indirectly very positive, of the Japanese culture as a model (besides the globalized craze for anime, manga, and J-Pop), as a space of liberty, a trigger of the nonconfessed desires, and an inspiration. It is a form of oblique and nuanced representation and a source of interpretation that expresses itself in an increasingly powerful voice within mainstream Taiwanese cinema and which, consequently, seems to reject the possibility of a menacing Chinese "reunification" in the future, orienting itself rather toward Japan—a Japan certainly imaginary, yet present in the collective subconscious. It is definitely not the case for all Taiwanese, this goes without saying; but I seem to hear a cry coming from Taiwan more and more often, and more and more powerfully, a nostalgic longing, with a maybe slightly masochistic trait, which informs us about the fear of PRC authoritarianism, but of the idleness of democracy, as well. A cry that says, "Give me back my colonizer!"

Notes

1   The most relevant reference is Wu Zhuoliu's 1945 novel *The Orphan of Asia* (*Ajia no koji*); he describes the psychological struggles of a Taiwanese intellectual growing up under Japanese rule, writing about self, national identity, and the anxiety of colonial consciousness.

2   A compelling novelization of the famous actress's life and influence on Asian culture can be found in Buruma (2008).

3   I am thankful to National Taiwan University Professor Sebastian Liao for his enlightening discussions of this subject.

4   For more on the concept of Retrocession (*Guangfu*), see Ghermani (2009b).

10

Reliving the Past: The Narrative Themes of Repetition and Continuity in Japan–Taiwan News Coverage

Jens Sejrup

Introduction

When Japan and the People's Republic of China (PRC) established official relations in September 1972, one of the consequences was the immediate termination of decades of mutual recognition and official relations between Japan and the Republic of China (ROC) on Taiwan. This new situation was codified in a "Joint Communique" between Beijing and Tokyo, a document that to this day serves as the basic framework for all political and diplomatic interaction between the two states. The Communique announced the intention of the two parties to "establish relations of perpetual peace and friendship," declared Japan's recognition of the PRC as "sole legal Government of China," and specified each party's position on the question of the status of Taiwan: "The Government of the People's Republic of China reiterates that Taiwan is an inalienable part of the territory of the People's Republic of China. The Government of Japan fully understands and respects this stand..." ("Joint Communique" 1972).

With this formulation, Japan reversed its "one-China policy" in the PRC's favor and discontinued all official interaction with Taipei. The relationship between the two island states was now of a private nature, their respective embassies became "representative offices" outside of the conventional diplomatic system (although with practically the same functions as before), and Japan joined the rapidly increasing number of countries that had severed ties with the ROC in favor of the PRC (Rawnsley 2000: 27). Switching from one "China" to the other was a choice based on *Realpolitik* and foreign policy objectives, but taking this step posed more complexities

I thankfully acknowledge the valuable comments and constructive suggestions I received from Denise Gimpel, Karl Gustafsson, Barak Kushner, Yoichi Nagashima, Ming-yeh Rawnsley, Jennifer Robertson, Marie Roesgaard, Agnes Schick-Chen, Elina Sinkkonen, Shogo Suzuki, and many others during my work on this piece. I am very grateful also to participants at conferences in Finland, Australia, and the United Kingdom where I presented different aspects and early drafts of the present chapter.

for the Japanese state and society than for other countries, given the special historical relationship between Taiwan and Japan. It meant the termination of official dealings with a territory still relatively recently ruled as a colony of the Japanese empire for fifty years and a society generally perceived to be far more amicably disposed toward Japan than any other in East Asia. The two most important events in twentieth-century Japan–Taiwan diplomatic history—"Retrocession" to the ROC in 1945 and discontinuation of official relations in 1972—were both essentially breaches of continuity, disruptions, transformations, and ends. They both marked the boundaries of distinct periods, each new phase increasing the political distance between them: Japanese direct control giving way to formal relations and formal relations giving way to mere informal interaction.

I have demonstrated elsewhere that a motif of repetition characterizes the narrative structure of news coverage of Japan–Taiwan relations in general (Sejrup 2012) and argue that this concept of repetition serves as a particularly useful analytical tool for thematically connecting and elucidating otherwise seemingly unrelated occurrences, news events, and phenomena in interactions between the two societies. Here I will direct my attention to the way influential Taiwanese politicians visiting Japan confront the problem of bilateral discontinuity in their public statements and conduct and how the media cover their presence in Japan through the application of narrative strategies of repetition and continuity. Unlike "regular" visitors, such guests attract discussion and media attention; their status as visitors is ambiguous and their activities in the host country are open to various levels of interpretation and public debate. My aim is to demonstrate how Japanese mass media either tend to portray visiting Taiwanese politicians as embodiments of bilateral alienation and difference or, conversely, let them appear as icons of continuity and mutual affinity across the divide. My claim is that the positioning of Taiwanese political characters in these opposing roles is intimately connected to a general drift toward repetition in these news sources—repetition of movement, of behavior, of assumptions, and of a longing toward narratives structured as returns, reiterations, and resurrections.

This study draws upon an extensive collection of original media sources from both Taiwan and Japan run by seven different national newspapers in the 2000–2008 period. All seven newspapers covered all the events I analyze here. Operating in one of the world's most newspaper-saturated societies, most of the Japanese national dailies studied here are sold through household or company subscription and generally deliver serious and sober-minded unsensationalist journalism (Cooper-Chen 1997; Freeman 2000). My collection of sources incorporates the whole spectrum of paid-for national dailies, ranging from the squarely right-wing *Sankei shimbun*, over the conservative *Yomiuri shimbun* and the liberal *Mainichi shimbun*, to the left-leaning *Asahi shimbun*. The *Sankei shimbun*, which is very well connected in Taiwan and extremely critical of Beijing, operates with an ideological worldview often resembling that of many prominent Japan-friendly Taiwanese politicians. At the other end of the spectrum, the *Asahi shimbun* takes a far less cynical and confrontational view of Japan–PRC relations, in fact so much so that Ming Wan has even characterized the *Asahi* as "the most pro-China newspaper in Japan" (Wan 2007: 170). Significantly, all the studied newspapers employ the repetition motif in their Taiwan coverage, although the *Sankei* and the *Yomiuri*, due primarily to the general political orientation of their respective editorial lines, tend to make even more extensive use of it than do the *Asahi* and the *Mainichi*.

The Taiwanese papers, on their side, operate in a fiercely competitive market where newsstand sales matter far more than subscriptions (Rawnsley and Rawnsley 1998; Fell 2005), a fact that accounts for the often highly antagonistic tone and attitude that exist between them. Two of the papers I have studied, *China Times* and *United Daily News*, are generally conservative and oriented toward eventual cross-strait unification, while the third one, *Liberty Times*, is liberal and sympathetic to political platforms advocating Taiwanese formal independence. A special relationship exists between *Liberty Times* and *Sankei shimbun* due to both the virtual ideological confluence of their respective views of the historical significance of Japanese colonial rule for Taiwan's process of modernization and their shared editorial antipathies toward the PRC. Thus, in many ways, relations between the two otherwise very different newspapers present a micro-illustration of larger political interconnections between the two island societies that Barak Kushner has described as a "relationship between otherwise unlikely bedfellows, the Japanese political right and the Taiwanese political left" (Kushner 2007: 796).

A witness to progress and surviving tradition: Lee Teng-hui's Japan visits in 2001 and 2004–2005

By far the biggest news story involving Taiwan and Japan in the first decade of the twenty-first century was the four visits to Japan (and the additional two aborted attempts to visit) by former ROC president Lee Teng-hui. A towering figure in Taiwanese politics, Lee was born in 1923, educated in the colonial Japanese school system and studied at Kyoto University during the war. He speaks fluent Japanese and was well-known for his avid admiration of Japanese culture, history, and literature. Originally an academic, his political career began when he was recruited by the Guomindang (KMT) to serve first as minister of agriculture, then mayor of Taipei in the late 1970s, and governor of Taiwan Province in 1981. In 1984 he advanced to the ROC vice presidency under Chiang Ching-kuo, whom he then succeeded as ROC president and KMT chairman in 1988. Lee was later re-elected in the first direct presidential election in 1996 and served a total of twelve years as the first-ever Taiwan-born ROC president before passing the reins to Chen Shui-bian of the Democratic Progressive Party (DPP) in 2000. Having resigned as KMT chairman, he then left the party and became a mentor figure for the new pro-independence party Taiwan Solidarity Union (TSU) after its founding in July 2001, "apparently turning into an outright supporter of Taiwan independence" (Schubert 2012: 77).

Lee's ideological move away from the KMT toward a far more independence-oriented position only aggravated his already difficult relationship with the PRC leadership. Denny Roy summarizes this development by stating that "Beijing holds Lee in particularly deep contempt, blaming him for attempting to set Taiwan on a path toward formal independence from China while he was president" (2006: 84), and Melissa Brown concurs, citing his "deliberate, if delicate, strategy of moving toward independence" (2004: 64). Certainly, the PRC came to regard him as a hardline separatist and traitor to the "Chinese" cause and consistently opposed him making any overseas visits. With reference to the Joint Communique, China made a habit of sternly reminding Japan that Beijing would consider any move on Tokyo's part to grant Lee an entry visa as a breach of the agreed commitment to "non-interference in [China's] internal affairs" and a danger to the "relations of perpetual peace and friendship" between the two countries ("Joint Communique").

Lee himself has often publicly acknowledged an identification with and admiration for things Japanese, and the mass media and researchers in Taiwan, Japan, and elsewhere usually ascribe his veneration of Japan to his having grown up under Japanese rule and received training and education in Japan as a young man. Lee's "nostalgia" for Japan and his desire to revisit the land of his formative years resurfaces time and again in the media sources collected here, and they are more often than not presented as the main motivation for his repeated attempts to obtain entry to Japan.

In 1985, while Lee was ROC vice president, he managed to make a visit to Tokyo and Yokohama, and later, during his presidency, he made unsuccessful attempts to join the 1994 Asia Summit in Hiroshima and the 1995 APEC meeting in Osaka. Having had in his last months as president in the fall of 2000 to relinquish his wish to participate in the Asia Open Forum in the Japanese city of Matsumoto, Lee soon after his resignation finally went ahead and applied for a visa, this time in order to receive a cardiac checkup at Kurashiki Central Hospital. Weeks of interministerial struggle and political and bureaucratic intrigue in Tokyo followed, along with official statements of ROC government support for Lee's application and repeated threats and protests from Beijing intensely covered by both Japanese and Taiwanese media. In the end, outgoing Japanese prime minister Mori Yoshirō, well known in Taiwan for his political sympathies for independence platforms like Lee's (Sejrup 2012: 759–60), effectively terminated this diplomatic–bureaucratic seesaw. He directly ordered Foreign Minister Kōno Yōhei (whose overt reluctance to challenge Beijing on this matter was in perfect consonance with his own ministry's influential PRC-oriented "China School") to end administrative procrastination and issue a "humanitarian" visa with strict limitations, just a few days before Mori himself stepped down and was succeeded by Koizumi Jun'ichirō.

When Lee and his wife finally arrived at Kansai International Airport with an entourage of assistants, secretaries, and security staff on April 22, 2001, a large crowd of enthusiastic supporters and media personnel received him in a jubilant atmosphere, here in *Yomiuri shimbun*'s account:

> [Lee] smiled calmly at the Taiwanese residents in Japan and media people welcoming him at Kansai Airport and at his hotel in downtown Osaka and thanked them repeatedly.... From the roadside of the airport freeway he was welcomed by about three hundred Taiwanese citizens gathered from all over the country and by Kyoto University students. As his limousine passed them, they waved banners with the words "Welcome, Mr. Lee Teng-hui" and flags, shouting "Banzai!" again

and again .... A source close to him says that Lee was deeply touched by today's welcome, saying that "I'm thankful to the point of tears that they care for me this much. I'm speechless." ("Taiwan kara" 2001)

In most sources, descriptions of Lee's "return to Japan" are soaked in pathos. People hug, onlookers are joyful that he prevailed in his quest for a visa, and interviewees wish for his medical recovery, while voices of dissent are also heard on the scene, angrily shouting reiterations of the PRC's viewpoint ("Ayumi" 2001). As the restrictions on his visa barred him from making political statements, Lee himself was confined to a role as beaming gentleman giving thanks, shaking hands, and receiving a flood of excited attention. Indeed, the coverage was so intense that Taiwanese daily *China Times* described Lee as more media-exposed than even Prime Minister-Elect Koizumi:

> Today, all front pages of every Japanese newspaper feature large color photos of Lee Teng-hui and his wife arriving at Kansai International Airport. Although the front page headline is that Japan's Liberal Democratic Party will elect Koizumi Jun'ichirō as its new president tomorrow, pictures of Lee Teng-hui figure more prominently than any of Koizumi. Anyone not knowing what each of the two looks like and not reading the captions could be forgiven for thinking that tomorrow Lee Teng-hui will be elected LDP president. ("Zai Ri chu" 2001)

The supposedly private nature of the visit notwithstanding, reporters and spectators literally crawled over each other later that day to follow the Lees around, the commotion prompting last-minute schedule changes:

> The original plan for the afternoon was to go to Osaka Mint to admire the Yayoi (...) cherry trees, but yesterday morning when Lee Teng-hui was out on a stroll along the riverside next to his hotel, Taiwanese and Japanese reporters chased him madly, pushing and squeezing so that it was nearly impossible for him to move a single step, let alone enjoy the scenery for all the reporters and microphones. Therefore, Lee's chief of staff cancelled the scheduled sightseeing trip, and having then coordinated with the media, changed the destination to the somewhat more spacious Osaka Castle. ("Li Denghui" 2001)

Actively catering to the media interest, politically silent Lee cooperated with the staging of his visit "for medical purposes" as a poignant return to the lost land of his youth. As no political statements were forthcoming, the media opted for focusing instead on the presumed emotional aspects of the trip, as can be seen in this passage from the front page of the *Yomiuri shimbun* evening edition of April 23:

> In Osaka on the twenty-third, Taiwanese Former President Lee Teng-hui (78) greeted a "Japanese morning" for the first time in sixteen years. Lee, who was born in Taiwan during Japanese rule, was educated in Japanese, and harbors an

exceptional love for Japan. On this Japan trip, restrictions apply as to where he can
go, but on that day he and his wife Tseng Wen-hui (75) took a stroll in the vicinity
of their hotel, looking as if spring in Japan, re-experienced after so long, filled their
hearts with joy.... "It's wonderful, there's a river just like the Tamsui River flowing
right in front of our room. I think we'll be quite comfortable here," Lee revealed to
his aides as he entered his room on the eleventh floor of the hotel on the evening of
the twenty-second. The Tamsui River flows through the northern part of Taiwan,
and Lee was born and raised close to it. ("Ri Tōki, Taiwan" 2001)

Several layers of returns and repetitions are constructed here—the Japan that
shaped Lee's childhood and youth, educated him, and fostered "exceptional love"
in him returns in a spring dawn: "Japanese spring" evokes deep emotion in the
Lees, apparently detectible from their appearance alone. "All the reporters and
microphones" that kept Lee from enjoying the scenery in the previous account seem
to have disappeared here, leaving the Lees alone by the river with their raging *mono
no aware*. Temporal concepts ("morning," "spring") are localized, indeed nationalized,
to become "Japanese," so that Lee, who has no particularly intimate past connection
to Osaka itself (he studied in Kyoto and did military service in Nagoya and Tokyo),
can still be emotionally affected as "Japanese mornings" and "Japanese springs" are
presumably to be experienced uniformly in any Japanese location[1] (spring is, literally,
"re-experienced after so long"). With the repetition of past experience thus achieved
on one level, another conceptual circle is drawn by the similarity of the river outside
the window with the Tamsui River in Taipei (repetition of geographical features,
likeness transcending distance), which again is connected to Lee's formative years,
so that a Taiwanese childhood is invoked in a Japanese location. Re-experiencing
this Japanese past compels even extra-Japanese elements in Lee's personal history to
resurrect through similarity with what he sees in Japan, resulting in an atmosphere of
emotional harmony and equilibrium ("I think we'll be quite comfortable here") and
the closure of another circle of repetition.

On his four trips to Japan during the period covered here, Lee is consistently shown
in a posture of contemplating the contrasts between past and present in Japan's physical
appearance.

Time and again, Lee returns to places changed and improved, and as such he
becomes both a witness to Japanese progress and development (the places are
always prettier, more dynamic, more developed than when he knew them) and a
bringer of continuity and historical perspective. Responding with astonishment
and awe to the changes he sees, Lee authenticates Japanese postwar development
as a continuation of the "old Japan" that he epitomizes in the media. Coupled with
his aura of scholarly intellect, his role as witness to progress within continuity often
takes on ideological proportions. In an interview with *Sankei shimbun*'s Taiwan
correspondent shortly after his return to Taipei after his second Japan visit over
New Year's in 2004–2005, Lee was asked about his impression of Japan and he
answered thus:

Japanese people living in Japan may not be fully aware of the changes, but ... what
I felt when I took a thorough look at Japan sixty years after the war was that its

traditions have not been lost in progress, but have undergone an *Aufhebung*.... The moral system of former times is being restored. ("Ri Tōki, Taiwan" 2005)

The rationale seems to be that despite change and development, traditions prevail in Japan, Lee's observation operating with the assumption that there are a given set of "traditions" and a "moral system of former times" characteristic of an ahistorical "prewar Japan." Thus, postwar and prewar time come to form two distinct and opposing blocs that are, however and quite fortunately, somehow *aufgehoben* and dissolved again. This line of thinking streamlines the image of an orderly, coherent, and timeless entity without inner conflict or development—an ideological view disguised as a historical fact, but without any historical validity.[2] Lee's contribution is then to witness the continuity of this image into modernity and to attest to the ongoing restoration of its "moral system" in conveniently borrowed Hegelian terms. Lee even claims to observe the true nature of Japan more acutely than the average Japanese person, whose ability to identify an instance of *Aufhebung* is apparently debilitated by his native presence in the very locus of its execution. The return of the witness thus symptomizes the return of the system that produced him.

In *The Location of Culture*, Homi K. Bhabha discusses precisely the role of *enunciation* in the ascription of models, systems, and traditions to already overdetermined modern individuals. Arguing that cultures are open-ended and in a constant state of negotiation and appropriation, he emphasizes the need to deconstruct on the level of language and enunciation, the ideological dimensions of postulating cultural practices to be of an original and exclusive nature. Claiming that identifications of cultural origins and purity, closures of social narratives, are in fact politically motivated ideological constructs, Bhabha's observations are useful in elucidating the function of Lee's role as witness to continuity:

> The enunciation of cultural difference problematizes the binary division of past and present, tradition and modernity, at the level of cultural representation and its authoritative address. It is the problem of how, in signifying the present, something comes to be repeated, relocated and translated in the name of tradition, in the guise of a pastness that is not necessarily a faithful sign of historical memory but a strategy of representing authority in terms of the artifice of the archaic. (Bhabha 1994: 51–2)

Professing to the continuation of past traditions through his self-professed ability to discern their *Aufhebung* through progress, Lee stages the present as the place where the pre-present (i.e. "eternal" Japanese values and dehistoricized Japaneseness) returns in the form of a repetition, a negation of loss, and a resurrection of the past.

Apart from his mere personal presence in Japan, which alone sufficed to generate enormous amounts of media attention and public debate in 2001, Lee intensified his aura of connectedness to Japanese culture and tradition on subsequent trips. However, the overall media interest in his visits fell markedly for each visit, he drew fewer and fewer front pages, and a fatigue with Lee's repeated visits seemed to hit the media in both Japan and Taiwan. After the severely restricted "medical trip" of 2001 and an aborted attempt to lecture at Keiō University in 2002, Lee found himself admitted to Japan in December 2004 as a tourist. Although he was still not allowed to make political statements or give press briefings, he clearly no longer needed to insist on a health "necessity" to visit. The PRC made the usual protests, but Japanese authorities took them less seriously than in 2001 when official threats and consternation over the supposed violation of the Joint Communique had resulted in the Chinese rescheduling a number of bilateral exchanges, most notably the postponement of an official Japan visit by Li Peng, chairman of the Standing Committee of the National People's Congress. However, although the Japanese foreign ministry granted Lee a visa for his 2004–2005 trip, which he himself referred to as his "nostalgic journey" (*huaigu zhi lü*) and which took him around central Japan ("Huangjun" 2004), the Koizumi government was still concerned about the possible diplomatic consequences of the trip. Chief Cabinet Secretary Hosoda Hiroyuki asked the media to show restraint in covering Lee's trip, and Foreign Minister Machimura Nobutaka instructed all Liberal Democratic Party (LDP) Diet members not to meet with Lee during his visit ("Ri Tōki, Zen" 2004; "Taichū-kankei" 2004).

The visit itself featured Lee and his immediate family (this time including the Lees' widowed daughter-in-law and granddaughter) traveling from one historic location to another: enjoying the view from Nagoya Castle toward Sekigahara, the site of the battle of 1600 where Tokugawa Ieyasu (1543–1616) decisively defeated the Toyotomi clan; visiting memorials to Kyoto School philosopher Nishida Kitarō (1870–1945) and hydraulic engineer Hatta Yoichi (1886–1942) as well as making traditional pottery in Kanazawa; enjoying the hot springs at the exclusive Kagaya Spa Resort; journeying along Lake Biwa; and finally sightseeing in Kyoto, where Lee had once been a student. The nature of the itinerary reinforced the already well-established association in the public mind between Lee and Japan's cultural, philosophical, and political history and, by extension, the historical ties between Japan and Taiwan.

A classic journey reenacted, a Yasukuni reunion: Lee Teng-hui's Japan visit in 2007

This association was pushed and stimulated onto a whole new level when Lee made his third and far more controversial visit in the summer of 2007. This time none of the original visa restrictions of 2001 applied anymore—Lee was free to talk to the media, speak publicly, and give lectures.[3] Having received a newly instituted honorary award in Tokyo, he set out on a trip through the Tōhoku region in imitation of seventeenth-century haiku poet Matsuo Bashō (1644–1694). An ardent admirer of Bashō and his magnum opus, the poetic travel diary *The Narrow Road to the Interior* (*Oku no hosomichi*), Lee had long before 2007 introduced the idea of making his own trip along the "narrow roads" in the footsteps of the great poet. It was, therefore, a jubilant Lee who could inform reporters of his plans for the upcoming journey. As the *Yomiuri shimbun* reported, "Lee said cheerfully: 'On the basis of *Bushidō* and *The Narrow Road to the Interior*, I want to study the daily life of the Japanese and their harmony with nature'" ("Ri Tōki, Taiwan-zen-sōtō rainichi" 2007).

Citing Bashō's book alongside Nitobe Inazō's classic *Bushido: The Soul of Japan* (1900) as foundational texts for understanding "the daily life of the Japanese," Lee once again reveals his dehistoricized view of an "eternal" Japan to be experienced in 2007 like Bashō saw it in 1689. His trip is to be structured as a real-life enactment of what Lee has read in old books, the assumption being that a textual "old Japan" could repeat itself naturally in experience. The notion is about as reasonable as touring the Scottish Isles today with an aim to see James Boswell's *Journal of a Tour to the Hebrides* (1786) reassert itself before one's eyes or taking a trip around Italy in order to prove Goethe's observations in his *Italian Journey* (1816). In Lee's world, there is one "Japanese" life, one "Japanese" harmony with nature, one "Japanese" way, awaiting his discovery, contemplation, and interpretation for his fellow Taiwanese citizens.

Having reached the scenic spot of Matsushima outside the city of Sendai in Miyagi Prefecture (Bashō traveled on foot and horseback along dirt roads, while Lee resorted to the comfort of the excellent Japanese railway system), Lee gave a public display of his own poetic skills in the stringent haiku form. *Yomiuri* described the scene as follows:

> After visiting Matsushima, Lee recited [his poem] "Oh Matsushima!/Its light and shades/so dazzling" in front of a group of reporters and said: "The sight of Matsushima is a beautiful sight unchanged for hundreds of years. Japanese culture is a wonderful culture whose spiritual aspects are in harmony with nature." ("'Matsushima'" 2007)

Composing a haiku in strict accordance with the formal five-seven-five syllable meter (*Matsushima ya, hikari to kage no, mabushikari*) and incorporating an adjective conjugated in classical rather than modern Japanese, Lee added further strength to his image as a master of Japanese tradition. The rhetorical composition of his subsequent remark was noteworthy: like Matsushima stays locked to its beauty across the ages, Japanese culture maintains constant spiritual harmony with nature. The "hundreds of years" in the first sentence insinuate a similar permanence to the relationship between "wonderful" Japanese culture and its natural surroundings—a reiteration of Lee's notion of Japanese tradition being retained in progress, but here the repetitive element consists in reiteration of classical aesthetic sensitivity induced by a particular canonical location whose natural constancy becomes a symbol of "eternal" Japanese ways. Furthermore, the act of visiting the place and making poetic statements is itself a repetition enacted specifically to reiterate the past visit of an illustrious wanderer poet of "old Japan" (note again, in Bhabha's terms (1994: 52), an instance of "representing authority in terms of the artifice of the archaic"), of re-enacting the past in order to rediscover and experience anew that nothing has changed, that continuity prevails.

Back in Tokyo after finishing about half of Bashō's historical itinerary, Lee played the most controversial trump of all on the morning of June 8. Throughout his visit Taiwanese and Japanese reporters had repeatedly asked him if he intended to visit the Yasukuni Shrine, where his elder brother, who was killed as a Japanese soldier in World War II, is listed among the spirits enshrined. Lee responded by indicating a wish to go, but would give no definite answer. Instead, he phrased his answers along sentimental lines like "The more you talk about my brother the more I feel like crying" and referred to his filial duties as a younger brother ("Ri Tōki, Taiwan-zen-sōtō: Bashō" 2007). As the *Sankei shimbun* reported,

> Lee expressed his intention to visit…the Yasukuni Shrine where his deceased brother Lee Teng-chin is enshrined under his Japanese name, Iwasato Takenori. His eyes welling up, he said: "Having come to Tokyo, it would be unbearable for me as a human being and as a younger brother not to go see my brother whom I haven't seen for over sixty years." ("Ri Tōki-shi" 2007)

Stressing an emotional and ethical obligation to go there, Lee reverses the conventional view of Yasukuni among non-Japanese East Asians (and many Japanese, as well): that the shrine celebrates war criminals, that it is a monument to disastrous Japanese imperialism, and that it symbolizes a lack of Japanese postwar soul-searching and coming to terms with the country's war responsibility. Instead, Lee intends to go there to "see" (or "meet," "*au*") his brother, that is, to close a circle of dispossession and bereavement by entering sacred space and thereby to transcend six decades of temporal distance and the divide between the living and the dead. In other words, Lee tries to legitimize politically the continued existence and retroactive symbolism of the Yasukuni Shrine by postcolonially reinterpreting it as a site of spiritual fraternal reunion.

Taiwanese and Japanese media covered the Yasukuni visit with much drama and excitement. Taiwan's *United Daily News* reported,

> Around ten o'clock this morning, Lee Teng-hui arrived at the special VIP side entrance to Yasukuni Shrine in Tokyo's Kudanshita area. Up to a hundred Taiwanese and foreign reporters had been waiting for him for a long time outside the shrine, helicopters dispatched by several television networks were hovering in the air, and the police were out in force to maintain order at the scene. The fuss resembled that of a Japanese prime minister's visit. ("Li Denghui canbai" 2007)

After the visit, Taiwan's *Liberty Times* explained how Lee informed the agitated media of its propitious outcome: "Giving interviews to the media, he said that as a result of this visit, his brother's soul can now enjoy good fortune in the nether world" ("Li canbai" 2007).

Taiwanese newspapers included several voices of opposition to Lee's Yasukuni visit spanning the entire political spectrum (though primarily in the form of KMT legislators and activists), arguing that Lee had gone too far and had shown disrespect for the people who suffered during Japanese colonization. The PRC also expressed regret over Lee's renegade "prettification of history" ("Beijing pi Li" 2007). Attempts were made to expose Lee as a hypocrite: The KMT-friendly *China Times* reported that Lee had never even bothered to visit his brother's memorial tablet at Taiwan's own Jihuagong Temple in Xinzhu County where war-dead Taiwanese are remembered, and editorialized that as a Presbyterian Christian, Lee should not believe in Shinto spirits ("Jihuagong" 2007). With this 2007 visit, Lee seemed to have reached a point where he was beginning to alienate all political camps in Taiwan with his adoring submission to the Japanese right wing. A *United Daily News* editorial from June 3 reproached him in a way typical for the general atmosphere in the Taiwanese media during the visit and asked him to make up his mind:

> For the sake of his own personal desire to visit Japan, Lee Teng-hui … will even use a memorial service for his dead brother as a political prop. This tour of worship has in fact only revealed more clearly the greed and ignorance in the mind of this retired old man. As he walks *The Narrow Road to the Interior* to muse over the past, Lee Teng-hui may wish to reconsider himself the meaning of this trip. Is he a great man of Taiwan or a clown of Japan? ("Li Denghui Riben" 2007)

Clearly, Lee's returns and repetitions, his reverence for Japanese tradition, and his enthusiasm for dehistoricized "eternal" Japanese ways are meant to fit into a mode of social orientation generally prevalent in Japan and often termed "nostalgia." It has been shown and discussed in a number of different studies that a nostalgic mood permeates Japanese popular culture, political discourse, commercial consumption, and so on (Iwabuchi 2002: 547–73; Kushner 2007: 793–820; Robertson 2007: 62–82). Here, I stress the intimate thematic connection between nostalgia and repetition, and define nostalgia as a "longing for repetition," my argument being that that is the way nostalgia is articulated in the structuring of media narratives. In fact, rather than treating nostalgia as a distinct and self-sufficient discursive motif in its own right, I consider nostalgia as one particular instance of the general and overarching logic of repetition that so thoroughly permeates these sources. The "longing for repetition" clearly discernible in these sources seems to relate to a prevailing mood of nostalgia in the newspaper-consuming market that my Japanese source texts are, of course, directed toward.

In Japan, the mass media generally treat newsworthy statements of Taiwan–Japan postcolonial affinity as a particularly poignant subfield of the much larger narrative complex of Tokyo–Beijing political differences and potential confrontation. To be sure, however, postcolonial nostalgia is not confined to the Japanese side only. In Taiwan's news media and politics, the notion of Taiwanese postcolonial nostalgia in itself makes up a controversial, politically contentious, and culturally significant theme (Sejrup 2012: 759). As the popularity of the 2014 colonial-era baseball film *KANO* suggests, there seems to be no end to the contemporary Taiwanese fascination with, and willingness to profit from and tweak "Chinese" sensibilities with, nostalgia for the colonial moment, as discussions of Taiwanese cultural production in both Andrew Morris's and Corrado Neri's chapters of this book reveal. It is, however, the case that Japanese media, irrespective of their overall editorial slant, employ the mode of repetition in news stories relating to Taiwan much more often, and uncritically, than vice versa. This indeed suggests that they operate in a social context and in a market where demand for nostalgic forms is larger and far less divisive than do their Taiwanese counterparts.

Reading the newspaper coverage of Lee's Japan visits, one is tempted to regard his different statements on the nature of Taiwan and Japan as somewhat insincere and as the results of more or less cynical calculations of how best to tap into Japanese nostalgia for political gain. Certainly, Lee is no fool. He has demonstrated remarkable tactical skills maneuvering across the Taiwanese political field, he has many achievements behind him, and his use of the media is often masterful. He knows how to stage himself and how to take advantage of the situation when favorable opportunities present themselves in the public mood. Most experts, therefore, take the view (as do the Chinese government and his pan-blue opponents) that his Japan trips were basically political campaigns meant to bolster Japanese support of Taiwanese independence (Lam 2004: 249–67; Wan 2007: 159–81). Lee can easily be shown to have a keen political interest in making the Japanese public like him and, by extension, Taiwan (perhaps even at the cost of sacrificing some of his own political support in Taiwan), but the ambiguity cannot be finally dissolved. The question here is not really if Lee means what he says but if what he does is effective, gets publicity, and creates momentum. Does he need to defend himself or does he achieve a balance and a consistency between his media-generated image and his words and deeds at public appearances? It is clear that Lee's role as witness to progress and continuity through repetition earns him advantages and offensive possibilities within the Japanese public sphere that have not transferred to other powerful Taiwanese politicians. For an illustrative example of a more orthodox "Chinese"–Japanese confrontation, I will now turn to current ROC president Ma Ying-jeou and his Japan visits in 2006 and 2007.

A stranger's visits, a friend's return: Ma Ying-jeou's and Frank Hsieh's Japan visits

It should be kept in mind that the PRC does not generally oppose ROC politicians' Japan visits, and its reason for protesting each time Lee went to Japan was not that a visit as such was a threat to the Joint Communique, but that it regards Lee as a separatist trying to drum up support for Taiwanese formal independence in Japan and, therefore, considers Japan as interfering in Chinese internal affairs when it lets him visit for whatever official reason. In fact, the PRC does not make that kind of loud protests very often—the DPP's candidate for the presidential election in 2008, Frank Hsieh (Xie Changting), visited Japan without diplomatic controversy in 2007, and Ma likewise toured Japan twice, in 2006 as Taipei mayor and KMT chairman and in 2007 as the KMT's presidential candidate, without Beijing's official interference.[4] The PRC played no dramatic role in the coverage of these visits, a fact that significantly sets those cases apart from Lee's where Beijing's threats and protests had a major effect on the way Japanese and Taiwanese media portrayed the decision-making process in Tokyo surrounding the visa question. Indeed, as chairman of the KMT, which is in favor of eventual cross-strait reunification and considers Taiwan Chinese, and as a consequence of his already well-established image in the Japanese media, Ma already faced ample challenges with Japanese public opinion as it were and posed no immediate danger to Beijing in terms of securing Japanese popular support for anything. An expert on the legal aspects of the Senkaku/Diaoyutai Islands dispute, Ma had previously uttered the view that Japanese claims to the islands were unjustified and he had also in the past expressed the view that Japan had still not learned from its history of aggression in the 1930s–1940s and, therefore, needed to confront its past in order to prevent such things from happening again. As a consequence, Japanese media had already labeled Ma "anti-Japanese" prior to his 2006 visit and now presented the visit as his attempt, as Taiwan's probable next president, to shed that label.

To Taiwanese media Ma explained his motives for going as part of an intercity exchange between Taipei and Yokohama (whose mayor at the time, Nakada Hiroshi, is a personal friend of Ma) and a desire to clarify his views to the Japanese: "to explain to the Japanese that he does not take an anti-Japanese stance and that his position on Japan is very clear, namely that mistakes can be forgiven but not forgotten" ("Shizhang" 2006). Despite having thus linked himself perhaps intentionally to Chiang Kai-shek's magnanimous postwar stance toward Japan, which Chih Huei Huang discusses in another chapter of this book, Ma came to occupy a position in the Japanese media as a Japan-skeptic and as a stranger to Japan exactly through a focus on his enumerations of things not to be repeated. In many ways, his image in Japan was shaped by his refusal to engage in the pathos of repetition as continuity. Ma's view was that Japan committed "mistakes" that must not be repeated, that Japan is not special and does not need to be measured by unique standards, that the Japanese prime minister should not repeat his Yasukuni visits, that the Senkaku/Diaoyutai Islands should not rightly be considered Japanese again, and so on. Perhaps unsurprisingly then, Ma found himself confronted by angry demonstrators outside his hotel, which Taiwan's *Liberty Times*, a DPP-friendly newspaper with little sympathy for Ma and the KMT, also made a point of covering with sensation and *Schadenfreude*:

> The chairman of the main group protesting against Ma Ying-jeou's Japan visit, The Association for Restoration of Japanese Sovereignty, Sakai Nobuhiko, said in a statement issued at the scene: "Ma Ying-jeou is like an agent of the PRC, a habitual criminal fabricating history and inciting anti-Japanese feelings." He also said that "Ma is the common enemy of the people of both Taiwan and Japan," while people held up banners exclaiming that Ma Ying-jeou was "not welcome." ("Riren kangyi" 2006)

His insistence on having been wrongly labeled "anti-Japanese" and having no intention to move the KMT still closer to China and further away from Japan notwithstanding, Ma failed to carve out a position for himself in the unenthusiastic public between that of the blatant "enemy of the people" (in the rhetoric of Mr. Sakai's right-wing citizens' group quoted above) and the enthusiastic witness to development within the authenticity of tradition. *China Times* evaluated the trip as a failure in terms of its PR objectives:

Japanese media reports on Ma Ying-jeou still focused on him as anti-Japanese and on the Yasukuni Shrine issue, and it seems he did not obtain the result he was after: the elimination of his "anti-Japanese" image…. This trip does not seem to have erased the impression among the general [Japanese] public that he is "anti-Japanese, pro-Chinese." ("Xiao Ma ge" 2006)

When he returned to Japan on another visit just sixteen months later in November 2007, he was now neither Taipei mayor nor party chairman, but the KMT's candidate for the 2008 presidential election, which he eventually went on to win by a large margin. This time he tried even harder to dispel his unpopularity, taking time off between meetings with politicians to give a public lecture at Kyoto's private Dōshisha University, where he declared himself neutral and curious toward Japan: "I am neither anti-Japanese nor pro-Chinese, I just want to really understand Japan" ("Ba Eikyū-shi" 2007). This came after days of media coverage where his attempts to reassure the Japanese media and public that if he were to become president he would pursue a policy of status quo in the Taiwan Strait and that unification with China was unrealistic virtually drowned in his constantly having to answer questions about his "anti-Japanese" opinions. As the *China Times* reported, "On the first day of KMT presidential candidate Ma Ying-jeou's visit to Japan, he voiced his frustrations to the Japanese media at the hotel where he is staying in Tokyo, saying: 'Please stop calling me anti-Japanese'" ("Ma: bie zai" 2007). Already firmly established as unfriendly to Japan, Ma is trapped in a vicious circle of repetition—the more he goes to Japan, the more opportunity the media have to present the image of Ma as a candidate who dislikes Japan and is disliked by the Japanese—precisely the image that Ma is trying to dispel by traveling to Japan. Significantly, there are demonstrations almost everywhere he goes, and his speech at Dōshisha gets little more attention than the angry mob in front of the university gate and a banner hung there telling him to "go home" ("Ma di Ri" 2007).

In sharp contrast to Ma's image problems in Japan, his rival for the presidency, the DPP's Frank Hsieh, received a much warmer welcome when he visited a month later. Hsieh studied law at Kyoto University in the 1970s, is fluent in Japanese, and likewise met with Taiwan-friendly politicians and gave a speech, managing to lecture at his Japanese alma mater. Japanese and Taiwanese media were both preoccupied with this curious phenomenon of Japan becoming a battleground in the Taiwanese election. Both sides speculated that while outgoing president Chen's foreign policy had meant a general deterioration of Taiwan's foreign relations, ties with Japan had actually improved, therefore making the candidates' handling of Japan an important factor in the election. That is a plausible explanation, but also problematic as Hsieh definitely defeated Ma in the PR battle over Japan but still lost the election nonetheless. However, unlike Ma, he actively played on the Lee-like repetition motifs of continuity, progress, and emotional attachment to Japan during his visit. He repeatedly stressed his Japanese educational background and declared himself fond of Japan, including, as the DPP-friendly *Sankei shimbun* reported, his "love [for] Japanese *enka* songs that call up emotions from the depths of the heart." ("Sha Chōtei-shi" 2007). While Ma had to distance himself from Lee Teng-hui politically, Hsieh positioned himself almost as Lee's successor and took advantage of his platform of sympathy in Japan.

A good example of how he did that was his lecture at Kyoto University which, it will be remembered, is also Lee's alma mater. *Liberty Times* celebrated

> the first time a Taiwanese political figure has been allowed entry to Kyoto University to lecture … Hsieh gave his entire speech in Japanese, and the venue was fully packed. Three years ago, Lee Teng-hui wanted to visit his alma mater, Kyoto University, but due to protests from China he could not even enter the gates. ("Xie: wo dangxuan" 2007)

Positioned as taking up Lee's thread even to the point of surpassing him vis-à-vis the Japanese, Hsieh pushed the similarities further in his Kyoto speech: "Lee Teng-hui is the only Kyoto University graduate to become president anywhere in the world; next year I will be the second Kyōdai graduate-turned-president" ("Xie: yuan" 2007).

Literally assuming for himself a role as Lee's heir, Hsieh repeats the posture of a bringer of continuity: when he wins the election Taiwan will once again be ruled by a Japanese-trained president, the shared connection to Japan and to Kyoto University being the link that connects the two reigns. Thus, continuity in Taiwanese political power can now be achieved largely through continuity in its links to Japanese culture and aesthetics.

Conclusion

The figure of the Taiwanese politician visiting Japan is interpreted in media narratives depending on his or her attitude toward the question of continuity and enthusiasm for Japan, his ability to credibly activate instances of repetition of the past, and of signaling that nothing has been lost, in words and deeds. What seems at first to be a case of positive versus negative repetition (Ma also repeats his points and his visits and the media repeat their view of him, one could argue) dissolves upon further investigation into a question of repetition versus difference (or nonrepetition): there is really no corresponding concept of negative repetition at play, as current ROC president Ma Ying-jeou's position is a denial of the value of repetition; he is unwilling or unable for political or other reasons to free himself of constant association with all that he wants Japan *not* to repeat, and he is, therefore, cast in the role of someone who wants Japan to break free of itself, to lose itself in projecting itself forward, and of one who would strip Japan of the pathos of roots, continuity, and tradition. Former president Lee Teng-hui and 2008 DPP presidential candidate Frank Hsieh, of course, do not celebrate Japanese violence or military aggression; rather, they are able through the use of repetition as continuity to reactivate fragments of "old Japan" in a positive and sentimentally rewarding way. They find themselves at home in Japan, while Ma is essentially different and communicatively trapped in that difference. It grows as he tries to overcome it.

The main attraction to the news media of this mode of repetition as continuity is that the Taiwanese visitor can be perceived as sensitive to "eternal" structures in Japan unnoticed by Japanese themselves and, therefore, serve to negate any lurking suspicions of fundamental breaks and fissures in the recent history of Japan–Taiwan relations and between "old" and contemporary Japan. Overindulgence in flattering the Japanese poses a real threat for a Taiwanese politician to alienate large domestic voter segments sensitive to "neo-colonial" attitudes. However, I demonstrate it to be a prerequisite for the successful execution of repetition as continuity that the visitor's emotional involvement in Japan appears credible and genuine and that he or she displays a willingness to regard Japan as a special place with its own unique character. Engaging in the pathos of positive Japanese continuity and confirming the value of "eternal" Japanese ways allows Taiwanese leaders to authenticate their status in the former colony and to posit a Taiwan that continues to be defined by its Japanese—not Chinese—past.

Notes

1   Homi K. Bhabha has analyzed in some detail the general phenomenon in postcolonial rhetoric of imagining national characteristics to emanate uniformly from all parts of national territory, calling it an instance of "turning Territory into Tradition" (1994: 213). I discuss a number of Bhabha's analytical approaches later in this chapter.

2   For more on this type of dehistorization and instrumentalization of history, see Sejrup (2012).

3   He was not, however, able to meet officially with Japanese political officeholders on the 2007 trip; this did not happen until he met with Okinawa prefecture governor Nakaima Hirokazu in Naha in September 2008.

4   The PRC seems to limit its strong opposition to visits by acting or former heads of government. Thus, it was "worried" about former prime minister Mori's visit to Taiwan in December 2003 on the rationale that an ex-government leader simply cannot make a visit without political overtones.

11

Drinking Modernity: Sexuality and the Sanitation of Space in Taiwan's Coffee Shops

Marc L. Moskowitz

In the summer of 2008 I took a trip from Taipei to a small village in Pingdong County, one of the poorest and most remote areas of Taiwan.[1] To get there I had to take the high-speed rail to a train to an unlicensed Greyhound-style "wild chicken" bus. The final stretch of the trip was in a storeowner's car—the driver sidelined with an unofficial taxi service in his personal car because licensed taxis were so few in that area. We were a 50-minute drive from the nearest branch of what I had thought to be the ubiquitous McDonald's franchise. There, a 5-minute walk from my destination was a 24-hour 7-Eleven market with four choices of prepackaged Starbucks coffee—cappuccino, caramel quandi, espresso, and latte. All of this was in a country that ten years earlier had almost no coffee shops, where the coffee to be had in teahouses tasted like instant coffee for NT$150 (US$4.50) a cup.

Coffee did not originate in East Asia; neither did Buddhism, baseball, or the Internet. Although not "Taiwanese" in origin, coffee shops still have become central in Taiwan's urban landscape. In many ways Taiwan was ready-made for coffee consumption. With long traditions of tea and teahouses, with workaholic tendencies beginning in primary school, and in an environment in which elite status is often embedded in Western symbology, Taiwan's modern coffee shop culture now seems like a natural development. Even twenty years ago, however, few could have predicted its current widespread popularity.

The history of coffee consumption in Taiwan is a vivid illustration of the ways that Japanese and American consumer cultures have vied to capture the hearts of Taiwan's populace and the contents of their wallets. The history of coffee in Taiwan raises several questions about the cultural influences of Japan and the United States: What do Japanese- and American-inspired coffee shop cultures say about class stratification or the opposing ideology of individualist egalitarianism? What are the gendered dimensions of public space? In what ways are consumers disciplined, in a very Foucauldian sense, by the behavioral expectations within these spheres? Historically, Japanese and American models of coffee shops differed in their views of class, gender hierarchies, hygiene, sexuality, and standardization. As the American model won out, Japanese corporate coffee houses emulated much of what Starbucks and other

American corporate competitors had to offer while still striving to maintain local choices about food and smoking. The ensuing history of coffee in Taiwan is intertwined with the cultural legacies of Japan and the United States. These two models of business and culture have at times been in competition and at times in symbiosis, but they are continually in dialogue within Taiwan's cultural sphere.

I should note from the outset that I compare and contrast Japan's influences on Taiwan's coffee culture with specifically American, rather than generally "Western," examples. I do use the terms "West" and "Western," however, to highlight an important yet symbolic construct that is used in Taiwan's envisioning of self and other, past and future.

Café culture was part of Japan's profound modern influence on their Taiwanese colony. Frequenting Japanese coffee shops spoke to a desire to participate not only in the culture of the metropolis but also in global trends. After 1945, as Chinese Nationalist rulers and educators worked to erase the imprints of Taiwan's colonial history, the United States became a powerful icon of modern global culture. Still, Japanese cinema, music, fashion, and a colonial nostalgia continue to have a tremendous influence on Taiwan's culture today. Its profound influence on Taiwan's coffee culture is less understood but is still a telling instance of the colonial legacy.

American coffee culture has captured the imagination of many of Taiwan's intellectuals as a central representation of Western modernity (Shen 2005: 79). American coffee shop and fast-food chains like Starbucks and McDonald's have built on the Japanese corporate model in Taiwan. They flaunt their brightly lit trademarks to demonstrate a symbolic capital that is far more embedded in elite status than in their countries of origin. American corporate coffee houses and fast-food chains have thereby been the central point of contrast to Japanese coffee traditions, which are themselves inspired by a range of elements from Chinese, Japanese, and American coffee and tea cultures.

Scholarship and popular press coverage on Taiwan often treat the "Chinese" elements (in religious or familial values, for example) as "true" Taiwanese culture, as opposed to Japanese- or Western-inspired innovations that are perceived to be somehow inauthentic. Yet something as seemingly "foreign" as coffee shops truly gives voice to the complex cultural hybridity of contemporary Taiwan. Taiwan's vibrant coffee culture highlights the ways that many people frame their own choices and commitments as forward-looking global participation. This stands in juxtaposition to weighty traditional expectations. It is only in exploring both created nostalgias and imagined futures that one can hope to truly understand Taiwan. Here I hope to question the implicit hierarchies of what we assume to be Taiwanese. To do so one must use a wider range of analysis that necessarily conceptualizes Japanese and American influences as being no more "foreign" than Chinese traditions.

Japan's legacy: Coffee shops as a sexualized sphere

Dutch merchants introduced coffee to Japan in the seventeenth century. In 1888 two "coffee-tea houses" opened in Tokyo, claiming to combine the best of the East and the

West in its exotic yet familiar atmosphere. Other Japanese coffee houses followed in the 1920s; these were opened primarily by Japanese people who had lived abroad and who wanted to create Parisian-style cafés in Japan (Pendergrast 1999: 269; Weinberg and Bealer 2002: 143–4).

In 1884 the British company Tait Marketing & Distribution (*Deji yanghang*) began growing coffee in Taiwan for export. The ownership and administration of its Taiwan branch was turned over to Japan when the island became a Japanese colony in 1895. During the colonial era, Japanese-style coffee houses called "tea-sipping stores" (*kissaten*) appeared. In Chinese culture, even into the Republican period, teahouses were associated with "lecherous shows." As with hostess clubs today, the teahouse was a place for businessmen and politicians to build alliances for their business dealings in an overtly masculinist environment (Goldstein 2003: 753; Wang 2008: 10).

As late as the 1930s most of Taiwan's coffee houses were Japanese-run (Wen 2014: 220); colonial businesses continued to grow coffee in Taiwan as well until 1937, when Taiwan's labor pool was reassigned to help with the Pacific War effort against China (Fan 2000: 46, 2001: 6). These Japanese coffee houses represented modernity and participation in global culture through the consumption of Western goods. Unlike European cafés, in which the waiters were primarily male, Japanese cafés were staffed with women (Wen 2014; White 2012: 49). The presence of female waitresses was seen as an abrupt transformation of the traditionally male-dominated public sphere, yet this site also was defined by traditional gender hierarchies.

Taiwan's early coffee shops drew on this erotically charged environment, featuring a mix of Japanese coffee traditions and Chinese teahouse precedents. These cultural mores were embedded in expectations of elite male privilege. This included the use of women as voyeuristic pleasure for men and the constant erotic potential that the waitresses presented. In many coffee shops from the Japanese era through the 1970s, a waitress's role was remarkably similar to women working in contemporary high-end hostess clubs. Coffee houses bragged about the beauty of their waitresses (White 2012: 47; Wen 2014) and a significant part of café waitresses' jobs was to keep the male clientele happy through erotically charged conversation (White 2012: 47–53, 65, 68). In the words of Merry White, coffee houses created a "trancelike" ethos in which "eroticism dominated over communication, fantasy over intellect" (2012: 47).[2]

Taiwan's coffee house waitresses played a very similar role to that of a Japanese geisha (Wen 2014: 190). As the coffee houses became more established in Taiwan, they were reconstructed to be more like taverns, even to the point that many of the waitresses were expected to dance with the guests (Wen 2014: 193, 208). Taiwan's coffee shop waitresses often had few other prospects. They were usually women whose families had died or who were running away from unwanted marriage arrangements. Coffee shops provided economic stability while allowing these women to avoid a drastic step into prostitution. Still, it was a highly stigmatized job and, as historian Shen Mengying has explained, at that time "a father would rather die than allow his own daughter to work as a coffee shop hostess." This tradition continued throughout the 1960s and 1970s in the "music coffee shops" (*yinyue kafeiting*), which housed the rather infamous "coffee women" (*kafei nülang*) who continued serving in the hostess tradition (Fan 2000: 53, 57, 2001: 74; Shen 2002: 114, 2005: 71).

By the late 1960s, the hypersexual-style coffee shop was falling out of vogue as hostess settings became increasingly bound to alcohol-related spheres. Yet one could see several caffeinated adaptations of this tradition in the following decades. In the 1970s, for example, "black coffee shops" (*hei kafeiting*) continued to link sensuality with coffee culture in dimly lit cafés that provided convenient make-out spots (Shen 2002: 73). In the 1980s these evolved into MTVs or private rooms one could rent to watch a movie. MTV rooms offered a relatively affordable place for trysts that, not coincidentally, included a complimentary cup of coffee or tea with the price of entry.[3] In the mid-1990s, there was also considerable sensationalistic news coverage on teahouses in Taizhong employing teenage girls who wore extremely skimpy clothing for the voyeuristic pleasure of the male customers.

In many ways, the contemporary distancing of coffee house culture from sexuality resulted in binding such activities more firmly to alcohol-related domains. To contemporary sensibilities, this is hardly surprising. Because alcohol is known to lower inhibitions, it is socially accepted that drinking will allow people to say and do things that might be censured in their daily lives. This provides especially important ammunition for women who must mediate between what are known as "virgin/whore" dichotomies (Moskowitz 2008: 327–35). If this sounds familiar to the English-speaking reader, it is because the values that create this particular tightrope for women to walk have largely been imported to Taiwan through American mass media. This is not to say that women in China and Taiwan traditionally did not have to mediate between contradictory expectations of being "good" and alluring. Yet many of the transitions in Taiwan's coffee houses would seem to point to the hegemonic paradoxes of Puritanism as ushered in by American missionaries and mass media. The separation of the hostess environment in Taiwan from Japanese coffee culture symbolically marked a greater equality of the sexes in the public sphere. Yet it also narrowed sexually charged behavior to alcohol-related domains that often served as strong reminders of continued patriarchal values. Desexualizing the world of coffee marked the victory of the American corporate coffee shop over the Japanese model as well as a growing degree of gender equality in the public sphere. Yet it also highlights the inheritance of American inconsistencies that attempt to censure sexuality while at the same moment celebrating it as a ubiquitous part of public discourse.[4]

In addressing these historical developments, it is easy to overlook the fact that coffee is a profoundly sensual experience that is embodied both through the physical effects of caffeine, its distinctive taste, and a range of auditory, olfactory, and tactile experiences that are distinctive to each coffee house. We should, therefore, be wary of teleological views that the traditional model of Japanese-style hostess coffee shops was somehow abnormal and that the American corporate model was a natural evolutionary result.

Creating taste: Coffee for the masses

In addition to changing domains of sexuality in the public sphere, coffee shops were a symbol of important shifts in Taiwan's political economy. In the 1930s, coffee shop clientele primarily consisted of Japanese or Taiwanese elites who had studied in Japan (Fan 2001: 42, 57). By 1943, coffee houses had split into two types: there were eight hostess-style coffee shops and seven Western-style coffee shops in Taipei that served the intelligentsia, including students, writers, and reporters (Shen 2005: 20–4, 30). The number of coffee shops increased from twenty-one in 1928 to eighty-seven in 1968 (Shen 2002: 51, 117). All of these coffee houses continued to be prohibitively expensive for most. In the 1950s, one cup of coffee cost a steep NT$15–70 (US$0.40–1.75) per cup when the average annual income in Taiwan was around US$150. In the mid-1970s, a cup of coffee in a high-end coffee shop in a hotel cost anywhere from NT$100 (US$2.50) to as much as NT$500 (US$12.50), while the average person in Taiwan spent approximately NT$40 (US$1.00) a day on food. These trends were closely related to the KMT's economic policies in their new home province. Part of the continued expense of coffee consumption was due to the high tariffs placed on imports in 1951 in order to encourage economic growth within Taiwan. In the early 1960s the coffee tariff was 120 percent; this was reduced to 60 percent in 1968. These costs were primarily borne by American businessmen and military personnel (Fan 2000: 49, 53, 2001: 7, 9, 46; Shen 2002: 42, 2005: 85).

In 1947, mainland immigrants who had fled the civil war opened their first coffee shops in Taiwan with the intent of serving a clientele of other Chinese expatriates. From 1949 through 1978, American soldiers stationed in Taiwan frequented some of Taipei's coffee shops; Taiwanese students, intellectuals, and other elite literati occupied others. Taiwan's coffee shop culture was part of many writers' and artists' envisioning of a new Westernized modernity. This trend continued through the 1950s and 1960s with a new modern literature movement that centered on coffee shop culture because of its modern globalized imagery (Fan 2000: 54, 2001: 59–60; Shen 2002: 84, 2005: 77).

Instant coffee was another important part of Taiwan's emerging coffee culture. Nescafé followed American troops who were stationed in Taiwan from 1947 to 1978 and became the first instant coffee brand to enter Taiwan's market (Fan 2001: 82, 95–6). Maxwell House followed in 1982 (Fan 2001: 82, 95–6). Japan's coffee industry was also profoundly influenced by instant coffee. In 1970s Japan, coffee production increased exponentially when General Foods and Nestle opened plants to produce instant coffee. By the mid-1970s there were 21,000 coffee shops in Tokyo alone and coffee sales generated US$100 million annually (Pendergrast 1999: 304–5). Historian Fan Ting has suggested that it was instant coffee advertisements that created a niche for mainstream coffee shop culture in Taiwan by promoting images of individual and social enjoyment of coffee (Fan 2001: 98–101). Drawing on Japan's long-standing relationship with Taiwan, in 1974 the Japanese-owned Honey Café (*Mifeng kafei*) became Taiwan's first coffee shop chain (Fan 2000:

57, 2001: 182). Primarily catering to businessmen, the Honey Café continued to be popular in Taiwan throughout the 1970s and 1980s.

In 1984, the first McDonald's opened in Taipei, featuring a NT$35 (US$0.83) cup of coffee with free refills. For the first time, coffee shop culture thereby became accessible to Taiwan's steadily growing middle class, which had a thirst for ways to mark its new social distinction as well as to enjoy the fruits of Taiwan's new flourishing economy. As the first Western food corporation allowed to open in Taiwan, McDonald's ushered in a range of new cultural mores for dining. It almost singlehandedly removed the traditional stigma of employment in service industries and introduced an intensified focus on hygiene, Taylorist production, and standardization. It also ushered in a new regime of egalitarian customer relations where a customer who spent NT$35 (US$1.06) on a small coffee was treated the same as someone who spent ten times that amount (Ho 1994; Watson 1997). Because of its modern image, affordability, and cleanliness, McDonald's became a place to study and pass time for a new generation with spending power and leisure time away from their parents.

In recent years, McDonald's has opened cafés in separate sections within its stores. These McCafés serve higher-end pastries and coffee in an effort to compete with Starbucks and Japanese-owned franchises. Yet from its arrival in Taiwan, McDonald's was already known for its coffee-shop ethos.[5] Students took advantage of the clean, air-conditioned environment by nursing a cup of coffee or tea for the day—a trend that continues in McDonald's and other American fast-food franchises such as Kentucky Fried Chicken. McDonald's allowed this as a localized set of customs that reflected its higher social standing in Taiwan.

Here too we must remember that Taiwanese appropriations of McDonald's as a coffee shop space came from customers' desire to recreate a cultural milieu that they had experienced traveling abroad, heard about from friends, or seen in foreign films. Yet Japanese-owned coffee shops, teashops that served Japanese-style coffee, and McDonald's restaurants constituted most people's first lived experience with coffee culture in Taiwan.

Between 1949 and 1978 coffee bean imports to Taiwan gradually rose to 500 metric tons a year. This rose by almost four times to 2,300 metric tons in the decade between 1987 and 1997, and doubled again to 5,000 metric tons in 1999. The sale of instant coffee rose from NT$1.2 billion (US$36.4 million) in 1987 to NT$4.76 billion (US$144.2 million) in 1999 (Fan 2001: 8, 110). As coffee consumption became more widespread in Taiwan, people's knowledge of coffee also grew. Magazines in the 1980s featured articles that instructed readers on the proper etiquette of coffee drinking (*kafei zhengque fangshi*) in terms reminiscent of ritualized tea ceremonies. In the 1990s the discussion shifted to how to discern between good- and bad-tasting coffee beans, and the particular differences between different kinds of blends. This marked a transition from an emphasis on the knowledge of ceremony and etiquette to familiarizing one's self with the quality of the coffee itself as a marker of sophistication (Fan 2001: 156, 186). In this sense, coffee consumption was but one part of an increasing cosmopolitanization of consumer culture in Taiwan.

By the late 1990s there were hundreds of coffee shops in Taiwan. Coffee culture had shifted from being exotic to an everyday experience for many. In 1990, Japan yet again paved the way for Taiwan's coffee shop culture when the Doutor Coffee Shop (*Luoduolun*) chain opened, featuring a NT$35 (US$1.06) cup of coffee. By 1995 the Japanese-owned Café House (*Zhenguo kafeiguan*) had already opened forty-six branches in Taiwan. In 1995 there were five coffee chains in Taiwan with a total of twenty-two shops; by 1999 there were 103 chains with a total of 469 shops (Fan 2000: 62, 64, 2001: 64). Taiwanese corporations such as 85°C and Eslite Bookstore were also making coffee culture more central to middle-class lives.[6]

The Eslite Bookstore chain opened its first 24-hour coffee shop in 1999 and explicitly represented this step as a way of pushing Taiwan into the culture of globalization. Its customers saw it as an important step in creating a more cultured Western-inspired modernity within Taiwan. Its coffee shops featured sandwiches and salads that were decidedly Western in appearance while still often localized in taste.

McDonald's followed suit by opening 24-hour franchises in 2005. This too had precedents in the form of Taiwan's restaurants, teahouses, and night markets that are open into the very late hours. It also drew on the model of 7-Eleven and other mini-marts that offer 24-hour service. Taiwan's 7-Eleven stores sell conspicuously Western goods ranging from Pringles potato chips to freshly cooked hot dogs at the same time that their customers can buy localized foods such as hot tea eggs or triangular rice and tuna seaweed rolls. 7-Eleven's coffee selection includes a machine that grinds coffee for each cup of cappuccino or latte. Its refrigerators house cans of localized flavors of coffee such as Mr. Brown's Coffee, which is heavily sweetened to meet local tastes. In combining these traditions, the 24-hour coffee shop and mini-marts symbolize a new urban modernity that is embedded in an imagery of Western efficiency. Yet the hours kept by service industries in the United States actually seem parochial by comparison.

The arrival of Starbucks arguably marked the beginning of Taiwan's contemporary coffee house era. Corporate interests and marketing strategies from Japan and Taiwan are surprisingly central to the Starbucks phenomenon as well. In Taiwan, Starbucks is managed by the Uni-President Enterprises Corporation (*Tongyi qiye*), which also supervises the Taiwan branches of the convenience store 7-Eleven, the formerly American company acquired by the Japanese corporation Itō-Yōkadō in the early 1990s. In 2014, there were 4,919 stores bearing the 7-Eleven moniker that served Taiwan's 23 million populace, as opposed to the 8,155 branches serving the entire United States—or eight times more of a presence proportionally ("7-11" 2014).

Drawing on its great success in localizing the American 7-Eleven for Japanese controlling interests, Uni-President consciously works to market Starbucks' American image (Tsai 1990: 151). People who frequent Starbucks in Taiwan clearly enjoy the American atmosphere. In the aforementioned survey in southern Taiwan, 19.6 percent of responding Starbucks customers said that they frequented Starbucks because the food and drinks tasted good—less than the 21.1 percent who responded that they went because they liked the English-language music or the 26.8 percent who responded that they went because of its overall reputation (Hsu, Liu, and Pan 2006: 71). Starbucks' success in Taiwan is, therefore, in large part directly associated with Japanese corporate precedents and Taiwanese marketing skills.

In many ways, the rise of Taiwan's coffee shops was a tangible symbol of its booming economy and increased exposure to the outside world. Taiwan's per capita GNP rose from US$145 in 1951 to US$8,111 in 1990 (Fan 2000: 49, 51, 59; Shen 2002: 63). Its per capita GDP rose to US$39,600 in 2013 (Central 2014). The number of Taiwanese who went abroad to study increased from 2,558 in 1971 to 26,371 in 1999. In 1980, almost half a million Taiwanese went abroad to travel. A decade later, this number had risen to 2.9 million and in 1999 almost 6.6 million (out of a population of 22 million) did so (Fan 2001: 92–3, 124, 127; Shen 2005: 102). This exposed Taiwan's elite and upper middle classes to alternative lifestyles and solidified an already growing commitment to continuing global identities through consuming transnationally produced goods in localized environments.

Far from driving out its competition, as many assume is happening in the United States, Starbucks has created a wider consumer base in East Asia that other firms draw on. Japan's Doutor Coffee franchise, for example, has very much benefited from Starbucks' success in generating a wider interest in coffee. Today Doutor boasts of having more than 1,200 coffee shops worldwide (2012). Doutor's executives have stated that they intentionally revamped its coffee shop's images to draw on the Starbucks customer base while also offering a more localized set of options that include local food choices (Lewis 2003: 13). This might include local meals such as curried chicken or fried pork on rice. The pastries are also far more localized. Although their ingredients are not available to the public, their pastries, like most desserts in Taiwan, seem to contain less cream and vanilla extract than their American counterparts. Doutor coffee shops also feature a smoking room, which provides a dramatic and localized alternative to the American food chains' antismoking policies.

Starbucks and other corporate coffee houses cater to Taiwan's enormous educated and cosmopolitan middle class. Indeed, one survey of Starbucks consumers in southern Taiwan found that 77.6 percent of its consumers were in, or had graduated from, university (Hsu, Liu, and Pan 2006: 70). Elite patrons also go to Starbucks, but there is also a range of small privately owned coffee shops in anonymous back streets that are often owned or frequented by pop stars and television and movie stars. More visibly located in main thoroughfares, fast-food chains such as Mister Donut, Dunkin' Donuts, Kentucky Fried Chicken, and McDonald's offer cheaper coffee alternatives while also allowing people to study for hours. In 2003 McDonald's also began to compete with the new coffee shop popularity by creating its own coffee shops, called McCafé, as a separate section in their restaurants. Even as Starbucks and other corporate coffee houses have boomed, these cheaper alternatives have held on to their niche in the market.

Coffee culture is both social and individualistic in that one can go to a coffee shop to meet with friends, but one can also go alone to read or simply to daydream. This is a marked difference from the traditional hostess-style coffee shop that was, by its very nature, a profoundly social space with no conceptual room for isolated individuals. In a sense, then, contemporary coffee shops thereby become emblematic of a new self-oriented (*ziwo*) identity valued for its space for authentic expression rather than the previous negative connotation of ego-driven selfishness. This new form of individualism marks a new urban identity that is particularly amenable to coffee symbology as both modern and global.[7] Yet as with so much else in Taiwan, labeling this as Western modernity would ignore much of what actually drives this culture. It is more accurate to call this a Western-inspired modernity, in which Taiwanese and Japanese business and cultural precedents are as much a part of these new manifestations as anything found in the West.

Shifting gender paradigms

As American and Japanese coffee house corporations adapt to new global standards in order to vie for their piece of Taiwan's market, it is easy to overlook the profound transformations in Taiwan's gendered public culture that this represents. Before the 1970s, the only women one was likely to find in Taiwan's traditional coffee houses were the coffee house hostesses described above or prostitutes who accompanied the male customers (Shen 2005: 145–8). From the 1970s to the mid-1980s, more "respectable women" began to frequent coffee shops, but only those from the upper elite could afford this luxury. Today, not only are women an integral part of coffee shop clientele, but they represent a slight majority: 60.4 percent of the consumers in southern Taiwan Starbucks branches are women, for example (Hsu, Liu, and Pan 2006: 70). To some degree, this may be less emancipatory than one might think, in that many women in Taiwan have more leisure time because of their continued exclusion from high-status, more time-consuming professions.[8] Yet it also points to a certain degree of equality for women who now have their own incomes and a place as consumers in the public sphere.

The shifting gender dynamic in Taiwan's coffee shops is a direct result of Taiwan's exponentially growing middle class and changes to the service economy in the 1980s (Yang 2004). This was both a reflection of, and the impetus for, women's widespread entrance into the workforce, which provided them with spending money of their own.

Anthropologist Karen Kelsky has suggested that it is structurally advantageous for Japanese women to embrace images of global modernity and its accompanying relative gender equality, whereas Japanese men benefit more from, and are more devoted to, traditional gender roles (Kelsky 2001; Ong 2006: 234). Because Taiwan's middle-class and elite women face many of the same challenges and opportunities, their choices in consumption are a reflection of similar attitudes toward the West. Women's consumption habits have become a vital part of Taiwan's economy—one that shapes Taiwan's gendered public sphere in profound ways. Coffee shops are not unique in this. Rather, they are but one of a range of public venues including restaurants, dance clubs, and shopping malls that provide visual testimony for the changing gender roles in Taiwan's public sphere.

The separation of sex and caffeine was tied into this new globalized set of perceptions in which coffee shifted from an exotic stimulant to just one of many beverages. In contrast, coffee's long-standing association with Western modernity has resulted in a clear victory for the corporate coffee house model.

Yet if these shifts in coffee culture mark a degree of gender equality in the public sphere, they also introduce their own set of control mechanisms. Large corporate coffee culture equalizes gender status to some degree, but corporate coffee houses' mechanized customer relations also presents an argument against modern coffee culture as innately emancipatory. American corporations have become infamous for their scripting, for example, in which the person serving the coffee or meal is expected to ask questions from a set of predetermined questions designed to encourage the consumer to buy more items and in larger servings (Ritzer 2007). In Taiwan, coffee shop employees still seem to have retained their right to express their personalities (and one might say their humanity) far more than their counterparts at the same institutions in the United States. Yet if Taiwan's branches of McDonald's and Kentucky Fried Chicken are anything to go by, it is only a matter of time before employees at both American and Japanese coffee chains in Taiwan are forced to completely limit their interactions to corporate-produced scripts as well.[9] One can still find less scripted interactions in individually owned coffee houses that are hidden in the back roads of urban Taipei. Yet, the coffee at these cafés is often three times the price of the offerings at Doutor or Starbucks. In many ways, choosing these more selective venues revives the elitist histories of coffee culture.

The new corporate model of coffee houses represents the sanitization of the coffee shop as part of the public sphere, which is but one part of a larger governmental and corporate control of public space in Taiwan. Examples of this phenomenon investigated recently by scholars include Taipei's Mass Rapid Transit subway system and the accompanying behavior control of Taiwan's citizenry (Lee 2007), betel nut consumption and governmental efforts to discourage betel nut chewing as unhygienic and backward (Liu 2006), and the corporate and governmental encroachment on Taiwan's night market culture that is accompanied by a sanitization of these public spaces (Yu 2004). The shifts in Taiwan's coffee house culture that I have presented above should, therefore, be seen less as a natural evolutionary step in a universal progress toward modern capitalism than as part of the hegemony of a new globalized sanitation of the public sphere.

Conclusion

As with so many other aspects of Taiwan's culture, it is important to remember that coffee is but one example of Western imagery being ushered in through the powerful presence of Japan's colonial regime. In this context, the border between many seemingly distinctive categories of East and West, local and global, quickly began to fray. Both Japanese and American coffee corporations sell the allure of Western modernity. This vividly illustrates the highly constructed nature of such imagery, and the ways that corporate structures both adapt to new cultural environments and form them.

As I noted above, although the modern coffee shop is an emblem of the emancipation of women through their presence in the public sphere, we should also remember that all of the sexual practices that once took place at coffee and tea houses can still be found today in alcohol-related locales. These alcohol-related spheres are also diversifying into public global styles of alcohol consumption—in pubs and clubs, for example, in addition to the East Asian model of hostess clubs in which one needs a personal introduction to gain access.[10] In this sense, Taiwan's governmental efforts to create a public sphere that reflects American and Japanese sanitized modernities have also solidified the exclusive and reciprocity-oriented gender constructions that hide behind hostess bars' closed doors.

Taiwan's contemporary coffee shops represent a new bifurcated culture in which alcohol-related spheres continue to be associated with sensuality, traditionalism, and male privilege, whereas coffee shops have come to represent modernity, participation in global lifestyles, and gender equality. Removing the sexually charged ethos from modern coffee shops is part of a larger sanitation process in which sensory experiences ranging from smoking to chewing betel nut to making loud noises are all prohibited from the coffee house's new domain. This disciplining of both employees and customers also marks the increasingly successful hegemony of puritanical tendencies introduced to Taiwan by American missionaries and mass-mediated culture.

It is, of course, impossible to have public spaces that are free of control mechanisms. Yet, in examining Taiwan's coffee culture, we must problematize the degree to which the traditional hostess-style coffee shop has come to be seen as an aberration or perversion and the corporate coffee shop is perceived to be the result of a natural evolution. In this cultural history, we are witness to coffee culture's transformation as a reflection of an intense sanitization process that ranges from a greater attention to hygiene, to prohibiting smoking, and to controlling employee behavior and speech. Excising earlier hypersexualized models of coffee house culture is an important, though unarticulated, part of this new set of disciplinary mechanisms, one that seems to have wrested the power from the Japanese legacy. Yet if one looks more closely, one sees the ways that Japanese coffee corporations have adapted to these new globalized values. In agreeing to sell images of Western-inspired global modernity, Japanese coffee franchises continue to have profound effects on Taiwan's gendered public space.

Modern corporate coffee shops are iconic representations of laudable goals of sanitation and health, gender and class equality. Yet this celebratory stance is also an indication of just how accustomed we have become to the velvet cage of standardization. This is not to say that the traditional Japanese hostess-style coffee shops were free of disciplinary structures. Yet one should keep the full range of these changes in mind—less as a nostalgic sense of loss than with an analytical eye to what has been exchanged, what has been merged, and what we choose to see. These new hybrid forms are neither completely Chinese, Japanese, or American—yet they contain elements of each in contemporary Taiwan's vibrant coffee culture.

Notes

1   I am grateful to Tom Gold and David Jordan for their insightful feedback on an earlier draft of this chapter. To express equivalent currency values, for any period before 1990, I use a NT$40:US$1 conversion rate; from 1990 to today, I use an average conversion rate of NT$33:US$1.

2   This model of the sensually charged café continues today in Japan (Bornoff 1991: 430–7; Galbraith 2013).

3   This also helps MTV owners avoid paying royalties for showing films.

4   My analysis here draws on Michel Foucault's ([1978] 1990) work on censorship and the heightened rhetoric of sexuality in Victorian-era Europe.

5   By 1996 there were 131 McDonald's restaurants in Taiwan; the number rose to 346 in 2006 (Lin 2006: 10).

6   IS Coffee, the Taiwan-owned thinly veiled imitation of Starbucks, was established in 1995 and had fifty shops in Taiwan by 2000 (Fan 2000: 63, 136). The Taiwan-owned 85°C Café currently has 326 stores in Taiwan with localized flavors such as salted coffee (Jennings 2009). Several American coffee chains arrived in the late 1990s: Seattle Coffee (*Xiyatu jipin kafei*) opened in 1997, also featuring a NT$35 cup of coffee, and Starbucks (*Xingbake*) opened in 1998, which had fifty shops by 2000, with this number increasing to 225 in 2009.

7   I have argued elsewhere that individualism is nothing new to Taiwan but, rather, the conceptualization of individualism and how it is expressed has shifted. For more on this and the shifting conceptions of *ziwo*, see Fan (2001: 147); Moskowitz (2005, 2007, 2010).

8   For more on the paradoxically liberatory aspects of gender exclusion in Japan, see Kelsky (2001); Kondo (1990); Ogasawara (1998).

9   This is not to say that hostess settings are free of scripting—their drinking games are designed to fill conversational gaps and the hostesses must make a constant effort to make men feel powerful, charming, and in control. On Japanese hostess clubs, see Allison (1994); on PRC karaoke bars, see Zheng (2006). Yet the degree to which scripting takes over customer relations in corporate coffee shops is intensified.

10   For more on the need for introductions to gain access to karaoke bars in the PRC, see Zheng (2006: 162). Avron Boretz has also written on the particularistic bonds that are formed in Taiwan's karaoke bars (2004).

Glossary

Aikoku fujinkai	愛國婦人會
aiyusen	隘勇線
Ajia no koji	アジアの孤児
Aoki Shūzō	青木周藏
Arai Ryohei	荒井良平
Arai Yoshio	新井良雄
Arakawa Hiroshi	荒川博
Arisan no kyōji	阿里山の俠児
Asahi shimbun	朝日新聞
au	会う
Awashima Chikage	淡島千景
Bai Chongxi	白崇禧
banchi	蕃地
banhei	蕃兵
banjin shoyōchi	蕃人所要地
banshanren	半山人
bao Diao yundong	保釣運動
baodao yunü	寶島玉女
baojia	保甲
Beiqing chengshi	悲情城市
benshengren	本省人
benshi	弁士
bentuhua	本土化
betsuri no uta	別離の歌
Bukonsho	撫墾署
Bushidō	武士道
Cai Bingchang	蔡炳昌
Cai Kuncan	蔡焜燦
Cai Zhong-han	蔡中涵
canyu Riqiao (zanyo Nikkyō)	殘餘日僑
Chang Mei-Yao	張美瑤
Chen Cheng	陳誠
Chen Huaien	陳懷恩
Chen Shui-bian	陳水扁
Chen Yanchuan	陳嚴川
Chen Yi	陳儀
Cheng Hsiao-tse	程孝澤
Chiang Ching-kuo	蔣經國
Chiang Kai-shek	蔣介石
Chiang Shu-Chen	蔣淑貞
Chien Wei-su	簡偉斯
chiji	知事

chō	廳
Dai Guohui	戴國煇
Dai wo qu yuanfang	帶我去遠方
Dakis Pawan (Guo Mingzheng)	郭明正
Dali Kakei	達屬·卡給
Daodejing	道德經
Deji yanghang	德記洋行
Deng Shian-yang	鄧相揚
dohi	土匪
dōka	同化
Dongjing Huaqiao huibao	東京華僑會報
doshū	土酋
Du Zhengsheng	杜正勝
Duosang	多桑
Edajima Heihachi	江田島平八
enka	演歌
Erdeng jingxing xunzhang (dashou)	二等景星勳章(大綬)
Ererba shijian	二二八事件
fan zuguo	返祖國
fanzu	番族
Fu Tian-yu	傅天余
Fukuda Takeo	福田赳夫
furigana	振り仮名
Gan'en suiyue	感恩歲月
Gao Shousou	高瘦叟
Gotō Shinpei	後藤新平
Gu Fengxiang	谷鳳翔
Guangfu	光復
gun	郡
Guoli Taiwan tushuguan	國立臺灣圖書館
Guomindang (KMT)	國民黨
Guoshi	國史
Haijiao qi hao	海角七號
Haixia liang'an fuwu maoyi xieyi	海峽兩岸服務貿易協議
Hakka	客家
Hanaoka Ichirō (Dakis Nomin)	花岡一郎
Hanaoka Jirō (Dakis Nawi)	花岡二郎
Hanjian	漢奸
Hao nan, hao nü	好男,好女
Hashiguchi Bunzō	橋口文藏
Hatta Yoichi	八田與一
Hayami Kunihiko	速水國彦
hei kafeiting	黑咖啡廳
hikiageru	引上げる/引揚げる
Hiyama Tetsusaburō	檜山鉄三郎
Hoklo	福佬
hokō	保甲
hokuban	北蕃
Hokufu (Beipu) Incident	北埔事件

hontōjin (bendaoren)	本島人
Hosoda Hiroyuki	細田博之
Hou Hsiao-hsien	侯孝賢
Huang Ba	黃霸
Huang Cong	黃蔥
Huang Daolin	黃道琳
Huang Shu	黃樹
Huang Wen-hsiung (Kō Bunyū)	黃文雄
Huaqiao	華僑
Hung Chih-yu	洪智育
Inō Kanori	伊能嘉矩
Ishizuka Eizō	石塚英藏
isshi dōjin	一視同仁
Itō-Yōkadō	イトーヨーカ堂
Iwasato Takenori	岩里武則
Jianan dazhen	嘉南大圳
Jiang Wenye (Kō Bunya)	江文也
Jiku Shō Min	竺紹珉
Jiyū minshutō	自由民主党
Jueming paidui	絕命派對
jukuban	熟蕃
Kabayama Sukenori	樺山資紀
kafei nülang	咖啡女郎
Kafei shiguang	咖啡時光
kafei zhengque fangshi	咖啡正確方式
kaishan fufan	開山撫番
kami	神
kansō (huansong)	還送
Kawahira Chōshin	川平朝申
Kawanakajima	川中島
Ke Mengrong (Kevin Ko)	柯孟融
keibu	警部
keibu-ho	警部補
keishu	警手
Kejia	客家
Kejiaren	客家人
kijunshiki	歸順式
kikoku	貴国
kissaten	喫茶店
Kitashirakawakyū seitō kinenhi	北白川宮征討紀念碑
Ko Wen-je	柯文哲
Kobayashi Yoshinori	小林善範
Kodama Gentarō	兒玉源太郎
Kōfuku no nōmin	幸福の農民
Koh Se-kai	許世楷
Koizumi Jun'ichirō	小泉純一郎
Kokumin eiyoshō	国民栄誉賞
Kokumin taiiku taikai	国民体育大会
kōminka (huangminhua)	皇民化

Kōshien	甲子園
Koyae Kyoko	小八重恭子
Kuo Chen-ti	郭珍弟
lāu-ōo-á	老芋仔
Lee Ah-long	李阿隆
Lee Teng-chin	李登欽
Lee Teng-hui	李登輝
Lei Zhen	雷震
Li Guanghui	李光輝
Li Peng	李鵬
Li Xianglan (Ri Koran)	李香蘭
Li Zhuoyu	李琢玉
Lianhebao	聯合報
Lianxi qu	練習曲
Liao Hsien-hao	廖咸浩
Liao Shou-chen	廖守臣
Lifa yuan	立法院
Lin Shuhao	林書豪
Liu Tianlu	劉天祿
liuyong (ryūyō)	留用
Lü Yanping	呂雁萍
Luoduolun	羅多倫
Ma Shuli	馬樹禮
Ma Ying-jeou	馬英九
Ma Zhixiang	馬志翔
Mabuchi Tōichi	馬淵東一
Machimura Nobutaka	町村信孝
Mainichi shimbun	毎日新聞
Marui Keijirō	丸井圭治郎
Matsunaga Tō	松永東
Matsuo Bashō	松尾芭蕉
Matsushima ya, hikari to kage no, mabushikari	松島や　光と影の　まぶしかり
Matsuzaki Shinji	松崎晋二
mei Ri	媚日
Miao Miao	渺渺
Mifeng kafei	蜜蜂咖啡
Minnan	閩南
minsheng	民生
Minzhu jinbudang	民主進步黨
minzu jingshen	民族精神
Miyanohara Tōhachi	宮ノ原籐八
Miyashita Heiko	宮下萍子
Mizuno Jun	水野遵
Mochiji Rokusaburō	持地六三郎
Mokkōban	木瓜蕃
Mona Ludaw	莫那·魯道
mono no aware	物の哀れ
Mori Ōgai	森鷗外
Mori Ushinosuke	森丑之助

Mori Yoshirō	森喜朗
Mu Gu (Sun Qingyu)	穆谷 (孫慶餘)
Murakami Yoshio	村上義雄
Musha jiken (Wushe shijian)	霧社事件
Mushaban	霧社蕃
Nagashima Shigeo	長嶋茂雄
naichijin	內地人
Nakada Hiroshi	中田宏
Nakahara Masao	中原正夫
Nakahara Torao (Tora)	中原寅雄 (虎)
Nakahata Kiyoshi	中畑清
Nakaima Hirokazu	仲井眞弘多
Nakamura Teruo	中村輝夫
nanban	南蕃
nanshin	南進
Nanshin Taiwan	南進臺灣
Nanshinkan	南進舘
Nanshō (Nanzhuang) Incident	南庄事件
naoding	腦丁
naozhang	腦張
Nishida Kitarō	西田幾多郎
Nitobe Inazō	新渡戸稲造
nuhua jiaoyu	奴化教育
Oh Sadaharu (Wang Zhenzhi)	王貞治
Oh Tetsujō (Wang Tiecheng)	王鐵城
Okamura Yasuji	岡村寧次
Okinawajin dōkyōkai	沖縄人同郷会
Oku no hosomichi	奥の細道
Ong Iok-tek	王育德
ongi gaikō	恩義外交
Oshikawa Norikichi	押川則吉
Ōta Masahiro	太田政弘
Ozaki Hotsuma	尾崎秀実
Ozawa Maria	小澤マリア
Ozu Yasujiro	小津安二郎
Pan Yuekang	潘月康
Peng Ming-min	彭明敏
Pingpuzu	平埔族
qianfan	遣返
qiansong	遣送
Qinmindang	親民黨
qipao	旗袍
rensageki	連鎖劇
Ri Aguai	日阿拐
riban	理蕃
Riban no tomo	理蕃の友
Riban shikō	理蕃誌稿
Richan chuli weiyuanhui	日產處理委員會
Rifu	日俘

Riji renmin	日籍人民
Riqiao (Nikkyō)	日僑
Riqiao guanli weiyuanhui	日僑管理委員會
ryū Tai Nikkyō gojokai	留台日僑互助会
Saideke Balai	賽德克·巴萊
Saideke guo	賽德克國
Saitō Otosaku	斉藤音作
Sakai Nobuhiko	酒井信彦
Sakigake!! Otokojuku	魁!!男塾
Sakuma Samata	佐久間左馬太
Sankei shimbun	産経新聞
Satō Haruo	佐藤春夫
Sayon no kane	サヨンの鐘
seiban	生蕃
seinendan	青年團
Senbatsu kōtō gakkō yakyū taikai	選抜高等学校野球大会
senpai	先輩
senryū	川柳
sewayaku	世話役
shanbao	山包
shashinchō	寫真帖
she	社
Shen Baozhen	沈葆禎
shengfan	生番
shengji maodun	省籍矛盾
Shi Ming	史明
Shimizu Hiroshi	清水宏
Shinajin	支那人
shisō	思想
shōchū	焼酎
Shōka jinjō kokumin shōgakkō	彰化尋常國民小學校
shokusan-bu	殖産部
shōrai kika	招来帰化
shoufan	熟蕃
Shu Chin-chiang	蘇進強
Socjima Tancomi	副島種臣
sokoku	祖國
Soong May-ling	宋美齡
Su Junxiong	蘇俊雄
Taibei huabao	臺北畫報
Taihokujō no enkaku	臺北城の沿革
Tainan shūritsu Kagi nōrin gakkō	台南州立嘉義農林學校
Tainan-shū Kokumin dōjō	台南州國民道場
Taishō	大正
Taiwan bukyoku	臺灣舞曲
Taiwan gongyō hōkoku seinentai	臺灣勤行報國青年隊
Taiwan jieguan jihua gangyao	臺灣接管計畫綱要
Taiwan jieguan jihua gangyao cao'an	臺灣接管計畫綱要草案
Taiwan Man'yōshū	台灣萬葉集
Taiwan nichinichi shinpō	臺灣日日新報

Taiwan ryokō annai	臺灣旅行案内
Taiwan sōtokufu toshokan	臺灣総督府圖書館
Taiwan takushoku kabushiki kaisha	臺灣拓殖株式會社
Taiwan tuanjie lianmeng	台灣團結聯盟
Taiwan weixin	台灣維新
Taiwan-ron	台灣論
Taiwanshi	台灣史
Taiwantō	臺灣島
Takahashi Dairiku	高橋大陸
Takasago	高砂
Takasago giyūtai	高砂義勇隊
Takasagozoku	高砂族
Takasagozoku seinendan	高砂族青年團
Takekoshi Yosaburō	竹越与三郎
Takun Walis (Qiu Jiancheng)	邱建堂
Tangshan	唐山
Tarokoban tōbatsu	太魯閣蕃討伐
Tasaka Tomotaka	田坂具隆
Tera Yudaw (Li Jishun)	李季順
Tianbian yi duo yun	天邊一朵雲
Tiaowu shidai	跳舞時代
Tokugawa Ieyasu	徳川家康
tongbao	同胞
tongshi	通事
Tongyi qiye	統一企業
Torii Ryūzō	鳥居龍藏
toyū	都邑
Tōzumi Tomi	当住登美
Tsai Ming-liang	蔡明亮
Tseng Wen-hui	曾文惠
tsūben	通辯
tsūji	通事
tsūyaku	通訳
tsūyakukan	通訳官
Uchida Kuichi	内田九一
Ueno Sen'ichi	上野專一
Umi no gōzoku	海の豪族
waishengren	外省人
Wang Gongzi	王恭子
Wang Jiasheng	王岬生
Wang Jinyi	王進益
Wang Shifu (Oh Shifuku)	王仕福
Wang Zhenzhi xuanshou Huaqiao houyuanhui	王貞治選手華僑後援會
Waseda jitsugyō gakkō	早稲田実業学校
Wei Te-sheng	魏德聖
Weili Incident	威利事件
Weixin xinwenbao	微信新聞報
Wu Zhuoliu	吳濁流
Wu Lianyi	吳連義

Wu Nianzhen	吳念真
Wushantou Dam	烏山頭水庫
Xi meng rensheng	戲夢人生
Xie Changting	謝長廷
Xie Dongmin	謝東閔
Xie Xuehong	謝雪紅
Xincheng (Shinjō) Incident	新城事件
Xingbake	星巴克
Xiyatu jipin kafei	西雅圖極品咖啡
Yamaguchi Yoshiko	山口淑子
Yamaji Katsuhiko	山路勝彦
Yamato-damashii	大和魂
Yami	雅美
Yang Jizhen	楊基振
Yasukuni	靖國
yi de bao yuan	以德報怨
Yin Haiguang	殷海光
yinyue kafeiting	音樂咖啡廳
Yomiuri shimbun	読売新聞
Yozakura Sumomo	夜桜すもも
Yuandong daxue	遠東大學
yuanxiang	原鄉
Yuanzhumin	原住民
Yuanzhuminzu	原住民族
Zhang Hexiang	張和祥
Zhanghua shi wudedian (butokuden)	彰化市武德殿
Zhenguo kafeiguan	真鍋咖啡館
Zhongguo qingnian fangong jiuguotuan	中國青年反共救國團
Zhongguo shibao	中國時報
Zhongguo wenhua daxue	中國文化大學
Zhongguodang mai Tai yuan	中國黨賣台院
Zhongguohua	中國化
Zhonghua minzu	中華民族
Zhonghua wenhua fuxing yundong	中華文化復興運動
Zhongyang tongxunshe	中央通訊社
Zhou Yi'e	周一鶚
zijue zizhi	自決自治
ziwo	自我
Ziyou shibao	自由時報
Ziyou xinwen	自由新聞
zizhi	自治
zuguo	祖國
zuguohua	祖國化

Bibliography

In Atayalic languages, including all three Sediq dialects, there are no surnames. Instead, people use their personal names, followed by the name of a parent (usually the father). Atayal authors are thus cited and referenced here according to their personal names, followed by the initial of the parent's name, with no comma.

Here is a note regarding citations of Chinese or Japanese publications with English subtitles: the English titles that accompany many of these publications often give insight to how an author or a publisher understood a certain work and are thus too valuable to discard or replace with our own objectively "more accurate" translations. Therefore, Chinese or Japanese publications that carry English subtitles are cited to include them in parentheses and italics, as follows: "*Kamera de mita Taiwan (Lure of Taiwan)*." This is opposed to publications for which we provide translations, which appear as, for example, "*Yijiusiwu xiamo* (The end of summer, 1945)," with unitalicized English translations. Likewise, the original English titles of articles are included within quotation marks, e.g. "Cong minzu guojia de moshi kan zhanhou Taiwan de Zhongguohua (The Sinicisation of Post-War Taiwan from the Perspective of Ethnic-State Patterns)."

Adas, M. (1989), *Machines as the Measure of Men: Science, Technology, and Ideologies of Western Dominance*, Ithaca: Cornell University Press.

Aki, T. (1982), "Hikiage senchū ibun" (A strange tale of shipboard repatriation), in Taiwan kyōkai (eds), *Taiwan hikiage shi: Shōwa nijūnen shūsen kiroku* (A history of repatriation from Taiwan: A record of the end of the war from Shōwa 20 [1945]), Tokyo: Zaidan hōren Taiwan kyōkai.

Allen, J. (2005), "Mapping Taipei: Representation and Ideology, 1626–1945," *Studies on Asia*, Series III, 2.2: 59–80, plus illustrations. http://studiesonasia.illinoisstate.edu/seriesIII/vol2-2.shtml [accessed 1 April, 2014].

———. (2007), "Taipei Park: Signs of Occupation," *Journal of Asian Studies*, 66.1: 159–99.

———. (2012), *Taipei: City of Displacements*, Seattle: University of Washington Press.

———. (2014), "Picturing Gentlemen: Japanese Portrait Photography in Colonial Taiwan," *Journal of Asian Studies*, 73.4: 1009–42.

Allen, S. (2005), "Establishing Autonomous Regions in the Republic of China: The Salience of International Law for Taiwan's Indigenous Peoples," *Indigenous Law Journal*, 4: 159–217.

Allio, F. (1998), "The Austronesian Peoples of Taiwan: Building a Political Platform for Themselves," *China Perspectives*, 18: 52–60.

Allison, A. (1994), *Nightwork: Sexuality, Pleasure, and Corporate Masculinity in a Tokyo Hostess Club*, Chicago: University of Chicago Press.

Alloula, M. (1986), *The Colonial Harem*, trans. M. Godzich and W. Godzich, Minneapolis: University of Minneapolis Press.

Andrade, T. (2008), *How Taiwan Became Chinese: Dutch, Spanish and Han Colonization in the Seventeenth Century*, New York: Columbia University Press.

Arai, R. (dir) (1942), *Umi no gōzoku* (Pirates of the Seas), Kyōto: Nikkatsu; Taihoku: Taiwan sōtoku.

Arisan Niitakayama keishoku shashinchō (Scenery of Ali and Niitaka Mountains) (1927), Tainan: Chūō shashinkan.

Atkins, E. (2010), *Primitive Selves: Koreana in the Japanese Colonial Gaze, 1910–1945*, Berkeley: University of California Press.

"Ayumi no saki, egao to kinchō—Taiwan no Ri Tōki zen-sōtō ga rainichi" (Smiles and tension lie ahead—Taiwan's former President Lee Teng-hui arrives in Japan) (2001), *Asahi shimbun*, April 23, morning ed.

"Ba Eikyū-shi, Dōshisha Dai de kōen—'Nihon o fukaku rikai shitai'" (Ma Ying-jeou gives speech at Dōshisha University—'I Want to Deeply Understand Japan') (2007), *Sankei shimbun*, November 22, morning ed.

Balandier, G. (1966), "The Colonial Situation: A Theoretical Approach," in I. Wallerstein (ed), *Social Change: The Colonial Situation*, New York: John Wiley and Sons.

"Bangqiu wang Wang Zhenzhi zai zuguo" (Baseball king Oh Sadaharu in the motherland) (1965), "Zhonghua minguo xinwen" (ROC News[reel]) 623.

"Bangqiu zhi wang liying pianpian, miyue huache xian dao Taiwan" (King of baseball and spouse make a graceful couple, honeymoon coach to Taiwan first) (1966), *Lianhebao (United Daily News)*, December 4: 3.

"Banjin banchi ni kansuru jimu oyobi jōkyō" (Conditions pertaining to the administration of Aborigines and Aborigine territories) (1900), *Taiwan zongdu fu gongwen leizuan shuweihua dang'an* (Taiwan Government-General official records, digital edition), July 1, 4625–5–3.

Barclay, G. (1954), *Colonial Development and Population in Taiwan*. Princeton: Princeton University Press.

———. (1958), *Techniques of Population Analysis*, New York: John Wiley & Sons, Inc.

Barclay, P. (2005a), "Bansan kōekijo ni okeru 'banchi' no shōgyōka to chitsujoka (Commodification and Control in the Aborigine Trading Posts)," *Taiwan genjūmin kenkyū* (Studies on Indigenous Peoples of Taiwan), 9: 70–109.

———. (2005b), "Cultural Brokerage and Interethnic Marriage in Colonial Taiwan: Japanese Subalterns and Their Aborigine Wives, 1895–1930," *Journal of Asian Studies*, 64.2: 323–60.

———. (2005c), "Profits as Contagion, Production as Progress: Trading Posts, Tribute, and Feasting in the History of Japanese-Formosan Relations, 1895–1917," in *International Symposium: Studies on Indigenous Peoples of Taiwan: Retrospect and Prospect in Japan und Taiwan*, Tokyo, Research Institute for Languages and Cultures of Asia and Africa, Tokyo University of Foreign Studies.

———. (2007), "Contending Centres of Calculation in Colonial Taiwan: The Rhetorics of Vindicationism and Privation in Japan's 'Aboriginal Policy', *Humanities Research*, XIV.1: 67–84.

———. (2008), trans., "Kondō Katsusaburō among Taiwan's Atayal/Sedeq Peoples, 1896–1930" [articles translated from the 1930–31 *Taiwan nichinichi shinpō*], *The View from Taiwan*, November 18. http://michaelturton.blogspot.com/2008/11/serial-i-kondo-katsusaburo-among.html [accessed February 25, 2014].

———. (2010), "Peddling Postcards and Selling Empire: Image-Making in Taiwan under Japanese Colonial Rule," *Japanese Studies*, 30.1: 81–110.

———. (2015), "Playing the Race Card in Japanese Governed Taiwan, or: Anthropometric Photographs as 'Shape-Shifting Jokers,'" in C. Hanscom and D. Washburn (eds), *The

Affect of Difference: Representations of Race in East Asian Empire, Honolulu: University of Hawai'i Press.

Barthes, R. (1977), *Image, Music, Text,* trans. S. Heath, New York: Hill and Wang.

———. (1981), *Camera Lucida: Reflections on Photography,* trans. R. Howard, New York: Hill and Wang.

"Baseball strikes out politics" (2003), *Taipei Times,* 14 November: 2. http://www.taipeitimes.com/News/taiwan/archives/2003/11/14/2003075755 [accessed June 10, 2014].

Baskett, M. (2008), *The Attractive Empire: Transnational Film Culture in Imperial Japan,* Honolulu: University of Hawai'i Press.

"Beijing pi Li—Guanfang ruan meiti ying" (Beijing criticizes Lee—government goes soft on him, media go hard) (2007), *Zhongguo shibao,* June 8, morning ed.

Bhabha, H. (1994), *The Location of Culture,* London: Routledge.

Bissell, W. (2005), "Engaging Colonial Nostalgia," *Cultural Anthropology,* 20.2: 215–48.

Booth, A. (2007), "Did It Really Help to be a Japanese Colony? East Asian Economic Performance in Historical Perspective," *The Asia-Pacific Journal: Japan Focus.* http://japanfocus.org/-Anne-Booth/2418 [accessed September 4, 2012].

Boretz, A. (2004), "Carousing and Masculinity: The Cultural Production of Gender in Taiwan," in C. Farris, A. Lee, and M. Rubinstein (eds), *Women in the New Taiwan: Gender Roles and Gender Consciousness in a Changing Society,* New York: M.E. Sharpe.

Bornoff, N. (1991), *Pink Samurai: Love, Marriage, and Sex in Contemporary Japan,* New York: Pocket Books.

Brown, M. (2004), *Is Taiwan Chinese? The Impact of Culture, Power, and Migration on Changing Identities,* Berkeley: University of California Press.

Buruma, I. (2008), *China Lover,* London: Atlantic Books.

Cai, K. (2001), *Taiwanjin to Nihon seishin* (Taiwanese people and the Japanese spirit), Tokyo: Nippon Kyōbunsha, 2001.

Cai, M. (2003), *Taiwan ni okeru Nihongo kyōiku no shiteki kenkyu, 1895–2002* (Historical study of Japanese language education in Taiwan, 1895–2002), Taibei: Daxin.

Central Intelligence Agency (2014), "The World Factbook: Taiwan," https://www.cia.gov/library/publications/the-world-factbook/geos/tw.html [accessed May 8, 2014].

Chang, C. (1968), "Zhongguo wenhua yu Zhongguo minzuxing" (Chinese culture and the nature of the Chinese people), in Y. Yang (ed), *Ruhe renshi Zhonghua wenhua fuxing yundong* (How to understand the Chinese Cultural Renaissance movement), Taibei: Wenyuan shuju.

Chang, L. (2003), "From Island Frontier to Imperial Colony: Qing and Japanese Sovereignty Debate and Territorial Projects in Taiwan, 1874–1906," Ph.D. Dissertation, Harvard University.

———. (2008), "From Quarantine to Colonization: Qing Debates on Territorialization of Aboriginal Taiwan in the Nineteenth Century," *Taiwan Historical Research,* 15.4: 1–30.

Chang, M. (1994), "Toward an Understanding of the Sheng-chi Wen-ti in Taiwan: Focusing on Changes after Political Liberalization," in C. Chen, Y. Chuang, and S. Huang (eds), *Ethnicity in Taiwan, Social, Historical and Cultural Perspectives,* Nankang: Institute of Ethnology, Academia Sinica.

———. (2000), "Ethnic and National Identities in Taiwan: On the Origins and Transformations of Taiwanese National Identity," *China Perspectives* 28: 51–70.

Chen, C. (1975), "The Japanese Adaptation of the *Pao-chia* system in Taiwan, 1895–1945," *Journal of Asian Studies,* 34.2: 391–416.

Chen, C., Chuang, Y., and Huang, S. (eds) (1994), *Ethnicity in Taiwan: Social, Historical, and Cultural Perspectives,* Nankang: Institute of Ethnology, Academia Sinica.

Chen, F. (2003), *Houzhimin Taiwan: Wenxueshilun ji qi zhoubian (Postcolonial Taiwan: Essays on Taiwanese literary history and beyond)*, Taibei: Maitian.

Chen, H. (dir) (2006), *Lianxi qu (Island Etude)*, Taibei: Zongheng.

Chen, K. (2005), "*A Borrowed Life* in *Banana Paradise*: De-Cold War/Decolonization, or Modernity and Its Tears," in C. Berry and F. Lu (eds), *Island on the Edge: Taiwan New Cinema and After*, Hong Kong: Hong Kong University Press.

Chen, P. (2008), "Ojisan pai duosang: Wu Nianzhen *Duosang*" (The Son filming his Father: Wu Nianzhen's *A Borrowed Life*), 19 December 2008. http://www.funscreen.com.tw/review.asp?RV_id=701 [accessed March 5, 2014].

Chen, W. (2014), *Yineng Jiaju: Taiwan lishi minzuzhi de zhankai* (Inō Kanori and the emergence of historical ethnography in Taiwan), Taibei: Taida chuban zhongxin.

Chen, Y. (2001), "Imperial Army Betrayed," in T. Fujitani, G. White, and L. Yoneyama (eds), *Perilous Memories: The Asia-Pacific War(s)*, Durham: Duke University Press.

Cheng, H. (dir) (2008), *Miao Miao*, Hong Kong: Zedong dianying.

Chiang, M. (2012), *Memory Contested, Locality Transformed: Representing Japanese Colonial 'Heritage' in Taiwan*, Leiden: Leiden University Press.

Chiayi City Government (2012), "The Film "KANO" which is based on the story of Jianong baseball team is about to start shooting & Sankei News from Japan interviews with Chiayi City Mayor Huang Ming-Hui" (July 30). http://www.chiayi.gov.tw/2011web/en/index.aspx?mid=97&rid=1471 [accessed December 4, 2012].

"Chicheng qiuchang fengbamian, gaoji jubang ba yi tian" (Galloping to the stadium and inspiring awe all around, holding the giant bat high and ruling the day) (1965), *Lianhebao*, December 4: 3.

"Chichibunomiya denka no Taiwan Onari" (Prince Chichibu's royal visit to Taiwan) (1925), *Taiwan jihō*, July.

Chien, W. and Luo, C. (dirs.) (2003), *Tiaowu shidai (Viva Tonal, the Dance Age)*, N.p.: Chien Wei-su and Kuo Chen-ti.

Chin, C. (2002), "Tailuge kang Ri zhanyi dui Deluguzu de lishi yiyi" (The historical significance of Taroko anti-Japanese battles of resistance for the Truku peoples), in C. Shih, S. Koh, and Pusin T. (eds), *Cong hejie dao zizhi: Taiwan Yuanzhuminzu lishi chongjian* (From reconciliation to autonomy: Reconstructing the history of Taiwan's Indigenous Peoples), Taibei: Qianwei.

Ching, L. (2000), "Savage Construction and Civility Making: The Musha Incident and Colonial Representations in Colonial Taiwan," *Positions*, 8.3: 795–818.

——. (2001), *Becoming Japanese: Colonial Taiwan and the Politics of Identity Formation*, Berkeley. University of California Press.

——. (2012), "Colonial Nostalgia or Postcolonial Anxiety: The Dosan Generation In-Between 'Restoration' and 'Defeat'," in R. King, C. Poulton, and K. Endo (eds), *Sino-Japanese Transculturation: From the Late Nineteenth Century to the End of the Pacific War*, Lanham, MD: Lexington Books.

"Chinki na bussan ni gokyō mo fukashi" (His Highness's interest in curious Aborigine products deepens) (1923), *Tokyo Asahi Shinbun*, April 18: 2.

Chou, W. (2000), "Shilun zhanhou Taiwan guanyu Wushe shijian de quanshi" (On postwar Taiwanese interpretations of the Wushe Incident), *Taiwan fengwu* (Taiwan folkways), 60.3: 11–57.

Christy, A. (1997), "The Making of Imperial Subjects in Okinawa," in T. Barlow (ed), *Formations on Colonial Modernity in East Asia*, Durham: Duke University Press.

Chuang, Y. (1994), *Jiazu yu hunyin: Taiwan beibu liang ge Min Ke cunluo zhi yanjiu* (Family and marriage: Hoklo and Hakka villages in North Taiwan), Nangang: Zhongyang yanjiuyuan Minzuxue yanjiusuo.

Clastres, P. (1977), *Society against the State*, Oxford: Blackwell.

Cohen, M. (1976), *House United, House Divided, the Chinese Family in Taiwan*, New York: Columbia University Press.

Comaroff, J.L. and J. Comaroff (2009), *Ethnicity, Inc.*, Chicago: University of Chicago Press.

The Conferees (1985), "The Relationship of Nutrition, Disease, and Social Conditions: A Graphical Presentation," in R. Rotberg and T. Rabb (eds), *Hunger and History*, Cambridge: Cambridge University Press.

Constable, N. (1996), *Guest People: Hakka identity in China and Abroad*, Seattle: University of Washington Press.

———. (2000), "Ethnicity and Gender in Hakka Studies," in C. Hsu (ed), *Juluo, zongzu yu zuqun guanxi, disijie guoji kejiaxue yantaohui lunwenji* (Community, lineage and ethnic relations: Proceedings of the International Conference on Hakkology), Nangang: Zhongyang yanjiuyuan Minzuxue yanjiusuo.

Conway, B. (2009), "Rethinking Difficult Pasts: Bloody Sunday (1972) as a Case Study," *Cultural Sociology*, 3.3: 397–413.

Cooper-Chen, A. (1997), *Mass Communication in Japan*, Ames: Iowa State University Press.

Corcuff, S. (2011), "Liminality and Taiwan Tropism in a Postcolonial Context: Schemes of National Identification among Taiwan's 'Mainlanders' on the Eve of Kuomintang's Return to Power," in T. Ngo and H. Wang (eds), *Politics of Difference in Taiwan*, New York: Routledge.

Costantini, L. (1994), "Introduzione," in Ō. Mori (ed), *L'Oca Selvatica*, Venezia: Marsilio.

Cromartie, W. with Whiting, R. (1991), *Slugging It Out in Japan: An American major leaguer in the Tokyo Outfield*, New York: Kodansha International.

Dai-ikkai Taiwan kokusei chōsa, yōran hyō, Taishō kyū nen (First census of Taiwan, summary tables, Taishō Year 9 [1920]) (1922), Taihoku: Taiwan sōtoku kambō, rinji kokusei chōsabu.

Dai-niji rinji Taiwan kokō chōsa kekka hyō, Taishō yo nen (Results of second provisional household census, Taishō Year 4 [1915]) (1918), Taihoku: Taiwan sōtoku kambō rinji kokō chōsabu.

Dai-niji rinji Taiwan kokō chōsa shūkei gempyō, zentō no bu, Taishō yo nen (Second provisional household census, detailed tables, entire island, Taishō Year 4 [1915]) (1917), Taihoku: Taiwan sōtoku kambō rinji kokō chōsabu.

Dai, G. (1989), *Taiwan zongtixiang: Zhumin, lishi, xinxing* (Macro study of Taiwan: Humanity, history, and mentality), trans. T. Wei, Taibei: Yuanliu.

Dali Kakei (2001), *Gaosha wangguo* (Kingdom of Taiwan Aborigines), trans. B. You and J. Nao, Taizhong: Chenxing.

Davidson, J. (1903), *The Island of Formosa Past and Present: History, People, Resources, and Commercial Prospects: Tea, Camphor, Sugar, Coal, Sulfur, Economical Plants, and Other Production*, London: McMillan & Company.

Dawley, E. (2006), "Constructing Taiwanese Ethnicity: Identities in a City on the Border of China and Japan," Ph.D. Dissertation, Harvard University.

Deng, S. (1998), *Wushe shijian* (The Wushe Incident), Taibei: Yushanshe.

DeRoo, R. (2002), "Colonial Collecting: French Women and the Algerian *cartes postale*," in E. Hight and G. Sampson (eds), *Colonialist Photography: Imag(in)ing Race and Place*, London: Routledge.

"Diyipi qiansong Riqiao quansheng da qiwan ren" (The first stage of deporting Overseas Japanese reached 70,000 people in the whole province) (1946), *Minbao*, March 1: 2.

"Doutor History" (2012). http://www.doutorcoffee.com.sg/history [accessed May 2, 2014].

Dower, J. (2000), *Embracing Defeat: Japan in the Wake of World War II*, New York: W.W. Norton & Co.

Dudziak, M. (2012), *War-Time: An Idea, Its History, Its Consequences*, Oxford: Oxford University Press.

Ericsson, N. (2004), "Creating 'Indian' Country in Taiwan," *Harvard Asia Quarterly*, 8.1: 33–44.

Eskildsen, R. (2002), "'Of Civilization and Savages': The Mimetic Imperialism of Japan's 1874 Expedition to Taiwan," *American Historical Review*, 107.2: 388–418.

Fan, J. (2011), *China's Homeless Generation: Voices from the Veterans of the Chinese Civil War, 1940s–1990s*, New York: Routledge.

Fan, T. (2000), "Cong "polilu" dao "xingbake"—Taiwan kafei wenhua lishi fenxi" (From "Bolero" to "Starbucks": An Analysis of Taiwan's History of Coffee Culture), *Chuanbo wenhua (Journal of Communication & Culture)*, 8: 41–77.

———. (2001), "Taiwan kafei xiaofei wenhua de lishi fenxi" (A Historical Analysis of Coffee Consumption in Taiwan), MA Thesis, Furen University.

Fell, D. (2005), "Political and Media Liberalization and Political Corruption in Taiwan," *China Quarterly*, 184: 875–93.

Ferguson, N. (2008), *The Ascent of Money: A Financial History of the World*, New York: Penguin Press.

Fix, D. (2006), "Reading the Numbers: Ethnicity, Violence, and Wartime Mobilization in Colonial Taiwan," in P. Liao and D. Wang (eds), *Taiwan Under Japanese Colonial Rule, 1895–1945: History, Culture, Memory*, New York: Columbia University Press.

———. (2009), "The Changing Contours of Lived Communities on the Hengchun Peninsula, 1850–1874," in L. Hung (ed), *Nations and Aborigines: History of Ethnic Groups in the Asia-Pacific Region*, Taipei: Institute of Taiwan History, Academia Sinica.

Forman, H. (1938), "Diary: Japan, Taiwan, Korea," *Harrison Forman Papers*, Box 1, Folder 7, Item 6. Special Collections and University Archives, University of Oregon Libraries.

———. (1941), "Letter to Editor," *Natural History*, 47.4: 182–83.

Foucault, M. ([1978] 1990), *The History of Sexuality: An Introduction, Volume 1*, trans. R. Hurley, New York: Vintage Books.

Freeman, L. (2000), *Closing the Shop: Information Cartels and Japan's Mass Media*, Princeton: Princeton University Press.

Fu, T. (dir) (2009), *Dai wo qu yuanfang (Somewhere I Have Never Travelled)*, Taibei: Lanyue dianying.

"Fujia qian jin bangqiu wang, yi ge meili, yi ge qiang" (Old-money family and a Baseball King, one beautiful and the other strong) (1966), *Lianhebao*, January 7: 3.

Fujii, S. (1997), *Lifan: Riben zhili Taiwan de jice: Meiyou paohuo de zhanzheng (yi)* (Ruling savages: Japanese governance on Taiwan: A war without gunfire, Vol. 1), Taibei: Wenyingtang.

———. (2001), *Taiwan Yuanzhumin shi: Zhengcepian (san)* (Taiwan Aborigine history: Policy, Vol. 3), Nantou: Taiwan wenxianguan.

Galbraith, P. (2013) "Maid Cafés: The Affect of Fictional Characters in Akihabara, Japan," *Asian Anthropology*, 12.2: 1–22.

Gao, P. (2011) "An Engineer with the Common Touch: Colonial Japan's Hatta Yoichi has found lasting respect and admiration in Taiwan," *Taiwan Review*, 61.10. http://goo.gl/YXo1zw [accessed October 4, 2011].

Gardella, R. (1999), "From Treaty Ports to Provincial Status, 1860–1894," in M. Rubinstein (ed), *Taiwan: A New History*, Armonk: M.E. Sharpe.

Gates, H. (1987), *Chinese Working-Class Lives: Getting By In Taiwan*, Ithaca: Cornell University Press.

Geismar, H. (2013), *Treasured Possessions: Indigenous Interventions into Cultural and Intellectual Property*, Durham: Duke University Press.

Ghermani, W. (2009a), "Histoire du cinéma taïwanais," *Monde chinois*, 17: 21–8.

———. (2009b), "What is Taiwanese Cinema?" in C. Neri and K. Gormley (eds), *Le Cinéma taïwanais/Taiwan Cinema*, Lyon: Asiexpo.

Ghosh, P. (2012), "Jeremy Lin: Chinese or Taiwanese?" *International Business Times*, February 20. http://www.ibtimes.com/jeremy-lin-chinese-or-taiwanese-214102 [accessed November 13, 2012].

Goldstein, J. (2003), "From Teahouse to Playhouse: Theaters as Social Texts in Early-Twentieth-Century China," *Journal of Asian Studies*, 62.3: 753–79.

Gordon, L. (1965), "Japan's Abortive Colonial Venture in Taiwan, 1874," *Journal of Modern History*, 37.2: 171–85.

Gotō danshaku sōbetsu kinenchō (Album commemorating Viceroy Gotō's departure) (1906), n.p.

Gotō, K. (2004), "Japan's Southward Advance and Colonial Taiwan," *European Journal of East Asian Studies*, 3.1: 15–44.

Goto, S. (1904), "Formosa, the Present Condition," in A. Stead (ed), *Japan By the Japanese*, New York: Dodd, Mead, and Company.

Greenough, S. (2009), *Looking In: Robert Frank's The Americans*, Washington: National Gallery of Art.

Guan, S. (1981), *Taiwan san bai nian* (300 years of Taiwan), Taibei: *Huwai shenghuo zazhi* she.

Guo, T. (1954), *Taiwan shishi gaishuo* (Summary of Taiwan historical events), Taibei: Zhengzhong.

Hall, S. (1996), "When Was 'The Post-Colonial'? Thinking At the Limit," in I. Chambers and L. Curti (eds), *The Post-Colonial Question: Common Skies, Divided Horizons*, New York: Routledge.

"Hanbilou ye zongtong" (Paying a visit to the President at the Blue Jade Mansion) (1966), *Lianhebao*, December 5: 2.

Hara, E. (2003) "Taiyaru Sedekku Taroko o meguru kizoku to meishō ni kan suru undō no tenkai (1)—Taroko ni okeru dōkō o chūshin ni" (The development of the campaign on the definition and naming of the Atayal, Sediq, Taroko, Part 1: Centered on Taroko tendencies), *Taiwan genjūmin kenkyū* (Taiwan Aborigine research), 7: 209–27.

———. (2004), "Taiyaru Sedekku Taroko o meguru kizoku to meishō ni kan suru undō no tenkai (2)—Nantō ken Sedekku no dōkō o chūshin ni" (The development of the campaign on the definition and naming of the Atayal, Sediq, Taroko, Part 2: Centered on Nantou Sediq tendencies), *Taiwan genjūmin kenkyū* (Taiwan Aborigine research), 8: 94–104.

Harrison, H. (2003), "Clothing and Power on the Periphery of Empire: The Costumes of the Indigenous People of Taiwan," *positions*, 11.2: 331–60.

Hashiguchi, B. (1895a), "Banmin ni shinamono keiyo no gi hōkoku" (On the propriety of distributing gifts to the Aborigines), in L. Huang (ed), *Taiwan sōtokufu banzoku jijō kōbun ruisan genbun* (Manuscripts of the official business of the Taiwan Government-General, related to conditions among Aborigine tribes), Vol. 1, Nangang: Zhongyang yanjiuyuan Minzuxue yanjiusuo bowuguan.

———. (1895b), "Taiwan Jijō" (Conditions on Taiwan), *Tokyo chigaku kyōkai hōkoku* (Tokyo Geographical Society report), 17.3: 309–38.

———. (1896), "Dakekan chihō seiban kaiken no tame shutchō jihōkoku" (A report on
   an outing to meet the Aborigines of the Dakekan region), in L. Huang (ed), *Taiwan
   sōtokufu banzoku jijō kōbun ruisan genbun* (Manuscripts of the official business of the
   Taiwan Government-General, related to conditions among Aborigine tribes), Vol. 1,
   Nangang: Zhongyang yanjiuyuan Minzuxue yanjiusuo bowuguan.
Hayashi, E. (1998), *Shōgen Taiwan Takasago giyūtai* (Testimony from the Taiwan Takasago
   volunteers), Tokyo: Sōfūkan.
Hayashi, M. (1979), "Ueno Sen'ichi: Nisshin sensō mae no Taiwan ninshiki no senkusha'
   (Ueno Sen'ichi: A Pioneer in the Conceptualization of Taiwan before the Sino-Japanese
   War," *Taiwan kin-gendaishi kenkyū* (Modern and contemporary Taiwanese historical
   research), 2: 30–60.
He, P. (dir) (1989), *Ganèn suiyue (Honor Thy Father)*, Taibei: Zhongyang dianying.
"'Heibaiji': Liben" (In black and white: Establishing the fundamentals) (1977), *Lianhebao*,
   September 2: 3.
"Heixiang fumao liyuan zaofeng 'Zhongguodang mai Tai yuan' " (Black box Service
   Agreement gets parliament sarcastically named "Parliament of the Chinese Party for
   Selling out Taiwan") (2014), *News.sina.com.tw (Xinlang xinwen)*, March 22. http://
   news.sina.com.tw/article/20140322/12040291.html [accessed April 8, 2014].
Hevia, J. (2003), *English Lessons: The Pedagogy of Imperialism in Nineteenth Century
   China*, Durham: Duke University Press.
Hirano, K. (2008), *Duosang de yinghua* (Father's cherry blossom), trans. F. Pan, Taibei:
   Miaosi.
Hirsch, M. (1997), *Family Frames: Photography, Narrative, and Postmemory*, Cambridge:
   Harvard University Press.
Ho, J. (He, C) (1994), "Taiwan de Maidanglaohua—kuaguo fuwuye ziben de wenhua luoji
   (The Cultural Logic of Capital: The Case of McDonaldization in Taiwan)," *Taiwan
   shehui yanjiu jikan (Taiwan: A Radical Quarterly in Social Studies)*, 16: 1–20.
"Hokuban no sensō" (War of the northern savages) (1898), *Taiwan nichinichi shinpō*,
   May 10.
Hou, H. (dir) (1993), *Xi meng rensheng (The Puppetmaster)*, Taibei: Niandai.
———. (dir) (2003), *Kafei shiguang (Café Lumière)*, Tokyo: Shochiku.
Hsia, C. (2002), "Theorizing Colonial Architecture and Urbanism: Building Colonial
   Modernity in Taiwan," trans. I. Chong, *Inter-Asia Cultural Studies*, 3.1: 7–23.
Hsieh, S. (1998), "On Three Definitions of Han Ren: Images of the Majority People in
   Taiwan," in D. Gladney (ed), *Making Majorities: Constituting the Nation in Japan,
   Korea, China, Malaysia, Fiji, Turkey, and the United States*, Stanford: Stanford
   University Press.
Hsu, C. (2000), *Juluo, zongzu yu zuqun guanxi, disijie guoji kejiaxue yantaohui lunwenji*
   (Community, lineage and ethnic relations: Proceedings of the International
   Conference on Hakkology), Nangang: Zhongyang yanjiuyuan Minzuxue yanjiusuo.
Hsu, S., Liu, H., and Pan, H. (eds) (2006), "Nan Taiwan Xingbake kafei xiaofeizhi pianhao,
   shenghuo xingtai yu shangpin yinxiang manyidu zhi guanxi yanjiu" (Research on
   southern Taiwan Starbucks Coffee consumers' preferences, lifestyle attitudes and
   product images as influence levels of satisfaction), *Dongfang xuebao* (Eastern journal),
   27: 66–80.
Hu, C. (2007), "Taiwanese Aboriginal Art and Artifacts: Entangled Images of Colonization
   and Modernization," in Y. Kikuchi (ed), *Refracted Modernity: Visual Culture and
   Identity in Colonial Taiwan*, Honolulu: University of Hawai'i Press.

Huang, C. (1989), "Tenrikyō no Taiwan ni okeru dendō to yuyō" (A discussion of evangelism and acceptance of Tenrikyō in Taiwan), *Minzokugaku kenkyū (Japanese Journal of Ethnology)*, 54.3: 292–309.

———. (2001), "The *Yamatodamashii* of the Takasago Volunteers of Taiwan: A Reading of the Postcolonial Situation," in H. Befu and S. Guichard-Anguis (eds), *Globalizing Japan: Ethnography of the Japanese Presence in Asia, Europe, and America*, London: Routledge.

———. (2003a), "Posutokoroniaru toshi no hijō: Taipei no Nihongo bungei katsudō ni tsuite" (The sadness of a postcolonial city: On Japanese literary activity in Taipei), in S. Hashizume (ed), *Ajia toshi bunkagaku no kanōsei* (The possibility of Asian urban cultural studies), Osaka: Seibundo.

———. (2003b), "The Transformation of Taiwanese Attitudes toward Japan in the Postcolonial Period," in N. Li and R. Cribb (eds), *Imperial Japan and National Identities in Asia, 1895–1945*, London: RoutledgeCurzon.

———. (2006a), " 'Sengo' Taiwan ni okeru irei to tsuitō no kadai: Nihon to no kanren ni tsuite" ("Postwar" issues of mourning and memorial in Taiwan: With relevance to Japan), in Kokusai shūkyō kenkyūjo (ed), *Gendai shūkyo 2006* (Contemporary religion: 2006), Tokyo: Tōkyōdō shuppan.

———. (2006b), "Taiwan ni okeru 'Nihon Bunkaron' ni mirareru tai Nichi kan" (Taiwanese Attitudes toward Japan and the "Japanese culture" discourse), *Ajia Afurika gengo bunka kenkyujo (Journal of Asian and African Studies)*, 71: 146–68.

———. (2009), "Zuqun bupingdeng, ruhe miping?" (How to balance the inequalities between ethnic groups?), *Ziyou shibao*, March 31, A12.

Huang, J. (2004), " 'Grand master Lee' takes on the younger generation," *Taipei Times*, November 17: 3. http://www.taipeitimes.com/News/taiwan/archives/2004/11/17/2003211409 [accessed September 11, 2013].

Huang, W. (Kō, B.) (2003), *Riben ruhe dizao Zhonghua Minguo?* (How did Japan create the Republic of China?), trans. Z. Xiao, Taibei: Qianwei. [Translation of *Kindai Chūgoku wa Nihon ga tsukutta* (Modern China was Created by Japan), Tokyo: WAC, 2002.]

Huang, Y. (2006), "Were Taiwanese Being 'Enslaved'? The Entanglement of Sinicization, Japanization, and Westernization," in P. Liao and D. Wang (eds), *Taiwan Under Japanese Colonial Rule, 1895–1945: History, Culture, Memory*, New York: Columbia University Press.

Huang, Y. and Xu, S. (eds) (2007), *Yang Jizhen riji shiliao xuanji* (Historical selections from the diary of Yang Jizhen), Taibei: Guoshiguan.

Huang, Z. (2001), *Taiwanlun fengbao* (The storm regarding 'On Taiwan'), Taibei: Qianwei.

——— (2009), "Kangzhan jieshu qianhou Jiang Jieshi de dui Ri taidu: "Yi de bao yuan" zhenxiang de tantao (Chiang Kai-shek in East Asia: The Origins of the Policy of Magnanimity toward Japan after World War II)," *Zhongyang yanjiuyuan Jindaishi yanjiusuo jikan (Bulletin of the Institute of Modern History, Academia Sinica)*, 45: 143–94.

"Huangjun shaowei huaigu lü, shiguang daoliu liushi nian" (The Imperial Army second lieutenant's nostalgic journey, turns back the clock sixty years) (2004), *Lianhebao*, December 28, morning ed.

Hughes, T. (1871–2), "Visit to Tok-e-Tok, Chief of the Eighteen Tribes, Southern Formosa," *Proceeding of the Royal Geographic Society*, New Series, 7: 1–19. Published in G. Dudbridge (ed), *Aborigines of South Taiwan in the 1880s*, Taipei: Shung Ye Museum of Formosan Aborigines and Institute of Taiwan History, Academia Sinica, 1999.

"Huiguo xinqing qingsong, bushi lai zhao nüyou" (Returning to his country [sic] in a relaxed frame of mind, not looking for a girlfriend) (1965), *Lianhebao*, December 5: 3.

Hung, C. (dir) (2008), *1895 (Blue Brave: The Legend of Formosa in 1895)*, Taibei: Qinglai yingshi.

Huyssen, A. (1995), *Twilight Memories: Marking Time in a Culture of Amnesia*, New York: Routledge.

Imagawa, R. (ed) (2006), *Suigyū: Ri Takugyoku senryū kushū* (Drunken cow: Selected *senryū* [poems] of Li Zhuoyu), Osaka: Shinyosha.

Inatomi, T. (1982), "Ryūyō seikatsu" (Kept-behind life), in Taiwan kyōkai (eds), *Taiwan hikiage shi: Shōwa nijūnen shūsen kiroku* (A history of repatriation from Taiwan: A record of the end of the war from Shōwa 20 [1945]), Tokyo: Zaidan hōren Taiwan kyōkai.

Inō, K. (1896), "Taiwan tsūshin dai rokkai" (Sixth communique from Taiwan), *Tokyo jinruigakkai zasshi (Journal of the Tokyo Anthropological Society)*, 11.121: 272–8 and 11.122: 299–313.

———. (ed) (1918), *Riban shikō dai ikkan* (Records of Aborigine administration, Vol. 1), Taihoku: Taiwan sōtokufu keisatsu honsho.

———. (1992), "Juntai nichijō" (Taiwan circuit journal), in K. Moriguchi (ed), *Inō Kanori no Taiwan tōsa nikki* (Inō Kanori's Taiwan expedition journals), Taipei: *Taiwan fūbutsu zasshi* sha.

Inoguchi, Y. (ed) (1921), *Riban shikō dai nikan* (Records of Aborigine administration, Vol. 2), Taihoku: Taiwan sōtokufu keimukyoku,.

Irie, T. and Hashimoto, S. (1896), "Taiwan banchi zatsuzoku" (Various customs in Taiwan Aborigine territory), *Fūzoku gahō* (Customs pictorial), 130: 26–32.

Ishiguro, N. (dir) (2009), *Pattenrai!! Minami no shima no mizu monogatari* (Hatta is coming!! The story of water in the southern island), Kanazawa: *Hokkoku shimbun* sha.

Ishimaru, M. (2008), "Taiwan Riben shidai de lifan jingcha" (Savage administration police in Japanese-era Taiwan), Ph.D. dissertation, National Chengchi University.

Itō, K. (1982), "Gakuto dai no owari" (The end of student days), in Taiwan kyōkai (eds), *Taiwan hikiage shi: Shōwa nijūnen shūsen kiroku* (A history of repatriation from Taiwan: A record of the end of the war from Shōwa 20 [1945]), Tokyo: Zaidan hōren Taiwan kyōkai.

Iwabuchi, K. (2002), "Nostalgia for a (Different) Asian Modernity: Media Consumption of 'Asia' in Japan," *positions*, 10.3: 547–73.

Japan Photographers Association (ed) (1980), *A Century of Japanese Photography*, New York: Pantheon Books.

Jennings, R. (2009), "Salt in your coffee? Taiwan cafe chain insists," *Reuters*, 27 February. http://goo.gl/MGlh6H [accessed June 10, 2014].

Jian (1965), "Wang Zhenzhi de 'xuanfeng'" (The Oh Sadaharu "whirlwind"), *Lianhebao*, December 13: 2.

Jiang, W. (2009), "Zhi Yue Taiji Riben bing Wu Lianyi zhi anli yanjiu" (Research into the case of Wu Lianyi, the Taiwanese solider of the Japanese Army stuck in Vietnam), unpublished paper. http://uibun.twl.ncku.edu.tw/chuliau/lunsoat/tiongbun/2009/ngoo-lian-gi.pdf [accessed May 11, 2011].

"Jiang zongtong jiejian Wang Zhenzhi fufu" (President Chiang receives Mr. and Mrs. Sadaharu Oh) (1966), *Weixin xinwenbao*, December 5, reprinted in *20 shiji Taiwan 1966 (20th Century Taiwan 1966)*, June 2001: 20.

"Jianju fu dalu, yi xin hui zuguo" (Resolutely refusing to travel to the mainland, returning [sic] to the motherland wholeheartedly) (1965), *Lianhebao*, December 5: 3.

"Jihuagong baoxiong lingwei—Li Denghui weiceng zhiji" (Lee Teng-hui has never visited his elder brother's memorial tablet at Jihuagong) (2007), *Zhongguo shibao*, June 2, Xinzhu morning ed.

Jiryū, Y. (1895), "Taiwan zakki: Seiban no kinkyō" (Miscellaneous notes from Taiwan: The recent state of the savages), *Tokyo Asahi shimbun*, October 12.

"Joint Communique of the Government of Japan and the Government of the People's Republic of China" (September 29, 1972). http://www.mofa.go.jp/region/asia-paci/china/joint72.html [accessed February 25, 2014].

"Junju Zhonggong ji Riben dianyingjie yaoqing, Wang Zhenzhi zizhuan shouquan wo pianshang paishe" (Harshly refusing invitations of Chinese Communist and Japanese film circles, Oh Sadaharu authorizes our film studios to shoot his memoir) (1985), *Lianhebao*, December 17: 9.

Ka, C. (1995), *Japanese Colonialism in Taiwan: Land Tenure, Development and Dependency, 1895–1945*, Boulder: Westview Press.

Kabayama, Y. (2003), "Nihon ni okeru Taiwanshi kenkyū no genjō to kadai" (The current state of, and challenges in, Taiwanese historical research in Japan), in Taiwan kenkyū bukai (Taiwan Research Group) (ed), *Taiwan no Kindai to Nihon* (Modern Taiwan and Japan), Nagoya: Chukyo University Institute of Social Science.

Kamera de mita Taiwan (Lure of Taiwan), Vol. 3 (1937), Taihoku: Taiwan Branch, Japan Tourist Bureau.

"Kappanzan bansha ni onari no Asakanomiya denka" (The Aborigine village on Mt. Kappan during Prince Asaka's royal visit) (1927), *Taiwan jihō*, December.

Katō, K. (2002), *Kaigai hikiage kankei shiryō shūsei* (Collection of documents related to overseas repatriation), Tokyo: Yumani shobō.

Kawahara, I. (1997), *Taiwan hikiage ryūyō kiroku* (Records of being kept-behind during repatriation from Taiwan), Tokyo: Yumani shobō.

Kawahira, C. (1982), "Ikoku kashita Okinawa e" (Loaned from a foreign country to Okinawa), in Taiwan kyōkai (eds), *Taiwan hikiage shi: Shōwa nijūnen shūsen kiroku* (A history of repatriation from Taiwan: A record of the end of the war from Shōwa 20 [1945]), Tokyo: Zaidan hōren Taiwan kyōkai.

Ke, D. (2005), *Bokoku wa Nihon, sokoku wa Taiwan: Aru Nihongozoku Taiwanjin no kokuhaku* (Motherland is Japan, fatherland is Taiwan: Confessions of a Taiwanese Japanophone), Tokyo: Sakuranohana.

"Keguan dui hongzhuang, ba jiu hua jiachang, huanyan qiuwang yunü zuopei, jishi you kong zai he yi bei" (Gentleman and lady chitchat over drinks, Jade Maiden helps welcome and entertain the Baseball King, when will they be able to have another drink?) (1965), *Lianhebao*, December 5: 3.

Kelly, W. (1998), "Learning to swing: Oh Sadaharu and the pedagogy and practice of Japanese baseball," in J. Singleton (ed), *Learning in Likely Places: Varieties of Apprenticeship in Japan*, New York: Cambridge University Press.

Kelsky, K. (2001), *Women on the Verge: Japanese Women, Western Dreams*, Durham: Duke University Press.

Kerr, G. (1965), *Formosa Betrayed*, Boston: Houghton Mifflin Company.

"Kikan Nikkyō ni tsugu" (Announcement regarding the deportation of Overseas Japanese) (1946), *Minbao*, April 1: 1.

Kikuchi, Y. (ed) (2007), *Refracted Modernity: Visual Culture and Identity in Colonial Taiwan*. Honolulu: University of Hawai'i Press.

Kinoshita, N. (2003), "The Early Years of Japanese Photography," in J. Junkerman (ed), *The History of Japanese Photography*, New Haven: Yale University Press.

Kip, K. (ed) (2009), *Disease, Colonialism, and the State: Malaria in Modern East Asian History*, Hong Kong: Hong Kong University Press.

Kleeman, F. (2003), *Under an Imperial Sun: Japanese Colonial Literature of Taiwan and the South*, Honolulu: University of Hawai'i Press.

Kleinman, A. (1980), *Patients and Healers in the Context of Culture*, Berkeley: University of California Press.

Ko, K. (dir) (2009), *Jueming paidui (Invitation Only)*, Taibei: Sanhe.

Kodama sōtoku gaisen kangei kinenchō (Album commemorating Governor-General Kodama's triumphant arrival) (1906), Taihoku: *Taiwan nichinichi shinpō* sha.

Koh, S. (1991), *Taiwan xin xianfa lun* (On Taiwan's new constitution), Taibei: Qianwei.

Kojima, Y. ([1915] 1996), *Fanzu xiguan diaocha baogaoshu, di yi juan, Taiyazu* (Report on savage tribal customs, Vol. 1: Atayal peoples), trans. Zhongyang yanjiuyuan Minzuxue yanjiusuo. Nangang: Zhongyang yanjiuyuan Minzuxue yanjiusuo.

Kondo, D. (1990), *Crafting Selves: Power, Gender, and Discourses of Identity in a Japanese Workplace*, Chicago: University of Chicago Press.

Kondō, M. (1992), "Taiwan sōtokufu no riban taisei to Musha Jiken" (The Taiwan Government-General's Aborigine administration policy and the Musha Incident), in S. Ōe (ed), *Kindai Nihon to shokuminchi: Teikoku tōchi no kōzō* 2 (Modern Japan and its colonies: The structure of imperial rule, Vol. 2), Tokyo: Iwanami Shoten.

———. (ed) (1993), Riban no Tomo *bessatsu, kaidai, satoshi, mokuji sakuin (Aborigine Administrators' Companion synopses, annotated bibliography, table of contents, index)*, Tokyo: Ryokuin shobō.

Kushner, B. (2007), "Nationality and Nostalgia: The Manipulation of Memory in Japan, Taiwan, and China since 1990," *International History Review*, 29.4: 793–820.

———. (2013), "Ghosts of the Japanese Imperial Army: The "White Group" (*Baituan*) and Early Post-war Sino-Japanese Relations," *Past and Present*, 218, Supplement 8: "Transnationalism and Contemporary Global History," 117–50.

Lagerwey, J. (ed) (2005), *Kejia chuantong shehui* (The traditional society of the Hakka), 2 vols, Beijing: Zhonghua shuju.

Lai, T., Myers, R., and Wou, W. (1991), *A Tragic Beginning: The Taiwan Uprising of February 28, 1947*, Stanford: Stanford University Press.

Lam, P. (2004), "Japan-Taiwan Relations: Between Affinity and Reality," *Asian Affairs*, 30.4: 249–67.

LaMarre, T. (2009), "Cine-Photography as Racial Technology: Tanizaki Jun'ichirō's Close-up on the New/Oriental Woman's Face," in R. Morris (ed), *Photographies East: The Camera and Its Histories in East and Southeast Asia*, Durham: Duke University Press.

Lamley, H. (1981), "Subethnic Rivalry in the Ch'ing Period," in E. Ahern and H. Gates (eds), *The Anthropology of Taiwanese Society*, Stanford: Stanford University Press.

Larsen, K. (2008), *Tradition, Treaties, and Trade: Qing Imperialism and Choson Korea, 1850–1910*, Cambridge: Harvard University Press.

Le Gendre, C. (1871), *Reports on Amoy and the Island of Formosa*, Washington: Government Printing Office.

———. (2012), *Notes of Travel in Formosa*, D. Fix and J. Shufelt (eds), Tainan: National Museum of Taiwan History.

Lee, A. (2007), "Subways as a Space of Cultural Intimacy: The Mass Rapid Transit System in Taipei, Taiwan," *China Journal*, 58: 31–55.

Leong, S. (1997), *Migration and Ethnicity in Chinese History: Hakkas, Pengmin and their Neighbors*, Stanford: Stanford University Press.

Lewis, L. (2003), "Japan's Coffee Kings and the Starbucks Effect," *J@pan Inc*, 49: 12–13.

"Li canbai Jingguo shenshe—'Ge ke xiang mingfu le'" (Lee visits Yasukuni Shrine—"My brother can enjoy good fortune in the nether world") (2007), *Ziyou shibao*, June 8.

Li, D. (1970), "Ju Tai waishengji renkou zhi zucheng yu fenbu" (Composition and distribution of the mainlander population in Taiwan), *Taibei wenxian*, 11-12: 62–86.

Li, D. (1995), *Xishuo kangzhan* (Details on the Anti-Japanese War of Resistance), Taibei: Yuanliu.

"Li Denghui canbai Jingguo, zhenzhang pimei shouxiang" (Lee Teng-hui visits Yasukuni, fuss comparable to a prime minister's visit) (2007), *Lianhebao*, June 8, morning ed.

"Li Denghui Riben xing: huang min you zi yi jin fanxiang?" (Lee Teng-hui's Japan trip: Imperial subject wanderer returning home gloriously?) (2007), *Lianhebao*, June 3, morning ed.

"Li Denghui you Daban cheng fa sigu youqing, zhi Riben tongyi zhanshi zhide xuexi" (Visit to Osaka Castle leads Lee Teng-hui to muse over the past—points out that the history of the Japanese War of Unification deserves study) (2001), *Zhongguo shibao*, April 24, morning ed.

Li, G. (BARZ) (2011), *Yijiusiwu xiamo* (The end of summer, 1945), Tainan: Guoli Taiwan lishi bowuguan.

Li, S. (2002), *Saⁿ-kha-a: Taiwanlun yu huangminhua pipan* ("Wanna-be": A critique of *On Taiwan* and Japanization), Taibei: Haixia xueshu.

Li, Y. (1965), "Yi bang weizhen Fusangdao, wanzhong zhengying mei qiuwang" (One bat awes Japan, a crowd of thousands competes to welcome the beautiful King of Baseball), *Lianhebao*, December 5: 3.

Li, Y. (1983), *Shandi xingzheng zhengce zhi yanjiu yu pinggu baogaoshu* (Mountain areas administrative policy research and evaluation report), Nantou: Taiwan sheng zhengfu minzhengting.

"Lin considering playing overseas if NBA lockout continues" (2011), *Focus Taiwan News Channel*, 4 August. http://focustaiwan.tw/news/aspt/201108040045.aspx [accessed June 10, 2014].

Lin, G. (ed) (2001), *Chunlei shengsheng: Bao Diao yundong sanshi zhounian wenxian xuanji* (Sounds of spring thunder: Selected documents on the 30th anniversary of the Protect Diaoyutai movement), Taibei: Renjian.

Lin, J. (2006), "KFC to double number of Taiwan Restaurants," *Taipei Times*, January 5: 10.

Lin, J. (2014), "Lian Zhan pi huangminhua guan san dai; Ke P: Zufu shengzuo Ribenren, bu shi ta de cuo" (Lien Chan's three-generation critique of "imperialization"; Professor Ko: It wasn't his fault that my grandfather was born a Japanese subject), *NOWnews*, November 17. http://www.nownews.com/n/2014/11/17/1508935 [accessed November 27, 2014].

Lin, M. (1997), *Cha, tang, zhangnao ye yu Taiwan zhi shehui jingji bianqian* (The tea, sugar and camphor industries and socioeconomic changes in Taiwan), Taibei: Lianjing.

Lin, Q. (2010), "Ha Ri, qin Ri, lian Ri? 'Bianchui dong Ya' de 'Riben qingjie'" (Being crazy about Japan, being close to Japan, loving Japan? The "Japan complex" in "East Asia's margins"), *Sixiang (Reflexion)*, 14, Special Issue: "Taiwan de Riben zhenghouqun" (Taiwan's Japan Syndrome), 139–59.

Lin, S. (2000), *Diyi minzu: Taiwan Yuanzhuminzu yundong de xianfa yiyi* (First peoples: The constitutional significance of Taiwan's Indigenous Peoples movement), Taibei: Qianwei.

Lin, S. (2005), "Jingdiansai, A-bian: Taiwan guanjun xiang" (World Baseball Classic: A-bian: Taiwan looks like a champion), *Zhongguo shibao*, December 23.

Linck-Kesting, G. (1978), "Ein Kapitel japanischer Kolonialgeschichte: Die Politik gegenüber der nichtchinesischen Bevölkerung von Taiwan," *Nachrichten der Gesellschaft für Natur- und Völkerkunde Ostasiens/Hamburg*, 123: 61–81.

———. (1979), *Ein Kapitel Chinesischer Grenzgeschichte: Han und Nicht-Han im Taiwan der Qing-Zeit 1683–1895*, Wiesbaden: Franz Steiner Verlag.

Liu, C. (2003), "Taiwanshi kenkyū no genjō to kadai" (The current state of, and challenges in, Taiwanese historical research), in Taiwan kenkyū bukai (Taiwan Research Group) (ed), *Taiwan no Kindai to Nihon* (Modern Taiwan and Japan), Nagoya: Chukyo University Institute of Social Science.

Liu, J. (2009), "Immanentism, Double Abjection, and the Politics of Psyche in (Post) Colonial Taiwan," *Positions*, 17.2: 261–87.

Liu, L. (2006), "Betel Nut Consumption in Contemporary Taiwan: Gender, Class and Social Identity," MA Thesis, Chinese University of Hong Kong.

Liu, M. (2009), *Prescribing Colonization: The Role of Medical Practices and Policies in Japan-Ruled Taiwan, 1895–1945*, Ann Arbor: Association for Asian Studies.

"Liu Tai Riqiao renshu an sanwan wuqian yinei" (The number of kept-behind Japanese is within 35,000) (1946), *Minbao*, March 19: 2.

Loa, I. (2014), "Lien Chan's 'bastard' barb bounces off Ko Wen-je," *Taipei Times*, November 23: 3. http://www.taipeitimes.com/News/taiwan/archives/2014/11/23/2003605105 [accessed November 27, 2014].

Loomba, A. (1998), *Colonialism/Postcolonialism*, London: Routledge.

Lu, J. (2003), *Taiwan houzhimin guozu rentong, 1950–2000* (Taiwan's postcolonial national identity, 1950–2000), Taibei: Maitian.

Lu, T. (2011), "A Cinematic Parallax View: Taiwanese Identity and the Japanese Colonial Past," *positions*, 19.3: 763–79.

"Lü Ri Huaqiao bangqiu mingxing, Wang Zhenzhi po Riben jilu" (Overseas Chinese baseball star, having traveled to Japan [*sic*], sets Japanese record) (1964), *Lianhebao*, September 8: 2.

Lunn, P. (1991), "Nutrition, Immunity, Infection," in R. Schofield, D. Reher, and A. Bideau (eds), *The Decline of Mortality in Europe*, Oxford: Oxford University Press.

Lupke, C. (2009), "Fractured Identities and Refracted Images: The Neither/Nor of National Imagination in Contemporary Taiwan," *positions*, 17.2: 243–59.

"Ma: bie zai jiao wo fan Ri pai" (Ma: Stop calling me anti-Japanese) (2007), *Zhongguo shibao*, November 22, morning ed.

"Ma di Ri xiaodu: wo bu fan Ri" (Ma arrives in Japan to disinfect his image: I'm not against Japan) (2007), *Ziyou shibao*, November 22.

Ma, S. (2009), "Found(l)ing Taiwanese: from Chinese Fatherland to Japanese Okasan," in C. Neri and K. Gormley (eds), *Le Cinéma taïwanais/Taiwan Cinema*, Lyon: Asiexpo.

Mabuchi, T. (1974), *Ethnology of the Southwestern Pacific: the Ryukyus-Taiwan-Insular Southeast Asia*, Taipei: Chinese Association for Folklore.

Mair, V. (2014), "A current neologism in Taiwan," *Language Log*, March 22. http://languagelog.ldc.upenn.edu/nll/?p=11239 [accessed April 8, 2014].

Mao, H. (2001), "Liuyiqi xuesheng shiwei jishi" (Record of the 17 June student demonstrations), in G. Lin (ed), *Chunlei shengsheng: Bao Diao yundong sanshi zhounian wenxian xuanji* (Sounds of spring thunder: Selected documents on the 30th anniversary of the Protect Diaoyutai movement), Taibei: Renjian.

Marshall, B. (1967), *Capitalism and Nationalism in Prewar Japan; the Ideology of the Business Elite, 1868–1941*, Stanford: Stanford University Press.

Martin, H. (1996), "The Hakka Ethnic Movement in Taiwan, 1986–1991," in N. Constable (ed), *Guest People: Hakka identity in China and Abroad*, Seattle: University of Washington Press.

Marui, K. (1914), *Buban ni kansuru ikensho, Bandō kyōiku ikensho* (Position paper regarding Aborigine pacification and the education of Aborigine children), Taihoku: Banmu honsho.

Marx, K. (1978), "Capital, Volume One" in R. Tucker (ed), *Marx-Engels Reader*, New York: W.W. Norton & Co.

Masaw M. (S. Liao) (1977), "Taiyazu dong Saidekequn de buluo qianxi yu fenbu (shang)" (Migration and distribution of the eastern Seediq group of the Atayal tribe, Part 1), *Zhongyang yanjiuyuan Minzu yanjiusuo jikan*, 44: 61–206.

———. (1978), "Taiyazu dong Saidekequn de buluo qianxi yu fenbu (xia)" (Migration and distribution of the eastern Seediq group of the Atayal tribe, Part 2), *Zhongyang yanjiuyuan Minzu yanjiusuo jikan*, 45: 81–212.

Masuya, S. (1935), "Banjin no keizai kannen to kanshū" (The economic customs and consciousness of the Aborigines), *Riban no tomo* (Aborigine administrators' companion), October 1: 8–9.

Matsuda, Y. (2006), *Taiwan ni okeru ittō dokusai Taisei no seiritsu* (On the establishment of one-party dictatorship in Taiwan), Tokyo: Keiō gijuku daigaku shuppankai.

Matsuoka, T. (2012), *Taiwan Genjūmin shakai no chihōka: Mainoriti no nijūsseiki* (The provincialization of Taiwan Indigenous society: Minority's twentieth century), Tokyo: Kenbun shuppan.

"'Matsushima, utsukushii'—Ri Tōki-shi ga raiken—Sendai-shichō-ra demukae" ("How beautiful Matsushima is!"—Lee Teng-hui visits Miyagi Prefecture—Sendai Mayor and others greet him) (2007), *Yomiuri shimbun*, June 3, morning ed.

McClintock, A. (1992), "The Angel of Progress: Pitfalls of the Term 'Post-Colonialism,'" *Social Text*, 31/32, Special Issue: "Third World and Post-Colonial Issues," 84–98.

McWilliams, W. (1975), "East Meets East: The Soejima Mission to China, 1873," *Monumenta Nipponica*, 30.3: 237–75.

"Meiren ru yu bang ru hong, fengyun ernü zong xiangfeng, Zhang Meiyao jin ying Wang Zhenzhi" (Beauty like jade, a bat like a rainbow, the man and woman of the moment finally meet, Chang Mei-yao to welcome Oh Sadaharu today) (1965), *Lianhebao*, December 4: 3.

Meyer, M. (1991), "'We Can Not Get a Living as We Used To': Dispossession and the White Earth Anishinaabeg, 1889–1920," *American Historical Review*, 96.2: 368–94.

Miller, B. (2003), *Invisible Indigenes: the Politics of Nonrecognition*, Lincoln: University of Nebraska Press.

Mizuno, J. (1930), "Seiban Shiki" (A savage diary), in Yagashiro Hideyoshi (ed), *Tairo Mizuno Jun Sensei* (Tairo Professor Mizuno), Nagoya: Tairokai.

Monbushō (ed) (1910), *Jinjō shōgaku chiri ken ni: jidō yō* (Standard elementary school geography, Volume 2: For youth), Tokyo: Monbushō.

Moore-Gilbert, B. (1997), *Postcolonial theory: contexts, practices, politics*, London: Verso.

Mori, U. (1917), "Taiwan shinrin to Banjin no kankei ni tsuite" (On the connection between the Aborigines and Taiwan's forests), *Taiwan jihō* (Taiwan news), 89: 9–19.

Morris-Suzuki, T. (2012), "Post-War Warriors: Japanese Combatants in the Korean War," *The Asia-Pacific Journal*, 10.31.1. http://japanfocus.org/-Tessa-Morris_Suzuki/3803 [accessed July 30, 2012].

Morris, A. (2004), *Marrow of the Nation: A History of Sport and Physical Culture in Republican China*, Berkeley: University of California Press.

———. (2010), *Colonial Project, National Game: A History of Baseball in Taiwan*, Berkeley: University of California Press.

Morris, R. (2009), "Photographies East: The Camera and Its Histories in East and Southeast Asia", in R. Morris (ed), *Photographies East: The Camera and Its Histories in East and Southeast Asia*, Durham: Duke University Press.

Moskowitz, M. (2005), "Magic Tricks, Midnight Grave Outings, and Transforming Trees: Performance and Agency in Taiwanese Religion," *Journal of Ritual Studies*, 19.1, special issue on "Asian Ritual Systems: Syncretisms and Ruptures": 19–30.

———. (2007), "Failed Families and Quiet Individualism: Women's Strategies of Resistance in Urban Taiwan," *Journal of Archaeology and Anthropology* 67: 157–84.

———. (2008), "Multiple Virginity, Barbarian Prince Charmings, and Other Contested Realities in Taipei's Foreign Club Culture," *Sexualities* 11.3: 327–35.

———. (2010), *Cries of Joy, Songs of Sorrow: Chinese Pop Music and its Cultural Connotations*, Honolulu: University of Hawai'i Press.

Musha tōbatsu shashinchō (Musha expedition photo album) (1931), Taihoku: Kyōshi shōkai.

Myers, R. (2009), "Towards an Enlightened Authoritarian Polity: The Kuomintang Central Reform Committee on Taiwan, 1950–1952," *Journal of Contemporary China*, 59: 185–99.

Nagano, S. and Kondō, M. (eds) (1999), *Nihon no sengo baishō* (Japanese postwar reparations), Tokyo: Keisō shobō.

Nanpō no kyoten: Taiwan (Southern base: Taiwan) (1944), Tokyo: *Asahi shimbun* sha.

Nanshin Taiwan (Southward expansion into Taiwan) (1935), Tokyo: Jitsugyō jidaisha and *Zaikai no Nihon sha*. [Released in DVD collection "Piange zhuandong jian de Taiwan xianying" *(Colonial Japanese Documentaries on Taiwan)*, Tainan: Guoli Taiwan lishi bowuguan, 2008.]

"Nanwang zuguo renqing wennuan" (The unforgettable warmth of the people of the motherland [*sic*]) (1966), *Lianhebao*, December 8: 3.

Neri, C. and Gormley, K. (eds) (2009), *Le Cinéma taïwanais/Taiwan Cinema*, Lyon: Asiexpo.

Newhall, B. (1964), *The History of Photography*, New York: Museum of Modern Art.

Niezen, R. (2003), *The Origins of Indigenism: Human Rights and the Politics of Identity*, Berkeley: University of California Press.

"Nikkyō ryū Tai tsūchijo juryōhō no ken" (Overseas Japanese accept the regulations for remaining in Taiwan) (1946), *Minbao*, April 12: 2.

Noble, D. (2002), *Death of a Nation: American Culture and the End of Exceptionalism*, Minneapolis: University of Minnesota Press.

Oehler, W. (1922), "Christian Work Among the Hakka," in M. Stauffer (ed), *The Christian Occupation of China*, Shanghai: China Continuation Committee.

Ogasawara, Y. (1998), *Office Ladies and Salaried Men: Power, Gender, and Work in Japanese Companies*, Berkeley: University of California Press.

Ogawa, S. (2009), "Hou Hsiao-hsien in Japan: From Taiwan Trilogy to Café Lumière," in C. Neri and K. Gormley (eds), *Le Cinéma taïwanais/Taiwan Cinema*, Lyon: Asiexpo.

Oh, S. (1976), *Tobeyo nekkyū* (Ball, heat, flight), Tokyo: Kodansha.

———. (1981), *Kaisō* (Reminiscences), Tokyo: Keibunsha.

Oh, S. and Falkner, D. (1984), *Sadaharu Oh: A Zen Way of Baseball*, New York: Times Books.

Oh, T. (1985), "Gan'en de suiyue: Wang Zhenzhi muqin de huiyilu" (Years of gratitude: Memoir of Oh Sadaharu's mother), trans. Q. Lin and C. Liao, serialized in 79 entries, *Minshengbao* (The people's livelihood newspaper), June 10–September 5.

Ohnuki-Thierney, E. (2002), *Kamikaze, Cherry Blossoms, and Nationalisms: The Militarization of Aesthetics in Japanese History*, Chicago: University of Chicago Press.

Okada, H. (1997), *"Hannichi" to "Shinnichi" no hazama: Kankoku, Taiwan kara mita Nihon* (Between anti-Japanese and pro-Japanese: Looking at Japan from Korea and Taiwan), Tokyo: *Tōyō keizai shinpō* sha.

————. (2009), *Taiwan no meiun: Mottomo shinnichitekina rinkoku* (Taiwan's destiny: The neighboring country that is closest to Japan), Tokyo: Yudachisha.

Omran, A. (1971), "The Epidemiologic Transition," *Milbank Memorial Fund Quarterly*, 44.4: 509–38.

Ong, A. (2006), *Neoliberalism as Exception: Mutations in Citizenship and Sovereignty*, Durham: Duke University Press.

Ong, I. (1970), *Taiwan: Kumon suru so no rekishi* (Taiwan: An agonizing history), Tokyo: Kōbundō.

Otani, B. (ed) (1914), "Sakuma sōtoku-kakka gaisen (Taihoku teishaba mae) Taishō sannen-do Taroko-ban tōbatsu (The Triumph of Governor-General Sakuma at Taihoku Station)," *Taiwan shashinchō* (Taiwan photographic monthly), 1.1: 22. http://digital. lafayette.edu/collections/eastasia/cpw-shashinkai/ts0022 [accessed November 9, 2014].

Ozaki, H. (1933), "Jūyō bijutsu no hozon to Taiwan no banzokuhin" (Preserving important artworks and Taiwan's Indigenous materials), *Riban no tomo* (Aborigine administrators' companion), April 1: 2.

Packard, R. (2007), *The Making of a Tropical Disease: A Short History of Malaria*, Baltimore: Johns Hopkins University Press.

Pan, C. (2005), "Xin huoban guanxi xia Taiwan Yuanzhuminzu zizhi wenti zhi yanjiu" (Research into Taiwan Aborigine autonomy under the new partnership), MA Thesis, Taiwan Normal University.

Parr, M. and Badger, G. (2004), *The Photobook: A History*, Vol. 1, London: Phaidon Press.

Pasternak, B. (1972), *Kinship and Community in Two Chinese Villages*, Stanford: Stanford University Press.

————. (1983), *Guests in the Dragon: Social Demography of a Chinese District, 1895–1946*, New York: Columbia University Press.

Peattie, M. (1984), "Japanese Attitudes toward Colonialism," in R. Myers and M. Peattie (eds), *The Japanese Colonial Empire, 1895–1945*, Princeton: Princeton University Press.

Pendergrast, M. (1999), *Uncommon Grounds: The History of Coffee and how it Transformed Our World*, New York: Basic Books.

Peng, M. (1972), *A Taste of Freedom: Memoirs of an Independence Leader*, New York: Holt, Rinehart, and Winston.

Peng, M. (2002), *Taiwan shixue de Zhongguo chanjie* (The China tangle in Taiwanese historiography), Taibei: Maitian.

Phillips, S. (2003), *Between Assimilation and Independence: The Taiwanese Encounter Nationalist China, 1945–1950*, Stanford: Stanford University Press.

President Chiang Kai-Shek: His Life Story in Pictures (1972), Taipei: Government Information Office, Republic of China.

"President confers medal of honor on baseball legend Oh" (2009), *The China Post*, 6 February. http://www.chinapost.com.tw/taiwan/intl-community/2009/02/06/194877/ President-confers.htm [accessed September 23, 2012].

Preston, S. (1976), *Mortality Patterns in National Populations: With Special Reference to Recorded Causes of Death*, New York: Academic Press.

Pu, W. (2002), "Wenhua rentong dui kuaguo qiye jingying zheng zhi yinxiang, Meishi xingbake yu zhongshi chichaqu" (Cultural identification towards international business strategies and influences: Comparative research on interest in American Starbucks and in drinking Chinese-style tea), MA Thesis, Central Taiwan Nursing Technology Institute.

Pusin T. (2002), "Cong Wushe shijian tan Yuanzhuminzu de zizhi" (From the Wushe Incident to a discussion about Aboriginal self-government), in C. Shih, S. Koh, and Pusin T. (eds), *Cong hejie dao zizhi: Taiwan Yuanzhuminzu lishi chongjian* (From reconciliation to autonomy: Reconstructing the history of Taiwan's Indigenous peoples), Taibei: Qianwei.

"Qiuwang zhi zongtongfu, qianming zhijing" (Baseball king to the Presidential Palace, autographs and greetings) (1965), *Lianhebao*, December 7: 3

"Quan Riben yiliu bangdui, bao simian liansheng xiongxin" (Japan's finest team has lofty ambitions for fourth straight title) (1968), *Lianhebao*, February 8: 6.

Rawnsley, G. (2000), *Taiwan's Informal Diplomacy and Propaganda*, Houndmills: Macmillan.

Rawnsley, G. and Rawnsley, M. (1998), "Regime Transition and the Media in Taiwan," *Democratization*, 5.2: 106–24.

Ren, Y. (2008), *Xiang xia zagen: Zhongguo Guomindang yu Taiwan difang zhengzhi de fazhan, 1949–1960* (Taking root: The Chinese Nationalist Party and the development of local politics in Taiwan, 1949–1960), Taibei: Daoxiang.

"Ri Tōki, Taiwan zen-sōtō ni kiku—Hōnichi wa seikō—'Shizuka na messeiji' ga shinrai-kankei tsuyomeru" (Interview with Taiwan's former President Lee Teng-hui—Japan visit a success—"quiet message" strengthens mutual trust) (2005), *Sankei shimbun*, January 13, morning ed.

"Ri Tōki, Taiwan-zen-sōtō—Nihon no haru ni kanmuryō—16-nen-buri no asa" (Taiwan's former President Lee Teng-hui—filled with emotion over Japanese spring—one morning after 16 years) (2001), *Yomiuri shimbun*, April 23, evening ed.

"Ri Tōki, Taiwan-zen-sōtō rainichi—Hamon yobu 'jiyū' na tabi—Chūgoku kensei suru kōen" (Taiwan's former President Lee Teng-hui in Japan—'unrestricted' travel creating sensation—will lecture [on need to] contain China) (2007), *Yomiuri shimbun*, June 2, morning ed.

"Ri Tōki, Taiwan-zen-sōtō: Bashō kinenkan ni—Tōkyō, Kōtō-ku" (Taiwan's former President Lee Teng-hui at Bashō Museum in Tokyo's Kōtō Ward) (2007), *Mainichi shimbun*, June 1, Osaka morning ed.

"Ri Tōki, Zen-Taiwan-sōtō no hōnichi-jitsugen—Totsuzen no yotei-henkō, genba konran—Tōrinuke yame Ōsaka-jō e" (Taiwan's former President Lee Teng-hui's Japan visit realized—sudden plan changes, confusion on site—dropping cherry tree stroll, off to Osaka Castle) (2001), *Mainichi shimbun*, April 24, Osaka morning ed.

"Ri Tōki, Zen-Taiwan-sōtō no rainichi—Hosoda Kanbōchōkan ga shuzai-jishuku o yōbō" (Taiwan's former President Lee Teng-hui visiting Japan—Chief Cabinet Secretary Hosoda requests media to abstain from covering visit) (2004), *Yomiuri shimbun*, December 21, morning ed.

"Ri Tōki-shi rainichi—Yasukuni 'sanpai shitai'" (Lee Teng-hui in Japan—"I want to visit" Yasukuni) (2007), *Sankei shimbun*, May 31, morning ed.

Riban shikō (Records of Aborigine administration) (1918–1938), editions 1–5, Taihoku: Taiwan sōtokufu keisatsu honsho.

"Riben xiaojie, Zhongguo taitai" (Japanese young lady, Chinese wife) (1966), *Lianhebao*, December 2: 3.

"Richan fangwu fen jiu an, kedao gaihui shou caijue" (For investigating confusing cases on the distribution of Japanese assets and property, report to the Committee for adjudication) (1946), *Minbao*, April 12: 2.

"Riren gongsi caichan bude shanzi maimai" (Assets of Japanese companies cannot be bought or sold without permission) (1945), *Minbao*, October 16: 1.

"Riren kangyi Ma 'fan Ri mei Zhong'" (Japanese protesting against Ma's "opposing Japan, toadying to China") (2006), *Ziyou shibao*, July 11.

"Riren xuesheng zhi dan shang ren" (Japanese student throws explosive, injures people) (1945), *Minbao*, November 9: 1.

Ritzer, G. (2007), *The McDonaldization of Society*, New York: Pine Forge Press.

Robertson, J. (2007), "It Takes a Village: Internationalization and nostalgia in postwar Japan," in D. Martinez (ed), *Modern Japanese Culture and Society*, Volume I, London: Routledge.

"Rongzhuang de Riren qiangdao qiangjie huowu zidongche" (Japanese in uniform steal and loot merchandise and automobiles) (1945), *Minbao*, October 31: 2.

Rosaldo, R. (1989), "Imperialist Nostalgia," *Representations*, 26, Special Issue: "Memory and Counter-Memory", 107–22.

Roy, D. (2006), "Stirring Samurai, Disapproving Dragon: Japan's Growing Security Activity and Sino-Japan Relations," in Y. Sato and S. Limaye (eds), *Japan in a Dynamic Asia: Coping with the New Security Challenges*, Lanham, MD: Lexington Books.

Ruan, M. (1992), *Youan jiaoluo de qisheng: Xunfang ererba sanluo de yizu* (Tears from a dark corner: Searching for the scattered descendants of February 28th), Taibei: Qianwei.

Rudolph, M. (2003), *Taiwans multi-ethnische Gesellschaft und die Bewegung der Ureinwohner: Assimilation oder kulturelle Revitalisierung?* Hamburg: LIT Verlag.

———. (2004), "The Pan-Ethnic Movement of Taiwanese Aborigines and the Role of Elites in the Process of Ethnicity Formation," in F. Christiansen and U. Hedetoft (eds), *The Politics of Multiple Belonging: Ethnicity and Nationalism in Europe and East Asia*, Aldershot, UK: Ashgate.

———. (2008), *Ritual Performances as Authenticating Practices: Cultural Representations of Taiwan's Aborigines in Times of Political Change*, Berlin: LIT Verlag.

Ryan, J. (1997), *Picturing Empire: Photography and the Visualization of the British Empire*, Chicago: University of Chicago Press.

"Sadaharu Oh named ambassador-at-large for sports" (2001), Central News Agency, November 13.

Safran, W. (1991), "Diasporas in Modern Societies: Myths of Homeland and Return," *Diaspora: A Journal of Transnational Studies*, 1.1: 83–99.

Sanbō, H. (ed) (1895), *Taiwan shi* (Taiwan records), Hiroshima.

Satō, E. (1982), "Hinomaru no shōhata o butte" (Waving small Hinomaru flags), in Taiwan kyōkai (eds), *Taiwan hikiage shi: Shōwa nijūnen shūsen kiroku* (A history of repatriation from Taiwan: A record of the end of the war from Shōwa 20 [1945]), Tokyo: Zaidan hōren Taiwan kyōkai.

Satō, H. (1998), "Musha," in I. Kawahara (ed), *Nihon tōchiki Taiwan bunka: Nihonjin sakka hinshū, bekkan (Naichi sakka)* (Taiwanese culture during Japanese colonial rule: Collected works of Japanese authors, appendix: Mainland authors), Tokyo: Rokuin shobō.

Schubert, G. (2012), "Taiwan's Political Evolution from Authoritarianism to Democracy and the Development of Cross-Strait Relations," in J. Damm and P. Lim (eds), *European Perspectives on Taiwan*, Wiesbaden: VS Verlag.

Sejrup, J. (2012), "Instrumentalized History and the Motif of Repetition in News Coverage of Japan-Taiwan Relations," *Pacific Affairs*, 85.4: 745–65.

Selbin, E. (1997), "Revolution in the Real World: Bringing Agency Back In," in J. Foran (ed), *Theorizing Revolutions*, New York: Routledge.

"7–11 Around the World" (March 31, 2014). http://www.sej.co.jp/company/en/g_stores. html [accessed May 2, 2014].

"Sha Chōtei-shi, hōnichi oe kitai—'Shinnichi-ha' Senkaku-mondai mo hairyo" (Frank Hsieh finishes Japan visit, returns to Taiwan—"pro-Japanese" considering even [Japanese position in] Senkaku Islands question) (2007), *Sankei shimbun*, December 20, morning ed.

Shashin kurabu: Ichimei Taiwan jimbutsu shashinchō (Photographs of the club: Album of famous people in Taiwan) (1901), Taihoku: Taiwan shūhō.

"Shelun: Richan fangwu chuli wenti" (Editorial: The problem of processing Japanese assets and property) (1946), *Minbao*, April 6: 1.

"Shelun: Songgui guo de Riqiao" (Editorial: The Overseas Japanese who are being sent home) (1946), *Minbao*, March 5: 1.

"Shelun: Taiwan weichang 'nuhua' " (Editorial: Taiwan was never "enslaved") (1946), *Minbao*, April 7: 1.

Shen, M. (2002), "Taibei kafeiguan: yi ge (wenyi) gonggong lingyu zhi jueqi fazhan yu zhuanhua (1930s-1970s) (The Coffee Shop in Taipei: The Rise, Change, and Transformation of Literary Public Sphere [from 1930s to 1970s])," MA Thesis, Chung Yuan Christian University.

———. (2005), *Kafei shidai: Taiwan kafeiguan bai nian fengsao* (The coffee age: One hundred years of the seduction of Taiwan coffee shops), Taibei: Yuanzu.

Shepherd, J. (1993), *Statecraft and Political Economy on the Taiwan Frontier, 1600–1800*, Stanford: Stanford University Press.

———. (2011a), "Regional and ethnic variation in mortality in Japanese colonial period Taiwan," in T. Engelen, J. Shepherd, and W. Yang (eds), *Death at the opposite ends of the Eurasian continent: Mortality trends in Taiwan and the Netherlands, 1850–1945*, Amsterdam: Aksant Academic Publishers.

———. (2011b), "Trends in mortality and causes of death in Japanese colonial period Taiwan," in T. Engelen, J. Shepherd, and W. Yang (eds), *Death at the opposite ends of the Eurasian continent: Mortality trends in Taiwan and the Netherlands, 1850–1945*, Amsterdam. Aksant Academic Publishers.

———, Pan, I., Kok, J., Engel, C., Engelen, T., and Brown, M. (2006), "Group Identity and Fertility: An Evaluation of the Role of Religion and Ethnicity in the Netherlands and Taiwan," in Chuang Ying-chang, Theo Engelen, and Arthur P. Wolf. (eds) *Positive or Preventive? Reproduction in Taiwan and the Netherlands, 1850–1940*, Amsterdam: Aksant Academic Publishers.

Shi, M. (1994), *Taiwanjin yonhyakunenshi* (Four hundred years of Taiwanese history), Tokyo: Shinsensha.

Shi, T. (1987), *Qingdai zai Tai Hanren de zuji fenbu he yuanxiang shenghuo fangshi* (Modes of livelihood in localities of ancestral registration and the distribution by provenance of the Han in Qing Taiwan). Taibei: Guoli Taiwan shifan daxue Dili xuexi.

Shiba, R. (1994), *Taiwan kikō* (Journal of travels in Taiwan), Tokyo: *Asahi shimbun*.

Shimizu, H. (dir) (1943), *Sayon no kane* (Sayon's bell), Tokyo: Shochiku; Taihoku: Taiwan sōtoku; Shinkyō: Manshu eiga kyōkai.

"Shizhang bu fan Ri, dan bu wang tamen de cuo" (Mayor is not anti-Japanese but doesn't forget their mistakes, either) (2006), *Zhongguo shibao*, July 8, morning ed.

Shufelt, J. (2010), "Imagining Formosa: Victorian Writings on Taiwan, 1860–1885," Ph.D. Dissertation, University of Sheffield.

Shui, B. (2001), "Huigu 'Baodiao'" (Looking back on the Protect Diaoyutai movement), in G. Lin (ed), *Chunlei shengsheng: Bao Diao yundong sanshi zhounian wenxian xuanji* (Sounds of spring thunder: Selected documents on the 30th anniversary of the Protect Diaoyutai movement), Taibei: Renjian.

Sima, S. (1964), "Fengmi Riben de bangqiu xuanshou Wang Zhenzhi" (Baseball player Oh Sadaharu, fashionable in Japan), *Lianhebao*, April 25: 2.

Simon, S. (2003), "Contesting Formosa: Tragic Remembrance, Urban Space, and National Identity in Taipak," *Identities: Global Studies in Culture and Power*, 10.1: 109–31.

———. (2007), "Paths to Autonomy: Aboriginality and the Nation in Taiwan," in C. Storm and M. Harrison (eds), *The Margins of Becoming: Identity and Culture in Taiwan*, Wiesbaden: Harrassowitz.

———. (2009), "Identité autochtone et lutte pour l'autodétermination: Le cas de la nation taroko à Formose," in Thibault Martin (ed), *Autochtonies. Vues de France et du Québec*, Québec: Presses de l'université de Laval.

———. (2010), "Negotiating Power: Elections and the Constitution of Indigenous Taiwan," *American Ethnologist*, 37.4: 726–40.

———. (2012), "Politics and Headhunting among the Formosan Sejiq: Ethnohistorical Perspectives," *Oceania*, 82.2: 164–85.

———. and Awi M. (2013), "Human Rights and Indigenous Self-Government: The Taiwanese Experience," in S. Bagchi and A. Das (eds), *Human Rights and the Third World: Issues and Discourses*, Lanham, MD: Lexington Books.

Siyat U. (S. Liu) (2004), *Gimi Ka Truk*u (*Zhao hui Tailuge*) (Recovering Taroko), Taibei: Hanlu tushu.

Smith, A. (2002), *The Wealth of Nations: Representative Selections*, Bruce Mazlish (ed), Mineola, NY: Dover Publications.

Sontag, S. (1973), *On Photography*, New York: Farrar, Straus, and Giroux.

Spector, R. (2007), *In the Ruins of Empire: The Japanese Surrender and the Battle for Postwar Asia*, New York: Random House.

Stoler, A. (1997), "Sexual Affronts and Racial Frontiers: European Identities and the Cultural Politics of Exclusion in Colonial Southeast Asia," in F. Cooper and A. Stoler (eds), *Tensions of Empire: Colonial Cultures in a Bourgeois World*, Berkeley: University of California Press.

Su, J. (2008), *Women dou shi waishengren: Dalu yimin duhai lai Tai si bai nian* (We are all mainlanders: 400 years of immigration from the mainland across the sea to Taiwan), Taibei: Taiwan donghua shuju.

Su, Y. (2004), *Zuihou de Taiwan zongdufu: 1944–1946 nian zhongzhan ziliao ji* (The Last Governor-General of Taiwan: A Compilation of Materials from the End of the War, 1944–1946), Taizhong: Chenxing chuban.

Suzuki, H. (2002), *Hyakunenme no kikyō: Ō Sadaharu to chichi Shifuku* (Returning home after a century: Oh Sadaharu and his father Shifuku), Tōkyō: Shōgakkan.

———. (2005), *Wang Zhenzhi bainian guixiang* (Oh Sadaharu returning home after a century), trans. S. Li, Taibei: Xianjue.

Tagg, J. (1993), *The Burden of Representation: Essays on Photographies and Histories*, Minneapolis: University of Minnesota Press.

Tai, E. (2014), "The Discourse of Intermarriage in Colonial Taiwan," *The Journal of Japanese Studies*, 40.1: 87–116.

Taibei xin xingxiang (New image of Taipei) (1981), Taibei: Taibei shi zhengfu.

"Taichū-kankei ni kuryo—Seifu, Jimin ni menkai jishuku-yōsei—Taiwan no Ri zen-sōtō ni biza" (Worries over China relations—government requesting LDP [Diet members] to abstain from meeting with Lee—visa to Taiwan's former President Lee) (2004), *Asahi shimbun*, December 22, morning ed.

Taihoku shiku kaihen jinen shashinchō (Album commemorating Taihoku city street renovations) (1915), Taihoku: n.p.

Taihoku teikoku daigaku Dozoku jinruigaku kenkyūshitsu (ed) (1935), *Taiwan Takasagozoku: keitō shozoku no kenkyū* (The Taiwan native tribes: a genealogical and classificatory study), Tōkyō: Tōkō shoin.

Taihoku-shū (Taihoku Prefecture) (ed) (1924), *Taihoku-shū ribanshi* (Record of Aborigine administration in Taihoku Prefecture), Taihoku: Taihoku-shū keimubu.

Tainan-shū Kokumin dōjō (Tainan Prefecture Civilian Dojo) (1943), Taihoku: Taiwan eiga kyōkai. [Released in DVD collection *Piange zhuandong jian de Taiwan xianying (Colonial Japanese Documentaries on Taiwan)*, Tainan: Guoli Taiwan lishi bowuguan, 2008.]

"Taipei mayor opens Japanese baseball game" (2001), Central News Agency, August 15.

Taiwan dabaike quanshu (Encyclopedia of Taiwan). http://taiwanpedia.culture.tw/ [accessed June 1, 2014].

Taiwan fūzoku to fūkei shashinchō (Album of Taiwan customs and scenery) (1903), Osaka: Taiwan shashinchō hakkōsho.

Taiwan gun gaisen kinen shashinchō (Album commemorating military triumph in Taiwan) (1896), Tokyo: Endō shashinkan.

"Taiwan jieguan jihua gangyao cao'an" (Draft outline for the takeover of Taiwan) (2000), in W. Kirby, M. Lin, J. Shih, and D. Pietz (eds), *State and Economy in Republican China: A Handbook for Scholars, Volume 2*, Cambridge: Harvard University Asia Center.

Taiwan jinkō dōtai tōkei (Vital statistics of Taiwan, 1905–1942) (1906–43), Taihoku: Sōtoku kambō tōkeika.

"Taiwan kara Ri Tōki-shi rainichi—Seishun no chi, saihō 'kotoba ga denai'" (Lee Teng-hui arrives in Japan from Taiwan—"speechless" upon revisiting the land of his youth) (2001), *Yomiuri shimbun*, April 23, morning ed.

Taiwan kyōkai (eds) (1982), *Taiwan hikiage shi: Shōwa nijūnen shūsen kiroku* (A history of repatriation from Taiwan: A record of the end of the war from Shōwa 20 [1945]), Tokyo: Zaidan hōren Taiwan kyōkai.

Taiwan meisho fūzoku shashinchō (Album of famous sites and local customs in Taiwan) (1903), Osaka: Taiwan meisho fūzoku shashinchō hakkōsho.

Taiwan meisho shashinchō (Album of famous sites in Taiwan) (1899), Taihoku: Taiwan shōpō.

Taiwan miyage shashinchō (Album of Taiwan souvenirs) (1902), Taihoku: Taiwan shōpō.

Taiwan sangyō ryakushi (A summary history of industry in Taiwan) (1895), Tokyo: Nōshōmu daijin kanbō bunsho-ka.

Taiwan shashinchō (Taiwan photo album) (1915), n.p.

Taiwan sheng xingzheng changguan gongshu tongji shi (eds) (1946), *Taiwan sheng wushiyi nian lai tongji tiyao, 1894–1945* (Compilation of Statistics for Taiwan Province for 51 years, 1894–1945), Table 58–8. http://twstudy.iis.sinica.edu.tw/twstatistic50/ [accessed October 20, 2012].

Taiwan shishō meikan (Survey of institutions and businesses in Taiwan) (1901), Taihoku: Nihitakasha.

Taiwan sōtokufu (Taiwan Government-General) (ed) (1912), *Riban gaiyō* (Summary of Aborigine administration), Taihoku: Taiwan sōtokufu minseibu banmu honsho.

Taiwan sōtokufu minseikyoku shokusanbu hōbun dai ikken dai ni satsu (Taiwan Government-General, Promotion of Industry Section, Report: Volume 1, Number 2) (1896), Tokyo: Taiwan sōtokufu minseikyoku shokusanbu.

Taiwan takushoku gachō (Picture album of the colonization of Taiwan) (1918), Tokyo: n.p.

"Taiwan tsūshin" (Communications from Taiwan) (1895), *Yomiuri shimbun*, September 30.

Taiwan zongdu guanfang linshi hukou diaochabu (comp) (1992), *Minguo sinian di er ci linshi Taiwan hukou diaocha gailanbiao* (Results of second provisional Taiwan household census, ROC Year 4 [1915]), Taibei: Jieyou chubanshe.

Takekoshi, Y. (1907), *Japanese Rule in Formosa*, trans. G. Braithwaite, London: Longmans, Green, & Co.

Takun W. (2010), "Taiwan Yuanzhuminzu yusheng houyi yanzhong de Wushe shijian" (The Wushe Incident in the eyes of surviving Taiwan Aboriginal descendants), *Taiwan yu haiyang Yazhou*, February 10, 2010. http://goo.gl/9lWXIO [accessed March 25, 2014].

Tamoto, H. (2012), "'Genjūmin kōgei' no hyōshō to seisaku o meguru ikkōsatsu: Taiwan Genjūmin no orimono fukkō o jirei ni" (An investigation of the representation and production of "Aborigine handicrafts": The revival of Indigenous Taiwanese textiles as a case study), *Shigaku (Mita shi gakkai)* (History [The Mita Historical Society]), 81.3: 91–113.

Tanaka, H. (1911), *Shin kyōkasho kiga no kaisetu oyobi toriatsukai hō: shūshin chiri rekishi no bu* (Explanations and instructions for the illustrations of the new textbooks: Ethics, geography and history section), Tokyo: Kōbundō.

Tanaka, S. (1993), *Japan's Orient: Rendering Pasts into History*, Berkeley: University of California Press.

Tang, L. (2005), "Huangyuan zhi quan: Hatta Yoichi" (A spring in the wasteland: Hatta Yoichi), in M. Cai (ed), *Taiwan bainian renwu zhi (The Record of Taiwan Great Men)*, Vol. 1, Taibei: Yushan.

Tasaka, T. (dir) (1927), *Arisan no kyōji* (The Braves of Mount Ali), Kyoto: Nikkatsu Taishōkun.

Tavares, A. (2005), "The Japanese Colonial State and the Dissolution of the Late Imperial Frontier Economy in Taiwan, 1886–1909," *Journal of Asian Studies*, 64.2: 361–85.

Taylor, J. (2004), "Colonial Takao: The Making of a Southern Metropolis," *Urban History*, 31.1: 48–71.

———. (2005), "Reading History Through the Built Environment in Taiwan," in J. Makeham and A. Hsiau (eds), *Cultural, Ethnic, and Political Nationalism in Contemporary Taiwan: Bentuhua*, New York: Palgrave Macmillan.

Tera Y. (C. Lee) (2003), *Muda Hakaw Utux (Zou guo caihong)* (Walking across the rainbow), Hualien: Tailugezu wenhua gongzuofang.

Thomas, N. (1991), *Entangled Objects: Exchange, Material Culture, and Colonialism in the Pacific*, Cambridge: Harvard University Press.

"Tianya hechu wu fangcao, mingyang haiwai si Qiaobao" (Fragrant grass blooms all over the world, four Overseas Chinese become famous across the seas) (1965), *Lianhebao*, March 16: 3.

Tierney, R. (2010), *Tropics of Savagery: The Culture of Japanese Empire in Comparative Frame*, Berkeley: University of California Press.

"Tizhuan liu ming xuesheng, canjia Juren lianqiu" (Six P.E. College students join Giants'
    training) (1968), *Lianhebao*, February 12: 6.
Tōban guntai kinen shashinchō (Album commemorating the military campaign against the
    savages) (1914), Taihoku: Taiwan *nichinichi shinpō*.
Tōbatsu guntai kinen shashinchō (Album commemorating the campaign of the military)
    (1913), Taihoku: Endo shashinkan.
Torii, R. (1910), *Études Anthropologiques: Les aborigènes de Formose*, *Journal of the College
    of Science* 28, Tokyo: Tokyo Imperial University.
Trefalt, B. (2003), *Japanese Army Stragglers and Memories of the War in Japan, 1950–1975*,
    London: RoutledgeCurzon.
Ts'ai, H. (2009), *Taiwan in Japan's Empire Building*, London: Routledge.
Tsai, M. (dir) (2005), *Tianbian yi duo yun (The Wayward Cloud)*, Taibei: Honggelin
    dianying.
Tsai, W. (1990), "Xingbakeren de danshen yi—dushi kafei xiaofei kongjian de jiedu (The
    Birth of Starbucker—To Analyze the Coffee Consumption Space of the Urban)," *Shida
    dili yanjiu baogao (Geographical Research)*, 32: 147–69.
Tsuchida, S. (2008), "Nihongo bēsu no kuriōru" (Japan-based creole), *Taiwan genjūmin
    kenkyū* (Taiwan Aborigine research), 12: 159–72.
Turner, F. (1994), "The Significance of the Frontier in American History," in John Mack
    Faragher (ed), *Rereading Frederick Jackson Turner: The Significance of the Frontier in
    American History, and Other Essays*, New York: H. Holt.
Ueno, S. (1892), "Taiwan-jima jissen roku" (A practical guide to Taiwan), *Tokyo chigaku
    kyōkai hōkoku* (Tokyo Geographical Society report), 13.11: 21–48.
Uesugi, M. (1992), "Takasagozoku e no jusan seisaku: kōeki seisaku o chūshin toshite"
    (On industrial tutelage for Aborigines: A study of trade policy), *Takachiho ronsō*
    (Takachiho [University] essays), 26.4: 51–129.
Umin, B. (Ma, Z.) (dir) (2014), *KANO*, Taibei: Guozi dianying.
Wakatsuki, Y. (1991), *Sengo hikiage no kiroku* (A record of postwar repatriation), Tokyo:
    Jiji tōshinsha
Walis N. and Yu, G. (2002), *Taiwan Yuanzhumin shi: Taiyazu shi pian* (Taiwan Aboriginal
    history: Atayal history), Nantou: Taiwan wenxianguan.
Walis U. (Q. Zhang) (2002), "Cong Saidekezu de chuantong zongjiao kan Wushe shijian:
    Yi ge Sediq de jiaodu" (Looking at the Wushe Inciddent from the perspective of Sediq
    traditional religion: A Sediq's angle), in C. Shih, S. Koh, and Pusin T. (eds), *Cong hejie
    dao zizhi: Taiwan Yuanzhuminzu lishi chongjian* (From reconciliation to autonomy:
    Reconstructing the history of Taiwan's Indigenous Peoples), Taibei: Qianwei.
Wan, M. (2007), "Japanese Strategic Thinking toward Taiwan," in G. Rozman, K. Togo,
    and J. Ferguson (eds), *Japanese Strategic Thought toward Asia*, New York: Palgrave
    Macmillan.
Wang, C. (2012a), "Ma has history wrong: Lee Teng-hui," *Taipei Times*, April 19: 3. http://
    taipeitimes.com/News/taiwan/archives/2012/04/19/2003530717 [accessed August 18,
    2012].
———. (2012b), "Lee declines invitation to Ma's inauguration," *Taipei Times*, May 18: 1.
    http://www.taipeitimes.com/News/front/archives/2012/05/18/2003533101 [accessed
    May 25, 2012].
Wang, D. (2008), *The Teahouse: Small Business, Everyday Culture, and Public Politics in
    Chengdu, 1900–1950*, Stanford: Stanford University Press.

Wang, M. (1996), "Shei de lishi: Zizhuan, zhuanji yu koushu lishi de shehui jiyi benzhi (Whose Memories: The Social Memory Essence of Biography, Autobiography and Oral History)," *Si yu Yan (Thought and Words)*, 34.3: 147–83.

Wang, M. (2006), *Taiyazu* (The Atayal peoples), Taibei: Sanmin.

Wang, S. (1994), *Qingdai Taiwan shehui jingji* (Political economy in Qing-era Taiwan), Taibei: Lianjing chuban.

Wang, X. (1996), *Shangwei wancheng de lishi: Bao Diao ershiwunian* (Unfinished history: 25 years of protecting the Diaoyutai Islands), Taibei: Haixia xueshu, 1996.

Wang, Y. (2008), "Shisansuo daxue de Yuanzhumin zhongxin" (Aboriginal centers in 13 universities), *Yuanzhuminzu jiaoyu qingbaozhi (Aboriginal Education World)*, 20: 20–9.

Wang, Z. (Oh, S.) (1977), *Wo de quanleida shengya* (My home run career)/*Feiyue kantai de qiu* (Balls flying over the grandstand), trans. S. Wu, Xinzhuang: Lüyuan.

"Wang Zhenzhi jin fanguo, xie xinniang du miyue" (Oh Sadaharu returning to the country today, accompanying his wife for honeymoon) (1966), *Lianhebao*, December 3: 3.

"Wang Zhenzhi xia yue chuwan hun, xie mei juan lai Tai du miyue" (Oh Sadaharu to marry next month, to bring beautiful wife to honeymoon in Taiwan) (1966), *Lianhebao*, November 27: 3.

Watson, J. (1997), "Introduction: Transnationalism, Localization, and Fast Foods in East Asia," in J. Watson (ed), *Golden Arches East: McDonald's in East Asia*, Stanford: Stanford University Press.

Watt, L. (2005), "Imperial Remnants: The Repatriates in Postwar Japan," in C. Elkins and S. Pedersen (eds), *Settler Colonialism in the Twentieth Century: Projects, Practices, Legacies*, New York: Routledge.

———. (2009), *When Empire Comes Home: Repatriation and Reintegration in Postwar Japan*, Cambridge: Harvard University Asia Center.

Weber, M. (1958), *The Protestant Ethic and the Spirit of Capitalism*, trans. T. Parsons, New York: Scribner.

Wei, D. and Gao, C. (eds) (2004), *Chuanyue shikong kan Taibei: Taibei jiancheng 120 zhounian: Guditu, jiuxinxiang, wenxian, wenwu zhan* (Viewing Taipei through time and space: 120th anniversary of Taipei City Wall: An exhibition of maps, images, documents, and historical relics), Taibei: Taibei zhengfu wenhuaju.

Wei, T. (dir) (2008), *Haijiao qi hao (Cape No. 7)*, Taibei: Guozi dianying.

———. (dir) (2011), *Saideke Balai (Warriors of the Rainbow: Seediq Bale)*, Taibei: Guozi dianying and Zhongying.

Weinberg, B. and Bealer, B. (2002), *The World of Caffeine: The Science and Culture of the World's Most Popular Drug*, New York: Routledge.

Wen, K. (2014), *Taiwan modeng kafeiwu (Taiwan Modern Café)*, Taibei: Qianwei.

Wetherall, W. (1981), "Public Figures in Popular Culture: Identity Problems of Minority Heroes," in C. Lee and G. De Vos (eds), *Koreans in Japan: Ethnic Conflict and Accommodation*, Berkeley: University of California Press.

White, M. (2012), *Coffee Life in Japan*, Berkeley: University of California Press.

White, R. (1991), *The Middle Ground: Indians, Empires, and Republics in the Great Lakes Region, 1650–1815*, Cambridge: Cambridge University Press.

Whiting, R. (2008), "Oh's career sparkled with achievements as player, manager (Part II)," *Japan Times Online*, October 30. http://www.japantimes.co.jp/text/sb20081030j2.html [accessed July 24, 2012].

Winichakul, T. (1994), *Mapped: A History of the Geo-Body of a Nation*, Honolulu: University of Hawai'i Press.

Wolf, A. (1995), *Sexual Attraction and Childhood Association: A Chinese Brief for Edward Westermarck*, Stanford: Stanford University Press.

Wolf, A. and Chuang, Y. (1994), "Fertility and Women's Labour: Two Negative (but Instructive) Findings," *Population Studies*, 48: 427–33.

Wolf, A. and Huang, C. (1980), *Marriage and Adoption in China, 1845–1945*, Stanford: Stanford University Press.

Wolf, E. (1982), *Europe and the People Without History*, Berkeley: University of California Press.

Worswick, C. (ed) (1979), *Japan: Photographs, 1854–1905*. New York: Penwick Publishing.

Wu, N. (dir) (1994), *Duosang (A Borrowed Life)*, Taibei: Changshu.

Wu, W. (1986), "Riju shiqi Taiwan di fangzu duanfa yundong" (The anti-footbinding and queue-cutting campaigns in Japanese-occupied Taiwan), in H. Qu and Y. Zhang (eds), *Taiwan shehui yu wenhua bianqian* (Social and cultural change in Taiwan), Volume 1, Nangang: Zhongyang yanjiuyuan Minzuxue yanjiusuo.

Wu, Z. (1994), *Taiwan lianqiao* (Taiwan forsythia), Taibei: Qianwei.

———. (2002), *The Fig Tree: Memoirs of a Taiwanese Patriot*, trans. D. Hunter, Bloomington: 1stBooks.

"Xiao Ma ge fang Ri, meili shise" (Our very own Ma's Japan visit—his charm turned pale) (2006), *Zhongguo shibao*, July 16, morning ed.

Xiao, X. and Huang, S. (2001), *Taiwan Kejia zuqunshi: Zhengzhipian* (History of the Taiwan Hakka: Politics), Nantou: Taiwan sheng wenxian weiyuanhui.

Xie, S. (2005), "Baodao xiezhen: Shancheng na yi duan bangqiu suiyue" (Treasure island portrait: That moment of baseball history from the Mountain City), Arts.ChinaTimes. com, 29 November. Posted to *Taiwan bangqiu weijiguan*, July 6, 2006. http://goo.gl/ P8fWCx [accessed June 23, 2014].

"Xie: wo dangxuan, Zhongguo jiu hui zhengshi Taiwan zhuti minyi" (Hsieh: When I'm elected, China will face Taiwan's independent public opinion) (2007), *Ziyou shibao*, December 17.

"Xie: yuan yu Zhongguo heping duihua" (Hsieh: I want peaceful dialogue with China) (2007), *Zhongguo shibao*, December 17, morning ed.

Xiulin xiang gongsuo (Xiulin County Office) (2014), *Tailugezu bainian zhanji* (A 100-year anniversary of the Taroko-Japan War). http://war.truku.tw/ [accessed November 9, 2014].

Xu, G. (2001), "Qishi niandai chu Han Hua liu Tai xuesheng bao Diao yundong de huiyi" (Recollections of Taiwan's Korean Chinese students from the early 1970s Protect Diaoyutai movement), in G. Liu (ed), *Chunlei shengsheng: Bao Diao yundong sanshi zhounian wenxian xuanji* (Sounds of spring thunder: Selected documents on the 30th anniversary of the Protect Diaoyutai movement), Taibei: Renjian.

Xu, Z. (2007), "Yuenan zuihou yige Taiwanbing" (The last Taiwanese soldier in Vietnam), *Ziyou shibao dianzibao (Liberty Times)*, January 6. http://www.libertytimes.com. tw/2007/new/jan/6/today-o3.htm [accessed September 28, 2011].

Yagashiro, H. (ed) (2008), *Sakuma Samata* (Sakuma Samata), Tokyo: Yumani shobō.

Yamaguchi, M. (1999), *Higashi Taiwan kaihatsushi: Karenkō to Taroko* (The history of the development of eastern Taiwan: Karenkō [Hualian] and Taroko), Tokyo: Chūnichi sankyō shishūn.

Yamaguchi, S. (2007), *Shirarezaru higashi Taiwan: Wansei ga tsuzuru mitotsu no Taiwanshi* (The unknown history of eastern Taiwan: Revealed by Taiwanese-born Japanese), Tokyo: Tendensha.

Yamaji, K. (2004), *Taiwan no shokuminchi tōchi: "Mushu no yabanjin" to iu gensetsu no tenkai* (Taiwan colonial rule: The development of the discourse of the "wild barbarians"), Tokyo: Nihon tosho sentā.

————. (2011), *Taiwan Taiyaru-zoku no hyaku-nen: Hyōryū suru dentō, dakō suru kindai, datsu shokuminchika e no michinori* (The Atayal century: A floating tradition, serpentine modernity, and the road to decolonization), Tokyo: Fūkyosha.

Yan, A. and Yang, K. (2004), *Yuanzhuminzu tudi zhidu yu jingji fazhan* (Aboriginal land systems and economic development), Banqiao: Daoxiang.

Yan, X. (2008), "Liuzhuan de guxiang zhi ying: Zhimindi jingyan xia zai Tai Riren de guxiang yishi, jiangou yu zhuanzhe" (Roaming one's hometown as a shadow: Hometown consciousness, construction and transition among Japanese with experience in colonial Taiwan), in M. Wakabayashi Masahiro (ed), *Kuayu qingnian xuezhe Taiwanshi yanjiu lunji* (Collection of Taiwan history research essays by young cross-disciplinary scholars), Taibei: Daoxiang.

Yanagimoto, M. (2000), *Taiwan senjūmin: Yama no onnatachi no "seisen"* (Taiwan Aborigines: the "holy war" of the women of the mountains), Tokyo: Gendai shokan.

Yang, I. (2004), "International Women's Magazines and the Production of Sexuality in Taiwan," *Journal of Popular Culture*, 37.3: 505–30.

Yang, N., Kasahara, M., Miyaoka, M., and Miyazaki, S. (2005), *Maboroshi no jinrui gakusha Mori Ushinosuke: Taiwan genjūmin no kenkyū ni sasageta shōgai* (The illusive anthropologist Mori Ushinosuke: A life dedicated to research of the Taiwan Indigenous Peoples), Tokyo: Fūkyōsha.

Yang, S. (2005), "Imagining the State: an Ethnographic Study," *Ethnography* 6.4: 487–516.

Yang, T. (1993), "Cong minzu guojia de moshi kan zhanhou Taiwan de Zhongguohua (The Sinicisation of Post-War Taiwan from the Perspective of Ethnic-State Patterns)," *Taiwan wenyi (Taiwan Literature)*, 138: 77–112.

Yang, Y. (2008), *Shangxiao de erzi: Waishengren, ni yao qu na'er?* (Colonels' sons: Where are you going, mainlanders?), Taibei: Huayan.

"Yazhou bangqiusai, jin zai Min jiemu" (Asian Baseball Championships open today in Southeast Asia) (1965), *Lianhebao*, December 4: 2.

"Yazhou bangqiusai, wo jibai Riben, zixingchedui jinwan fan Tai" (Asian Baseball Championships: We beat Japan; cycling team returns to Taiwan tonight) (1965), *Lianhebao*, December 8: 2.

Yee, A. (2001), "Constructing a Native Consciousness: Taiwan Literature in the 20th Century," *China Quarterly*, 165: 83–101.

Yeh, B. (2012), "The empire smiles back: Taiwan's Japanese cherry festival," *Taipei Times*, March 26: 2. http://www.taipeitimes.com/News/taiwan/archives/2012/03/26/2003528744 [accessed March 31, 2014].

Yen, S. (1965), *Taiwan in China's Foreign Relations, 1836–1874*, Hamden, CN: The Shoe String Press.

Yoshimura, M. (2007), "Weaving and Identity of the Atayal in Wulai, Taiwan," MA Thesis, University of Waterloo.

Yu, S. (2004), "Hot and Noisy: Taiwan's Night Market Culture," in D. Jordan, A. Morris, and M. Moskowitz (eds), *The Minor Arts of Daily Life: Popular Culture in Taiwan*, Honolulu: University of Hawai'i Press.

Yu, W. (1977), "Wang Zhenzhi pan zuguo xiaojiang, nuli lianqiu wei guo zheng guang" (Oh Sadaharu hopes that the little generals of the motherland will work hard and practice to win glory for the nation), *Lianhebao*, September 2: 3.

"Zai Ri chu you Li: Xiaci yao qu Riben dongbei *Ao zhi xidao*" (Lee traveling in Japan: Next time I want to go to Japan's northeast [to travel] *The Narrow Road to the Interior*) (2001), *Zhongguo shibao*, April 23, evening ed.

"Zanryū Nikkyō ni tsugu" (Announcement regarding the Japanese detritus) (1946), *Minbao*, April 21: 1.

Zeng, J. (2005), *1945 Poxiao shike de Taiwan: bayue shiwuri hou jidongde yibai tian* (1945, the moment of daybreak in Taiwan: The stirring hundred days following August 15), Taibei: Lianjing.

Zeng, W. and Yu, J. (2004), *Taiwan bangqiu wang (Baseball King of Taiwan)*, Taibei: Woshi.

Zhang, L. (1997), "Zai Xinjiapo, Yuenan Yazhuang congshi shouyi yanjiu gongzuo zhi huiyi" (Memories of animal disease research work in Singapore and Nha Trang, Vietnam), in W. Zhou (ed), *Taiji Ribenbing zuotanhui jilu bing xiangguan ziliao* (Record of Conference on Japan's Taiwanese Soldiers and related information), Nangang: Zhongyang yanjiuyuan Taiwanshi yanjiusuo choubeichu.

Zhao, M. (1965), "Wenqi Gongzi, ban ru mi" (When asking [Oh] about Kyoko, he becomes enigmatic), *Lianhebao*, December 6: 3.

Zheng, C. (1995), *Les Austronésiens de Taïwan: à travers les sources chinoises*, Paris: Harmattan.

———. (1998), *Taiwanjin moto shiganhei to Daitōa sensō* (Taiwanese volunteers and the Great East Asian War), Tokyo: Tendensha.

Zheng, T. (2006), "Cool Masculinity: Male Clients' Sex Consumption and Business Alliance in Urban China's Sex Industry," *Journal of Contemporary China*, 15.46: 161–82.

"Zhongguo zhi mingyun (2)" (China's Destiny, Part 2) (1945), *Minbao*, October 11: 1.

"Zongtong gao Ri jingjijie fangwentuan" (President speaks to Japanese economic delegation) (1965), *Lianhebao*, December 11: 2.

Index

Made in the USA
Columbia, SC
27 August 2017